Assurance, Risk and Governance: an International Perspective

Second Edition

Michael Büchling, Dannielle Cerbone, Marianne Kok, Warren Maroun, Gary Marques, Talya Segal and Zakiyyah Varachia

University of the Witwatersrand, School of Accountancy

juta

Assurance, risk and governance: An international perspective

First published 2019
Second edition 2021

Juta and Company (Pty) Ltd
First Floor
Sunclare Building
21 Dreyer Street
Claremont
7708
PO Box 14373, Lansdowne 7779, Cape Town, South Africa

© 2021 Juta and Company (Pty) Ltd

ISBN: 978 1 48513 161 8
eISBN: 978 1 48513 162 5 (WebPDF)

Project manager: Valencia Wyngaard-Arenz
Proofreader: Deidre Du Preez
Typesetter: Wouter Reinders
Cover designer: Riedewaan Toffar
Typeset in Arial 11pt

CONTENTS

Chapter 1: Assurance, risk and governance 1

1   Introduction 1

2   References 5

PART A

Chapter 2: Regulatory environment for audit and assurance 7

1   Introduction 7

2   The need for laws, regulations, standards and other guidance 7

3   International standard-setting bodies 9

4   Public monitoring and review 10

5   Corporate governance and audit committees 13

6   Governance of ethics 15

7   Governance of information technology (IT) risks 16

8   Summary 16

9   References 16

Chapter 3: Code of Professional Conduct 20

1   Introduction 20

2   Structure of the Code 20

3   Fundamental principles and the conceptual framework 23

4   Fundamental principles 23

5   Conceptual framework 25

6   Identifying threats to compliance with the fundamental principles 25

7   Evaluating threats to fundamental principles 27

8   Addressing threats to fundamental principles 28

9   Professional accountants in public practice 29

10 International independence standards 34

11 International accounting bodies and their codes of conduct 40

12 ACCA 41

13 ICAS 41

14 ICAEW 41

15 CIMA 41

16 AICPA 42

17 SEC 42

18 SAICA 43

19 Summary 43

20 References 43

Chapter 4 : Laws and regulations **45**

1   Introduction 45

2   Legal requirements applicable to a company 45

3   Management and auditors' responsibilities 47

4   Summary 52

5   References 52

Chapter 5: Money laundering **54**

1   Introduction 54

2   The concept and mechanics of money laundering 55

3   The accountant's role 57

4   Ethics 58

5   Customer Due Diligence (CDD) 59

6   The responsibilities of auditors with regards to money laundering 60

7   International efforts to combat money laundering 63

8   Summary 64

9   References 65

Chapter 6: Fraud and error **68**

1   Introduction 68

2   The expectation gap 69

3   Responsibilities of management and the auditor 71

4   Professional judgement, professional scepticism and the audit 76

5   Defining fraud 78

6   How fraud is committed 80

7   Responsibilities of the auditor in terms of ISA 240 86

8   Summary 89

9   References 89

Chapter 7: Ensuring audit quality **94**

1   Introduction 94

2   Understanding of quality control 95

3   Ensuring quality at the firm level 96

4   Ensuring quality at the engagement level 102

5   Indicators of audit quality 102

6   External regulation and audit quality 104

7   Summary 106

8   References 107

Chapter 8: Professional liability **111**

1   Introduction 111

2   Auditor liability 111

3   A South African Context 115

4   Reducing or limiting liability 116

5   Case law related to auditor liability 117

6   Transnational audits 118

7   Summary 119

8   References 120

PART B

Chapter 9: Client acceptance and continuance 122

1   Introduction 122

2   Tendering 123

3   Client acceptance process 128

4   ISA 210 – Agreeing on the terms of audit engagements 136

5   Regulatory requirements 138

6   Summary 143

7   References 144

Chapter 10: Introduction to business and audit risk 147

1   Introduction 147

2   Understanding risks in the entity 148

3   How the auditor performs a risk assessment 153

4   Summary 154

5   References 154

Chapter 11: Understanding the entity 156

1   Introduction 156

2   Understanding the client 156

3   Summary 171

4   References 171

Chapter 12: Overall and assertion level risk 173

1   Introduction 173

2   The components of audit risk 173

3   Significant audit risks 176

4   Summary 179

5   References 179

Chapter 13: Responding to audit risk 181

1   Introduction 181

2   Materiality terms and applications 181

3   Auditor response 183

4   Audit evidence 196

5   Summary.. 198

6   References.. 198

Chapter 14: Group audits **200**

1   Introduction.. 200

2   Group audits and audit risk.. 201

3   Understanding the component auditor 210

4   Consolidation processes... 215

5   Communicating and concluding 216

6   Summary.. 217

7   References.. 218

Chapter 15 – Placing reliance on the work of others **219**

1   Introduction.. 219

2   Opening balances.. 219

3   Written representations... 221

4   Using the work of an expert 224

5   Reliance on internal audit 227

6   Summary.. 232

7   References.. 232

Chapter 16: Audit of estimates... **234**

1   Introduction 234

2   Nature of estimates 234

3   Auditor's requirements in terms of ISA 540R 236

4   Applicability of specific IFRSs 259

5   Summary.. 263

6   References.. 263

PART C

Chapter 17: Completion activities... **265**

1   Introduction.. 265

2   Evaluating misstatements... 265

3   The auditor's responsibilities relating to going concern 269

4   Subsequent events 269

5   Conclusion analytics 270

6   Summary.. 270

7   References 270

Chapter 18: Reporting... **273**

1   Introduction.. 273

2   The different outputs of the audit process.. 273

3   Communicating with those charged with governance... 275

4   The auditor's report (ISA 700)... 277

5   The opinion on financial statements 279

6   Other modifications to the audit report (ISA 706).. 284

7   Critical/key audit matters (KAM) (ISA 710) 286

8   Summary.. 288

Appendix A.. 288

Appendix B 292

Appendix C 293

9   References.. 293

PART D

Chapter 19 Outsourcing.. 298

1   Introduction 298

2   Definitions 299

3   Regulatory requirements, codes of best practice and code of ethics 299

4   Requirements for entering into an outsourcing arrangement 303

5   Advantages and disadvantages 303

6   Outsourcing of IT functions.. 305

7   Implications of outsourcing for an external audit engagement 306

8   Summary.. 313

9   References.. 313

Chapter 20: Internal audit 315

1   Introduction 315

2   Evolution of internal audit 315

3   Audit services and types of reviews.. 326

4   The need for an IAF 329

5   The role of internal audit in enterprise risk management (ERM) 334

6   Characteristics of an effective IAF 336

7   The internal audit process 340

8   Summary 343

9   References.. 344

Chapter 21: Other types of assurance engagements 349

1   Introduction 349

2   Key definitions.. 351

3   Types of assurance... 351

4   Assurance provided by different assurance services.. 360

5   Non-assurance services 367

6   Reporting on assurance (attest and direct) engagements..................................... 371

7   Summary... 376

8   References.. 377

Chapter 22: Performance indicators and the public sector **382**

1   Introduction 382

2   Measuring performance information 383

3   The audit of performance information 385

4   Reporting on performance information 389

5   Integrated report of performance 391

6   Summary.. 394

7   References.. 394

Chapter 23: The future of the audit profession **398**

1   External regulation of the profession and recent technical developments............... 398

2   Assurance on extended forms of corporate reporting 401

3   Changes in technology 402

4   Areas for future research 404

5   References.. 404

Chapter 1: Assurance, risk and governance

1. Introduction

The use of some form of independent assurance has become more widespread. The assurance market has expanded from traditional financial statement audits to include, for example, the assurance of different types of environmental, social and governance reporting (ESG assurance); systems and operations audits; forensic investigations and public sector performance audits (Power, 1994; Farooq & De Villiers, 2018). As expected, this has gone hand-in-hand with an expansion of the service offerings of the large accounting and auditing firms (O'dwyer, Owen & Unerman, 2011) and a proliferation of technical standards designed to define the nature and scope of the work performed by the professional accountant (see, for example, Dillard, 2011; Iaasb, 2015; Maroun, 2017).

The 'audit explosion' has received considerable attention from the academic community (Power, 1994, p. 1). Drawing on agency theory, the external audit provides a useful monitoring tool which can lower agency costs and increase the value of the firm (Jensen & Meckling, 1976). In this way, the demand for early forms of an independent attest function reflected the fact that this was 'an efficient method of monitoring contracts between managers and those supplying capital' (Watts & Zimmerman, 1983, p. 626). This was especially true, following the emergence of the company as a legal person separate from its owners and an increase in the size and complexity of modern businesses. The result is that, when lawmakers decided to mandate the audit of financial statements in the early 20th century, this merely confirmed what had become an already established business practice (ibid).

Central to the auditor's ability to reduce agency costs is the fact that the auditor is independent of the audit client and sufficiently competent to detect misstatements in the financial statements (Watts & Zimmerman, 1983; Kaplan & Ruland, 1991). Independence and technical expertise have also contributed significantly to the legitimacy of the audit profession. Efforts to regulate 'acceptable' behaviour; define knowledge templates and control access to the industry have become defining features of the audit profession, leading it to secure and maintain public trust (Chandler, Edwards & Anderson, 1993; Edwards, 2001). This has been complemented by the modern risk-based audit model. The codification of process followed to identify, quantify and respond to risks allows an otherwise interpretive exercise (Dillard, 2011) to be framed as a rational technical process which commands the confidence of non-expert users (see, for example, Humphrey & Moizer, 1990; Power, 2003). The result is external audit has become such an integral part of contemporary society that its application in other areas, such as sustainability or integrated reporting and the management of operational performance, has been accepted with little contestation (O'dwyer et al., 2011).

1

While the prior research has provided an important perspective on the development and proliferation of different types of assurance services, it is not without its limitations. Most notably, the academic literature has focused significantly on the development of theory (Hay, 2015). Agency and legitimacy theory are common examples. Audit practice, including the practical issues encountered when attempting to test and express an opinion on the subject matter of an assurance engagement are less seldom considered (considered Bell, Marrs, Solomon & Thomas, 1997; Peecher, Schwartz & Solomon, 2007). Related closely to this, most of the prior auditing research is informed by a positivist philosophy. This stresses the need to study external audit by drawing inferences from objective (and usually mathematical) analysis of underlying data (Maroun & Jonker, 2014). Examples include: studies on audit quality based on changes in the amount of litigation against or the size of the audit firm (Francis, 2004); experimental studies designed to simulate auditor judgement decisions (Seifert, Sweeney, Joireman & Thornton, 2010; Soni, Maroun & Padia, 2015) and studies on how legal systems, governance frameworks and firm characteristics predict the use of ESG assurance (Simnett, Vanstraelen & Chua, 2009; Peters & Romi, 2014). This collection of work has provided important insights into the drivers and implications of external audit at the macro-level but it stops short of shedding light on the intricacies of the processes followed to test and express an opinion on the subject matter of an assurance engagement (Power, 2003; Khalifa, Sharma, Humphrey & Robson, 2007). As a result, this book takes a more pragmatic approach. It shifts the attention from theoretical and methodological models to the practical nature of the external audit and other assurance services as part of a combined assurance framework.

Combined assurance:

> 'incorporates and optimises all assurance services and functions so that, taken as a whole, these enable an effective control environment; support the integrity of information used for internal decision-making by management, the governing body and its committees; and support the integrity of the organisation's external reports' (Iod, 2016, p. 10).

From this perspective, external audit is not just a statutory requirement. As argued by Watts and Zimmerman (1983), external audit can lower agency costs by enhancing and/or signalling the reliability of a client's financial statements. At the same time, the test procedures used to support the opinion on the financial statements can also provide useful information to managers about the integrity of the controls put in place to protect an organisation's assets. This is especially true when external audit services are complemented by an internal audit function. Internal audit can be used to support or enhance the test procedures performed by an external audit (Iaasb, 2009). Perhaps more important is the role which internal audit can play by expanding the scope of assurance procedures to include the systems, processes and functions of an organisation which would not have been considered by the external auditor (Coetzee & Lubbe, 2014; Iod, 2016). This is becoming increasingly relevant when considering that traditional audit services focus exclusively on a client's financial statements. Key information which is being reported in environmental, sustainability and integrated reports will not form part of a financial statement audit despite the role which assurance can play in enhancing the reliability of these reports (Iirc, 2014; Cohen & Simnett, 2015; Maroun & Atkins, 2015). As a result, combined assurance recognises the importance of complementing the external audit of financial statements with a well-resourced internal audit function and other types of external assurance services. This is not only essential for safeguarding the quality of information being reported to stakeholders outside of the financial statements; assurance can also be used to enhance the accuracy, completeness and reliability of the data, systems and processes being used to support internal decision-making (see Simnett & Huggins, 2015; Iod, 2016; Maroun, 2017).

To explore the potential of external assurance in more detail, Part A of this book examines how assurance (focusing initially on external audit) forms part of a broader system of corporate governance. This is followed by Part B which deals with the technical features of an audit engagement. Part C examines other types of assurance services which may be used to complement the audit of financial statements. This is summarised in Figure 1.

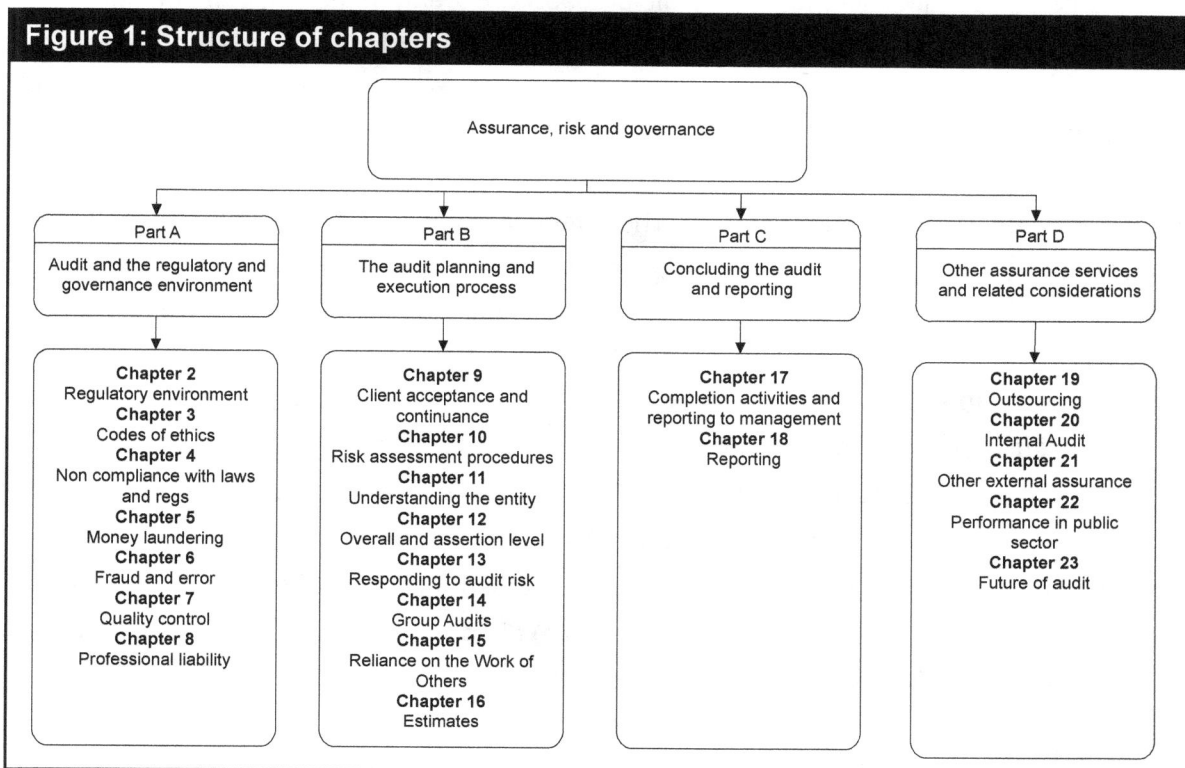

Figure 1: Structure of chapters

The remainder of this book is organised as follows. Part A examines the international regulatory environment. It explains how regulation is being used increasingly to ensure the quality of external audit (and other types of assurance services). Chapter 2 provides examples of external regulatory measures and discusses the structure and mandate of the standard-setters responsible for codifying assurance practice. Chapters 3 and 4 explain the relevance of ethics and the importance of responding to ethical dilemmas for the sound functioning and credibility of the external assurance model. This includes a review of the fundamental principles informing the code of ethics issued by the International Federation of Accountants and guidance on how these practices are applied. The role of international accounting bodies and regulators in advancing or safeguarding ethics in the profession is also discussed. This is followed by a review of the role played by auditors in combatting money laundering (Chapter 5) and in preventing or detecting fraud (Chapter 6); the importance of quality control (Chapter 7) and the legal implications for deficient audit practice (Chapter 8).

Part B deals with the technical standards issued by the International Auditing and Assurance Standards Board dealing with the planning and execution of the audit of financial statements. Chapter 9 details the client acceptance and continuance process, including the application of the applicable ethical principles discussed in Chapter 3. Chapters 10 to 13 examine how an auditor assesses the risk that financial statements are materially misstated; the methods used to collect sufficient and appropriate audit evidence to mitigate audit risk and how any misstatements identified during the audit process are dealt with. Chapter 14 deals with the planning and execution of group audits. How auditors place reliance on the work of others (Chapter 15) and the process followed when testing estimates (Chapter 16) are also considered.

Part C focuses on concluding the audit. The effects of identified misstatements on financial statements are evaluated. This is followed by a discussion on how the auditor communicates key findings/issues to those charged with an organisation's governance.

Part D complements the details on the audit of financial statements by discussing other types of assurance engagements. The final part of the book opens with an explanation of outsourcing arrangements (Chapter 19) and the operation of internal audit in the private sector (Chapter 20). The requirements of the applicable professional standards are discussed and examples of when different assurance services are relied on are provided in Chapter 21. The role of external assurance in a public sector context is dealt with in Chapter 22. Chapter 23 concludes and identifies areas for future research.

2. References

Bell, T.B., Marrs, F.O., Solomon, I. and Thomas, H., 1997. Auditing Organizations Through a Strategic System Lens: The KPMG Business Measurement Process. sl: KPMG LLP.

Chandler, R., Edwards, R. & Anderson, M.'Changing Perceptions of the Role of the Company Auditor, 1840–1940'. *Accounting and Business Research,* 23. 92 (1993) pp 443–459.

Coetzee, P. & Lubbe, D. 'Improving the Efficiency and Effectiveness of Risk-Based Internal Audit Engagements'. *International Journal of Auditing,* 18. 2 (2014) pp 115–125.

Cohen, J. R. & Simnett, R. 'CSR and Assurance Services: A Research Agenda'. *AUDITING: A Journal of Practice & Theory,* 34. 1 (2015) pp 59–74.

Dillard, J. 'Double Loop Learning; or, Just Another Service to Sell: A Comment on "The Case of Sustainability Assurance: Constructing a New Assurance Service"'. *Contemporary Accounting Research,* 28. 4 (2011) pp 1267–1277.

Edwards, J. R. 'Accounting regulation and the professionalization process: A historical essay concerning the significance of P. H. Abbott'. *Critical Perspectives on Accounting,* 12. 6 (2001) pp 675–696.

Farooq, B. & De Villiers, C. 2018. Assurance of sustainability and integrated reports. *In:* DE VILLIERS, C. J. (ed.) *Sustainability Accounting and Integrated Reporting.* Oxfordshire, UK: Taylor & Francis.

Francis, J. R. 'What do we know about audit quality?'. *The British Accounting Review,* 36. 4 (2004) pp 345–368.

Hay, D. 'The frontiers of auditing research'. *Meditari Accountancy Research,* 23. 2 (2015) pp 158–174.

Humphrey, C. & Moizer, P. 'From techniques to ideologies: An alternative perspective on the audit function'. *Critical Perspectives on Accounting,* 1. 3 (1990) pp 217–238.

IAASB 2009. ISA 610 Using the Work of Internal Auditors. *In:* South African Institute of Chartered Accountants (ed.) *SAICA Members' Handbook.* 2009 ed. Pietermaritsburg: LexisNexis.

IAASB. 'Exploring assurance on integrated reporting and other emerging developments in external reporting'. (2015), https://www.iaasb.org/publications/exploring-assurance-integrated-reporting-and-other-emerging-developments-external-reporting-0 (10 September 2020).

IIRC. 'Assurance on <IR>: An introduction to the discussion. IIRC assurance paper.' (2014), https://integratedreporting.org/resource/assurance/ (10 September 2020).

IOD, *King IV Report on Corporate Governance in South Africa,* (Lexis Nexus South Africa, Johannesburg, South Africa, (2016).

Jensen, M. C. & Meckling, W. H. 'Theory of the firm: Managerial behavior, agency costs and ownership structure'. *Journal of Financial Economics,* 3. 4 (1976) pp 305–360.

Kaplan, S. E. & Ruland, R. G. 'Positive theory, rationality and accounting regulation'. *Critical Perspectives on Accounting,* 2. 4 (1991) pp 361–374.

Khalifa, R., Sharma, N., Humphrey, C. & Robson, K. 'Discourse and Audit Change: transformations in methodology in the professional audit field'. *Accounting, Auditing and Accountability Journal,* 20. 6 (2007) pp 825–854.

Maroun, W. 'Assuring the integrated report: Insights and recommendations from auditors and preparers'. *The British Accounting Review,* 49. 3 (2017) pp 329–346.

Maroun, W. & Atkins, J. 2015. The Challenges of Assuring Integrated Reports: Views from the South African Auditing Community. *In:* ACCA (ed.). London: The Association of Chartered Certified Accountants.

Maroun, W. & Jonker, C. 'Critical and interpretive accounting, auditing and governance research in South Africa'. *Southern African Journal of Accountability and Auditing Research,* 16. 1 (2014) pp 51–62.

O'dwyer, B., Owen, D. & Unerman, J. 'Seeking legitimacy for new assurance forms: The case of assurance on sustainability reporting'. *Accounting, Organizations and Society,* 36. 1 (2011) pp 31–52.

Peecher, M. E., Schwartz, R. & Solomon, I. 'It's all about audit quality: Perspectives on strategic-systems auditing'. *Accounting, Organizations and Society,* 32. 4–5 (2007) pp 463–485.

Peters, G. F. & Romi, A. M. 'The association between sustainability governance characteristics and the assurance of corporate sustainability reports'. *Auditing: A Journal of Practice & Theory,* 34. 1 (2014) pp 163–198.

Power, M. K., *The Audit Explosion,* (Demos, London, (1994)

Power, M. K. 'Auditing and the production of legitimacy'. *Accounting, Organizations and Society,* 28. 4 (2003) pp 379–394.

Seifert, D. L., Sweeney, J. T., Joireman, J. & Thornton, J. M. 'The influence of organizational justice on accountant whistleblowing'. *Accounting, Organizations and Society,* 35. 7 (2010) pp 707–717.

Simnett, R. & Huggins, A. L. 'Integrated reporting and assurance: where can research add value?'. *Sustainability Accounting, Management and Policy Journal,* 6. 1 (2015) pp 29–53.

Simnett, R., Vanstraelen, A. & Chua, W. F. 'Assurance on Sustainability Reports: An International Comparison'. *The Accounting Review,* 84. 3 (2009) pp 937–967.

Soni, F., Maroun, W. & Padia, N. 'Perceptions of justice as a catalyst for whistle-blowing by trainee auditors in South Africa'. *Meditari Accountancy Research,* 23. 1 (2015) pp 118–140.

Watts, R. L. & Zimmerman, J. L. 'Agency Problems, Auditing, and the Theory of the Firm: Some Evidence'. *Journal of Law and Economics,* 26. 3 (1983) pp 613–633.

PART A

Chapter 2: Regulatory environment for audit and assurance

1. Introduction

High profile corporate failures exposed several weaknesses in corporate governance systems and the functioning of external audit (Bazerman et al., 2002; Unerman and O'Dwyer, 2004). One of the most significant outcomes is the erosion of trust in the audit profession and the increased use of laws and regulations to maintain confidence in the external audit process (Shaked and Sutton, 1981; Unerman and O'Dwyer, 2004; Black, 2008). For example, the Sarbanes Oxley Act was introduced in the USA to deal with, among other things, the quality of external audit services (Carrington, 2010). In the UK, the Financial Reporting Council is responsible for the development and enforcement of accounting and auditing standards (Ronen, 2002). In South Africa, the Independent Regulatory Board for Auditors carries out the monitoring and review of the local audit profession (Auditing Profession's Act [APA], 2005) while the Financial Reporting Investigations Panel is an example of an external body which carries out reviews of listed companies' financial statements to ensure high-quality financial reporting (Louw and Maroun, 2017).

Financial crises and corporate failures are not the only reasons for the increased reliance on external regulation (Porter, 1993; Francis, 2004; Peecher et al., 2007; DeFond and Lennox, 2011; Humphrey et al., 2011; Porter et al., 2012; DeFond and Zhang, 2014; Porter et al., 2014). Companies are becoming more complex and frequently operate in multiple jurisdictions. This has resulted in the need for new laws, regulations and standards to ensure minimum levels of audit and financial reporting quality (Humphrey et al., 2011). Those charged with an organisation's governance are also being expected to fulfil a more proactive monitoring and review function in terms of codes of corporate governance (Monks and Minow, 2003; Maroun and Jonker, 2014; Nag, 2015; IOD, 2016).

Against this backdrop, Chapter 2 provides an overview of how the assurance function is regulated and the role of assurance as part of the broader corporate governance system. This is followed by an overview of the international standard-setting bodies in Section 3 and examples of monitoring and compliance bodies in Section 4.

2. The need for laws, regulations, standards and other guidance

Historically, the audit profession has relied on a self-regulatory system to ensure minimum levels of audit quality (Unerman and O'Dwyer, 2004). The profession codified accounting and auditing practice to provide standards on how to compile and audit financial statements.

This went hand-in-hand with peer reviews of audit and accounting practice by professional bodies, rigorous examinations to control entry to the profession and efforts to define what constituted professional behaviour (for details see Chandler et al., 1993; Pentland, 1993; Power, 1994; Edwards, 2001; Zeff, 2003). Collectively, these measures allowed members of the audit profession to be seen as an elite group of experts who could be trusted (Unerman and O'Dwyer, 2004; Khalifa et al., 2007).

Successive (and high profile) corporate failures changed this. The taken-for-granted legitimacy of the audit profession was questioned and, as part of the this, the ability of the self-regulatory system to ensure the quality of audit engagements was called into question (Anderson and Ellyson, 1986; Unerman and O'Dwyer, 2004; Bazerman and Moore, 2011). The result has been a significant increase in the number of laws and prescriptions to provide an external or arms-length basis for regulating the audit profession.

In South Africa, the APA sets out the legislative requirements with which an auditor must comply. These include, for example, prohibitions on the rendering of certain non-audit services and a duty to report instances of fraud or theft by those charged with governance to the regulator (IRBA[1]). The APA also clarifies the circumstances in which an auditor is regarded as being negligent or guilty of an offence because of non-compliance with laws and regulations (refer to Chapter 8).

The Audit Directive and Regulation (2016) in the European Union (EU) has regulatory requirements for the auditors of public interest entities. It specifies mandatory audit firm rotation and the prohibition of non-audit services. In the EU, the directive sets out policies and procedures which each jurisdiction is required to follow to allow for harmonisation of the auditing profession throughout the EU. Each jurisdiction establishes its legislation to regulate the profession and to impose a duty to report on any non-compliance with laws and regulations. The EU Eighth Directive on company law, for example, requires that persons carrying out statutory audits must be approved by EU member states (Deumes et al., 2012). These auditors are also required to comply with all standards set by the IAASB and IESBA.

Under the Australian Securities and Investments Commission Act, (2001), an auditor is required to comply with the auditing standards and pronouncements set out by the regulator (AUASB[2]). Such regulation includes the duty to report any instances of fraud and/or non-compliance with laws and regulations committed by directors and those charged with governance to the regulator.

---

1   Independent Regulatory Board for Auditors.
2   Auditing and Assurance Standards Board.

In the United Kingdom, the Financial Reporting Council (FRC) is the independent regulator for corporate reporting and governance. The FRC is responsible for audit quality review and professional oversight. In the USA, the Public Company Accounting Oversight Board (PCAOB) establishes laws and regulations (SOX, 2002) with which auditors are required to comply. These include the need to test controls and report any deficiencies in controls to the regulator.

As a general rule, auditors are required to comply with the applicable laws and regulations and to report any non-compliance with laws and regulations committed by management to the relevant regulator. In addition to reporting responsibilities, regulations also require the external assurance function to comply with approved auditing standards (as approved and issued by the respective regulatory body). In many jurisdictions, these are the International Standards on Auditing issued by the International Auditing and Assurance Standards Board (IAASB), a board of the International Federation of Accountants (IFAC). This is discussed in more detail in Section 3.

3.   International standard-setting bodies

The International Federation of Accountants delegates authority to several different boards (or committees), with each taking responsibility for a different sector. Table 1 provides details:

Table 1: IFAC boards and their purpose	
Board	**Purpose**
IAASB	The International Auditing and Assurance Standards Board set high-quality international standards for auditing, assurance and quality management which aim to strengthen public confidence in the global profession.
IAESB	The International Accounting Education Standards Board sets standards for professional accountancy education which deal with matters such as technical competence and professional skills, values, ethics, and attitudes
IESBA	The International Ethics Standards Board for Accountants sets high-quality, internationally appropriate ethics standards for professional accountants, including auditor independence requirements.
IPSASB	The International Public Sector Accounting Standards Board develops standards, guidance, and resources for use by public sector entities around the world for the preparation of general-purpose financial statements.

Adapted from IFAC (2020)

The IAASB and the IESBA are the main international bodies which set standards which apply to the external assurance function (IFAC, 2020). The IAASB is responsible for the development of assurance standards which are applied by external auditors, providing assurance over historical annual financial statements, interim financial statements and other information. The IESBA developed and amended the Code of Ethics which applies to professional accountants (this is discussed in more detail in Chapter 3). Figure 1 illustrates the different standards which apply to auditors and which the IFAC board is responsible for setting the standards.

Figure 1: IFAC Structure

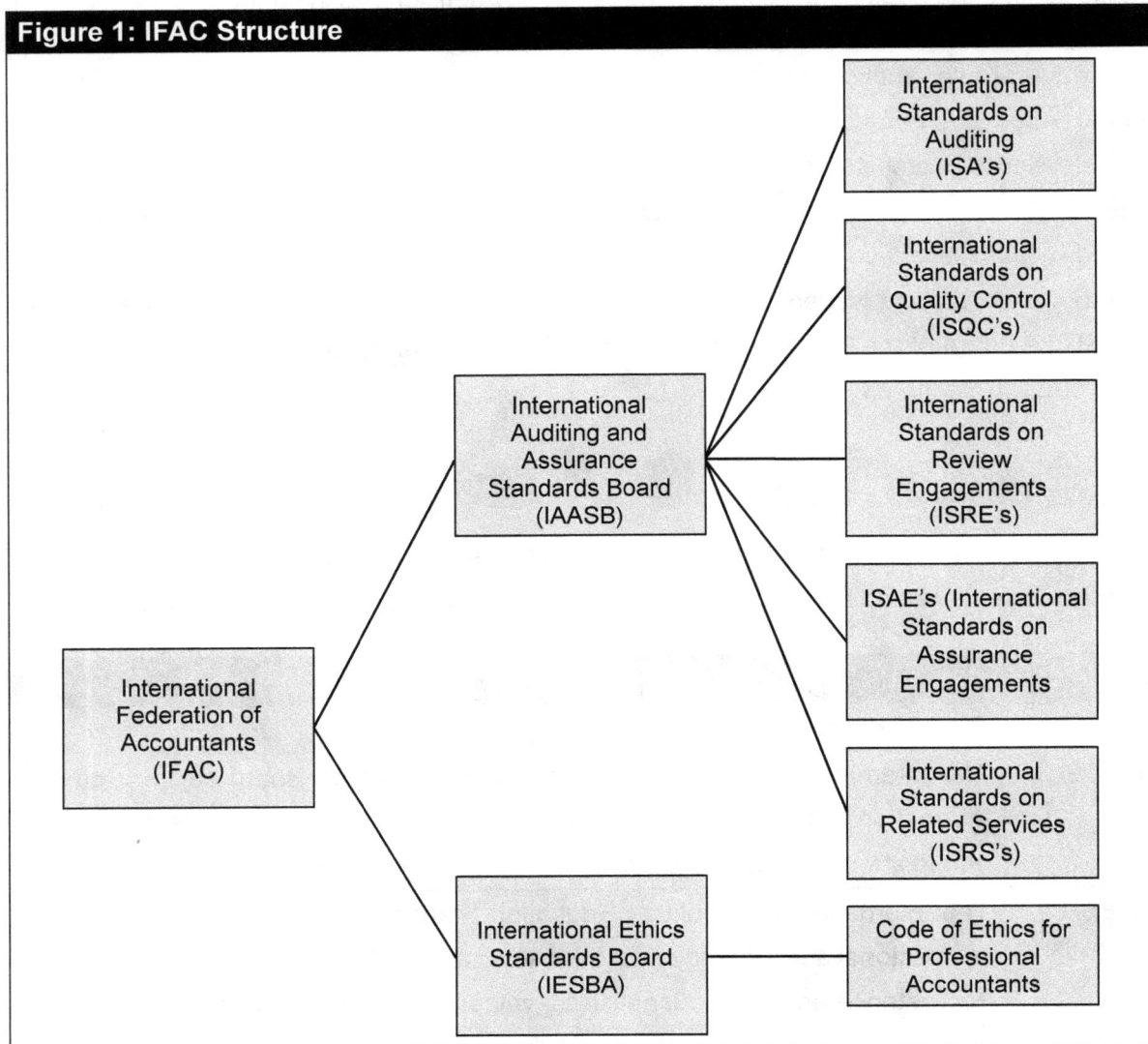

IFAC, 2020

4. Public monitoring and review

The Public Interest Oversight Board (PIOB) exercises oversight for all of the IFAC's public interest activities including standard-setting bodies (such as the IAASB) (IFAC, 2020).

The PIOB has the following responsibilities:

- Monitoring standard-setting bodies.
- Overseeing the nomination of individuals to the boards of these bodies.
- Co-operation with national supervisory authorities.

The PIOB is in place to ensure that there is public oversight of the IFAC. This means that they exist to increase confidence in investors and the public that the IFAC is responding properly to the public interest (IFAC, 2010).

Other examples of public oversight include the Recognised Supervisory Board (RSB) in Europe, the International Regulatory Board for Auditors (IRBA) in South Africa and the Public Company Accounting Oversight Board (PCAOB) in the USA. All such bodies are mandated to review the quality of audits performed by registered auditors (Sommer Jr, 2000). Over time, there has been an erosion in the integrity of audit quality. Such oversight reduces this erosion and enhances audit integrity, resulting in higher audit quality (Sommer Jr, 2000). Refer also to Chapter 7.

4.1 SOX and the USA

The Sarbanes-Oxley Act (SOX) was introduced in 2002 for any US company listed on a registered stock exchange in the US. SOX applies to:

- US public traded companies which file reports with the Securities and Exchange Commission (SEC);
- US public accounting firms which audit these companies; and
- Subsidiaries of US public companies even if these are foreign companies, for example, AngloGold Ashanti.

SOX is also relevant for foreign companies listed on the New York Stock Exchange (NYSE). For example, SASOL and Gold Fields are listed on both the Johannesburg Securities Exchange (JSE) and NYSE. As a result, both companies are required to comply with SOX. SOX is effective for companies with financial year-end on or after 15 November 2004 (with a market capitalisation greater than $75m) and for all other US public companies with financial years ended on or after 15 July 2005.

SOX was enacted in response to major corporate scandals, particularly Enron and WorldCom. It was introduced to restore the public's trust in corporate accounting and reporting (Unerman and O'Dwyer, 2004; Carrington, 2010). Some of the main provisions aimed at addressing audit quality are summarised in Part A; Chapter 7: Audit Quality.

In the USA, the Public Company Accounting Oversight Board (PCAOB) has the power to perform inspections of audit firm's engagements to ensure that these are being executed according to applicable professional standards and regulatory requirements. (Bishop et al., 2013).

- 'PCAOB inspections focus on how a firm conducted selected audits and on the effectiveness of the firm's quality control policies and procedures. Inspections are designed to identify whether there are deficiencies in how the accounting firm performs public company audits and whether there are weaknesses in its quality controls over public company auditing' (Centre for Audit Quality (2012).
- The results of inspection processes are publicly available, including the name of the applicable audit firms and weaknesses identified by the PCAOB (Bishop et al., 2013).

4.2 The FRC in the UK

The Financial Reporting Council (FRC) is responsible for the regulation of auditors, accountants and actuaries in the United Kingdom. The FRC sets the codes for corporate governance and stewardship codes. The code of corporate governance applies to all companies listed on the London Securities Exchange. Public interest entities, which include government institutions, are also required to comply with the code (FRC, 2016b; FRC, 2016a; FRC, 2016c). Such regulation includes establishing policies and procedures for the appointment of auditors, the determination and manner of application of technical, ethical and other standards and monitoring of statutory auditors and audit work through inspections. The inspections and monitoring of statutory auditors are conducted in order to enhance audit quality in the UK (FRC, 2016b; FRC, 2016a; FRC, 2016c).

The FRC also monitors the work of audit firms. Quality reviews focus on the FTSE 350 as well as on audit services provided to entities which are of public interest (FRC, 2015). Quality reviews focus on, among other things:

'[T]he appropriateness of key audit judgments made in reaching the audit opinion and the sufficiency and appropriateness of the audit evidence obtained. ...Reviews of firm-wide procedures are wide-ranging in nature and include an assessment of how the culture within firms impacts on audit quality.' (FRC, 2015).

The results of the FRC's inspections are communicated to the audit firm, which is required to take appropriate corrective action, if necessary. Inspection findings can also be referred to an enforcement unit which has the power to impose additional sanctions on auditors (FRC, 2015).

4.3 EU Audit directive and regulation in the EU

In the European Union (EU), each jurisdiction (such as Germany, France) establishes its codes of corporate governance and auditing profession legislation. However, the European Commission is responsible for harmonising these codes and the legislation to ensure that there is some form of consistency across the jurisdictions.

The European Commission has set out the following areas for harmonisation:

Board structure:The Commission acknowledged the coexistence of different board models deeply rooted in national legal systems, stating that it would not pursue board-structure harmonization.

Shareholder identification and engagement:The Commission recommended better mechanisms for companies to identify shareholders and to enhance shareholder engagement. The plan strengthens transparency rules for institutional investors, including disclosure of institutional investors' voting and better shareholder control over related-party transactions. The Commission intends to investigate whether employee share ownership should be encouraged.

Disclosure: The Commission recommended that corporate governance reporting be improved, especially concerning explanations for not applying code provisions. This particularly includes the disclosure of board diversity policy, risk-management policies, remuneration policies and individual remuneration of directors and shareholder voting on the remuneration policy and the remuneration report.

(The European Commission, 2005)

4.4 The IRBA in South Africa

In South Africa, the IRBA performs inspections of audit firms. These inspections are designed to measure compliance of audit firms with the core aspects of ISQC 1. In addition, the inspections also measure compliance against the ISA's and other regaultions at the engagement level (IRBA, 2014). Similar to the approach followed by the FRC, findings are communicated to the audit firm and measures to address any weaknesses or problems are discussed. The IRBA also publishes the results of the inspection process. Unlike the PCAOB, this is done on an aggregate rather than on a per-firm-basis (IRBA, 2014, p. 5).

5.   Corporate governance and audit committees

Corporate governance is the system by which companies are directed and controlled (Solomon, 2010). According to agency theory, shareholders (principals) of an organisation and its management body (agents) have conflicting interests, with the result that a system of checks and balances is required to mitigate losses (Jensen and Meckling, 1976). Good corporate governance forms part of this. An effective corporate governance system can be used to align the objectives of agents and principals, monitor management's performance and introduce controls to prevent, detect or correct fraud, errors or system failures (Solomon, 2010).

There are several codes of corporate governance internationally. In the United Kingdom, the UK Corporate Governance Code provides standards of good practice regarding board leadership and effectiveness, accountability, remuneration and relations with shareholders (FRC, 2016c). In South Africa, the King IV Report on Corporate Governance (King–IV) recommends similar standards of good governance (IOD, 2016). However, the listing requirements of a jurisdiction will often require compliance with these codes (as in the UK and South Africa) (Love and Klapper, 2002; Maroun and Cerbone, 2020). There are several similarities when comparing jurisdictions and these include the composition and function of audit committees and the establishment and operating of internal controls.

5.1 Audit committees

A central theme in all governance codes is the need for a board of directors to establish an audit committee (Love and Klapper, 2002). In general, this committee must comprise of a majority of independent non-executive directors. The definition of a non-executive director is largely consistent throughout the various codes (Imhoff, 2003; IOD, 2016). A non-executive director typically does not engage in the day-to-day management of the organisation but is involved in policymaking and planning exercises (Imhoff, 2003).

The advantages of establishing an audit committee include:

- Increasing confidence in the credibility and objectivity of financial reports (Imhoff, 2003; IOD, 2016).
- An audit committee can be used to balance the authority of the board of directors by holding the board of directors accountable for the quality of financial reporting and the controls in place to safeguard an organisation's resources (King, 2016). An audit committee can also segregate duties. For example, an audit committee can be tasked with appointing an external auditor, rather than appointing the executive directors whose performance may be subject to testing by external auditors (either directly or indirectly) (Imhoff, 2003; IOD, 2016).
- In establishing an audit committee, executive directors can devote their attention to the management of the company (Imhoff, 2003).

- There is a body to which the internal auditors will be accountable. This allows for the internal audit function to operate more effectively as it is held accountable to a monitoring body (Raghunandan et al., 2001). There is a large body of research which suggests that effective corporate governance, in this case, having an audit committee in place, reduces agency costs, leading to lower costs of capital and higher firm value (Christopher, 2010; Solomon, 2010).

The role and responsibilities of audit committees will vary from jurisdiction to jurisdiction. There are, however, several common functions. These include:

- The committee should be made up of 3 or more independent non-executive directors;
- Reviewing the internal control functions;
- Monitoring the effectiveness of the company's internal audit function;
- Reviewing and monitoring the external auditor's independence and objectivity;
- Developing and implementing a policy on the engagement of the external auditor to supply non-audit services; and
- Reporting to the board of directors as to how it has discharged its responsibilities, assessed the effectiveness of the audit process and how the external auditor's independence and objectivity have been safeguarded.

5.2 Internal control effectiveness

The first step in establishing an environment of effective internal control is to establish the recommended practice in the relevant code of corporate governance (Spira and Page, 2003). The codes of corporate governance require committees to be established: who are responsible for monitoring and reviewing an organisation's risk management and the design, implementation and effectiveness of an entity's controls (see, for example, IOD, 2016). They include the establishment of a risk committee which will be responsible for identifying, quantifying and assessing the risks to which an entity is exposed (see, for example, IOD, 2016a). An entity will also establish an internal audit function, often overseen by the audit committee (see, for example, Companies Act No 71 of 2008; IOD, 2016).

6. Governance of ethics

Ethical leadership is crucial to the functioning of an entity. Ethical leadership is exemplified by integrity, competence, accountability, fairness and transparency (see, for example, IOD, 2016). Implementing such principles into an entity's governance structure will promote a culture of ethical behaviour. Ethical behaviour by senior management is in the best interest of the stakeholders of the organisation as long-term growth is promoted by ethical behaviour (Fogarty, 2009; King and Atkins, 2016).

The code of corporate governance in South Africa, King IV, recommends the practice that an ethics committee (referred to as a social and ethics committee in King IV) be established which oversees the reporting on organisational ethics, responsible corporate citizenship, sustainable development and stakeholder relationships (IOD, 2016). King IV requires the ethics committee to progress beyond compliance with the creation of value (IOD, 2016). This is achieved through the committee being comprised primarily of independent non-executive directors to ensure that an independent assessment is being performed (IOD, 2016).

7. Governance of information technology (IT) risks

Because of the continuing growth of and integration between business and IT, several risks, predominantly business continuity risks, arise (Raghupathi, 2007). The codes of corporate governance have evolved to cater for the risks a company is exposed to because of IT. King III and King IV required the establishment of an IT Steering Committee and a Chief Information Officer role (IOD, 2016). The duties of this type of committee include responding to the ever-changing IT environment to mitigate the risks arising, as well as taking advantage of business opportunities arising because of such changes in the IT environment (IOD, 2016). Refer to Chapter 17 on further developments in the auditing profession for more information with regard to IT.

8. Summary

- In conclusion, this chapter gives a brief history of how the auditing profession has come to be regulated and a summary of how it is regulated and why.
- There is an international body responsible for ensuring that the profession is regulated.
- It then mandates and requires each jurisdiction to establish its own regulatory oversight body. This is to assist the profession in improving the quality of audits, as well as provide a regulatory body, used in times of failures or crises in the profession.
- The chapter also focuses on the audit client and the need for the audit client to establish practices of good corporate governance which include the establishment of audit committees and a system of effective internal control.
- This is done to mitigate the risks to which the entity is exposed, resulting in the entity achieving its business strategy which would include long-term growth and profitability.

9. References

Anderson, G. D. & Ellyson, R. C. 1986. Restructuring Professional Standards: The Anderson Report. *Journal of Accountancy,* 162 (3), 92–104.

APA 2005. Auditing Profession Act No. 26 of 2005. *APA*. Republic of South Africa.

Bazerman, M. H., Loewenstein, G. & Moore, D. A. 2002. Why good accountants do bad audits. *Harvard business review,* (80), 96–102, 134.

Bazerman, M. H. & Moore, D. 2011. Is it time for auditor independence yet? *Accounting, Organizations and Society,* 36 (4–5), 310–312.

Bishop, C. C., Hermanson, D. R. & Houston, R. W. 2013. PCAOB Inspections of International Audit Firms: Initial Evidence. *International Journal of Auditing,* 17 (1), 1–18.

Black, J. 2008. Forms and Paradoxes of Principles-Based Regulation. *Capital Markets Law Journal,* 3 (4), 425–457.

Carrington, T. 2010. An analysis of the demands on a sufficient audit: Professional appearance is what counts! *Critical Perspectives on Accounting,* 21 (8), 669–682.

Centre for Audit Quality. 2012. Guide to PCAOB Inspections. Available: http://thecaq.org/sites/default/files/guidetopcaobinspections.pdf [Accessed 10 October 2017].

Chandler, R., Edwards, R. & Anderson, M. 1993. Changing Perceptions of the Role of the Company Auditor, 1840–1940. *Accounting and Business Research,* 23 (92), 443–459.

Christopher, J. 2010. Corporate governance–A multi-theoretical approach to recognizing the wider influencing forces impacting on organizations. *Critical Perspectives on Accounting,* 21 (8), 683–695.

Companies Act No. 71 of 2008. Republic of South Africa: Government Printers.

DeFond, M. & Zhang, J. 2014. A review of archival auditing research. *Journal of accounting and economics,* 58 (2–3), 275–326.

DeFond, M. L. & Lennox, C. S. 2011. The effect of SOX on small auditor exits and audit quality. *Journal of Accounting and Economics,* 52 (1), 21–40.

Deumes, R., Schelleman, C., Vander Bauwhede, H. & Vanstraelen, A. 2012. Audit firm governance: Do transparency reports reveal audit quality? *Auditing: A Journal of Practice & Theory,* 31 (4), 193–214.

Edwards, J. R. 2001. Accounting regulation and the professionalization process: A historical essay concerning the significance of P. H. Abbott. *Critical Perspectives on Accounting,* 12 (6), 675–696.

Fogarty, T. J. 2009. Corporate Governance and Ethics. *Issues in Accounting Education,* 24 (2), 253.

Francis, J. R. 2004. What do we know about audit quality? *The British Accounting Review,* 36 (4), 345–368.

FRC 2015. *The Financial Reporting Council* [Online]. Available: https://www.frc.org.uk/Home.aspx [Accessed 1 December 2015].

FRC 2016a. Scope and Authority of Audit and Assurance Pronouncements.

FRC 2016b. UK Code of Corporate Governance.

FRC 2016c. The UK corporate governance code. *London, September.*

Humphrey, C., Kausar, A., Loft, A. & Woods, M. 2011. Regulating Audit beyond the Crisis: A Critical Discussion of the EU Green Paper. *European Accounting Review,* 20 (3), 431–457.

IFAC 2010. Definition of Transnational Audit. *TAC Guidance Statement 1*. New York: [IFAC].

IFAC 2020. *International Standard Setting Boards* [Online]. Available: https://www. international-standards.org/ [Accessed 20 May 2020].

Imhoff, G. 2003. Accounting quality, auditing and corporate governance.

IOD 2016. *King IV Report on Corporate Governance in South Africa*, Lexis Nexus South Africa, Johannesburg, South Africa.

IRBA 2014. IRBA Manual of Information. Johannesburg, South Africa: Independent Regulatory Board for Auditors.

Jensen, M. C. & Meckling, W. H. 1976. Theory of the firm: Managerial behavior, agency costs and ownership structure. *Journal of Financial Economics,* 3 (4), 305–360.

Khalifa, R., Sharma, N., Humphrey, C. & Robson, K. 2007. Discourse and Audit Change: transformations in methodology in the professional audit field. *Accounting, Auditing and Accountability Journal,* 20 (6), 825–854.

King, M. 2016. Comments on: *Integrated reporting*, GARI Conference, Henley on Thames, United Kingdom. 23 October.

King, M. & Atkins, J. 2016. *The Chief Value Officer. Accountants Can Save the Planet,* Abingdon, Oxon, United Kingdom, Greenleaf Publishing Limited.

Louw, A. & Maroun, W. 2017. Independent monitoring and review functions in a financial reporting context. *Meditari Accountancy Research,* 25 (2), null.

Love, I. & Klapper, L. F. 2002. *Corporate governance, investor protection, and performance in emerging markets*, The World Bank.

Maroun, W. & Cerbone, D. 2020. *Corporate Governance in South Africa*, Walter de Gruyter GmbH & Co KG.

Maroun, W. & Jonker, C. 2014. Critical and interpretive accounting, auditing and governance research in South Africa. *Southern African Journal of Accountability and Auditing Research,* 16 (1), 51–62.

Monks, R. A. & Minow, N. 2003. Corporate Governance. 3rd. London, Blackwell.

Nag, T. 2015. Corporate Governance in South Africa. *Corporate Governance, Responsibility and Sustainability.* Springer.

Peecher, M. E., Schwartz, R. & Solomon, I. 2007. It's all about audit quality: Perspectives on strategic-systems auditing. *Accounting, Organizations and Society,* 32 (4–5), 463–485.

Pentland, B. T. 1993. Getting comfortable with the numbers: Auditing and the micro-production of macro-order. *Accounting, Organizations and Society,* 18 (7), 605–620.

Porter, B. 1993. An empirical study of the audit expectation-performance gap. *Accounting and business research,* 24 (93), 49–68.

Porter, B., Ó hÓgartaigh, C. & Baskerville, R. 2012. Audit Expectation-Performance Gap Revisited: Evidence from New Zealand and the United Kingdom. Part 1: The Gap in New Zealand and the United Kingdom in 2008. *International Journal of Auditing,* 16 (2), 101–129.

Porter, B., Simon, J. & Hatherly, D. 2014. *Principles of External Auditing,* West Suzzex, John Wiley & Sons.

Power, M. K. 1994. *The Audit Explosion,* London, Demos.

Raghunandan, K., Rama, D. V. & Read, W. J. 2001. Audit committee composition,"gray directors," and interaction with internal auditing. *Accounting horizons,* 15 (2), 105–118.

Raghupathi, W. 2007. Corporate governance of IT: A framework for development. *Communications of the ACM,* 50 (8), 94–99.

Ronen, J. 2002. Post-enron reform: Financial-statement insurance and GAAP revisited. *Stan. JL Bus. & Fin.,* 8, 39.

Shaked, A. & Sutton, J. 1981. The Self-Regulating Profession. *Review of Economic Studies,* 48, 217–234.

Solomon, J. 2010. *Corporate Governance and Accountability, Third Edition,* West Susex, United Kingdom, John Wiley and Sons Ltd.

Sommer Jr, A. 2000. The Public Oversight Board. *Journal of Accountancy,* 190 (3), 84.

Spira, L. F. & Page, M. 2003. Risk management: The reinvention of internal control and the changing role of internal audit. *Accounting, Auditing & Accountability Journal,* 16 (4), 640–661.

The European Commission (2005). Corporate Governance, Innovation and Economic Performance in the EU CGEP.

Unerman, J. & O'Dwyer, B. 2004. Enron, WorldCom, Andersen et al.: a challenge to modernity. *Critical Perspectives on Accounting,* 15 (6–7), 971–993.

Zeff, S. A. 2003. How the U.S. accounting profession got where it is today: Part I. *Accounting Horizons,* 17 (3), 189–205.

Chapter 3: Code of Professional Conduct

1. Introduction

Professional accountants are held to a high standard of ethical conduct by users of financial statements (Duska et al., 2018). Stakeholders of companies rely on financial information, prepared by professional accountants, in making decisions. Errors and misstatements in financial information have a detrimental effect on stakeholders' wealth and wellbeing (Porter et al., 2014; Duska et al., 2018). The reliance placed on financial information has resulted in the need for auditors to assure the financial statements to provide a higher level of confidence in the information presented by management (Porter et al., 2014). Given the prominence and effect which these two professions have in financial markets, professional accountants and auditors must conduct themselves in line with these expectations, as well as act in the public interest. To ensure this, various accounting and auditing bodies have created codes of conduct to which members of their relevant professional body are bound (Sutton, 1993; Zeff, 2003; Porter et al., 2014; Duska et al., 2018).

IFAC published its first *Code of Ethics for Professional Accountants* in 1996, with the last major revision in 2018. The Code of Ethics, although published by IFAC, is developed by the International Ethics Standards Board for Accountants (IESBA) which functions under the authority of IFAC (IESBA, 2019a). In the United States, the American Institute of Certified Public Accountants created and adopted a separate code which applies to professional accountants in the United States. This chapter deals mainly with IESBA's *Code of Ethics for Professional Accountants* (referred to as the Code). The chapter also provides examples of codes of best practice from different jurisdictions and deals with some of the similarities in these codes.

2. Structure of the Code

A code of professional ethics establishes ethical requirements for members of a profession. It provides standards for describing and assessing ethical behaviour in order to facilitate accountability for professional conduct. This is achieved by, *inter alia,* providing terms of reference for members' conduct, guidance on day-to-day decision making and resolution of ethical difficulties and recommendations for addressing unethical conduct (Kretzchmar et al., 2012).

A code of ethics should promote responsibility in the interest of bolstering the trust which stakeholders vest in the profession and, in turn, its continued existence (Rossouw and Vuuren, 2016). Codes of ethics have become a defining feature of the accounting and auditing professions (Kretzchmar et al., 2012). The Code states that, 'a distinguishing mark of the accountancy profession is its acceptance of the responsibility to act in the public interest', (IESBA, 2019a, p. 16). The Code makes it clear that a professional accountant should not place the needs of an individual or organisation above those of the public.

In order to ensure that there is no uncertainty regarding the responsibilities of the professional accountant, the Code is structured in four parts, each addressing different services which are rendered by a professional accountant. The structure is shown in Figure 1 below:

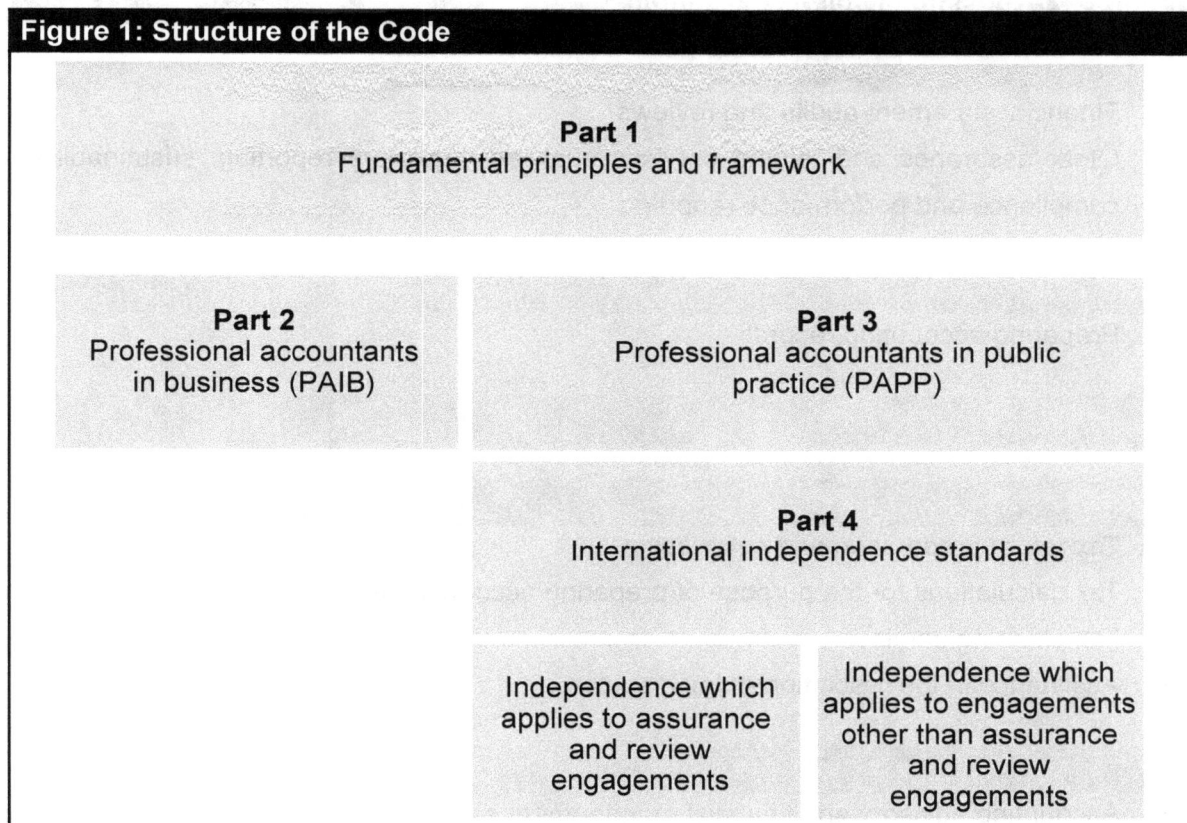

Figure 1: Structure of the Code

Part 1
Fundamental principles and framework

Part 2
Professional accountants in business (PAIB)

Part 3
Professional accountants in public practice (PAPP)

Part 4
International independence standards

Independence which applies to assurance and review engagements

Independence which applies to engagements other than assurance and review engagements

(IESBA, 2019a)

Part 1 explains the conceptual framework which is generally applicable to all professional accountants (IESBA, 2019a). Part 2 elaborates on how the conceptual framework applies to professional accountants in business. This includes professional accountants employed by a public practice firm (ie an audit firm) performing professional services pursuant to their relationship with the firm and those providing professional services in the following sectors:

- Commerce, trade and industry;
- The public sector;
- Education;
- Not-for-profit sectors; or
- Regulatory or professional bodies.

(IESBA, 2019a)

The Code does not provide detailed guidance on what is meant by 'professional services'. The South African amended-code includes the following as examples of professional services which, in the authors' opinion, should be broadly applicable in other jurisdictions: audit, reviews, other assurance and related services, accounting services, company statutory services, taxation services and management consulting and advisory services (For more examples, refer to SAICA, 2019, pp. 27–28).

Figure 2: Professional services examples

Audit, review and other assurance and related services
- Financial statement audits and reviews
- Other assurance and related services such as regulatory reporting, sustainability, compliance and performance reporting

Accounting services
- Preparing accounting records

Company statutory services

Taxation services
- Tax return preparation and submission
- Tax calculations for the purpose of preparing accounting entries
- Tax planning services
- Assistance in the resolution of tax disputes

Management consulting and advisory services
- Accounting advisory and financial management services
- Business performance services
- Internal audit, risk and compliance services, reviews and monitoring of internal controls
- Corporate finance services, mergers and acquisitions, valuations
- Corporate recovery services, liquidation and insolvency
- Financial risk management services, actuarial services, banking and risk advisory
- Information techonology advisory services
- Forensic services, dispute advisory and resolution, ethics and integrity monitoring, fraud risk management

Part 3 of the Code applies to professional accountants who are in public practice and provide professional services, other than assurance services. Should professional accountants provide assurance services, Part 4A and B will apply. Part 4A details the applicable independence rules when the professional accountant carries out audit or review engagements. Part 4B details independence rules which apply when the professional accountant provides assurance services other than audit or review engagements (IESBA, 2019a). Refer to Chapter 21 for examples of assurance engagements other than audit or review engagements.

Each section in the Code starts by outlining the respective requirements and application material. The application material goes into considerable detail on specific practices which are or are not acceptable with multiple examples, suggestions and illustrations.

3. Fundamental principles and the conceptual framework

The Code follows a conceptual approach to managing ethics which is achieved through the application of the conceptual framework. The framework requires professional accountants to identify, evaluate and address threats to compliance with the fundamental principles, rather than merely comply with pre-defined rules. (Kretzchmar et al., 2012).

4. Fundamental principles

Table 1 below summarises the fundamental principles (see IEASB, 2019, para 110.A1).

Table 1: Fundamental principles	
Fundamental principle	**Requirement**
Integrity	• A professional accountant should be straightforward and honest in all professional and business relationships. • The accountant must be truthful and not knowingly be associated with reports, returns, communications or other information which (1) contains false information; (2) contains statements or information provided recklessly or (3) omits or obscures required information where such omission or obscurity will be misleading.
Objectivity	• A professional accountant should not allow bias, conflict of interest or the undue influence of others to compromise professional or business judgements.

►

Table 1: Fundamental principles	
Fundamental principle	**Requirement**
Professional competence and due care	• A professional accountant has a duty to maintain professional knowledge and skill at the level required to ensure that a client or employing organisation receives appropriate competent services based on current legislation, standards and legislation. • This will require the professional accountant to take reasonable steps to ensure that those working in a professional capacity under their authority have appropriate training and supervision. • A professional accountant is not permitted to continue with an engagement which they are not competent to perform unless advice and assistance are obtained to ensure that the applicable service is carried out satisfactorily.
Confidentiality	• A professional accountant should not disclose confidential information acquired as a result of his professional or business relationships unless there is a legal or professional right or duty to disclose such information. • Confidential information should not be used for the personal advantage of the professional or third parties. • The professional accountant will take steps to ensure that the confidentiality of the information is maintained.
Professional behaviour	• In addition to complying with the relevant laws and regulations, a professional accountant should avoid any action which discredits the profession.

Adapted from IESBA (2019a)

The Code provides guidance to professional accountants in situations where complying with one fundamental principle can create conflicts with one or more of the other fundamental principles. For example, in complying with a law or regulation requiring a matter to be reported to an external party, the professional accountant will breach the principle of confidentiality while complying with the principle of professional behaviour. However, the Code does permit such disclosure and provides examples of when these disclosures may be appropriate:

- Disclosure is required by law;
- Disclosure is permitted by law and is authorised by the client or the employing organisation; and

- There is a professional duty or right to disclose, when not prohibited by law:
  - To comply with quality reviews performed by regulatory authorities;
  - To respond to an inquiry or investigation;
  - To protect the professional interest of a professional accountant in legal proceedings; or
  - To comply with technical and professional standards, including ethics requirements.

(Refer to IESBA, 2019a, pp. 21–22)

While the Code contains numerous examples and prescriptions, the professional accountant is still required to apply professional judgement when resolving ethical conflicts. The Code also allows the professional accountant to consult, even anonymously, with:
- Others within the firm or organisation;
- Those charged with corporate governance of the client;
- A professional body;
- A regulatory body; or
- Legal counsel.

(IESBA, 2019a)

5. Conceptual framework

Different threats to the compliance with fundamental principles may arise from the day-to-day activities of a professional accountant. The conceptual framework in the Code requires the professional accountant to:

- Identify threats to compliance with the fundamental principles;
- Evaluate the threats; and
- Address relevant threats by eliminating or reducing them to an acceptably low level.

The professional accountant must exercise professional judgement when applying the conceptual framework. This requires the professional accountant to remain alert for new information and to changes in facts and circumstances when identifying and evaluating threats to the fundamental principles (Kretzchmar et al., 2012; Knechel and Salterio, 2016; IESBA, 2019a). Professional judgement is a skill and is the operationalisation of the professional accountant's knowledge, obtained from past experiences and training, to reach an appropriate conclusion.

6. Identifying threats to compliance with the fundamental principles

The threats to the fundamental principles are explained in Table 2. In order to identify the threats, the accountant is required to gather all the facts and circumstances related to the professional activity, interest or relationship which may compromise compliance with the fundamental principles (IESBA, 2019a). The Code provides examples of facts or circumstances which give rise to threats but it is not intended to be read as an exhaustive list of potential ethical concerns (IESBA, 2019a). Once these threats have been identified, it is necessary to evaluate and address them (Section 7 and 8).

Table 2: Threats to fundamental principles		
Threat	**Explanation**	**Examples**
Self-interest threat	*The threat that a financial or other interest will inappropriately influence a professional accountant's judgement or behaviour.*	• Financial involvement with a client • Close family or personal relationship with a director or senior executive of a client • Overreliance on professional services fee • Receipt of goods or hospitality from the client
Self-review threat	*The threat that a professional accountant will not appropriately evaluate the results of a previous judgement made or an activity performed by the accountant, or by another individual within the accountant's firm or employing organization, on which the accountant will rely when forming a judgement as part of performing a current activity.*	• Performed tax calculations for the client which will be used for the financial statements • Performed a valuation for the client which is used in the financial statements • Designing and implementing a new accounting application to be used by an audit client
Advocacy threat	*The threat that a professional accountant will promote a client's or employing organization's position to the point that the accountant's objectivity is compromised.*	• Supporting a client in a legal dispute and testifying on behalf of the client

▶

Table 2: Threats to fundamental principles		
Threat	**Explanation**	**Examples**
Familiarity threat	The threat that because a long or close relationship with a client or employing organization, a professional accountant will be too sympathetic to their interests or too accepting of their work.	• Long tenure with an audit client or close relationships with management at the audit client • Past relationships with members of a client
Intimidation threat	The threat that a professional accountant will be deterred from acting objectively because of actual or perceived pressures, including attempts to exercise undue influence over the accountant.	• Aggressive attitudes toward the professional services provider or team members • Threats to replace the professional accountant with another if differences are not resolved in favour of the client

(Jakubowski et al., 2002; Kretzchmar et al., 2012; Porter et al., 2014; IESBA, 2019a)

7. Evaluating threats to fundamental principles

In evaluating the threats to the fundamental principles, the professional accountant should consider whether or not a threat is at an acceptable level. In determining whether the threat is at an acceptable level, the professional accountant will apply the *reasonable and informed third party test (IESBA, 2019a)*. This requires the professional account to consider all facts and circumstances which would have been considered by a reasonable and informed party in concluding. The considerations should be taken into account from the perspective of the third party who will weigh all facts and circumstances the professional accountant knows, or is reasonably expected to know, at the time that the conclusions are made (IESBA, 2019a).

The considerations can include qualitative and/or quantitative factors which may be relevant in evaluating the threat to the fundamental principles. For example:

- Corporate governance requirements;
- Educational, training and experience requirements for the profession (such as continuous professional development programmes);
- Laws, regulations or ethical obligations; or
- Professional or regulatory monitoring and disciplinary procedures.

(Porter et al., 2014; IESBA, 2019a)

Should the professional accountant become aware of any additional information, the threat needs to be re-evaluated and appropriate responses developed and implemented.

8. Addressing threats to fundamental principles

Once the threats to the fundamental principles have been identified and evaluated, appropriate safeguards should be introduced to reduce any risks to an acceptably low level (IESBA, 2019a). There are two broad categories of safeguards namely, safeguards created by the profession, legislation or regulation and safeguards in the work environment.

These are summarised in Table 3:

Table 3: Examples of safeguards	
Safeguard	**Explanation**
Safeguards created by the profession, legislation or regulation	
Education and training	Educational training, professional development and training for members (CPD)
Regulation	Regulatory disciplinary procedures for members
Reviews	Professional reviews of work performed by other professional accountants.
Safeguards in the work environment	
Safeguards in the work environment are intended to deal with specific threats identified by professionals in the conduct of their work. Such appropriate safeguards are summarised as follows:	
Involving another accountant to review the work undertaken.	The work performed by the auditor or the accountant can be reviewed by another party, be it a professional accountant, auditor or any other professional. This can ensure that threats to the fundamental principles can be mitigated.
Consulting an independent third party.	If the accountant or auditor feels that there is a threat to his/her independence, then consulting with an independent third party who can provide an unbiased assessment of the facts and circumstances may mitigate the threat.

▶

Table 3: Examples of safeguards	
Safeguard explanation	
Discussing ethical issues with those charged with governance of the client.	Directors and other senior managers are those who are charged with a company's governance. If a accountant or auditor feels there is a threat to one of the fundamental principles, discussing these ethical matters with the directors and others charged with governance will allow the accountant or auditor to arrive at a solution which will mitigate the threat.
Involving another firm to perform or reperform part of the engagement.	In an assurance engagement, if the auditor feels that there is a threat to one of the fundamental principles, the audit partner can engage another firm to perform the part of the engagement again.
Rotating senior team personnel.	If the auditor feels that there is a threat to the fundamental principles (such as self-review or familiarity threats), the senior members of the team can be rotated in order to mitigate the threat.

(Adapted from Falk et al., 1999; Jakubowski et al., 2002; Kretzchmar et al., 2012)

9. Professional accountants in public practice

Part 3 applies to accountants in public practice, whether or not they provide assurance services. The Code does not provide for every circumstance the accountant may encounter and requires the accountant to be alert to any facts or circumstances which may cause ethical issues (IESBA, 2019a). The Code requires the professional accountant to apply the conceptual framework, as discussed in Section 3. The Code makes provision for accountants in public practice performing professional activities pursuant to their relationship with the firm and requires these professional accountants to comply with Part 2.

In addressing threats, the following general safeguards can be applied:

Figure 3: Safeguards applied to professional accountants in public practice

Assignment of additional resources to complete the required tasks	Appointing appropriate reviewers who are not members of the team to review the work or provide guidance	Appointing different partners and engagement teams with seperate reporting lines for the provision of non-assurance services to an assurance client
Involving another firm to perform or re-perform part of the engagement	Disclosing to clients any referral fees or commission arrangements received for recommending sercvies or products	Separating teams when dealing with matters of a confidential nature

Adjusted from IESBA (2019a)

Below is a summary of each section applicable to accountants in public practice with examples of threats and safeguards to reduce those threats:

Table 4: Summary of select provisions of the code

Section	Summary
310: Conflicts of interest	An accountant will not permit a conflict of interest to compromise professional business judgement. Examples of where a conflict of interest can arise include: • Providing advice to two clients at the same time to acquire the same company and the advice may be relevant to the parties' competitive positions; • Providing services to a seller and a buyer in relation to the same transaction; and • The interests of the accountant with respect to a matter and the interests of the audit client are in conflict. For example, the professional accountant advises an audit client to invest in a company of which the accountant's spouse is the owner. A self-interest threat to an auditor's independence arises when there is a conflict of interest. A number of other threats to the fundamental principles can also arise. For example, the client may obtain

▶

Table 4: Summary of select provisions of the code	
Section	**Summary**
	confidential information and is bound to comply with the fundamental principles of confidentiality to not make the information publicly available. When a conflict of interest arises, the professional accountant must determine whether or not the conflict requires specific disclosure and if explicit consent is necessary when addressing the threat. Factors to consider include: • The circumstances creating the conflict of interest • The parties which may be affected • The nature of the issues which may arise • The potential for the matter to develop in an unexpected manner. Disclosure and consent might take the following forms: • Inclusion of general disclosure in the standard terms and conditions for the engagement which states that the professional accountant does not provide professional services exclusively to any one client • Disclosure of the circumstances of the particular conflict to the affected client. When disclosing a potential conflict, the accountant should be careful not to breach confidentiality. For this reason, an engagement can only be accepted if: • The firm will not act in an advisory role for clients in adversarial positions on the same matter • Measures are in place to ensure that confidentiality of information is maintained • A reasonable third party would be likely to conclude that it is appropriate for the firm to accept or continue the engagement without any undue prejudice to any of the parties.

►

Table 4: Summary of select provisions of the code	
Section	**Summary**
320: Professional appointments	The acceptance of a new audit client gives rise to several threats to the fundamental principles. Upon accepting a new audit client, the auditor must apply the requirements of ISQC 1 in determining the threats to ethical requirements. The Code requires the auditor to do the following when accepting a new audit client: • Contact the previous auditor • Inquiring from the previous auditor whether or not there are any reasons to refrain from accepting the audit client • Obtain information from other sources as to the integrity of the proposed client's management. The client acceptance process is discussed in more detail in Chapter 9.
321: Second opinions	A self-interest threat to competence and due care arises when the accountant is requested to provide a second opinion. This is because the accountant may base an opinion on a different set of facts and circumstances or on incomplete information. Safeguards which can address the self-interest threat include: • Obtaining the client's written permission to obtain information from the existing or predecessor accountant • Describe the limitations surrounding any opinion in communications with the client • Providing the existing or predecessor accountant with a copy of the opinion.
330: Fees and other types of remuneration	The accountant must assess the amount and nature of the remuneration received from audit clients. This includes the following: • The level of audit fee – an accountant is not unethical by charging a fee lower than another accountant does provided that the quoted fee is not so low that it will impair the auditor's ability to conduct the audit according to the applicable professional standards • Contingent fees are fees based on some form of outcome being achieved. The accountant may not charge contingency fees for assurance engagements

►

Table 4: Summary of select provisions of the code	
Section	**Summary**
	• Referral fees could give rise to a self-interest threat to independence and professional behaviour as the accountant may focus their attention on the generation of fees rather than from the applicable professional services. The accountant will not charge contingency fees for the preparation of an original or amended tax return as this creates an unacceptably high self-interest threat. Refer to Section 4 below for independence requirements.
340: Gifts and hospitality	The accountant must assess the nature, value and intention of the gift received from a client as this may create self-interest, familiarity or intimidation threats, especially to integrity, objectivity and professional behaviour. In particular, the accountant will not: • Offer, or encourage others to offer any inducement that a reasonable and informed third party will be likely to conclude is made with the objective of improperly influencing the behaviour of the recipient or of another individual • Accept any offer or inducement which a reasonable and informed third party will be likely to conclude is made with the objective of improperly influencing the behaviour of the recipient or of another individual. In order to evaluate threats to the applicable fundamental principles, the accountant must consider, for example: • The nature, frequency, value and cumulative effect of the inducement • When the inducement is offered relative to any action or decision that it might influence • Whether the inducement is a customary or cultural practice. Should the inducement or gift pose a threat to the fundamental principles, the auditor must consider informing management of the firm or those charged with governance of the client of the offer or inducement. It may also be necessary to amend or terminate the business relationship with the client.

▶

Table 4: Summary of select provisions of the code	
Section	**Summary**
350: Custody of assets	An auditor must not hold any money as a custodian unless permitted by law as this can create a self-interest threat.
360: Responding to non-compliance with laws and regulations	An accountant may detect non-compliance with laws or regulations during the execution of professional services for a client. The non-compliance may create threats to the fundamental principles. If non-compliance is identified, the professional accountant is required to perform the following: • Understand that there is an act of non-compliance. Often this is obtained by seeking legal advice • Discuss the matter with the management of the entity • Assess management's response to the non-compliance • If the answer is inadequate, the professional accountant is required to contact their respective regulator. In South Africa, this means assessing whether a reportable irregularity must be reported to the Independent Regulatory Board for Auditors. In the UK, the matter may need to be referred to the Financial Reporting Council. Refer to Chapters 4, 6 and 8 where the application of this section is discussed.

Adjusted from IESBA (2019a)

10. International independence standards

The independence standards which accompany the Code are divided into two sections:

- Part 4A refers to independence requirements which apply to an audit or a review engagement and
- Part 4B refers to the independence requirements applicable to an assurance engagement other than a review or an audit engagement.

As discussed in Section 4, the accountant is required to be independent of their client. This requires independence in mind and independence in appearance. Independence in mind is defined as the state of mind which permits the expression of a conclusion without being affected by influences which compromise professional judgement. Independence in appearance requires the professional accountant to avoid circumstances which, in the opinion of a reasonably informed third party, would undermine the integrity, objectivity or professional scepticism of the professional account or the respective firm (Porter et al., 2014; IESBA, 2019a).

The Code mandates that independence must be maintained during the engagement period and the period covered by the financial statements. For example, should an entity become an audit client during or after the period covered by the financial statements on which the firm will express an opinion, the firm will determine whether any threats to independence are created by:

- Financial or business relationships with the audit client during or after the period covered by the financial statements but before accepting the audit engagement; or
- Previous services provided to the audit client by the firm or a network firm.

The independence rules also make reference to public interest entities. Public interest entities have a wide range of stakeholders and are usually listed on recognised stock exchanges[1]. In making this assessment, the professional accountant must consider whether the company is a financial institution, the entity's size and the number of employees. In a South African context, these will be listed companies, state-owned entities, entities with a large number of stakeholders, banks, pension funds and investment houses (SAICA, 2019). The guidelines which apply to the Code for professional accountants in South Africa, require the professional accountant *firm* to develop a framework or definition to classify a client as a public interest entity, which should include consideration of the following factors:

- The nature of the business, for example, holding of assets in a fiduciary capacity for a large number of stakeholders;
- Number of equity or debt holders;
- Size of the company; or
- The number of employees.

Given the different methods which can be employed by an accountant, each firm should develop its own definition or set criteria to determine whether an entity is a public interest entity or not[2]. This is essential to each service that a professional accountant (or firm) renders as some services may be prohibited. Table 5 provides a summary of the specific circumstances by which an auditor's independence may be threatened. In some circumstances, the threats to independence are so severe that no safeguard exists to reduce the threat to an acceptably low level.

---

1   The IESBA has received requests for further clarification on the definition of a recognised stock exchange and what is meant by a public interest entity. This was added to their agenda and a project was approved in December 2019. It is expected that this definition will be expanded on significantly given the requests from various stakeholders in the future (IESBA, 2019b).

2   In developing this criteria, the professional accountant and firm should take into consideration any laws or juristic requirements.

Table 5: Independence requirements in terms of Part 4	
Section	**Summary**
410: Fees	The relative size of the fee charged to each client must be assessed. This is because a self-interest and intimidation threats arise where a client's fee makes up a large proportion of the firm's total fees. For example, an auditor may compromise integrity and objectify and undermine independence in order to avoid losing the audit client. Where an audit client is a public interest entity and the audit fee is 15% or more of the total fees for two consecutive years, the auditor must disclose this fact to their audit client and consider whether or not there are any threats to the fundamental principles. • Overdue fees may create a self-interest threat to professional competence and due care because the auditor may not perform the audit to sufficiently high standards when fees are overdue. When a significant part of fees due from an audit client remain unpaid for a long time, the firm must determine: whether the overdue fees may be equivalent to a loan to the client; and • Whether it is appropriate for the firm to be re-appointed or continue the audit engagement.
411: Compensation and evaluation policies	This section deals with the possibility of an audit firm's compensation policy, creating a threat to the fundamental principles. For example, an audit team member's performance evaluation or compensation may be based on selling non-audit services to an audit client. In determining whether or not a self-interest threat arises, the auditor must assess the following: • What proportion of total compensation is made up of the sale of such services; • The role of the individual on the audit team; and • Whether or not the sale of non-assurance services impacts the promotion decisions of the audit firm. Key audit partners may not be compensated for the sale of non-assurance services.

▶

Table 5: Independence requirements in terms of Part 4	
Section	**Summary**
430: Actual or threatened litigation	In circumstances where litigation between an auditor and audit client arises, intimidation and self-interest threats to the fundamental principles can result. The auditor must consider the materiality of the litigation and whether or not it relates to a prior audit. This can result in the auditor being intimidated by the audit client or using confidential information to assist in supporting the auditor's position in the event of litigation.
510: Financial interests	Auditors may not hold a financial interest in firms they are auditing. This creates a self-interest threat to independence which is so severe that no safeguards can be applied to reduce the threat. Where an immediate family member[3] holds a financial interest in an audit client, the auditor must assess whether or not there are any self-interest threats to the fundamental principles. Safeguards may include removing the individual from the audit or requesting the family member to dispose of the interest in the entity. A self-interest threat can also arise when a close family member of an audit team has a direct or material indirect financial interest in an audit client. When evaluating the threat, the auditor should consider the nature of the relationship between the audit team member and the close family member, whether or not the financial interest is direct or indirect and the materiality of the financial interest to the close family member. Safeguards may include removing the individual from the audit, requesting the family member to dispose of the interest in the entity or having the work performed by the affected audit team member reviewed.
511: Loans and guarantees	If the audit client is a lending institution, a self-interest threat to independence can arise if a loan granted to the auditor or the audit firm is not under normal economic circumstances. The auditor or their immediate family may not accept a loan or guarantee of any form from their audit client if their audit client is not a lending institution.

▶

---

3   Immediate family includes spouses (or equivalent) and dependents. Close family members include parents, children or siblings.

Table 5: Independence requirements in terms of Part 4	
Section	**Summary**
520: Business relationships	Close business relationships may create self-interest and intimidation threats to independence. However, the buying of goods and services does not create a threat to an audit firm's independence provided that the purchase is made under normal business circumstances and is at arm's length.
521: Family and personal relationships	Family or personal relationships between the auditor and a client's staff may give rise to self-interest, familiarity or intimidation threat to the fundamental principles. The factors to consider when evaluating the significance of the threats include, for example, the individual's responsibilities on the audit and the role of the family member at the audit client. For example, if the family member is the director of an audit client, a self-interest and familiarity threat to the fundamental principles arises which is so severe that the audit team member should be removed from the audit.
522: Recent service with an audit client	• Service during the period covered by the audit report – the individual cannot be a part of the audit team if they served as director of the audit client or were in a position to exert significant influence over the preparation of the financial statements. • Service prior to the period covered by the report: this may create threats to the fundamental principles if the audit team member was a director or was in a position to exert significant influence over the preparation of the financial statements. Safeguards can include detailed reviews by a more senior individual of the audit team member's work.
523: Serving as a director or officer of an audit client	The auditor must not serve as a director or an officer of an audit client.

▶

Table 5: Independence requirements in terms of Part 4	
Section	**Summary**
524: Employment with an audit client	• Former audit partner: self-review and intimidation threats may arise. The auditor can implement safeguards such as changing the audit plan and/or assigning more experienced staff to the engagement. • For audit firm employee: if the audit firm's employee will take up employment with the audit client, the employee should no longer form part of the audit team. • Public interest entities and key audit partners: independence is compromised and the only safeguard is that the audit partner ceases to be the audit partner for a period of 12 months prior to accepting the new position at the audit client.
525: Temporary personnel assignments	The provision of audit staff may result in self-review and advocacy threats to independence. If assigning audit staff to a client results in the audit client's policies and procedures becoming similar to those of the audit firm or *vice versa* then the threat is significant and no safeguard can be applied.
540: Long association of personnel	• The individual: the length of the individual's relationship with the audit client and how long the individual has been an engagement team member can compromise the individual's independence. • The audit client: the auditor should consider whether or not there have been material changes at the client. For example, a change in a client's senior management can reduce the threat to an auditor's independence. • Public interest entities: The audit partner, engagement quality control/review partner or any other key audit partner cannot serve in that role for more than seven cumulative years. After the seven-year period, a cooling-off period applies after which the individual may not serve in the respective role for a further stipulated period. • Mandatory firm rotation has been implemented by both South Africa and the UK to address the risk of long association of firms with their clients.
601: Accounting and bookkeeping services	These services include the provision of preparation of accounting records or financial statements, recording transactions and payroll services. The auditors cannot provide such services as they will create a self-review threat to independence which is so severe that no safeguard can reduce this threat to an acceptably low level. They can provide these services if they are routine in nature.

▶

Table 5: Independence requirements in terms of Part 4	
Section	**Summary**
602: Administrative services	Administrative services are routine or day-to-day transactions. They require little professional judgement and, as a result, do not create material threats to the auditor's independence.
603: Valuation services	The provision of valuation services may create self-review threats to independence. The auditor can mitigate the risks by ensuring that the individual providing the valuation service is not part of the audit team. If, however, the client is a public interest entity, the auditor cannot provide valuation services.
604: Tax services	In general, these services create self-review threats to independence. Where a company is a not a public interest entity, safeguards to reduce the threats to independence include ensuring that the individual preparing the tax work is not part of the audit team and additional monitoring/ review. If the entity is a public interest entity, the audit firm cannot perform certain tax services to its audit clients. For example, the audit team will not be able to do tax calculations which relate to the financial statements.
605: Internal audit services	These services can include the monitoring and designing of internal controls, evaluating the operating effectiveness of internal controls and reviewing compliance with laws and regulations. If the auditor assumes the managerial responsibilities of the audit client, no safeguards can be implemented to reduce threats to the fundamental principles to acceptably low levels. In addition, if an entity is a public interest entity, internal audit services cannot be provided.
606: Information technology systems services	If the auditor assumes managerial responsibilities for a client's information technology systems (ITS), no safeguards can reduce threats to independence to an acceptably low level. In addition, if the entity is a public interest entity, ITS cannot be provided.

11. International accounting bodies and their codes of conduct

This section provides a brief review of codes of ethics issued by the following accounting bodies/regulators:

- Association of Chartered Certified Accountants (ACCA)
- Institute of Chartered Accountants of Scotland (ICAS)

- Institute of Chartered Accountants in England and Wales (ICAEW)
- Chartered Institute of Management Accountants (CIMA)
- American Institute of Certified Public Accountants (AICPA)
- Securities and Exchange Commission (SEC)
- South African Institute of Chartered Accountants (SAICA).

12. ACCA

The ACCA code of conduct follows a fundamental principles-conceptual-based approach. The code iterates that it is not sufficient for members only to comply with the examples of circumstances set out in the code but that members must also follow the fundamental principles for each ethical consideration and circumstances which arise (ACCA, 2020).

13. ICAS

The ICAS code establishes five fundamental principles applicable to all professional accountants (see Section 4 above) (ICAS, 2020). This conceptual framework approach iterates the need for professional accountants to use their professional judgement to identify and evaluate threats in compliance with the fundamental principles (Kretzchmar et al., 2012; FRC, 2019; ICAS, 2020).

14. ICAEW

The preamble to the ICAEW code of conduct discusses the fact that chartered accounts are expected to demonstrate the highest standards of professional conduct and to take into consideration the public interest (ICAEW, 2020). Public trust is maintained through ensuring a high standard of ethical conduct (Kretzchmar et al., 2012; ICAEW, 2020).

The code helps ICAEW members meet this ethical standard by providing them with a set of ethical guidelines which they can follow (Kretzchmar et al., 2012). In a fashion similar to the other accounting bodies, the ICAEW follows the fundamental principles approach (ICAEW, 2020). The ICAEW reinforces its commitment to the code by disciplining members who do not comply with the code (Kretzchmar et al., 2012; ICAEW, 2020).

15. CIMA

The CIMA code of conduct requires all CIMA members and registered students to maintain and uphold the highest standards of ethical conduct and professional behaviour (CIMA, 2020). Members and students are expected to refrain from any conduct or behaviour which can bring the profession into disrepute and to maintain and uphold the principles of equal opportunity and fundamental human rights (CIMA, 2020). The institute encourages its members to be good and responsible professionals and to behave in a manner befitting of professional accountants (CIMA, 2020).

CIMA's code of ethics is based on the International Federation of Accountants (IFAC) code of ethics which was developed with input from CIMA and other global accountancy bodies (CIMA, 2020). The CIMA code also follows the fundamental principles approach which requires members to follow the conceptual framework approach in assessing threats to independence (Kretzchmar et al., 2012; Rossouw and Vuuren, 2016; CIMA, 2020).

16. AICPA

The preamble to the AICPA code states that members should be self-disciplined and adhere to the spirt of codes of professional conduct and ethics and not only to explicit regulations (AICPA, 2020). The principles embodied in the AICPA code express and illustrate the profession's recognition of its responsibilities to the public, clients and colleagues (AICPA, 2020). The code aims to inform and guide members in the performance of their professional duties and to enshrine the principles of commitment to honourable behaviour, even if this is at the expense of personal advantage (Kretzchmar et al., 2012; AICPA, 2020).

The rules contained in the AICPA code seek to address many situations but cannot address all relationships or circumstances which may arise (AICPA, 2020). The member is guided to evaluate whether that relationship or circumstance can lead a reasonable and informed third party who is aware of the relevant information to conclude that there is a threat to the member's compliance with the rules (AICPA, 2020). In considering and evaluating this threat, the member should apply the conceptual framework approach (AICPA, 2020).

17. SEC

The SEC uses an Ethics Counsel which is responsible for administering the Commission's Ethics Program. The Ethics Counsel serves as Counsellor to the Commission and its staff regarding all ethical and conflict of interest questions and acts as the Commission's liaison on such matters with the Human Resources Office, the Office of Government Ethics, the Office of the Inspector General and the Department of Justice (GPO, 2020). The Ethics Counsel's responsibility includes receiving and reviewing allegations of misconduct by a Commission employee (GPO, 2020).

The Counsel refers matters involving management questions to division directors, office heads, or regional directors and matters involving alleged or apparent employee misconduct to the Office of the Inspector General (GPO, 2020). Complaints which appear to involve violation of federal criminal statutes (and are not frivolous) are referred to the Inspector General for further referral to the Department of Justice (GPO, 2020). The Councel will also draft rules and regulations as necessary to implement to the Commission's Ethics programme (GPO, 2020). The approach adopted by the SEC is more rules-based and procedural than the fundamental principles and frameworks applicable to other accounting bodies (GPO, 2020).

18. SAICA

The SAICA code of conduct is structured under the fundamental principles and is aligned to the majority of the other codes discussed above (see IESBA (2019a)). In the preamble to the SAICA Code of Professional Conduct (CPC) it is stated that a distinguishing characteristic of the accountancy profession is that accountants should accept the responsibility to act in the public interest (SAICA, 2019) . The CPC aims to guide the AGA (SA) and the chartered accountant in his/her conduct so as to ensure compliance with the fundamental principles of the code in terms of the conceptual approach(SAICA, 2019). It is not possible to identify and define each and every threat to compliance with the fundamental principles and, as a result, the code follows a principles-based approach for managing ethics (SAICA, 2019).

19. Summary

This chapter examines the code of ethics for professional accountants and auditors. It does this by analysing the fundamental principles necessary for a professional accountant to work in a professional environment (IESBA, 2019a). Specifically, the focus of this chapter is:

- The threats to the fundamental principles are explored with specific consideration of the safeguards which need to be implemented to ensure compliance (Kretzchmar et al., 2012).
- Conflicts on the application of fundamental principles are analysed and considered (IAASB, 2016).
- The various international accounting bodies and the different codes of ethics which they follow.

20. References

ACCA. 2020. *Code of Ethics and Conduct* [Online]. Available: https://www.accaglobal. com/gb/en/about-us/regulation/ethics/acca-code-of-ethics-and-conduct.html [Accessed 20 September 2020].

AICPA. 2020. *AICPA Code of Professional Conduct* [Online]. Available: http://pub.aicpa.org/ codeofconduct/ethicsresources/et-cod.pdf [Accessed 31 August 2020 2020].

CIMA. 2020. *CIMA Code of Ethics for Professional Accountants* [Online]. Available: https:// www.cimaglobal.com/Professionalism/Ethics/CIMA-code-of-ethics-for-professional- accountants/ [Accessed 28 September 2020 2020].

Duska, R. F., Duska, B. S. & Kury, K. W. 2018. *Accounting ethics*, John Wiley & Sons.

Falk, H., Lynn, B., Mestelman, S. & Shehata, M. 1999. Auditor independence, self-interested behavior and ethics: some experimental evidence. *Journal of Accounting and Public Policy,* 18 (4–5), 395–428.

FRC. 2019. *FRC Revised Ethical Standards 2019* [Online]. Available: https://www.frc.org.uk/ auditors/audit-assurance/standards-and-guidance/current-ethical-standards [Accessed 1 October 2020 2020].

GPO, U. S. 2020. *Electronic Code of Federal Regulations* [Online]. Available: https://www. ecfr.gov/cgi-bin/text-idx?SID=168e0f8e4d5f2f5b9e8ca3c60a71db45&mc=true&tpl=/ ecfrbrowse/Title17/17cfr200_main_02.tpl [Accessed 1 October 2020].

IAASB 2016. ISA 220: Quality Control for an Audit of Financial Statements.

ICAEW. 2020. *ICAEW Code of Ethics* [Online]. Available: https://www.icaew.com/technical/ ethics/icaew-code-of-ethics/icaew-code-of-ethics [Accessed 1 August 2020].

ICAS. 2020. *ICAS code of Ethics* [Online]. Available: https://www.icas.com/__data/assets/ pdf_file/0008/2006/F8001-ICAS-Code-of-Ethics.pdf [Accessed 15 August 2020].

IESBA 2019a. Code of ethics for professional accountants. *SAICA Members' handbook.* Pietermaritzburg: LexisNexis.

IESBA 2019b. Defintions of listed entity and public interest entity.

Jakubowski, S. T., P.Chao, Huh, S. K. & Maheshwari, S. 2002. A Cross-Country Comparison of the Codes of Professional Conduct of Certified/CharteredAccountants. *Journal of Business Ethics,* 35 (2), 111–129.

Knechel, W. R. & Salterio, S. E. 2016. *Auditing: Assurance and risk*, Taylor & Francis.

Kretzchmar, L., Prinsloo, F., Prozesky, M., Rossouw, D., Sander, K., Siebrits, J. & Woerman, M. 2012. *Ethics for Accountants and Auditors,* South Africa, Oxford University Press.

Porter, B., Simon, J. & Hatherly, D. 2014. *Principles of External Auditing,* West Suzzex, John Wiley & Sons.

Rossouw, D. & Vuuren, L. V. 2016. *Business Ethics,* South Africa, Oxford University Press.

SAICA 2019. Code of ethics for professional accountants. *SAICA Members' handbook.* Pietermaritzburg: LexisNexis.

Sutton, S. G. 1993. Toward an Understanding of the Factors Affecting the Quality of the Audit Process. *Decision Sciences,* 24 (1), 88–105.

Zeff, S. A. 2003. How the U.S. accounting profession got where it is today: Part I. *Accounting Horizons,* 17 (3), 189–205.

Chapter 4 : Laws and regulations

1. Introduction

Entities are required to comply with a variety of laws and regulations when conducting their business operations. The types of laws and regulations applicable to an entity will have different consequences for a company. Similarly, the type of industry in which an entity operates will also have an impact on the laws and regulations an entity is required to comply with. Certain laws and regulations may have an impact on the financial statements, whether directly or indirectly and will need to be considered by the auditor during the audit. Other laws and regulations do not have an impact on the financial statements but are critical to an entity's operations.

This chapter will explain the auditors' responsibility under laws and regulations. The chapter begins with an introduction to laws and regulations (Section 2), followed by management and auditors' responsibilities (Section 3). As part of the auditors' responsibilities, it will include a discussion around the auditors' response when non-compliance is identified (Section 3.3) and the reporting obligations when non-compliance is noted (Section 3.4).

2. Legal requirements applicable to a company

The auditor cannot conduct an audit without considering the laws and regulations which govern the entity being audited (KPMG, 2016). Although the responsibility of compliance with relevant laws and regulations rests with management, the auditor is responsible for issuing an appropriate opinion on the financial statements. This cannot happen unless the relevant legal and regulatory requirements have been taken into account (Maroun, 2015; KPMG, 2016). In addition, the auditor also needs to consider the responsibility imposed by the non-compliance with laws and regulations (NOCLAR) provisions (Chapter 3).

2.1 Legal requirements

Each company needs to consider the relevant laws and regulations applicable to its organisation and its listing jurisdiction, if applicable. Some industries are more regulated than other industries and the impact of laws and regulations can differ. Certain laws and regulations have a direct impact on the financial statements as these laws and regulations impact the amounts recognised and measured in the financial statements (IAASB, 2017, para 2). Other laws and regulations impact the financial statements as non-compliance may result in fines, penalties, and litigation which can have an indirect material impact on the financial statements (IAASB, 2017, para 2). These are some of the factors which the auditor needs to consider when completing the audit.

For example, each business will be required to conduct its human resources function in accordance with relevant and applicable labour legislation (Barker, 2003). Companies which operate in specific fields, such as engineering and health, will also be required to comply with applicable and relevant laws and regulations around health and safety, as well as environmental laws and regulations (Brauer, 2016; IAASB, 2017). Companies will also be required to conduct their business within the company and other specific legislation relevant to each country, for example, in South Africa the Companies Act 2008 will be relevant and in the USA, companies will be required to adhere to the corporate law requirements relevant to the state/s in which they are operating (Pfeiffer and Timmerbeil, 2008). In the UK companies will need to adhere to the Companies Act 2006 (CA 06) which is a consolidation of all previous company law provisions (CIMA, 2006).

2.2 Non-compliance

In terms of ISA 250 para 12, the definition of non-compliance has been updated to reflect the changes made to the IESBA's Code of Ethics for Professional Accountants relating to non-compliance.

Non-compliance is defined as acts of omission or commission by the entity, either intentional or unintentional, committed by the entity, or by those charged with governance, by management or by other individuals working for or under the direction of the entity, which is contrary to the prevailing laws or regulations. Non-compliance does not include personal misconduct (unrelated to the business activities of the entity) (IAASB, 2017, para 12).

Personal conduct which relates to the business activities will be categorised as non-compliance (IAASB, 2017, para A9).

Non-compliance can be categorised within two categories for the purpose of conducting an audit:

1. Laws and regulations which have a direct impact on material amounts reflected and disclosed in the financial statements. These laws and regulations impact: the measurement of amounts in the financial statements; the disclosure of the amounts or both the measurement and disclosure.
2. Laws and regulations which do not impact the measurement or disclosure of amounts directly, but, if non-compliance occurs it may result in fines, penalties, and litigation. This non-compliance may have a significant impact on the financial statements as it may result in the entity not being able to continue as a going concern. This may be due to the severity of fines instituted or because of the revocation of trading licenses.

(IAASB, 2017, para 6)

Some of the types of laws and regulations which would fall in these two categories are, for example, laws relating to fraud, corruption, money laundering, data protection, taxation, securities markets and trading, pension funds, compilation of financial statements and environmental protection (IAASB, 2017, para A6).

3. Management and auditors' responsibilities

3.1 Managements' responsibilities

It is managements' responsibility, with oversight from those charged with governance, to ensure that the company complies with the relevant laws and regulations applicable to an entity in the conduct of its operations and activities (IAASB, 2017, para 3). The following table illustrates the policies and procedures which may be implemented by management to prevent and detect non-compliance with laws and regulations per ISA 250R, para A2:

Table 1: Policies and procedures to ensure compliance	
Compliance policy	**Description**
Monitoring	Oversight and monitoring of policy by management, ensuring signed review and oversight.
Internal control	Implementation and operation of appropriate internal control systems which may be incorporated into the work programmes of internal audit and the audit committee.
Code of conduct	Inclusion in the company's code of conduct are sections highlighting the importance of staff adherence to required laws and regulations relating to the entity.
Training of staff	Implementation of training policies to ensure that employees are trained in the relevant sections of the code.
Legal advice	Engagement with attorneys and other legal advisers to assist in monitoring specific legal requirements and specific laws and regulations.
Register	Maintaining a register of specific and significant laws with which the entity must comply and updating this register regularly to ensure that all laws and regulations are complied with.

(IAASB, 2017)

3.2 Auditor's responsibilities

The auditor is responsible to obtain sufficient and appropriate evidence that the financial statements are free from material misstatement whether due to fraud or error

(IAASB, 2009, para 11). Based on this premise, the objectives of the auditor concerning laws and regulations are as follows per ISA 250R, para 11:

- To obtain sufficient appropriate audit evidence regarding compliance with the provisions of the laws and regulations applicable to financial statements;
- To perform specific audit procedures to identify instances of non-compliance with other laws and regulations that may have a material effect on the financial statements; and
- To respond appropriately to identified or suspected non-compliance with relevant laws and regulations.

(IAASB, 2017)

In addition to the above, the auditor may have additional responsibilities in terms of laws, regulations and relevant ethical requirements which may go beyond the responsibilities noted in ISA 250 (IAASB, 2017, para 9). This may include the steps noted in the IESBA's Code of Ethics applicable to non-compliance. In terms of laws, the auditor may have a responsibility to report certain non-compliance with relevant legislation. For example, in South Africa, the auditor may have to report certain types of non-compliance if the requirements of the Auditing Profession Act are not met.

Even though the audit may be properly planned and executed, a risk of material misstatement still exists that non-compliance with certain laws and regulations may be undetected by the auditor (IAASB, 2017, para 5). There are inherent limitations which exist such as:

- Entities are subject to many laws and regulations which spread across different areas such as labour laws, environmental laws, health and safety laws, tax laws and the governance of companies. As a result, there could be laws and regulations which impact the operating aspects of an entity rather than the financial statements.
- Management may be intentionally involved in non-compliance with laws and regulations which may result in management deliberately attempting to conceal such non-compliance through collusion or fraud.
- Ultimately the decision on whether an act is deemed to be non-compliant is determined by a court of law.

(IAASB, 2017, para 5)

3.3 Auditors' consideration of compliance with laws and regulations

The auditor will have to become familiar with the relevant laws and regulations which apply to the entity being audited (SAICA, 2017). The auditor obtains information on laws and regulations when the auditor gathers evidence regarding the understanding of the entity in accordance with ISA 315 as discussed in Chapter 11. This enables the auditor to familiarise himself with the relevant laws and regulations which apply to the entity being audited (SAICA, 2017). As part of this process, the auditor will gain an understanding of the laws and regulations applicable to the entity, as well as the compliance with such laws and regulations (ISA 250, para 13). The auditor will engage with a client's management to: identify key laws and regulations which impact the entity, identify and evaluate policies and procedures for ensuring compliance with laws and regulations and policies to identify litigation and claims (HTK, 2017; IAASB, 2017).

The auditor's considerations will also depend on the types of non-compliance indicated under 3.1 namely non-compliance which impacts the financial statements directly and non-compliance which may have an indirect impact on the financial statements. Regarding laws and regulations which have a direct impact on material amounts reflected in the financial statements, the auditor is required to obtain sufficient and appropriate evidence regarding compliance with the provisions of such laws (IAASB, 2017, para 14). Regarding non-compliance with other laws and regulations which may have an indirect material impact on the financial statements, the auditor will inquire of management or those charged with governance whether the entity is in compliance with such laws and regulations. The auditor will also inspect correspondence with the relevant authorities (IAASB, 2017, para 15).

For both types of non-compliance, the auditor must remain alert for non-compliance during the performance of the audit (IAASB, 2017, para 8). In addition to management inquiries, additional substantive procedures such as inspecting minutes of meetings for evidence of non-compliance with laws and regulations and sending confirmations to the client's legal counsel will be executed (ISA 250, para 16 and para A15) (HTK, 2017; IAASB, 2017). A management representation letter will also be obtained indicating that all known non-compliance which may impact the financial statements has been disclosed by management (IAASB, 2017, para 17).

There are other factors at the client which may also provide further evidence of non-compliance. The diagram below illustrates further indicators:

Figure 1 – Indicators of non-compliance

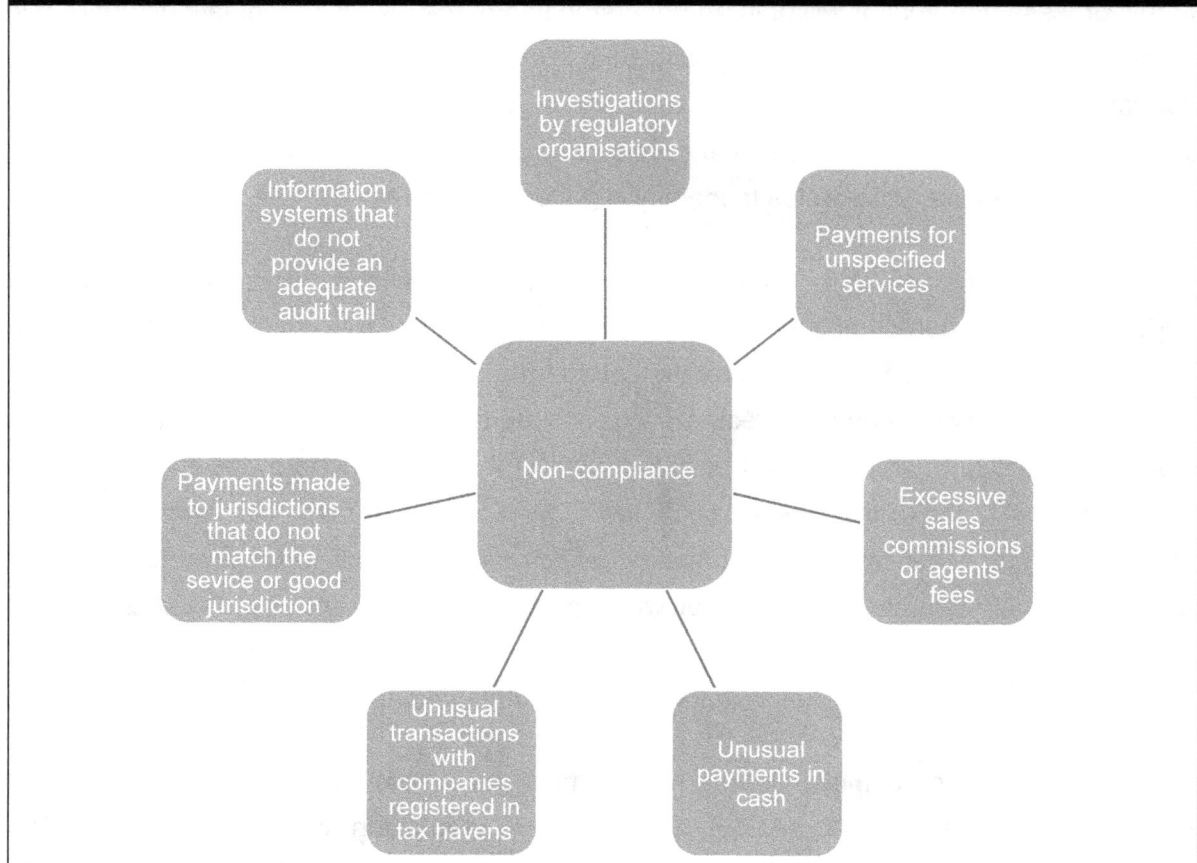

(HTK, 2017)

3.4 Response to identified or suspected non-compliance

If the auditor detects instances of non-compliance, the following is required of the auditor to obtain more information on the matter:

- The auditor must obtain an understanding of the non-compliance and the nature of what has occurred (ISA 250R, para 19);
- The auditor must obtain further information to evaluate the effects of this on the financials (ISA 250R, para 19). This includes the consideration of whether there may be fines, penalties, and litigation, the impact on the disclosure required and the impact on the fair presentation of the financial statements (ISA 250R, para A19);
- The auditor will discuss the suspected non-compliance with management or those charged with governance unless prohibited; and
- The auditor must consider the implications of identified or suspected non-compliance on other aspects of the audit such as the risk assessment and the integrity of management (ISA 250R, para 22).

(IAASB, 2017)

If sufficient information regarding the suspected non-compliance cannot be obtained, the auditor will need to consider the impact of this on the audit opinion (IAASB, 2017, para 27).

3.5 Reporting of the identified or suspected non-compliance

Unless the matter is clearly inconsequential, the auditor must communicate the non-compliance to management and those charged with governance (IAASB, 2017, para 23). If the auditor suspects that management or those charged with governance are involved in the non-compliance, the auditor should communicate the matter to the next higher level of authority within the entity, such as an audit committee or supervisory board (IAASB, 2017, para 25). If the auditor has concluded that the non-compliance has a material effect on the financial statements and this has not been adequately reflected in the financial statements, the auditor may need to modify the audit opinion in accordance with ISA 705 (IAASB, 2017, para 28) (For details on modifications to the audit report, please refer to Chapter 18).

The auditor may also need to consider reporting the non-compliance to an appropriate authority outside the entity (IAASB, 2017, para 29). This is dependent on the laws and regulations applicable to both the jurisdiction and the industry. In some industries, for example, the financial sectors, some laws require the reporting of certain non-compliances which the auditor will need to be aware of to respond appropriately.

Considerations for different jurisdictions

In Europe, the European Union (EU) has introduced auditing legislation, effective 17 June 2016, which requires the statutory auditor of a Public Interest Entity (PIE) who has reasonable grounds to suspect that irregularities including fraud may occur or have occurred, to do the following:

- Firstly, inform the audited entity; and
- Secondly, invite the entity to investigate the matter and take appropriate measures to deal with and prevent any recurrence of such irregularities (KPMG, 2016).

If the audited entity does not investigate the matter or take sufficient appropriate action, then the statutory auditor will be required to inform the Competent Authority (KPMG, 2016). Member States may require additional information from the statutory auditor, provided that it is necessary for effective financial market supervision as provided for in national law (KPMG, 2016).

In the UK, the Money Laundering Regulations (2007) (ICAEW, 2017) and provisions of the Proceeds of Crime Act (2002) (ICAEW, 2002) require auditors within the regulated sector to report suspected money laundering activity and adopt rigorous client identification procedures and appropriate anti-money laundering procedures (FRC, 2017). In the public sector, there may be additional audit responsibilities with respect to the consideration of laws and regulations which may relate to the audit of financial statements or may extend to other aspects of the entity's operations (FRC, 2017).

In South Africa, the South African Institute of Chartered Accountants (SAICA) has added additional sections to the SAICA code of professional conduct which deals specifically with non-compliance with laws and regulations (SAICA, 2017). These sections consider when there is a legal right of disclosure by the auditor, also considering that compliance with relevant legislation such as Protection of Information Act 84 of 1982 needs to be maintained (SAICA, 2017). An important consideration to note is that the auditor is not required to rectify, remediate, or mitigate the non-compliance; the sole responsibility rests with management (SAICA, 2017).

In certain situations, the auditor may have a statutory duty to report the matter to a professional or regulatory body. An example is a possible reportable irregularity which needs to be reported to IRBA as per the Auditing Profession Act (APA) (2005). A reportable irregularity is any unlawful act or omission committed by management which has caused or is likely to cause material financial loss to the entity or is fraudulent or amounts to theft or represents a material breach of any fiduciary duty to the entity (2005).

4. Summary

Management has certain responsibilities towards an organisation regarding compliance with laws and regulations. However, the auditor also has specific responsibilities to ensure that an appropriate audit opinion is issued. The auditor needs to take cognisance of management's responsibilities and the auditor's responsibilities to ensure that the appropriate response is provided if incidences of non-compliance to laws and regulations are noted.

5. References

2005. Auditing Profession Act. South Africa.

Barker, F. 2003. *The South African Labour Market*, Van Schaik Publishers.

Brauer, R. L. 2016. *Safety and health for engineers*, John Wiley & Sons.

CIMA 2006. UK company Law – Topic Gateway Series No.14.

FRC 2017. International Standard on Auditing (UK) 250 Section A: Consideration of Laws and Regulations in an Audit of Financial Statements.

HTK 2017. Consideration of laws and regulations in an audit of financial statements. *Assurance Notes*. HTK Consulting.

IAASB 2009 International Standard on Auditing 200 : Overall Objectives of the Indepdendent Auditor and the Conduct of an Audit in Accordance with International Standards on Auditing. *SAICA Members' Handbook*. Pietermaritsburg: LexisNexis.

IAASB 2017. International Standard on Auditing 250: Consideration of laws and regulations in an audit of financial statements. *SAICA Members' Handbook*. Pietermaritsburg: LexisNexis.

ICAEW 2002. Proceeds of Crime Act 2002.

ICAEW 2017. The Money Laundering, Terrorist Financing and Transfer of Funds (Information on the Payer) Regulations 2017.

KPMG 2016. EU audit reform – what you need to know.

Maroun, W. 2015. Reportable irregularities and audit quality: Insights from South Africa. *In: Accounting Forum*, 2015. Elsevier, 19–33.

Pfeiffer, D. G. & Timmerbeil, D. S. 2008. US – American Company Law – An Overview. Available: http://www.zjs-online.com/dat/artikel/2008_6_122.pdf [Accessed 11 August 2017].

SAICA 2017. NOCLAR – Seminar (Ethics and AA).

Chapter 5: Money laundering

1. Introduction

Financial crime includes fraud, corruption, bribery, money laundering and insider trading (Accountancy Europe, 2017). Regulatory bodies and governments are constantly updating their regulations to address growing concern of financial crime, for example:

- The IAASB updated ISA 250 dealing with non-compliance to laws and regulations (IAASB, 2017);
- The International Ethics Standards Board for Auditors (IESBA) Code of Ethics updated its S360 dealing with responding to non-compliance with laws and regulations (IESBA, 2018);
- The amendment to the South African Financial Intelligence Centre Act (2001) was promulgated in 2017 (South African Government, 2017);
- The United Kingdom's Money Laundering and Terrorist Financing (Amendment) Regulations 2019 came into effect on 10 January 2020 (Intstitute of Financial Accountants, 2019); and
- The USA's Department of Treasury announced in February 2020 their national strategy to combat terrorist and other illicit financing which provides a roadmap to modernise the USA's anti-money laundering/countering the financing of terrorism regime to make it more effective and efficient (Finextra, 2020).

This chapter explores the auditor's inherent responsibility to identify and investigate money laundering activities, taking into account changes to international codes of ethics, current auditing standards and certain regulatory requirements and, ultimately, to report any suspected money laundering activities.

This chapter is organised as follows: Section 2 examines definitions of money laundering and how common money laundering schemes work. Section 3 explores the involvement of the accountant in the activity of money laundering. Section 4 explores how ethics apply to accountants and auditors in this context. Section 5 refers to the requirements surrounding customer due diligence, otherwise known as 'know your customer'. Section 6 deals with the auditor's responsibilities to stop money laundering and the abuse of the system. Section 7 explores international measures to combat money laundering and the scope of criminal offences related to money laundering.

2. The concept and mechanics of money laundering

There are numerous definitions of money laundering, varying according to the legal system of the respective jurisdiction. According to Unger and Busuioc (2007), money laundering involves a process where the source of illegally obtained proceeds is made to appear legal. Buchanan (2004, p. 117) adds that money laundering makes use of financial systems to make the proceeds of crime appear legitimate and 'to render the proceeds re-usable for other purposes' (for details see Mitchell et al., 1998; Levi, 2002; Serio, 2004; Alldridge, 2008; Compin, 2008; Schneider and Windischbauer, 2008; Irwin et al., 2011; Financial Action Task Force, hereafter referred to as FATF, 2012; Muhammad, 2014; Ahmad, 2015; Masciandaro, 2017). These widely used definitions have, however, been criticised as they do not take into account the participants involved in money laundering, the flow of money or behavioural aspects involved in the money laundering process (Gilmour, 2016).

The money laundering process starts once the proceeds of crime enter the financial system, whether by a bank (Irwin et al., 2011) or other instruments (for example, Bitcoin) (Bryans, 2014). The money laundering process is explained in Table 1 below.

Table 1: Process of money laundering	
Stage	**Explanation**

Placement	• Placement refers to the proceeds of crime being placed in the financial or other systems to disguise the origin or nature of the proceeds.
	 • The purpose is to ensure that suspicion will not be aroused when depositing the cash at a bank or other financial institutions and to avoid detection of the cash deposits.
	 • The bulk of the cash is converted into smaller denominations of currency to make cash more 'portable'.
	 • Examples include:
	   – Lots of different people depositing small amounts of money into one account (referred to as 'smurfing').
	   – Disguising the proceeds as gambling profits.
	   – Using the proceeds to purchase hard foreign currency and smuggling the currency into another country.

▶

Table 1: Process of money laundering	
Stage	**Explanation**

Layering	• Layering is the process used to disguise the origin of the proceeds and remove any audit trail which can expose the proceeds as illegally obtained.
	• This is done by introducing a series of financial transactions to the firm. These transactions recur and do not appear to be out of the ordinary for the organisation's business model. Because of their uniform nature they are mistaken for part of the legitimate economic activity of the firm.
	• Examples of layering techniques include:
	  – The use of shell or front companies to make the transactions seem legitimate.
	  – The use of fraudulent invoices to support the occurrence of the cash generating transactions.
	  – Fraudulent sales or purchases.

Integration	• Integration takes places once the money has been laundered and the real origin is completely disguised and reintroduced by legitimate means into the economy.
	• During this part of the process, a complex set of financial transactions can be used to re-integrate funds with the formal part of the economic activities of the individual or the firm.
	• Examples of integration include:
	  – Purchasing of capital investment properties.
	  – Purchasing jewellery.
	  – Investments into capital markets.

Adapted from Reuter (2004), Buchanan (2004); Alldridge (2008);
Irwin et al. (2011); Qureshi (2017)

Per Table 1, financial transactions are used to introduce the illicit funds into the economic activities of the company. To detect this, the accountant or auditor needs to have a thorough understanding of the accounting policies and practices of the respective firm (Compin, 2008).

3. The accountant's role

Compin (2008) states that there are three levels of financial crime which impact the level of knowledge accountants have to have in order to properly layer and integrate the funds. This is illustrated in Table 2 below:

Table 2: Degree of accounting knowledge required in the different levels of crime		
Type of crime	**Explanation**	**Degree of accounting knowledge required**
Unorganised crime	• Simple crimes, such as theft, are committed by the potential money launderer. • There is also no urgency or need for capital accumulation. • There are also no formal structures involved (as would be the case in organised crime).	There is no need for complicated accounting knowledge as the profits are consumed immediately. These activities usually involve simple accounting schemes or breaches of internal controls.
Organised crime	• Crimes become more serious and can include acts of bribery and extortion. • Accountants and lawyers are placed in the middle, managing the revenues and the business.	As the transactions become more organised and the proceeds long-term, an intermediate accounting knowledge (together with a knowledge of law) is required for accountants. This is because of the proceeds of crime being re-invested in legal ventures to hide the source of the proceeds.
Organised crime networks	• High profile crimes (such as procurement fraud, dealing in illicit substances and arms trafficking) take places across a wide network of crime syndicates.	Accounting knowledge required is advanced as the crime network has to make decisions based on accounting information. Accounting knowledge is also required to ensure that the revenues generated by the crime syndicate will appear to be legitimate.

Adapted from Philippsohn (2001), Compin (2008)

Table 2 illustrates the various levels at which crime take places and the accounting knowledge which is required for each level of crime. Within the different levels of crime there can be various activities which generate the illicit proceeds. These activities require accountants to assist in the creation of complicated accounting transactions to ensure that the real origin of the cash is concealed (Compin, 2008). With accountants playing a vital role in the laundering of money, the question is: are there any ethical codes which prohibit accountants from taking part in these transactions or activities?

4. Ethics

The International Ethics Standards Board (IESBA) Code of Ethics is applicable to professional accountants. This code applies to, among others, auditors in the UK (FRC, 2016; ICAEW, 2018) and South Africa (IRBA, 2018). In terms of this code, accountants and auditors are required to adhere to the fundamental principles of objectivity, professional competence and due care, professional behaviour, integrity and confidentiality (IESBA, 2018)[1]. By applying the fundamental principle of professional behaviour in instances in which there is a suspicion of money laundering, accountants and auditors may not take part in any act to launder money.

With the inclusion of s360 of the Code of Ethics (also referred to as responding to non-compliance with laws and regulations (NOCLAR)), the role of the professional accountant in reporting on money laundering has also been clarified. Should the accountant become aware of any instances of money laundering, the matter has to be reported to an appropriate authority[2] (FRC, 2017; IRBA, 2017; IESBA, 2018).

Most countries have reporting responsibilities which require an auditor to report suspected illegal activities to investigative authorities. South Africa (The Audit Professions Act, 25 of 2004), the United Kingdom (Money Laundering Activities Regulations 2007; The Terrorism Act, 2000) and Australia (Anti-Money Laundering and Counter-Terrorism Financing Act 2006) are examples of when the auditors (and accountants in certain instances) have to report suspicious activity to a regulatory body. In this way, auditors have, in effect, a whistleblowing responsibility and an important role to play in protecting society from the effects of money laundering (Maroun, 2013; Maroun and Atkins, 2014a; Maroun and Atkins, 2014b; Maroun and Solomon, 2014a; Maroun, 2015).

The terms 'corruption', 'financial crime' and 'money laundering' have been specifically included in both the IESBA (2018) Code of Ethics s360 and the IAASB (2017) revised ISA 250 (Accountancy Europe, 2017). A professional accountant is obliged to report known or suspected non-compliance with laws/regulations to an appropriate authority for the purpose

---

1   The fundamental principles are discussed in detail in Chapter 3.
2   This can be management, those charged with governance or appropriate regulatory authority.

of s360 of the Code of Ethics and to a body specified in the applicable statute[3].

5. Customer Due Diligence (CDD)

Financial institutions are most at risk of being used in money laundering activities. As a result, they are often expected by stakeholders and required by statute to have systems and processes in place for preventing and detecting money laundering (Isa et al., 2015). One of the most essential preventative anti-money laundering controls is customer due diligence (FATF, 2012).

Because of the complicated processes used to hide the identity of the individuals involved in money laundering, financial institutions are prohibited from keeping anonymous accounts or accounts under fictitious names (FATF, 2012). To ensure that financial institutions comply with these requirements, CDD procedures should be performed when (FATF, 2012):

- Establishing business relations;
- Carrying out occasional transactions above the applicable designated threshold determined by applicable law or regulations;
- There is a suspicion of money laundering or terrorist financing; or
- The financial institution has doubts about the veracity or adequacy of previously obtained customer identification data.

The FATF (2012) requires countries to determine, according to their legal framework, the nature and timing of actions which have to be taken to combat money laundering. For example, the Money Laundering Regulations (2007) in the United Kingdom (2007) and the Financial Intelligence Centre Act 38 of 2001 in South Africa (South African Government, 2001) require CDD to be performed on both new and existing clients for all financial institutions. The UK and South Africa, both adopting the FATF recommendations in their jurisdictions, have the following steps to be taken by financial institutions (de Koker, 2006; FATF, 2012):

- Identify the customer and verify independent source documents, data or information on customer's identity using reliable information, such an as official government issued identification document;
- Identify the beneficial owner and take reasonable measures to verify the identity of the beneficial owner, so that the financial institution is satisfied that it knows who the beneficial owner is. For legal persons and arrangements this should include financial institutions understanding the ownership and control structure of the customer;

---

3   S360 of the Code of Ethics requires the auditor to gain an understanding of the known or suspected non-compliance. The auditor needs to be cautious that, in the process of doing so, the perpetrator is not alerted to the fact that he/she has been detected as this could compromise any formal investigation and result in adverse legal implications.

- Understand and, as appropriate, obtain information on the purpose and intended nature of the business relationship; and
- Conduct ongoing due diligence on the business relationship and scrutinise transactions throughout the course of that relationship to ensure that the transactions being conducted are consistent with the institution's knowledge of the customer, their business and risk profile, including, where necessary, the source of funds.

Where the financial institution is unable to comply with the applicable laws and regulation, it should not be permitted to open an account for the customer, commence business relations or perform the respective transaction (de Koker, 2006). Where applicable, the financial institution should terminate the business relationship and should consider making a suspicious transactions report[4] in relation to the customer (ibid).

6. The responsibilities of auditors with regards to money laundering

The audit process, as discussed in Part B, consists of 4 stages:

1. Client acceptance and continuance.
2. Planning the audit engagement.
3. Executing the audit plan.
4. Completion and reporting.

Table 3 summarises the impact of money laundering regulations, applicable legislation and the requirements of professional codes of conduct on the audit process.

---

[4] A suspicious transaction report should be made and reported to the assigned regulator when there are reasonable grounds to suspect that funds are the proceeds of a criminal activity (Financial Action Task Force, 2012).

Table 3: Impact of money laundering on the audit process	
Stage of the audit	**Impact on the audit**
Client acceptance and continuance (also refer to Chapter 9)	• The auditor is required to evaluate the integrity of management, including whether or not the client is possibly involved in money-laundering activities (ISQC 1 para A19). Should the risk of the client taking part in money laundering activities be high, the auditor should not accept the audit engagement (IRBA, 2011; FRC, 2017). • This will require the auditor to perform a due diligence check on the client to ensure that the client is not suspected (or has been suspected) of taking part in money laundering activities (de Koker, 2006; FRC, 2017). • The auditor should include in the engagement letter the fact that the auditor has a responsibility to report any money laundering and related activities to the regulator (IRBA, 2011; FRC, 2017).
Planning the audit engagement (also refer to Chapters 10–12)	The auditor will be expected to gain an understanding of the following: • The industry and operations of the entity to determine if the entity is operating in an industry in which there is high money laundering risk (ISA 315R); • The controls implemented in the entity which can prevent, detect or correct any activities related to money laundering (ISA 315R); • The procedures established by the client to ensure compliance with laws and regulations, especially anti-money laundering controls (ISA 250R para 13); • If there have been any instances of non-compliance with laws and regulations (usually based on enquiry with management and inspection of correspondence with regulatory bodies and internal communications) (ISA 250R para 15 and 16); or • Any risks of non-compliance with laws and regulations (ISA 250R para 13 – 18) including, in the auditor's view, the risk of fraud or money-laundering activities taking place (refer to Chapter 6 for fraud considerations).

▶

Table 3: Impact of money laundering on the audit process	
Stage of the audit	**Impact on the audit**
Executing the audit plan (also refer to Chapter 13)	• The auditor, as part of performing his/her audit procedures, should determine if the company is being used to launder money (ISA 250R para 15). • Where instances of non-compliance with money laundering laws have been identified, the auditor needs to obtain an understanding of how and why the non-compliance occurred and determine its effect on the financial statements (ISA 250R para 19). This can include detailed discussion with management, except when the auditor is prohibited from engaging with management on the suspected fraud/money laundering because of prevailing laws or regulations (see ISA 250R para 20). • In instances where money laundering is detected, the auditor has to re-assess the risk of material misstatement and the extent of reliance placed on management representations. Given the nature of money laundering and how transactions can be structured to hide the proceeds of crime, auditors will have to apply a high level of professional scepticism (see ISA 250R para 22 & ISA 240 para 13). • The auditor should develop audit procedures to test if active and inactive bank accounts have been opened (and are being managed) in accordance with the applicable regulatory framework (see Section 5). • Acknowledging the complex accounting which can be used to engage in money laundering, the auditor will have to develop advanced data analytics to determine if there are instances in which the transactions have been structured to hide cash transactions (Holzenthal, 2017).

▶

Table 3: Impact of money laundering on the audit process	
Stage of the audit	**Impact on the audit**

Completion and reporting (also refer to Chapter 9, 16 and 17)	• In instances where there was non-compliance with money laundering laws, the auditor should determine if the company will continue as a going concern (IRBA, 2011; FRC, 2017).
	
	• The auditor will have to determine if the financial statements are materially misstated because of money laundering or fraud and determine the impact of on the auditor's report (IRBA, 2011; FRC, 2017).
	
	• Where instances of non-compliance have been identified, the auditor has to report the non-compliance to the appropriate authority. The appropriate authority is for example:
	
	   – South Africa: Independent Regulatory Board of Auditors (IRBA, 2011) & Financial Intelligence Centre (South African Government, 2017)
	
	   – United Kingdom: Financial Reporting Council (FRC, 2017)
	
	   – Australia: The Australian Auditing and Assurance Standards Board (AUASB, 2016).

7. International efforts to combat money laundering

In an era characterised by globalisation, the fight against money laundering has become a matter of international importance. This is especially true for countries which have been impacted by terrorism (Dolar and Shughart, 2011; Muhammaddun Mohamed and Ahmad, 2012). With terrorism being funded by activities such as illegal weapons trade, smuggling of illicit substances and prostitution, the international community has had to develop appropriate measures to combat these (Vaithilingam and Nair, 2009; Dolar and Shughart, 2011). The USA, UK, Australia and the EU are examples of jurisdictions which have implemented laws to combat money laundering. Most of the regulations affect the banking industry, as explained in Section 5 (Vaithilingam and Nair, 2009; Dolar and Shughart, 2011; Isa et al., 2015).

One of the biggest breakthroughs in the fight against money laundering is the creation of the Financial Action Task Force (FATF), an intergovernmental agency (FATF, 2012). The goal of FATF is:

'setting standards and to promote effective implementation of legal, regulatory and operational measures for combating money laundering, terrorist financing and the financing of proliferation, and other related threats to the integrity of the international financial system' (FATF, 2012).

The FATF recommendations were endorsed by over 180 countries and most of the signatories have already adopted the recommendations (FATF, 2012; Isa et al., 2015; Oke, 2016). These require countries to enforce Customer Due Diligence Procedures at all financial institutions to ensure that customers can be identified and are not anonymous, as explained in Section 5. In addition, the FATF recommendations require that all foreign politically exposed persons[5] (PEP's) should also be subject to the customer due diligence checks.

More broadly, the FATF recommends that each country identifies, assesses, and understands its money laundering and terrorist financing risks and responds to the risks with adequately funded systems to combat money laundering and associated terrorist activities (FATF, 2012). The mechanisms used by the country, together with the relevant laws and regulations, must make it possible for the country to work with other jurisdictions and international institutions to investigate international crime networks (such as terrorist organisations). Related to this, money laundering, terrorism and terror-financing activities should be criminalised, as has been done in almost all countries across the globe (South African Government, 2017; Finextra, 2020).

8. Summary

- To define money laundering can become complex because of varying legal frameworks in different jurisdictions. As most money laundering activities will have an impact on the financial statements, the auditor has a responsibility to identify possible money laundering risks in a company.
- Once the risks have been identified, the auditor has to test for any possible material mis-statement and report the non-compliance with money laundering laws to the appropriate authority in each jurisdiction.
- The auditor not only has a responsibility to report in terms of laws and regulation, but also has an ethical responsibility to report the matters.
- As a result the auditor, plays an important role as a whistleblower , reporting non-compliance and ensuring management is held accountable (Maroun and Gowar, 2013; Maroun and Atkins, 2014b; Maroun and Solomon, 2014a; Maroun and Solomon, 2014b).

---

5   A politically exposed person (PEP) is defined by the Financial Action Task Force (FATF) as an individual who is or has been entrusted with a prominent public function (FATF, 2012)

9. References

Accountancy Europe 2017. Auditor's role in fighting financial crime. *Standing up to fraud, corruption and money laundering.* Brussels: Accountancy Europe.

Ahmad, N. M. 2015. Money laundering using investment companies. *Journal of Money Laundering Control,* 18 (4), 438–446.

Alldridge, P. 2008. Money laundering and globalization. *Journal of law and society,* 35 (4), 437–463.

AUASB 2016. ISA 250 Consideration of Laws and Regulations in an Audit of Financial Statements. *ISA 250.*

Bryans, D. 2014. Bitcoin and money laundering: mining for an effective solution. *Ind. LJ,* 89, 441.

Buchanan, B. 2004. Money laundering—a global obstacle. *Research in International Business and Finance,* 18 (1), 115–127.

Compin, F. 2008. The role of accounting in money laundering and money dirtying. *Critical Perspectives on Accounting,* 19 (5), 591–602.

de Koker, L. 2006. Money laundering control and suppression of financing of terrorism: Some thoughts on the impact of customer due diligence measures on financial exclusion. *Journal of Financial Crime,* 13 (1), 26–50.

Dolar, B. & Shughart, W. F. 2011. Enforcement of the USA Patriot Act's anti-money laundering provisions: Have regulators followed a risk-based approach? *Global Finance Journal,* 22 (1), 19–31.

FATF 2012. *International standards on combating money laundering and the financing of terrorism & proliferation: the FATF recommendations,* FATF/OECD.

Finextra. 2020. *US Treasury sets out to modernize AML rules* [Online]. Finextra. Available: https://www.finextra.com/pressarticle/81419/us-treasury-sets-out-plans-to-modernise-aml-rules [Accessed 21 May 2020].

FRC 2016. Scope and Authority of Audit and Assurance Pronouncements.

FRC 2017. International Standard on Auditing (UK) 250 (Revised). *ISA 250.*

Gilmour, N. 2016. Understanding the practices behind money laundering–A rational choice interpretation. *International Journal of Law, Crime and Justice,* 44, 1–13.

Holzenthal, F. 2017. Five trends shaping the fight against financial crime. *Computer Fraud & Security,* 2017 (3), 5–9.

IAASB 2017. ISA 250R: Consideration of laws and regulation in an audit of financial statements. *Student Handbook 2019/2020.* Pietermaritsburg: LexisNexis.

ICAEW. 2018. *ICAEW Code of Ethics* [Online]. [Accessed 8 August 2018].

IESBA 2018. Handbook of the International Code of Ethics for Professional Accountants *Including International Independence Standards* New York: International Federation of Accountants (IFAC).

Intstitute of Financial Accountants. 2019. *Money Laundering Regulations 2019* [Online]. London: Institute of Financial Accountants. Available: https://www.ifa.org.uk/technical-resources/aml/whistleblowing/money-laundering-regulations-2019 [Accessed 2020].

IRBA 2011. A guide for Registered Auditors – Combating Money Laundering and Financing of Terrorism.

IRBA 2017. Non-Compliance with Laws and regulations.

IRBA 2018. Proposed Revised and Restructured IRBA Code of Professional Conduct.

Irwin, A. S. M., Choo, K. K. R. & L, L. 2011. An analysis of money laundering and terrorism financing typologies. *Journal of Money Laundering Control,* 15 (1), 85–111.

Isa, Y. M., Sanusi, Z. M., Haniff, M. N. & Barnes, P. A. 2015. Money Laundering Risk: from the bankers' and regulators perspectives. *Procedia Economics and Finance,* 28, 7–13.

Levi, M. 2002. Money laundering and its regulation. *The Annals of the American Academy of Political and Social Science,* 582 (1), 181–194.

Maroun, W. 2013. *Investigating the role of reportable irregularities in South African audit.* King's College London (University of London).

Maroun, W. 2015. Reportable irregularities and audit quality: Insights from South Africa. *In:* Accounting Forum, 2015. Elsevier, 19–33.

Maroun, W. & Atkins, J. 2014a. Section 45 of the Auditing Profession Act: Blowing the whistle for audit quality? *The British Accounting Review,* 46 (3), 248–263.

Maroun, W. & Atkins, J. 2014b. Whistle-blowing by external auditors in South Africa: Enclosure, efficient bodies and disciplinary power. *Accounting, Auditing & Accountability Journal,* 27 (5), 834–862.

Maroun, W. & Gowar, C. 2013. South African Auditors Blowing the Whistle without Protection: A Challenge for Trust and Legitimacy. *International Journal of Auditing,* 17 (2), 177–189.

Maroun, W. & Solomon, J. 2014a. Whistle-blowing by external auditors: Seeking legitimacy for the South African Audit Profession? *Accounting Forum,* 38 (2), 109–121.

Maroun, W. & Solomon, J. 2014b. Whistle-blowing by external auditors: Seeking legitimacy for the South African Audit Profession? *In:* Accounting Forum, 2014b. Elsevier, 109–121.

Masciandaro, D. 2017. *Global financial crime: terrorism, money laundering and offshore centres,* Taylor & Francis.

Mitchell, A., Sikka, P. & Willmott, H. 1998. Sweeping it under the carpet: The role of accountancy firms in moneylaundering. *Accounting, Organizations and Society,* 23 (5–6), 589–607.

Muhammad, U. K. 2014. Anti-money laundering regulations and its effectiveness. *Journal of Money Laundering Control,* 17 (4), 416–427.

Muhammaddun Mohamed, Z. & Ahmad, K. 2012. Investigation and prosecution of money laundering cases in Malaysia. *Journal of Money Laundering Control,* 15 (4), 421–429.

Oke, T. 2016. Money laundering regulation and the African PEP: case for tougher civil remedy options. *Journal of Money Laundering Control,* 19 (1), 32–57.

Philippsohn, S. 2001. Money laundering on the internet. *Computers & security,* 20 (6), 485–490.

Qureshi, W. A. 2017. An Overview of Money Laundering in Pakistan and Worldwide: Causes, Methods, and Socioeconomic Effects. *U. Bologna L. Rev.,* 2, 300.

Reuter, P. 2004. *Chasing dirty money: The fight against money laundering,* Peterson Institute.

Schneider, F. & Windischbauer, U. 2008. Money laundering: some facts. *European Journal of Law and Economics,* 26 (3), 387–404.

Serio, J. D. 2004. Fueling global crime: the mechanics of money laundering. *International Review of Law, Computers & Technology,* 18 (3), 435–444.

South African Government 2017. Financial Intelligence Centre Amendment Act, 2017. Cape Town: South African Government

Unger, B. & Busuioc, E. M. 2007. *The scale and impacts of money laundering,* Edward Elgar Publishing.

United Kingdom 2007. Money Laundering Regulation 2007.

Vaithilingam, S. & Nair, M. 2009. Mapping global money laundering trends: Lessons from the pace setters. *Research in International Business and Finance,* 23 (1), 18–30.

Chapter 6: Fraud and error

1. Introduction

The Association of Certified Fraud Examiners (ACFE) estimates that companies lose approximately 5% of their revenue to fraud each year (ACFE, 2018; ACFE, 2020). Although it is impossible to quantify the total economic benefits lost due to fraud[1], it is important to quantify the damage done in order to understand the phenomenon better (ACFE, 2018; ACFE, 2020). Using its 5% estimate, the ACFE estimated that the total global economic benefits lost amounted to approximately USD 4.5 trillion (ACFE, 2018; ACFE, 2020). When examining the actual cost of known occupational fraud, the ACFE found that losses from 2504 reported cases amounted to USD 3.6 billion *(ibid)*. This number may be understated as the information used related only to reported cases. According to PwC (2018); PwC (2020), only 47% of companies are aware that they have been victims of economic crime.

Even though companies are becoming more aware of fraud and other economic crimes, the problem of detection and prevention remains (PwC, 2018; ACFE, 2020). At a technical legal level, it is often difficult to define fraud and prosecute offenders. Also, while companies are making investments in fraud detection and prevention, the amount being spent on these measures may exceed the total value lost because of fraud (ACFE, 2018; PwC, 2018; ACFE, 2020; PwC, 2020). Where this is not the case, the ACFE found that in many organisations, anti-fraud business managers still have to make a business case for implementing fraud prevention measures, including the development of an internal control system to mitigate the risk of fraud[2] (ACFE, 2020).

This chapter adds to the literature on the steps taken to mitigate the impact of fraud on organisations and, in particular, on the external auditor's responsibility for preventing and detecting fraud. The chapter deals with the following:

- The expectation gap, focusing specifically on the assumption that auditors are expected to seek out and detect every instance of fraud (section 2);
- The difference between the responsibilities of management and the auditors (section 3);
- Professional judgement, professional scepticism and the audit (section 4);
- A brief overview of fraud and its mechanics (section 5 and section 6);
- The responsibilities of the auditor in terms of ISA 240 (section 7); and
- The future role of auditors (section 8).

---

1   This is based on a large number of limiting factors which make it difficult to accurately calculate the total loss due to fraud.
2   Interestingly, once the relevant measures were in place, the cost of fraud reduced, which indicates that controls can decrease the cost of fraud for a company.

2. The expectation gap

External auditors play an important role in the broader corporate governance system (DeZoort and Harrison, 2018). Given the importance of the external audit function, both South Africa's and the UK's codes on corporate governance stress how independent internal and external audit functions are important for ensuring the quality of financial statements and safeguarding an organisation's assets (Solomon, 2010; IoD, 2016). However, even when a company has internal and external audit functions in place, it can still fall victim to economic crime. This gives rise to significant criticism concerning the audit profession, especially by non-experts (Ruhnke and Schmidt, 2014; Jeppesen, 2016; DeZoort and Harrison, 2018). The debate about whether or not auditors should be expected to detect and prevent fraud and how this informs the broader objective of a financial statement audit is often explained in terms of an 'audit expectation gap' (Porter, 1993; Hassink et al., 2009; Porter et al., 2012).

Liggio (1974, p. 27) defines the expectation gap as the difference between the expected level of performance 'as envisioned by the independent accountant and by the user of financial statements'. Hassink et al. (2009) add that the expectation gap exists because of the unrealistic expectations which broader society has regarding the responsibilities of auditors. It can also be a function of deficient audit practice or limitations in the audit model which society may reasonably expect to be addressed (Porter, 1993; Hassink et al., 2009) This is represented using the model developed by Porter (1993) reproduced as Figure 1:

Figure 1: The audit expectation gap

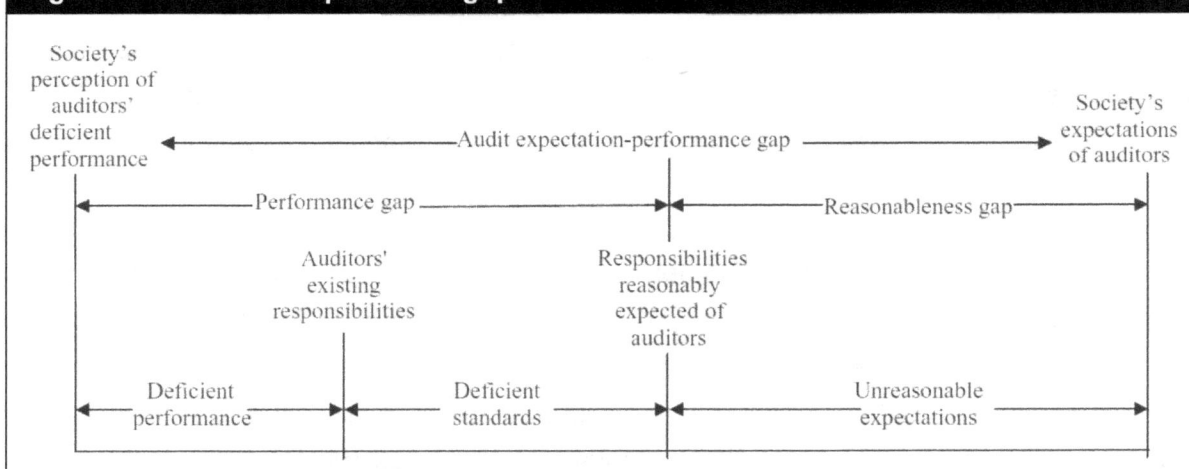

Sourced from Porter (1993, p. 50)

Figure 1 shows that the expectation gap comprises the performance and the reasonableness gap. The performance gap refers to the difference between the 'expected and perceived standard of auditors' existing duties, as expected and perceived by society' (Porter, 1993, p. 57). Hassink et al. (2009) add that the performance gap is widened in cases where corporate governance structures have failed to ensure the independence of the audit function.

Examples of this include instances where directors or management place pressure on the auditors not to report any irregularities to the appropriate bodies or where there is evidence of a close relationship between the auditor and management (Hassink et al., 2009). The performance gap is not limited to the procedures which the auditor performs but includes the independence of the audit function. This is supported by the fact that the performance gap can be attributed to the poor performance by the auditor and deficient auditing standards.

Deficient performance refers to the difference in the 'expected standards of performance of auditors' existing duties and the auditors perceived performance, as expected and perceived by society' (Porter, 1993). Of importance is the term 'perceived' as this can be linked to the perceived independence of the auditor. This can also be seen in the fact that auditors have to be independent in mind and appearance (IESBA, 2017). If the independence of the auditor is perceived as being impaired, society's trust in external audit is undermined and the integrity of the respective company's governance structure may be called into question (Porter et al., 2014).

The performance of the auditor is directly impacted by the audit standards with which the auditor has to comply before issuing an audit report (see IAASB, 2009a). There is a tension between auditors and the expectations of the standards setters (Curtis and Turley, 2007). This tension is referred to as the standards gap (Porter, 1993; Hassink et al., 2009; Porter et al., 2012). The standards gap exists because the standard-setter expects auditors to perform their procedures in line with laws, regulations and professional promulgations but this is not always the case (Porter, 1993; Porter et al., 2012). Curtis and Turley (2007) show that the technical divisions of audit firms, more often than not, require the audit teams to perform procedures which they may not see as reasonable. This may be because of, for example, the availability of resources or limitations of the client's accounting systems (Curtis and Turley, 2007).

In contrast, the reasonableness gap refers to stakeholders' expectations as it relates to the auditor's responsibilities (Hassink et al., 2009). Porter (1993) defined the reasonableness gap as 'a gap between what society expects auditors to achieve and what they can reasonably be expected to accomplish.' Hassink et al. (2009) add that the reasonableness gap usually involves unrealistic expectations of the auditor's responsibilities relating to fraud.

Porter et al. (2012) found that stakeholders expect the auditor to accept responsibility for the following:

- Preparation of financial statements;
- Absolute assurance over the financial statements;

- The absence of any misstatements when an unqualified audit report is issued; and
- The execution of fraud detection and prevention measures.

These responsibilities are more than those specified by ISA 200 which stresses that a reasonable assurance engagement provides a high (but not absolute) level of assurance (IAASB, 2009a) and ISA 240 which explains that the auditor is not expected to prevent or detect every instance of fraud (IAASB, 2009e). On the contrary, management is responsible for taking steps to prevent and detect fraud. At the same time, the auditor is primarily concerned with whether or not the financial statements are materially misstated. The responsibilities of managers and auditors in connection with fraud are discussed in Section 3 below.

3.   Responsibilities of management and the auditor

Responsibility for implementing controls to prevent, detect and correct misstatements (including fraud) rests solely with the management of an organisation (Porter, 1993; Hassink et al., 2009; IAASB, 2009e; Porter et al., 2012). Management includes those charged with a company's corporate governance (IAASB, 2009e). As a result, when there is a weakness or lack of controls, there may be a failing corporate governance system at the company (Hassink et al., 2009).

In the case of fraud, management and those charged with corporate governance should emphasise fraud prevention and detection. This will require an effective system of internal controls, independent monitoring and review processes and a culture of honesty and ethics within the organisation. According to ISA 240 (IAASB, 2009e), those who are responsible for an organisation's governance, should ensure that there are safeguards in place to prevent controls being overridden or bypassed by management to commit fraud (IAASB, 2009e). Codes on corporate governance take a similar position (see, for example, IOD, 2016, Solomon, 2010).

In contrast, the auditor is not responsible for the implementation of the controls at an organisation. The auditor's responsibility is to perform procedures over the financial statements to ensure that the financial statements are free from material misstatement, whether due to fraud or error. However, as stated in ISA 200 (IAASB, 2009a) and ISA 240 (IAASB, 2009e), audit procedures have inherent limitations and may not detect misstatements. This is especially relevant when it comes to fraud because of the sophistication of a fraud scheme and deliberate steps taken to conceal the fraud (Labuschagne and Els, 2006; IAASB, 2009e; Power, 2013; Porter et al., 2014; DeZoort and Harrison, 2018).[3]

---

3   For example, documents being manipulated or forged and the skilfulness of the fraudster (IFAC, 2010).

Even though the auditor is not expected to detect fraud, the auditors should apply a level of professional scepticism and be alert to the possibility that a client's financial statements may be misstated (IFAC, 2010a). For this purpose, the ISA's require an auditor to identify fraud risk factors (IAASB, 2009g; IAASB, 2009e). These factors can be an indication that fraud has been committed by management and that, as a result, more detailed or extensive test procedures need to be performed on the affected balances and transactions (IAASB, 2009e; IAASB, 2009g).

Once the fraud risk factors have been identified, the auditor should obtain an understanding of the relevant controls related to the fraud risk and assess the risk of misstatement (IAASB, 2009e). Where there is a significant risk of fraud, the auditor will need to adjust the nature, timing and extent of planned audit procedures on the applicable balances and transactions. This is discussed in more detail in Chapter 13. In this way, while the auditor is not responsible for the design and implementation of controls to prevent or detect fraud, the auditor is required to demonstrate how the risk of fraud has been taken into account in the planning and execution of the audit engagement.

The determination of the auditor's responsibilities concerning the prevention and detection of fraud has developed over several years. To better understand how the responsibilities have developed, Table 1 provides a summary of the relevant case law from different jurisdictions.

Table 1: Summary of case law and implications for the audit profession		
Country	**Findings**	**Implication**
Course Case: Leeds Estate Building and Investment Co v Sheppard		
United Kingdom	The auditors have to examine the records on which the financial statements are based and satisfy themselves about the existence and approximate value of the firm. Auditors must not merely ensure the arithmetical correctness of the financial statements but must also determine their 'substantial accuracy'.	Auditors do not serve management and must perform procedures to ensure that the financial statements are substantially correct.

▶

Table 1: Summary of case law and implications for the audit profession		
Country	Findings	Implication
Re London General Bank Ltd: Ex parte Theobald (No 2)		
United Kingdom	The business of an auditor is to determine, by performing various audit procedures, that the financial statements under examination are an accurate reflection of the current state of the entity. The court added that the duty of an auditor is limited to this examination. The court stressed that auditors must exercise reasonable care and skill when performing their audit procedures. Unless there is anything which causes suspicion, the auditor is not responsible for uncovering errors or fraud. The court also found that auditors must express an opinion on the financial statements, even when it is a negative opinion.	If the auditors should identify fraud risks or risks that may lead to errors, the auditor has a duty to examine the related accounts to determine if there are errors or fraud. Should there then not be any fraud or risk associated with errors, there is no duty to investigate further.
Court Case: Re Kingston Cotton Milll		
United Kingdom	The court found that '...an auditor is not bound to be a detective... or to approach his work with the foregone conclusion that there is something wrong...as auditors are watchdogs and not bloodhounds.'	The auditor should only respond to fraud once there is an indication that fraud is taking place and should not perform the audit thinking that fraud has taken place. This case illustrates that auditors have to apply a level of professional scepticism when fulfilling their responsibilities.

▶

Table 1: Summary of case law and implications for the audit profession		
Country	Findings	Implication
Court Case: London Oil Storage Co v Seaar Hasluck and Co		
United Kingdom	Auditors are required to protect the interests of the company and shareholders by being watchful and taking reasonable care, as the company and shareholders rely on the auditor to protect their interests. Auditors are required to go beyond the financial records of the client for evidence to support their opinion about the truth and fairness of the financial statements.	This case confirms that the auditor plays an important role in reducing agency costs. Although an auditor is not expected to perform an audit with the objective of detecting fraud, once a fraud is detected, the auditor is required to investigate the matter and resolve it.
Court Case: International Laboratories vs Dewar		
Canada	Where there is nothing to arouse suspicion and the fraud was conducted using carefully laid out plans, the auditor cannot be held liable for failing to detect the fraud.	The auditor should identify fraud risk factors and only develop procedures to respond to the risks. The auditor is not expected to perform procedures to detect fraud where there are no indications of fraud risk.
Court Case: Pacific Acceptance Corporation v Forsyth		
Australia	The court took a strong stance against the profession as a whole, requiring the updating of auditing standards based on the requirements of modern society. This is probably because the	As stated by Gibson and Arnold (1981), the profession has had to ensure that the requirements of auditing standards adapt according to the requirements of society.

▶

Table 1: Summary of case law and implications for the audit profession		
Country	**Findings**	**Implication**
	court judged the auditor using a reasonable man and *not* a reasonable auditor test. The court also found that auditors should not simply rely on the internal controls of a company but should first gain an understanding of the controls and test whether the controls are operating effectively (Kujinga, 2009).	

(Adapted from 1885; 1895; 1904; Rabel, 1944; 1970; Kujinga, 2009; Edwards and Chandler, 2013; Chapple and Mui, 2015)

There have been numerous cases dealing with the auditor's responsibility for preventing and detecting fraud. Table 1 is not intended to be exhaustive (see also Chapter 8 for a detailed review of auditor liability). The principles from the selected case law can be summarised as follows:

- The auditor should act with professional scepticism, taking into account the possibility that financial statements may be misstated due to fraud (see ISA 240 para 12 in IAASB, 2009e).

- The auditor does not have to assume that fraud has occurred in every instance but should assess the relevant fraud risk factors. If the auditor concludes that there is a risk of misstatement because of fraud, appropriate testing procedures will need to be performed to reduce this risk to an acceptably low level (See ISA 240 para 8 and 16 in IAASB, 2009e).

- The auditor is not responsible for performing procedures to detect fraud, especially in cases where there is no reasonable indication of a risk of misstatement because of fraud (See ISA 240 para 5–7 in IAASB, 2009e).

- If fraud is detected, the auditor has to investigate the fraud and resolve the issue. The auditor cannot assume that the fraud is isolated. It will be necessary to re-evaluate the assessed risk of misstatement and planned audit approach for other parts of the engagement (See ISA 240 para 35–37 and A51–53 in IAASB, 2009e).

- The implications of the fraud for the audit opinion should be taken into account (see Chapter 9 for further details). Depending on the jurisdiction, the auditor may also have a duty to report the fraud to the applicable regulator (see also Chapters 3 and 5) (See ISA 240 para 38 and A56 in IAASB, 2009e).

- In all cases, the auditor is required to act with professional scepticism. The auditor does not assume that management is inherently dishonest but, at the same time, must corroborate information provided by the client to ensure that it is accurate and complete (See ISA 240 para 13 in IAASB, 2009e).

4. Professional judgement, professional scepticism and the audit

4.1 What is professional judgement?

The auditor's professional judgement is applied in deciding which procedures are to be performed. To be able to make appropriate judgements, auditors should rely on their experience and draw on their integrity, objectivity and professional scepticism (CHIŞ and Achim, 2014). Professional judgement is viewed as an obligation instilled in an auditor through the auditor's training, knowledge and experience (CHIŞ and Achim, 2014). Having the appropriate level of professional judgement is considered to be a key factor in ensuring a 'successful' audit (Hurtt et al., 2013). Professional scepticism is seen as a cornerstone of professional judgement as auditors would need to rely on this in performing the audit appropriately (Nelson, 2011).

4.2 What is professional scepticism?

Professional scepticism refers to the auditor having an attitude which includes a questioning mind, being aware of and alert to conditions which may indicate possible misstatement and making a critical assessment of audit evidence (IAASB, 2009e; Hurtt et al., 2013). Professional scepticism includes being alert to contradictory audit evidence obtained at various stages throughout the audit, as well as being alert to information which brings into the question the reliability of documents and responses to inquiries to be used as audit evidence (Vinten et al., 2005) (IAASB, 2009b). It also involves the auditor being aware of and alert to conditions which may indicate possible fraud as well as circumstances that suggest the need for audit procedures in addition to those required by the ISA's (IAASB, 2009a; Nelson, 2011).

The auditor must maintain this attitude of professional scepticism in order to ensure that no ethical boundaries are crossed and that he/she is continually alert to any possible ethical contraventions (Jakubowski et al., 2002). Professional scepticism is important as it reduces the risk of overlooking unusual entries, over-generalising when drawing conclusions from audit observations, or using inappropriate assumptions in determining the nature, timing and extent of the audit procedures and the evaluation of the results (IAASB, 2009b; BKR, 2012).

Evidence obtained in an audit is a critical component of forming the basis for the audit opinion, and professional scepticism is, therefore, very important in questioning contradictory audit evidence, especially in consideration of fraud identification (IAASB, 2009a; Nelson, 2011). The auditor is not required or even expected to disregard the past experience of the honesty and integrity of management and those charged with governance (IAASB, 2009f). All the same, the auditor's professional scepticism is very important in assessing and considering risks of material misstatement because of fraud as there may have been a change in circumstances (IAASB, 2009d; IAASB, 2009c).

Professional scepticism is necessary at the engagement acceptance stage, as well as at the audit response stage (Vinten et al., 2005; BKR, 2012). The auditor can manage this through the authentication of documents, increasing the quantity of evidence obtained in higher risk areas, performing more substantive analytical procedures and confirming audit evidence directly with third parties, as well as using the work of an expert to assess the authenticity of certain documentation (IAASB, 2009d; BKR, 2012).

In order to assess whether or not an audit has been planned and performed with an attitude of professional scepticism will require the evaluation of audit documentation (Nelson, 2011) (BKR, 2012). In examining the documentation, an evaluation can be ascertained of the nature and sources of audit evidence obtained, a link can be drawn between the type of audit evidence and whether or not that evidence strenghtens the probability of the audit being performed with an increased attitude of professional scepticism (IAASB, 2009h; BKR, 2012).

From a philosophical standpoint, professional scepticism can be viewed as a multi-dimensional individual characteristic (Hurtt et al., 2013). As an individual characteristic, professional scepticism can be both a trait and a state (BKR, 2012). This means that professional scepticism can be viewed as a relatively stable enduring aspect of an individual and can also be viewed as a temporary condition of an individual triggered by situational variables evident in an audit (Vinten et al., 2005). Professional scepticism in auditing can be seen as a hybrid concept constituting the epistemic and psychological aspects of cognition (CHIŞ and Achim, 2014). The epistemic aspect can be viewed as either a positive or negative approach which the auditor should adopt prior to designing the actual audit approach (BKR, 2012). The psychological aspect is related to the auditor's disposition to ask a pertinent question in an audit setting (Vinten et al., 2005). This aspect deals with measuring the depth and breadth of the auditor's questioning mind (Nelson, 2011; BKR, 2012).

Because the auditor has to apply a level of professional scepticism throughout the audit, and especially with regard to fraud, the auditor has to have an understanding of the nature of fraud (Vona, 2012). Having this understanding will assist in identifying any possible fraud risk factors. The next section will investigate the nature of fraud with a focus on the different factors which can indicate if there is a fraud.

5.1 The legal definition of fraud

According to Wells (2017), fraud is a crime in which gains are made using deceptive means. Brooks et al. (2017) add that fraud is an intentional act in which a financial advantage will be obtained, either in the present or future, without the knowledge of the victim. Petraşcu and Tieanu (2014) add that fraud is the product of irregularities, committed with intention, either through not communicating information or violating obligations or embezzling money.

In England, Lord Herchell stated in *Derry v Peek* (1889) that '... Fraud is proved when it is shown that a false representation has been made (1) knowingly or (2) without belief in its truth, or (3) recklessly, careless whether it be true or false.' Lord Herchell later stated that dishonesty is a requisite for fraud. Stating that an accused is knowingly making a false representation indicates that intention is required to prove fraud. In S v Friedman (1996), the South African court stated that the definition of fraud, albeit wide, does not make it impossible to determine which acts fall within its definition.

In *S v Gardener* (2011), the South African court stated that 'fraud consists in unlawfully making, with intent to defraud, a misrepresentation which causes actual prejudice or which is potentially prejudicial to another.' The finding of the court shows that actual losses are not required but that just proving potential losses is sufficient. This requirement is also found in the United Kingdom in the Fraud Act (2006), which states that following are considered to be a fraud:

1. A person who intentionally makes a misrepresentation (or plans to make such representation) which will lead to a gain for the perpetrator but a loss to another;
2. A person who does not disclose information to another, even when there is a legal obligation to disclose such information, which leads to a gain for the perpetrator but a loss to another; or
3. A person, who is in a position to protect the financial interests of another person, dishonestly and intentionally abuses the power which comes with the position to make a gain for himself, but a loss for another. This includes where an omission takes place.

The ACFE is of the view that the most pervasive form of fraud is occupational fraud. This is described as the use of one's occupation for personal benefit, through the intentional abuse or misappropriation of the employing organisation's resources or assets (ACFE, 2018). This definition is distinguished from the previous definitions as it pertains to fraud committed against persons employed by the company. This definition is also applied to ISA 240 (IAASB, 2009e, p. 159), which defines fraud as:

'an intentional act by one or more individuals among management, those charged with corporate governance, employees, or third parties, involving the use of deception to obtain an unjust or illegal advantage.'

As can be seen above, the definition of fraud is wide and varies among sources and jurisdictions. There are, however, common elements which make up the concept of fraud:

1. There is willful intent to misrepresent a fact or facts;
2. The misrepresentation will be to the advantage of the perpetrator;
3. The misrepresentation will be to the prejudice of another; and
4. Prejudice can be either potential or actual.

In the context of an audit, fraud can be committed by an employee, third party, directors of a company, those charged with governance or even a customer (Hassink et al., 2009; IAASB, 2009e; Power, 2013; Reurink, 2016; Brooks et al., 2017; Wells, 2017).

Not all misstatements are fraud; errors frequently occur when preparing financial statements Per IAS 8 (IFRS, 2018), errors include mathematical mistakes, incorrect application of accounting policies, oversight or misunderstanding of facts. A mistake is unintentional and would not be regarded as a fraud.

The auditor needs to make a differentiation between fraud and error as fraud has to be reported to the appropriate authority in terms of section 360 of the Code of Professional Conduct (IESBA, 2019). However, it must be emphasised that auditors are not legal experts. Whether a suspected act can be regarded as fraud is a determination which only a court of law can make. As a consequence, auditors have to identify any indications (also referred to as red flags) that fraud is taking place. This can be done through the identification of fraud risk factors but this does require an understanding of the nature of fraud. Section 5.2 explores the factors which can assist the auditor in identifying if there are any fraud risks.

5.2 Fraud risk factors

As fraud is a legal determination, auditors have to look for 'red flags' when performing their audit procedures to assist them in identifying possible risks of material misstatement (Lou and Wang, 2011; Gullkvist and Jokipii, 2013; Boyle et al., 2015; Lokanan, 2015; Huang et al., 2016). The factors are often explained in terms of the fraud triangle (Lou and Wang, 2011; Lokanan, 2015) developed by Cressey (1953) to explain why people commit fraud. The fraud triangle has been criticised as being too narrow, given the fact that fraud is so multifaceted and can become so complex that it cannot be reconciled to any given framework (Lokanan, 2015). Nevertheless, the fraud triangle is a useful means to aid auditors to identify the risk that financial statements may be misstated owing to fraud.

The elements of the fraud triangle are: incentives/pressure, opportunity and rationalisation to commit fraud (Cressey, 1953; Lou and Wang, 2011; Boyle et al., 2015; Lokanan, 2015; Huang et al., 2016). Examples of incentives or pressures to commit fraud include (Lou and Wang, 2011; Boyle et al., 2015; Lokanan, 2015; Huang et al., 2016):

1. The pressure to meet targets of third parties;
2. Management's personal finances are threatened by the company not meeting performance targets; or
3. Economic and financial stability of the company is under threat from external forces.

Huang et al. (2016) assert that the opportunity for fraud exists in companies with weak internal control systems. In this environment, corrupt management can commit fraud without the risk of being detected (Lokanan, 2015). Also, as management is responsible for designing and operating internal controls, they are in a position to override or bypass or exploit weaknesses in controls to commit the fraud.

The perpetrator can rationalise committing fraud in a variety of ways (Lokanan, 2015). The following are common reasons for people to rationalise committing fraud (Lou and Wang, 2011; Boyle et al., 2015; Lokanan, 2015; Huang et al., 2016):

1. A belief that, by committing fraud, others may benefit;
2. A belief that everyone is committing fraud and that the act is, as a result, acceptable;
3. A belief that the person deserves the proceeds of the fraud as a reward for his/her hard work;
4. A belief that no-one will be negatively affected by fraud; or
5. A belief that there is no choice but to commit the fraud because of to pressure exerted on the individual.

Although the list is not complete, auditors can use the above to identify possible fraud risks. In identifying any pressure on management or incentives to commit fraud, the auditor will be able to identify the balances or classes of transactions which might be manipulated. The next section will explore how fraud is committed.

6. How fraud is committed

The ACFE (2016, 2018, 2020) state that fraud can be categorised into three distinct categories:

- Corruption;
- Misappropriation of assets; or
- Financial statement manipulation.

ISA 240, the main standard dealing with the auditor's responsibility regarding fraud, does not refer explicitly to corruption. Some authors regard fraud and corruption as two separate crimes (see Labuschagne and Els, 2006) where others regard them as interconnected. Jeppesen (2016) states that excluding corruption from the definition of fraud shows that standard setters do not see corruption as fraud, but rather as a non-compliance with laws and regulations issue. This is evidenced – according to Jeppesen (2016) – by the inclusion of crimes, such as collusion, in ISA 250 (see IAASB, 2017). With the inclusion of collusion in ISA 250 as an example of non-compliance with laws and regulations, regulators have included corruption as something the auditor needs to be aware of when performing the audit (see Shleifer and Vishny, 1993; Olsen and Torsvik, 1998; Khan, 2006; IAASB, 2017).

6.1 Corruption

As in the case of fraud, whether an act is regarded as corrupt or not, is a legal determination with each jurisdiction having a different definition of corruption. However, a common thread appears in all of the definitions of corrupt activity. A gift, either monetary or otherwise[4], is presented by one person to another person with the objective of altering the behaviour of the recipient of the gift. This view holds in the United Kingdom (2010), South Africa (2004), Australia (1995) and the US (2012). Each country has specific criteria which have to be met before a transaction is seen as corrupt. A detailed review of the relevant legislation is beyond the scope of this chapter. Instead, this chapter uses the typology developed by the ACFE (2016, 2018, 2020) to categorise corruption into different corrupt activities which may take place within an organisation (reproduced in Figure 2).

Figure 2: Types of Corrupt Activities

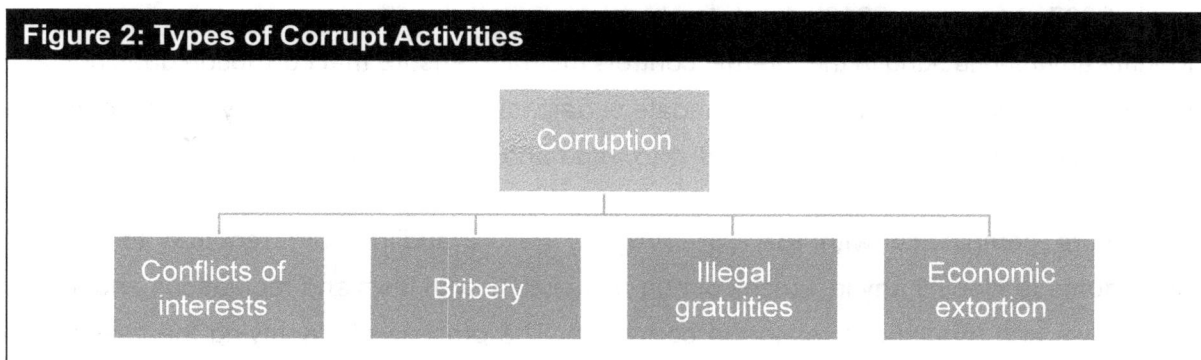

Adapted from ACFE (2016, 2018, 2020)

A conflict of interest arises when someone *can* abuse his/her position to gain advantage with purchase and sale schemes by which a kickback is received by the corrupt official (Catchick, 2014; Jeppesen, 2016). Bribery is a clear example of corruption as there is 'the offering, promising, giving, accepting or soliciting of any advantage as an inducement for an

---

4   This can include promises, assets, omission of information, not acting in a way required by law, regulations or the job
      description of the employee.

action which is illegal or a breach of trust' (Transparency International, 2013; Catchick, 2014; Jeppesen, 2016). When a bribe is being offered, the intention is to have someone act in a way which is contrary to their nature or responsibilities (Tackett, 2010). Illegal gratuities are amounts which are paid where the intention is not to influence any decision (Ketz, 2006) and are usually given as a token of goodwill or friendship, making this form of corruption more challenging to prove (Tackett, 2010). Economic extortion is when threats are made to the person to ensure advantage is obtained (Hauser, 2018).

Each type of corrupt activity illustrated in Figure 2 above usually involves efforts to bypass internal controls and conceal the corruption from managers, those charged with an organisation's governance and from the auditors (Khan, 2006). Also, even if an audit is carried out to the highest standards, inherent limitations in the audit process mean that not every misstatement (whether because of fraud or error) will be detected (IAASB, 2009a; IAASB, 2009e). It is also important to keep in mind the principals from the *Kinston Cotton Mill* case (see Table 1 in Section 2): the auditor is not supposed to audit financial statements with a foregone conclusion that there is corruption taking place within the company. While the auditor will be expected to identify possible risks which can indicate that corruption is taking place (see ISA 240 and ISA 250 for further details) the auditor cannot reasonably be expected to identify every instance of corrupt activity.

Nevertheless, auditors can play an important role in identifying instances of corrupt activities by focusing on where the opportunity exists as most jurisdictions require companies to implement controls to prevent corruption (Khan, 2006; Labuschagne and Els, 2006; Everett et al., 2007; Jeppesen, 2016). As stated by Khan (2006), auditors are in a unique position to identify anything lacking in the internal controls meant to ensure that corruption does not take place in a company. The ISAs also mandate certain minimum procedures by which an auditor responds to the risk of misstatement due to fraud and, in turn, corruption.

To ensure compliance with ISA 250 (IAASB, 2017), auditors are required to perform procedures to identify any instances of non-compliance with laws and regulations and, in this case, laws and regulations related to corruption. The process of identifying the risks which can indicate non-compliance with laws and regulations related to corruption is no different from the process required for other examples of non-compliance with laws and regulations. If corruption is identified, the auditor has to report the non-compliance to the appropriate authority, taking into account statutory reporting obligations in the applicable jurisdiction and s360 of the IESBA Code of Conduct (IAASB, 2017). Refer Chapters 3 and 5 for the processes required.

6.2 Misappropriation of assets

The ACFE (2018) defines misappropriation of assets as a:

'scheme in which an employee steals or misuses the employing organization's resources (eg, theft of company cash, false billing schemes, or inflated expense reports.'

According to ISA 240 (ISA 240 para A5 in IAASB, 2009e), misappropriation of assets:

'involves the theft of an entity's assets and is often perpetrated by employees in relatively small and immaterial amounts. However, it can also involve management who are usually more able to disguise or conceal misappropriations in ways that are difficult to detect '

The majority (57%) of reported fraud cases involve some form of asset misappropriation. The most common schemes, and those which present most risk include cheque and payment tampering, billing schemes, non-cash schemes, cash larceny, payroll schemes, skimming and register reimbursements (ACFE, 2018). The common schemes are explained below in Table 2:

Table 2: Summary of common asset misappropriation schemes	
Scheme	**Definition**
Cheque and payment tampering	Cheque and payment tampering schemes involve both external parties and employees of a company in which cash, electronic or otherwise, is stolen by altering payment details. This can involve changing details of cheques, changing banking details of suppliers to those of employees, voiding of cheques after making payment (Singleton and Singleton, 2010; Pedneault et al., 2012; Wells, 2017; ACFE, 2018).
Billing schemes	Billing schemes refer to schemes where the company pays a fraudulent disbursement based on falsified invoices, inflated invoices or invoices for goods and services unrelated to the entity. Examples include employees requesting disbursements for personal expense, employees using fictitious companies with the employees' details to submit invoices to the entity for payment (Singleton et al., 2006; Singleton and Singleton, 2010; Albrecht et al., 2011; ACFE, 2018).

Table 2: Summary of common asset misappropriation schemes	
Scheme	**Definition**
Non-cash schemes	These schemes involve the theft or misuse of any item which is not cash. Examples of this are using the assets of the entity for personal gain, theft of inventory and theft of confidential client information (Kranacher et al., 2010; ACFE, 2016; Wells, 2017; ACFE, 2018).
Cash larceny	These schemes involve employees of the company stealing cash after the receipt of the cash has been recorded in the accounting records. Examples include employees stealing cash before the amounts are deposited at a bank/into a bank account, lapping schemes in which cash from debtors is stolen after receipt and other debtors' receipts are allocated to the account (Kranacher et al., 2010; ACFE, 2016; Wells, 2017; ACFE, 2018).
Payroll schemes	These schemes involve the employees claiming fraudulent reimbursements from the company using incorrect or falsified information. These schemes include the overtime claimed but not worked, ghost employee schemes, falsifying hours worked etc. (Singleton et al., 2006; Singleton and Singleton, 2010; Albrecht et al., 2011; ACFE, 2016; ACFE, 2018).
Skimming	Skimming schemes take place when cash is received before the transaction is accounted for on the accounting application of the company (Kranacher et al., 2010; ACFE, 2016; Wells, 2017; ACFE, 2018).
Register reimbursements	This is when the cash register system is manipulated to conceal a fraudulent removal of cash, for example, when a cash sale is reversed to disguise the theft of cash by an employee (Kranacher et al., 2010; ACFE, 2016; Wells, 2017; ACFE, 2018).

6.3   Financial statement manipulation

The ACFE defines financial statement fraud as 'a scheme in which an employee intentionally causes a misstatement or omission of material information in the organisation's financial reports.' ISA 240 para A2 defines financial statement manipulation as intentional attempts to omit or misstate amounts or disclosures in the financial statements (IAASB, 2009e). Singleton and Singleton (2010) add that financial statement fraud can include schemes to manipulate both financial and non-financial information. For the purposes of this chapter, financial statement fraud refers to any attempt to manipulate the financial statements of the company, either through omission or intentional misstatement of financial or non-financial information.

According to the ACFE (2016; 2018), there are five common schemes used to manipulate financial statements. These have been summarised in Table 3 below.

Table 3: Financial statement fraud schemes	
Scheme	**Explanation**
Timing differences	These schemes involve accounting for a transaction (usually a sale) before the recognition criteria have been met. This is done to show increased earnings of the company by recognising, for example, sales before the performance obligations have been met or delaying the recognition of expenses (Kranacher et al., 2010; Wells, 2017).
Fictitious revenue	This is the fraudulent recognition of revenue when the requirements of the accounting standards have not been met. The purpose is to increase the earnings of the company and potentially the assets (Singleton et al., 2006; Kranacher et al., 2010; Singleton & Singleton, 2010; Wells, 2017).
Concealed liabilities and expenses	These schemes require that the liabilities (and associated expenses) are only recognised in the next financial year or not at all. Another method employed for these schemes is to move the liability to other entities within a complex group of companies[5] (Singleton et al., 2006; Singleton and Singleton, 2010).
Improper asset valuations	These schemes require that assets are not disclosed at the correct values or overvaluing assets, for example, disclosing inventory at the cost when the net realisable value is lower than cost (Kranacher et al., 2010).
Improper disclosures	Improper disclosure relates to the manipulation of both financial and non-financial information which will distort the interpretation of the financial statements. This includes not disclosing all liabilities, related party transactions or not disclosing all of the required accounting policies (Singleton et al., 2006; Kranacher et al., 2010; Manning and CFE, 2010; Singleton and Singleton, 2010).

There are not many schemes which can be employed to manipulate financial statements. However, the auditor has to be able to apply financial accounting knowledge to determine if the principles contained in accounting frameworks have been applied. Once the auditor has identified the risk factors, then he/she has to perform procedures in terms of the ISA's to investigate the matter further. The next section will explore the procedures which the auditor has to perform concerning fraud.

---

5   This was used by Parmelat to move a large number of liabilities to subsidiaries in the Caribbean (Singleton et al., 2006; Singleton & Singleton, 2010).

ISA 240 is the primary reference for the auditor's responsibility in connection with fraud; in particular, the standard sets out the basic procedures the auditor has to perform in determining the risk of fraud. These different aspects need to be understood by the auditor and he/she should respond to the fraud risk.

7.1 Risk assessment procedures

ISA 240 para 17 and 19 requires the auditor to perform risk assessment procedures to determine if there is a fraud risk by making enquiries of management and, where relevant, internal audit (IAASB, 2009e). To ensure that the risk assessment process is effective, ISA 240 para 15 requires the audit engagement team to discuss in detail where the financial statements might be susceptible to fraud, drawing on the collective experience of the audit team (IAASB, 2009e). ISA 240 para 16 requires that the risk assessment procedures should be performed when the auditor is gathering evidence to understand the entity and its internal control environment (IAASB, 2009e). This process is discussed in more detail in Chapter 10. The auditor should determine the following (see ISA 240 in IAASB (2009e)):

1. The process management has a process in place to assess the risk of fraud in the financial statements, including the nature, timing and extent of such assessments;
2. The process which management follows to identify and respond to any risk of fraud in the entity. An understanding should also be obtained regarding any specific risks of fraud which management has identified or which have been brought to management's attention by employees or other parties;
3. The communication sent to the entity's employees regarding management's view on ethics and business practises; and
4. Communication sent to those charged with governance regarding the processes followed by management for identifying and responding to risks of fraud in the entity.

In terms of ISA 240 para 17 and 21, to ensure that the information obtained from management is accurate, the auditor can make enquiries from other employees in the entity and of those charged with the audit client's governance (IAASB, 2009e). The exception to the latter is if those charged with governance are all executive management. The auditor also has to perform analytical procedures to identify any unusual or unexpected relationships. According to ISA 240 para 23, this can be used to inform the assessment of the risk of material misstatements due to fraud (IAASB, 2009e) and may also provide evidence to corroborate or refute details obtained from discussions with management.

Once the auditor has gained an understanding of the entity and its control environment, the auditor will be required to identify and evaluate any fraud risk factors which have been identified (See ISA 240 para 24 in IAASB, 2009e).

7.2 Identification and assessment of the risks of material misstatement due to fraud

ISA 240 para 25 requires the auditor to assess the risk of material misstatement because of fraud at the overall financial statement level, as well as at the assertion level for each class of transactions, balances and disclosures (IAASB, 2009e). In particular, the auditor has to assess the fraud risk for each revenue stream of the entity and each assertion related to each revenue line. This is based on the rebuttable presumption that there is fraud in the revenue of the entity, as stated in ISA 240 para 26 (IAASB, 2009e). Should the fraud risk in revenue be rebutted, the auditor has to document the considerations taken into account in rebutting the fraud risk (ibid).

For each of the fraud risks which have been identified, the auditor should assess the risk as significant in terms of ISA 315R (refer to Chapters 10 and 11 on risk assessment in planning of the audit) and obtain an understanding of the controls related to the fraud risk (See ISA 240 para 27 in IAASB, 2009e).

7.3 Responding to the fraud risk

Once a fraud risk has been identified, the auditor should respond appropriately to the risk by designing overall procedures to test for material misstatements due to fraud. Auditors are required to:

1. Assign personnel who have the necessary skill, knowledge and experience to the affected section and provide adequate supervision;
2. Evaluate the accounting policies to determine if the accounting policies are subjective or would lead to fraudulent financial reporting; and
3. Incorporate an element of unpredictability in the nature, timing and extent of audit procedures to decrease the detection risk of the auditor (ie lower the probability of not detecting a material misstatement due to fraud).

(See ISA 240 para 29 in IAASB, 2009e)

ISA 240 para 31 specifically requires the auditor to identify the risk of management override of controls and to respond to these risks (IAASB, 2009e). The standard requires the auditor to perform audit procedures over the following:

1. Journal entries recorded in the general ledger and any other adjustments made to the financial statements[6];

2. Any accounts or amounts which require a significant amount of estimation as this could indicate bias, leading to further fraud risks; and

3. Any significant transactions that are outside the normal course of business activities of the entity.

(See ISA 240 para 31 in IAASB, 2009e)

7.4 Evaluating audit evidence

As part of the process of concluding the audit,

'[T]he auditor shall evaluate whether analytical procedures that are performed near the end of the audit, when forming an overall conclusion as to whether the financial statements are consistent with the auditor's understanding of the entity, indicate a previously unrecognised risk of misstatement due to fraud (ISA 240, para 34).'

In terms of ISA 240 para 35, the auditor should determine if any misstatements identified are due to fraud (IAASB, 2009e). Should the misstatement be caused by fraud, the auditor has to perform the following procedures (See ISA 240 para 36 – 38 IAASB, 2009e):

1. Reassess the reliance placed on management representations, considering that the fraud might not be an isolated event;

2. Reassess if the risk of material misstatement due to fraud made during the planning stages of the audit is still applicable and determine if the nature, timing and extent of audit procedures need to be revised to address any additional fraud risks (refer to Chapter 13 for more details on the nature, timing and extent of audit procedures);

3. The auditor needs to determine if the fraud is material to the financial statements. In the case where the fraud is material, the auditor needs to adjust the audit report accordingly (refer to Chapter 18 on Reporting);

4. The auditor needs to determine the legal requirement and if the fraud should be reported to an appropriate authority[7];

---

6   ISA 240 requires the auditor to perform, not only audit procedures on the journals processed which affect year-end balances, but also on journals processed during the reporting period. This is because journals processed during the year can also be used to conceal fraud with implications for the year-end balances. The auditor should focus on the following journals: those outside the course of normal business, manual journals or journals which do not make logical sense.

7   As fraud is specifically mentioned in NOCLAR, the auditor has to report the fraud to the appropriate authority. This is discussed in more detail in Chapter 3.

5. The auditor needs to report any fraud to those charged with governance and supply them with any information regarding the fraud, which is material in the judgement of the auditor. This is, however, impacted by legal requirements of each jurisdiction and the process; and

6. The auditor needs to determine if the engagement team will continue with the audit or withdraw. It is suggested that legal opinion be obtained in these circumstances to determine if it would be possible to withdraw from the engagement.

8. Summary

- Auditor's responsibilities regarding fraud have developed over several years, requiring the auditors to perform procedures to address the fraud risk on an audit engagement.
- The audit should be conducted with an attitude of professional scepticism which embodies the concept of auditing using professional judgement. The auditor has to apply a level of professional scepticism throughout the audit and especially with regards to fraud.
- The auditor has to identify the risk of material misstatement because of fraud by taking into consideration any incentives management have to commit the fraud, opportunities which exist within the organisation which make fraud possible and any ways in which management can rationalise the fraud taking place.
- Fraud can take place to hide corrupt activities, misappropriation of assets and financial statement manipulation.
- The auditor should assess any fraud risk as a significant risk and perform substantive test of details.
- Auditors in the future should employ more data analytics and other analytical procedures to identify fraud risks.

9. References

1885. Leeds Estate Building and Investment Co v Sheppard (1887) L 119. *United Kingdom.*

1889. Derry v Peek (1889) 14 AC 337.

1895. In re London General Bank Ltd ex parte Theobald (No 2) [1895] 2 Ch 673. *United Kingdom.*

1904. London Oil Storage Co v Seaar Hasluck and Co (1904). *United Kingdom.*

1970. Pacific Acceptance Corporation v Forsyth (1970) 92 WN (NSW) 29. *Australia.* New South Wales – Supreme Court.

1995. Criminal Code Act 1995. *Division 70.* Australia.

1996. S v Freedman (1) 1996 (1) SACR 181 (W). *South Africa.* High Court.

2004. Prevention and combatting of corrupt activities Act. South Africa.

2006. Fraud Act. *Chapter 35.* United Kingdom.

2010. Bribery Act. *Chapter 23.* United Kindom.

2012. A Resource Guide to the FCPA: U.S. Foreign Corrupt Practices Act.

ACFE 2016. Report to the nations on occupational fraud and abuse. Association of Certified Forensic Examiners.

ACFE 2018. Report to the Nations 2018.

ACFE 2020. Report to the Nations 2020.

Albrecht, W. S., Albrecht, C. O., Albrecht, C. C. & Zimbelman, M. F. 2011. *Fraud examination*, Cengage Learning.

BKR 2012. Professional skepticism in an audit of financial statements – staff questions and answers. South Africa.

Boyle, D. M., DeZoort, F. T. & Hermanson, D. R. 2015. The effect of alternative fraud model use on auditors' fraud risk judgments. *Journal of Accounting and Public Policy,* 34 (6), 578–596.

Brooks, G., Tunley, M., Button, M. & Gee, J. 2017. Fraud, error and corruption in healthcare: a contribution from criminology.

Catchick, P. 2014. Conflict of Interest: Gateway to Corruption. *In:* ACFE European Fraud Conference, Research Paper, 2014.

Chapple, L. E. & Mui, G. Y. (2015). Social audit failure: Legal liability of external auditors. In *Social Audit Regulation* (pp. 281–299): Springer.

CHIŞ, A. O. & Achim, A. M. 2014. Professional Judgement: The Key to a Successful Audit. *SEA: Practical Application of Science,* 2 (3).

Cressey, D. R. 1953. Other people's money; a study of the social psychology of embezzlement.

Curtis, E. & Turley, S. 2007. The business risk audit–A longitudinal case study of an audit engagement. *Accounting, Organizations and Society,* 32 (4), 439–461.

DeZoort, F. T. & Harrison, P. D. 2018. Understanding auditors' sense of responsibility for detecting fraud within organizations. *Journal of Business Ethics,* 149 (4), 857–874.

Edwards, J. & Chandler, R. A. 2013. *British Audit Practice 1884–1900 (RLE Accounting): A Case Law Perspective*, Routledge.

Everett, J., Neu, D. & Rahaman, A. S. 2007. Accounting and the global fight against corruption. *Accounting, Organizations and Society,* 32 (6), 513–542.

Gibson, R. W. & Arnold, R. 1981. The development of auditing standards in Australia. *Accounting Historians Journal,* 8 (1), 51–65.

Gullkvist, B. & Jokipii, A. 2013. Perceived importance of red flags across fraud types. *Critical Perspectives on Accounting,* 24 (1), 44–61.

Hassink, H. F., Bollen, L. H., Meuwissen, R. H. & de Vries, M. J. 2009. Corporate fraud and the audit expectations gap: A study among business managers. *Journal of International Accounting, Auditing and Taxation,* 18 (2), 85–100.

Hauser, C. 2018. Fighting Against Corruption: Does Anti-corruption Training Make Any Difference? *Journal of Business Ethics,* 1–19.

Huang, S. Y., Lin, C. C., Chiu, A. A. & Yen, D. C. 2016. Fraud detection using fraud triangle risk factors. *Information Systems Frontiers*, 1–14.

Hurtt, R. K., Brown-Liburd, H., Earley, C. E. & Krishnamoorthy, G. 2013. Research on auditor professional skepticism: Literature synthesis and opportunities for future research. *Auditing: A Journal of Practice & Theory,* 32 (sp1)**,** 45–97.

IAASB 2009a. ISA 200: Overall objectives of the independent auditor and the conduct of an audit in accordance with international standards on auditing. *SAICA Members Handbook.* Pietermartizburg: LexisNexis.

IAASB 2009b. ISA 200: Overall objectives of the independent auditor and the conduct of an audit in accordance with international standards on auditing. *SAICA Members' Handbook.* 2009 ed. Pietermaritzburg: LexisNexis.

IAASB 2009c. ISA 220: Quality Control for Audits of Historical Financial Information. *SAICA Members' Handbook.* 2009 ed. Pietermaritzburg: LexisNexis.

IAASB 2009d. ISA 240: The auditor's responsibility realting to fraud in an audit of financial statements. *SAICA Members' Handbook.* 2009 ed. Pietermaritzburg: LexisNexis.

IAASB 2009e. ISA 240: The auditor's responsibility realting to fraud in an audit of financial statements. *SAICA Members' Handbook.* 2009 ed. Pietermaritsburg: LexisNexis.

IAASB 2009f. ISA 315 R: Identifying and Assessing the Risks of Material Misstatement. *SAICA Members' Handbook.* 2009 ed. Pietermaritzburg: LexisNexis.

IAASB 2009g. ISA 315: Identifying and assessing the risk of material misstatement through understanding the entity and its environment. *SAICA Members' Handbook.* 2009 ed. Pietermaritsburg: LexisNexis.

IAASB 2009h. ISA 500 Audit Evidence. *SAICA Members' Handbook.* 2009 ed. Pietermaritzburg: LexisNexis.

IAASB. (2017). Glossary. In *Handbook of International Quality Control , Auditing, Review, Other Assurance , and Related Services Pronouncements.*

IESBA 2017. Code of ethics for professional accountants. *SAICA Members' handbook.* Pietermaritzburg: LexisNexis.

IESBA 2019. Code of ethics for professional accountants. *SAICA Members' handbook.* Pietermaritzburg: LexisNexis.

IFRS 2018. IAS 8: Accounting policies, changes in accounting estimates and errors. *IAS 8.* London: IFRS Foundation.

IoD 2016. King IV Report on Governance for South Africa 2016. Institure of Directors Southern Africa.

Jakubowski, S. T., P.Chao, Huh, S. K. & Maheshwari, S. 2002. A Cross-Country Comparison of the Codes of Professional Conduct of Certified/CharteredAccountants. *Journal of Business Ethics,* 35 (2)**,** 111–129.

Jeppesen, K. K. 2016. The role of auditing in the fight against corruption. *The British Accounting Review.*

Ketz, J. E. 2006. *Accounting Ethics: Crisis in accounting ethics*, Taylor & Francis.

Khan, M. A. 2006. Role of audit in fighting corruption. In: Comunicação apresentada na Conferência: Ethics, Integrity, and Accountability. In the Public Sector: Re-building Public Trust in Government through the Implementation of the UN Convention against Corruption: Russia, 2006.

Kranacher, M. J., Riley, R. & Wells, J. T. 2010. *Forensic accounting and fraud examination*, John Wiley & Sons.

Kujinga, B. 2009. Reasonable care and skill – the modern scope of the auditors' duty. *GAA Accounting*.

Labuschagne, H. & Els, G. 2006. Corruption and fraud: any lessons for the auditor? *Meditari Accountancy Research,* 14 (1), 29–47.

Liggio, C. D. 1974. Expectation gap-accountants legal Waterloo. *Journal of contemporary business,* 3 (3), 27–44.

Lokanan, M. E. 2015. Challenges to the fraud triangle: Questions on its usefulness. *Accounting Forum,* 39 (3), 201–224.

Lou, Y. I. & Wang, M. L. 2011. Fraud risk factor of the fraud triangle assessing the likelihood of fraudulent financial reporting. *Journal of Business & Economics Research (JBER),* 7 (2).

Manning, G. A. & CFE, E. 2010. *Financial investigation and forensic accounting*, CRC Press.

Nelson, M. W. 2011. A model and literature review of professional skepticism in auditing.

Olsen, T. E. & Torsvik, G. 1998. Collusion and renegotiation in hierarchies: a case of beneficial corruption. *International Economic Review,* 413–438.

Pedneault, S., Silverstone, H., Rudewicz, F. & Sheetz, M. 2012. *Forensic accounting and fraud investigation for non-experts*, John Wiley & Sons.

Petraşcu, D. & Tieanu, A. 2014. The role of internal audit in fraud prevention and detection. *Procedia Economics and Finance,* 16, 489–497.

Porter, B. 1993. An empirical study of the audit expectation-performance gap. *Accounting and business research,* 24 (93), 49–68.

Porter, B., Ó hÓgartaigh, C. & Baskerville, R. 2012. Audit Expectation-Performance Gap Revisited: Evidence from New Zealand and the United Kingdom. Part 1: The Gap in New Zealand and the United Kingdom in 2008. *International Journal of Auditing,* 16 (2), 101–129.

Porter, B., Simon, J. & Hatherly, D. 2014. *Principles of External Auditing,* West Suzzex, John Wiley & Sons.

Power, M. 2013. The apparatus of fraud risk. *Accounting, Organizations and Society,* 38 (6), 525–543.

PwC 2018. Global Economic Crime Survey 2018: Pulling fraud out of the shadows.

PwC 2020. Ecomic Crime – When the boardroom becomes the battlefield. *PwC's Global Economic Crime and Fraud Survey – 7th South Afrian Edition.* 7th ed.

Rabel, F. K. 1944. Auditing standards and procedures in the light of court decisions. *Michigan Law Review,* 42 (6), 1009–1036.

Reurink, A. 2016. Financial fraud: A literature review. MPIfG Discussion Paper.

Ruhnke, K. & Schmidt, M. 2014. The audit expectation gap: existence, causes, and the impact of changes. *Accounting and Business research,* 44 (5), 572–601.

Shleifer, A. & Vishny, R. W. 1993. Corruption. *The quarterly journal of economics,* 108 (3), 599–617.

Singleton, T. W. & Singleton, A. J. 2010. *Fraud auditing and forensic accounting,* John Wiley & Sons.

Singleton, T. W., Singleton, A. J., Bologna, G. J. & Lindquist, R. J. 2006. *Fraud auditing and forensic accounting,* John Wiley & Sons.

Solomon, J. 2010. *Corporate Governance and Accountability, Third Edition,* West Susex, United Kingdom, John Wiley and Sons Ltd.

Tackett, J. A. 2010. Bribery and corruption. *Journal of Corporate Accounting & Finance,* 21 (4), 5–9.

Transparency International 2013. Business principles for countering bribery: a multi-stakeholder initiative.

Vinten, G., Payne, E. A. & Ramsay, R. J. 2005. Fraud risk assessments and auditors' professional skepticism. *Managerial Auditing Journal.*

Vona, L. W. 2012. *Fraud risk assessment: Building a fraud audit program,* John Wiley & Sons.

Wells, J. T. 2017. *Corporate fraud handbook: Prevention and detection,* John Wiley & Sons.

1. Introduction

Professional auditing standards state that audit quality is achieved by issuing an appropriate opinion of a client's financial statements (IAASB, 2009a; Hayes et al., 2014). The International Auditing and Assurance Board (IAASB) have two standards dedicated to audit quality at both the overall and firm level (ISQC 1) and the engagement level (ISA 220) (IAASB, 2009a; IAASB, 2011a). However, there is no guarantee that regulation by way of ISA's or legislative requirements will result in improved audit quality practice and reports (see, for example, Carcello et al., 2011; Maroun and Jonker, 2014; Carlin et al., 2018). For example, mandatory audit partner rotation under the Sarbanes-Oxley Act (SOX) may not necessarily yield actual quality gains (Myers et al., 2003). Similarly, there is no assurance that the prohibition on the rendering of non-audit services, a common feature in multiple jurisdictions, leads to improved audit quality (LIM and TAN, 2008; Liao et al., 2013).

Prior academic research has used different proxies for 'measuring audit' quality. One of the seminal studies on audit quality defined audit quality with reference to the size of the audit firm (DeAngelo, 1981b). DeAngelo (1981b) argues that ce*teris paribus,* barriers to entry allow an audit firm to earn 'client-specific quasi-rents' with the result that larger firms have 'more to lose' than their smaller counterparts (p. 184). Logically, larger firms are also more likely to have the financial, human and intellectual capital to execute audit engagements to a higher standard than firms do with constrained resources (Francis, 2004; PCAOB, 2013). They can charge a premium for their services (Peel and Makepeace, 2012) and report lower levels of litigation risk (Palmrose, 1988). Companies which are audited by one of the Big N[1] firms also tend to have higher quality corporate reports[2], lower information asymmetry and, in turn, lower costs of capital (Francis and Krishnan, 1999; Fernando et al., 2010a; Francis, 2011). These findings reaffirm the view that the size of an audit firm is a sound predictor of audit quality.

Size of the audit firm is not, however, the only indicator of audit quality. Both large and small firms have experienced audit failures (PCAOB, 2013). Large firms may also establish barriers of entry in order to limit competition, something which may also have adverse implications for audit quality (Francis, 2011). As a result, an alternate stream of research considers how the experience of an engagement team (Peecher et al., 2007) and engagement leader (Nagy, 2012), as well as the experience which an audit firm has accumulated in a particular industry

---

[1] The use of 'N' is to substitute for the largest firms in any given period. As at 2020, these firms are PwC, EY, KPMG and Deloitte.

[2] This is normally measured in terms of earnings quality such as the measure of discretionary accruals or other indicators of earnings management.

(Francis, 2004; Jenkins et al., 2006), positively influences audit quality (see also Ferguson et al., 2003; Francis et al., 2005). This is complemented by prior research on the relevance of independence for audit quality.

DeAngelo (1981a), for example, examines how low-balling may compromise independence and the auditor's willingness or ability to detect and report misstatements in financial statements. Similarly, the impact of rendering non-audit services to an audit client (Frankel et al., 2002; European Commission, 2010; Quick, 2012), rotation of the engagement leader (Firth et al., 2012) and mandatory firm rotation (Gavious, 2007; Daniels and Booker, 2011) on auditor independence and quality has been dealt with in detail in Chapter 3. How a company's corporate governance mechanisms can be used to safeguard auditor independence and improve audit quality has also been considered and incorporated in codes of best practice (Solomon, 2010; IOD, 2016).

This chapter complements the prior academic research by providing a more technical (and internally-focused) review on audit quality. This is done through an analysis of the relevant standards which deal with audit quality control systems at the firm (ISQC 1) and engagement level (ISA 220) (IAASB, 2009b; IAASB, 2009a). Audit quality indicators used by different international or regulatory bodies to demonstrate how the technical requirements can be operationalised are also considered.

Section 2 will provide an overview of audit quality and quality control systems. Section 3 will discuss the different quality control systems which should be implemented by audit firms. Section 4 will discuss quality control systems which can apply at the engagement level. Section 5 addresses the IAASB's audit quality indicators which are used as proxies for audit quality. Section 6 will provide an overview of the various methods used by regulators or international bodies to ensure audit quality.

2. Understanding of quality control

DeAngelo (1981a) defines audit quality as 'the market-assessed joint probability that a given auditor will both detect a breach in the client's accounting system and report the breach'. This definition is binary, suggesting that the auditor will either report a breach or not and does not take into account the value of assurance services in the preparation of a set of financial statements (see, for example DeFond and Zhang (2014)). The value of the audit can be found in better financial reporting, with the auditor ensuring that the financial statements do not only comply with the applicable financial reporting standards but also faithfully reflect the economics of the company (DeFond and Zhang, 2014). The result of this process is an audit report, containing an audit opinion expressing that the financial statements are free from material misstatements. However, to ensure reliance can be placed upon this report, auditors have to ensure that the work performed by the firm and the audit meet specified criteria, as set out by international bodies or regulators (see, for example Palmrose (1988); Imhoff (2003); Carrington (2010); Fernando et al. (2010b); IAASB (2011b); Deumes et al. (2012); Porter et al. (2014); Lamoreaux (2016).

Quality control in an auditing and assurance context is defined as policies and procedures which are in place to ensure that an appropriate audit opinion is issued and, in so doing, all ethical requirements, regulations and legislation have been complied with (ISQC 12009b). In order for this to be achieved, the auditing firm will need policies and procedures in place, for example, ensuring that the those employed have the appropriate knowledge and experience to execute their duties.

The applicable standards which require compliance with principles of quality control are International Standards on Quality Control 1: Quality Control for firms which perform audits and reviews of financial statements, and Other Assurance and Related Services Engagements (ISQC 1) and International Standards on Auditing 220: Quality control for an audit of financial statements (ISA 220). ISQC 1 and ISA 220 are similar standards. ISQC 1 applies to the audit firm as a whole and across all forms of assurance engagements. ISA 220 deals specifically with the requirement to maintain the quality of audits of historical financial information, that is, at engagement level (IAASB, 2016a).

3. Ensuring quality at the firm level

According to ISQC 1, an audit firm is responsible for its system of quality control for audits and reviews of financial statements and other assurance and related services engagements. Different personnel at an audit firm (typically senior management, engagement leaders and those charged with the firm's governance) are responsible for establishing and maintaining the firm's system of quality control. Also, they must comply with all requirements of ISQC 1 unless not applicable. Additional requirements may need to be established in addition to ISQC 1's requirements for fulfilment of an objective of ISQC 1 (ISQC 12009b).

The objective of ISQC 1 is for audit firms to establish and maintain a system of quality control to provide reasonable assurance that (see ISQC 1; Paragraph 11 in IAASB (2009b):

- The firm and its personnel comply with professional standards and applicable legal and regulatory requirements; and
- Reports issued by the firm or engagement partners are appropriate in the circumstances.

The core principles of ISQC 1 are summarised in Table 1.

Table 1: Summary of principles contained in ISQC 1	
Quality development	**Details**
Leadership responsibility	• The firm should promote a culture of professional excellence and recognise audit quality as essential (ISQC 1, para 18). • The governing body accepts ultimate responsibility for the firm's system of quality control (ISQC 1, para 18). • The firm's policies and procedures require those responsible for driving quality to have the necessary expertise (ISQC 1, para 19).
Relevant ethical standards	• Covered in Chapter 3. • Reinforces the fundamental principles (ISQC 1, para A7) and the need for effective monitoring, reviewing and training related to ethical compliance (ISQC 1, para A8). • Independence is of specific importance. Firm-wide policies are needed to ensure independence standards, define appropriate safeguards and ensure effective communication of the need for independence (ISQC 1, para 21–25).
Client acceptance and continuance (also refer to Chapter 9)	• Policies and procedures are needed to ensure that the firm accepts and retains engagements which it is competent to perform, can adhere to ethical standards for and is satisfied that the client does not lack integrity (ISQC 1, para 26). • Acceptance/continuance policy should cover the identification and communication of conflicts of interest (ISQC, para 27–28). • Factors related to firm competency are addressed in ISQC 1 para A18. • Client integrity is dealt with in more detail in ISQC 1 para A19–A20.
Human resources	• Specific considerations regarding the appointment of the engagement team and engagement partner (ISQC 1, para 30–31). • Specific considerations relating to the competency of the engagement team (ISQC 1, para A31).

►

Table 1: Summary of principles contained in ISQC 1	
Quality development	**Details**

Engagement performance	• Policies to ensure that adequate consultation takes place on importance/high risk/subjective issues (ISQC 1, para 34).
	 • Policies for the establishment of quality control review process and the circumstances in which quality control reviews are required (ISQC 1, para 35).
	 • Specific matters to be taken into account as part of the quality control review process (ISQC 1, para 37).
	 • Eligibility as a quality control reviewer (ISQC 1, para 39–41). This includes implementing policies and procedures to cover the degree to which the QCR can be consulted with and to ensure that:
	   – the quality control reviewer (QCR) has the necessary qualifications;
	   – the QCR is objective concerning the audit; and
	   – there is adequate documentation as to the QCR, their findings and policies and procedures.
	 • Policies for adequate supervision and review of staff (ISQC 1, para 32 & A34–A35).

Monitoring	• Focuses on the review of the firm's quality control system on a cyclical basis by suitably experienced partners who are not involved in the engagements under review (ISQC 1, para 48).

Adapted from IAASB (2016b)

3.1 Elements of a system of quality control

The elements of quality control are shown in Figure 1 below:

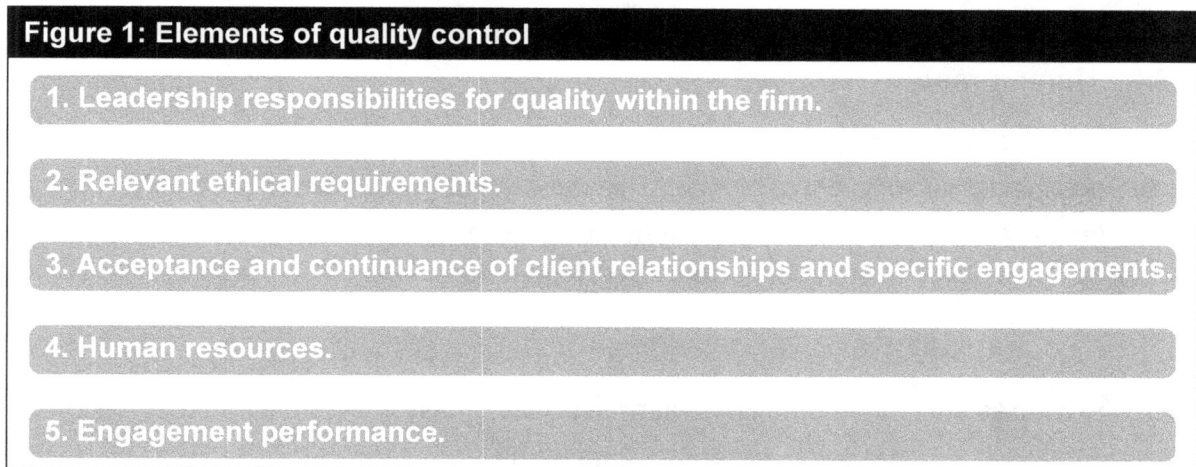

Figure 1: Elements of quality control

1. Leadership responsibilities for quality within the firm.

2. Relevant ethical requirements.

3. Acceptance and continuance of client relationships and specific engagements.

4. Human resources.

5. Engagement performance.

3.2 Leadership responsibilities for quality within the firm

The firm's chief executive officer or the firm's managing board of partners will assume ultimate responsibility for the firm's system of quality control. In order to assume this responsibility, these parties will need to have sufficient and appropriate experience, ability and authority (IAASB, 2016b).

3.3 Relevant ethical requirements

The firm and its personnel must comply with the relevant ethical requirements (IAASB, 2016b). As an example, the firm must communicate its independence requirements to its personnel to identify and evaluate circumstances and relationships which create threats to independence and to take appropriate action (IAASB, 2016b). Also, the engagement partner should provide information about the client and engagement to evaluate the impact on independence requirements and firm personnel shall promptly notify the firm of circumstances and relationships that create a threat to independence (IAASB, 2016b).

3.4 Acceptance and continuance of client relationships and specific engagements

The firm should establish policies and procedures for the acceptance and continuance of client relationships and specific engagements. The client acceptance and continuance process is discussed in more detail in Chapter 9. Briefly, the objective of the client acceptance and continuance process is to provide a firm with reasonable assurance that it will only undertake or continue relationships and engagements if the firm:

- is competent to perform the engagement and has the capabilities, including time and resources, to do so;

- can comply with relevant ethical requirements; and
- has considered the integrity of the client and does not have information that would lead it to conclude that the client lacks integrity (IAASB, 2016b).

3.5   Human resources

The firm should establish policies and procedures designed to provide it with reasonable assurance that it has sufficient personnel. This means that the personnel have the necessary competence, capabilities and commitment to ethical principles to perform engagements following professional standards and applicable legal and regulatory requirements (IAASB, 2016b).

Also, the policies and procedures on human resources should enable the firm or engagement partners to issue reports which are appropriate in the circumstances. In order to do so, the engagement partner must have the appropriate competence, capabilities, and authority to perform his/her role and responsibilities should be clearly defined and communicated (IAASB, 2016b).

3.6   Engagement performance

The firm should establish policies and procedures designed to provide it with reasonable assurance that:

- engagements are performed following professional standards and applicable legal and regulatory requirements;
- the firm or the engagement partner issues reports which are appropriate in the circumstances;
- appropriate consultation takes place on difficult or contentious matters; and
- sufficient resources are available to enable an appropriate consultation.

Figure 2 details the policies and procedures described in the preceding paragraph. ISQC 1 refers to these policies and procedures as quality control reviews. This list is not exhaustive and sets out the requirements of ISQC 1 (IAASB, 2016b).

Figure 2: Policies and procedures for quality control

Engagement quality control review required for:

- All audits of financial statements of listed entities.
- All other audits and reviews when a firm believes a quality control review is required.

The quality control review should include:

- Discussion of significant matters with the engagement partner.
- Review of the financial statements or other subject matter, information and the proposed report.
- Review of selected engagement documentation made by the engagement team and the conclusions it reached.
- Evaluation of the conclusions reached in formulating the report and consideration of whether the proposed report is appropriate.

Criteria for the eligibility of engagement quality control reviewers:

- The technical qualifications required to perform the role, including the necessary experience and authority; and
- The degree to which an engagement quality control reviewer can be consulted on the engagement without compromising the reviewer's objectivity.

Adapted from (IAASB, 2016b).

3.7 Monitoring

The firm should establish a monitoring process designed to provide reasonable assurance that the policies and procedures relating to the system of quality control are relevant, adequate, and operating effectively (IAASB, 2016b). This process will include an ongoing consideration and evaluation of the firm's system of quality control. In order to facilitate this, the responsibility for the monitoring process should be assigned to a partner or partners or other persons with sufficient and appropriate experience and authority in the firm to assume the responsibility (IAASB, 2016b).

ISQC 1 requires that the firm will communicate, at least annually, the results of the monitoring of its system of quality control to engagement partners and other appropriate individuals within the firm. This communication will be sufficient to enable the firm and these individuals to take prompt and appropriate action where necessary in line with their defined roles and responsibilities (IAASB, 2016b). Figure 2 above illustrates the policies and procedures for quality control.

4. Ensuring quality at the engagement level

ISA 220 is premised on the basis that the firm is subject to ISQC 1 or to national requirements which are, at least, as demanding (2009a, p. para 2). Within the context of the firm's system of quality control, engagement teams have a responsibility to implement quality control procedures which apply to the audit engagement. ISQC 1 requires that quality control policies and procedures be implemented through the audit firm, including policies and procedures for assurance and non-assurance related services. ISA 220 is more specific in that it applies to the need for quality control policies and procedures on specific audit engagements. Figure 3 summarises the requirements of ISA 220. The requirements of ISA 220 are very similar to those in ISQC 1.

Figure 3: ISA 220 requirements

Audit partner must take responsibility for the quality of the engagement (ISA 220, para 8).

The engagement team should remain continuously alert for threats to independence and must implement safeguards as necessary (ISA 200, para 9–10).

The engagement leader should ensure that firm policies have been applied appropriately in the accepting/continuing with the specific engagement (ISA 220, para 12–13 & A8–A9).

Individuals allocated to the engagement team should have the necessary competency and resources (ISA 220, para 14 & A10–A11).

Processes should be put in place and communicated to the engagement team to ensure adequate consultation, review and supervision takes place (ISA 220, para 15–18).

Where applicable, implement effective quality review processes. This would apply if the entity is a public interest entity or listed on a recognised stock exchange (ISA 200, para 19–21)).

Adapted from ISA 220 in IAASB (2009a)

5. Indicators of audit quality

The Advisory Committee on the Auditing Profession (ACAP) in the USA wanted auditing firms to provide periodic reporting on audit quality factors in order for market participants to observe audit quality which will result in differentiation between audit firms. If this data are publicly available, audit firms may be incentivised to increase their audit quality. Similar public disclosure of the PCAOB audit firm inspection results in negative publicity for the audit firms involved.

Audit quality is difficult to define. From research, the following definitions or sub-sections have been identified:

- A high-quality audit is one performed 'per generally accepted auditing standards'. This will ensure that audited financial statements and related disclosures are prepared following an acceptable financial reporting framework and are not materially misstated because of fraud or errors (DeAngelo, 1981 cited in Bedard, Johnstone & Smith, 2010).
- Audit quality is 'the market assessed joint probability that a given auditor will both discover a breach in a client's accounting system and report the breach.' (DeAngelo, 1981 cited in Bedard, Johnstone & Smith, 2010).
- Higher audit quality is 'greater assurance, which requires more audit work' (Carcello et al., 2002 cited in Bedard, Johnstone & Smith, 2010).
- The IAASB Framework for Audit Quality (2014) describes the term 'audit quality' as encompassing certain key elements which create an environment which maximises the likelihood that quality audits are performed consistently.

Bedard, Johnstone & Smith (2010) devised a list of measurable inputs and outputs with regards to audit quality. These inputs and outputs are a culmination of international research relating to audit quality. The authors divided the inputs and outputs into engagement-level indicators and firm-level indicators. The following table summarises their interpretation:

Table 2: Input summary

Measurable inputs	Measurable outputs
Engagement-level Indicators	
Audit hours	Accuracy of audit opinion
Training hours	Accounting and auditing enforcement releases detailing individual acts indicating low audit quality
Personnel assignment	
Audit fees	Client discretionary accruals and other earnings quality measures
Audit partner tenure	Length of service of the engagement leader
Tailoring of audit tests to reflect client risk	Compliance with applicable assurance standards
Audit budgeting	Budgeted and actual hours spent on an engagement
Individual auditor industry specialisation	Length of service

►

Table 2: Input summary	
Measurable inputs	**Measurable outputs**
Firm-level indicators	
Audit firm size	Litigation and related costs
Audit firm industry specialisation	Inspection activities and report results
Audit firm tenure	Peer review results
Audit firm independence	Internal inspection results
Audit firm compensation plans	Results from internal engagement inspections are considered in annual performance evaluations

If public disclosure of client information on this list should be regulated, it could result in the resignation of audit firms where there is a high risk associated with the client. Such resignations will have an effect on the investors of the risky organisation and impact on the financial markets.

6. External regulation and audit quality

ISQC 1 and ISA 220 form part of a self-regulatory system, requiring audit firms to take responsibility for the quality of their audit engagements. This self-regulatory approach to audit quality is, to an increasing extent, being complemented by arms-length regulation. The most well-known example is the introduction of the Sarbanes Oxley Act (2002) (SOX) in the US which, inter-alia, is designed to regulate auditor independence and quality. Other jurisdictions, including the UK, the EU and South Africa have also taken steps to regulate their audit professions. A brief overview of the external regulatory environment is provided below.

6.1. SOX and the US

SOX was enacted in response to major corporate scandals, particularly Enron and WorldCom. It was designed to restore the public's trust in corporate accounting and reporting (Unerman and O'Dwyer, 2004; Carrington, 2010).

In the US, the Public Company Accounting Oversight Board (PCAOB) has the power to perform inspections of an audit firm's engagements to ensure that these are being executed according to applicable professional standards and regulatory requirements. (Bishop et al., 2013).

- 'PCAOB inspections focus on how a firm conducted selected audits and on the effectiveness of the firm's quality control policies and procedures. Inspections are designed to identify whether there are deficiencies in how the accounting firm performs public company audits and whether there are weaknesses in its quality controls over public company auditing' (Centre for Audit Quality (2012).

- The results of inspection processes are publicly available, including the name of the applicable audit firms and weaknesses identified by the PCAOB (Bishop et al., 2013).

6.2. The FRC in the UK

The Financial Reporting Council (FRC) is responsible for the regulation of auditors, accountants and actuaries in the United Kingdom (UK). The FRC establishes the codes for corporate governance and stewardship. The UK Corporate Governance Code (Code) is applied to all companies listed on the London Securities Exchange. Public interest entities, which include government institutions and listed entities, are also required to comply with the Code.

The FRC also monitors the work of audit firms. Quality reviews focus on the Financial Times Stock Exchange (FTSE) 350, as well as on audit services provided to entities which have high public interest (FRC, 2015). Quality reviews focus on, *inter alia:*

'...the appropriateness of key audit judgments made in reaching the audit opinion and the sufficiency and appropriateness of the audit evidence obtained. ...Reviews of firm-wide procedures are wide-ranging in nature and include an assessment of how the culture within firms impacts on audit quality.' (FRC, 2015).

The results of the FRC's inspections are communicated to the audit firm which is required to take appropriate corrective action. Where necessary, inspection findings can also be referred to an enforcement unit which has the power to impose additional sanctions on auditors (FRC, 2015).

6.3. EU Audit Directive and Regulation in the EU

In the European Union (EU), each jurisdiction (such as Germany, France, etc.) establishes its codes of corporate governance. However, the European Commission is responsible for harmonising these codes to ensure that there is some form of consistency across the jurisdictions.

The European Commission has set out the following areas for harmonisation (The European Commission, 2001):

'Board structure — The Commission acknowledged the coexistence of different board models deeply rooted in national legal systems, stating that it would not pursue board-structure harmonisation.'

'Shareholder identification and engagement—The Commission recommended better mechanisms for companies to identify shareholders and to enhance shareholder engagement. The plan strengthens transparency rules for institutional investors, including disclosure of institutional investors' voting and better shareholder control over related-party transactions. The Commission intends to investigate whether employee share ownership should be encouraged.'

'Disclosure —The Commission recommended that corporate governance reporting be improved, especially concerning explanations for not applying code provisions. This particularly includes the disclosure of board diversity policy, risk-management policies, remuneration policies and individual remuneration of directors, and shareholder voting on the remuneration policy and the remuneration report.'

The EU Audit Directive and Regulation is the regulation which governs the auditing profession in the European Union (EU). Each jurisdiction is responsible for regulating audit firms and such regulations are in line with the EU Audit Directive and Regulation (The European Commission2001).

7. Summary

There are several studies which confirm the importance of these inspection processes for improving audit quality. For example, DeFond and Lennox (2011, p. 22) find that SOX has resulted in more scrutiny of audit practice and has increased the cost of performing a poor audit engagement. Gipper et al. (2015) and Shroff (2015) argue that inspections by an independent regulator strengthens users' confidence in the subject matter of assurance engagements while Offermanns and Peek (2011) present evidence on the positive effect which inspection processes have had on market risk and share prices (see also Church and Shefchik, 2011; Bishop et al., 2013; Lamoreaux, 2016). While much of this research is based in the US, it is reasonable to assume that a well-functioning external regulatory mechanism can result in similar benefits in other jurisdictions.

There have been some criticisms of inspections performed by an external regulator. For example, Lennox and Pittman (2010) and Hilary and Lennox (2005) argue that PCAOB inspections are focused on compliance, instead of dealing with whether or not the spirit of auditing standards and regulation is being adhered to. Others feel that inspections lead to a 'trade-off of expertise for independence' (Defond, 2010, p. 105) because of the emphasis placed on independence rules rather than on the internal management of audit firms. On average, however, the prior research suggests that independent inspections can encourage accountants and auditors to apply the requirements of professional standards more diligently, (Church and Shefchik, 2011; Canning and O'Dwyer, 2013; Louw and Maroun, 2017) and result in more reliable audit opinions (Canning and O'Dwyer, 2013; Canning and O'Dwyer, 2016).

8. References

Bishop, C. C., Hermanson, D. R. & Houston, R. W. 2013. PCAOB Inspections of International Audit Firms: Initial Evidence. *International Journal of Auditing,* 17 (1), 1–18.

Canning, M. & O'Dwyer, B. 2016. Institutional work and regulatory change in the accounting profession. *Accounting, Organizations and Society,* 54, 1–21.

Canning, M. & O'Dwyer, B. 2013. The dynamics of a regulatory space realignment: Strategic responses in a local context. *Accounting, Organizations and Society,* 38 (3), 169–194.

Carcello, J. V., Hollingsworth, C. & Mastrolia, S. A. 2011. The effect of PCAOB inspections on Big 4 audit quality. *Research in Accounting Regulation,* 23 (2), 85–96.

Carlin, D., Robert, K. W. & Robyn, M. 2018. Public Oversight of Audit Firms: The Slippery Slope of Enforcing Regulation. *Abacus,* In press (0).

Carrington, T. 2010. An analysis of the demands on a sufficient audit: Professional appearance is what counts! *Critical Perspectives on Accounting,* 21 (8), 669–682.

Centre for Audit Quality. 2012. Guide to PCAOB Inspections. Available: http://thecaq.org/ sites/default/files/guidetopcaobinspections.pdf [Accessed 10 October 2017].

Church, B. K. & Shefchik, L. B. 2011. PCAOB inspections and large accounting firms. *Accounting Horizons,* 26 (1), 43–63.

Daniels, B. W. & Booker, Q. 2011. The effects of audit firm rotation on perceived auditor independence and audit quality. *Research in Accounting Regulation,* 23 (1), 78–82.

DeAngelo, L. E. 1981a. Auditor independence, 'low balling', and disclosure regulation. *Journal of Accounting and Economics,* 3 (2), 113–127.

DeAngelo, L. E. 1981b. Auditor size and audit quality. *Journal of Accounting and Economics,* 3 (3), 183–199.

DeFond, M. & Zhang, J. 2014. A review of archival auditing research. *Journal of accounting and economics,* 58 (2–3), 275–326.

DeFond, M. L. & Lennox, C. S. 2011. The effect of SOX on small auditor exits and audit quality. *Journal of Accounting and Economics,* 52 (1), 21–40.

Deumes, R., Schelleman, C., Vander Bauwhede, H. & Vanstraelen, A. 2012. Audit firm governance: Do transparency reports reveal audit quality? *Auditing: A Journal of Practice & Theory,* 31 (4), 193–214.

European Commission. 2010. Green Paper on Audit Policy: Lessons from the Crisis. Available: http://europa.eu/rapid/pressReleasesAction. do?reference=MEMO/10/487&format=HTML&aged=0&language=EN&guiLanguage=en [Accessed 2 April 2011].

Ferguson, A., Francis, J. R. & Stokes, D. J. 2003. The Effects of Firm-Wide and Office-Level Industry Expertise on Audit Pricing. *Accounting Review,* 78 (2), 429–448.

Fernando, G., Abdel-Meguid, A., Elder, R. & Lubin, J. 2010a. Audit quality attributes, client size and cost of equity capital'. *Review of Accounting and Finance,* 9 (4), 363–381.

Fernando, G. D., Abdel-Meguid, A. M. & Elder, R. J. 2010b. Audit quality attributes, client size and cost of equity capital. *Review of Accounting and Finance.*

Firth, M., Rui, O. M. & Wu, X. 2012. How Do Various Forms of Auditor Rotation Affect Audit Quality? Evidence from China. *The International Journal of Accounting,* 47 (1), 109–138.

Francis, J. R. 2004. What do we know about audit quality? *The British Accounting Review,* 36 (4), 345–368.

Francis, J. R. 2011. A Framework for Understanding and Researching Audit Quality. *Auditing: A Journal of Practice & Theory,* 30 (2), 125–152.

Francis, J. R. & Krishnan, J. 1999. Accounting Accruals and Auditor Reporting Conservatism. *Contemporary Accounting Research,* 16 (1), 135–165.

Francis, J. R., Reichelt, K. & Wang, D. 2005. The Pricing of National and City-Specific Reputations for Industry Expertise in the U.S. Audit Market. *Accounting Review,* 80 (1), 113–136.

Frankel, R. M., Johnson, M. F. & Nelson, K. K. 2002. The relation between auditors' fees for nonaudit services and earnings management. *The accounting review,* 77 (s-1), 71–105.

FRC. 2015. *The Financial Reporting Council* [Online]. Available: https://www.frc.org.uk/Home. aspx [Accessed 1 December 2015].

Gavious, I. 2007. Alternative perspectives to deal with auditors' agency problem. *Critical Perspectives on Accounting,* 18 (4), 451–467.

Gipper, B., Leuz, C. & Maffett, M. 2015. Public audit oversight and reporting credibility: Evidence from the PCAOB inspection regime. National Bureau of Economic Research.

Hayes, R., Wallage, P. & Gortemaker, H. 2014. *Principles of auditing: An introduction to international standards on auditing,* Pearson Higher Ed.

Hilary, G. & Lennox, C. 2005. The credibility of self-regulation: Evidence from the accounting profession's peer review program. *Journal of Accounting and Economics,* 40 (1), 211–229.

IAASB 2009a. ISA 220: Quality Control for Audits of Historical Financial Information. *SAICA Members' Handbook.* 2009 ed. Pietermaritsburg: LexisNexis.

IAASB 2009b. ISQC1: Quality Control for Firms That Perform Audits and Reviews of Historical Financial Information, and Other Assurance and Related Services. *SAICA Members' Handbook.* Pietermartisburg: Lexis Nexis.

IAASB 2011a. Audit quality an IAASB perspective. IFAC.

IAASB 2011b. Audit quality: an IAASB perspective. IFAC.

IAASB 2016a. ISA 220: Quality Control for an Audit of Financial Statements.

IAASB 2016b. ISQC 1: Quality Control for firms.

Imhoff, G. 2003. Accounting quality, auditing and corporate governance.

IOD 2016. *King IV Report on Corporate Governance in South Africa*, Lexis Nexus South Africa, Johannesburg, South Africa.

Jenkins, D. S., Kane, G. D. & Velury, U. 2006. Earnings quality decline and the effect of industry specialist auditors: An analysis of the late 1990s. *Journal of Accounting and Public Policy*, 25 (1), 71–90.

Lamoreaux, P. T. 2016. Does PCAOB inspection access improve audit quality? An examination of foreign firms listed in the United States. *Journal of Accounting and Economics*, 61 (2), 313–337.

Lennox, C. & Pittman, J. 2010. Auditing the auditors: Evidence on the recent reforms to the external monitoring of audit firms. *Journal of Accounting and Economics*, 49 (1), 84–103.

Liao, Y., Chi, W. & Chen, Y. 2013. Auditor economic dependence and accounting conservatism: evidence from a low litigation risk setting. *International Journal of Auditing*, 17 (2), 117–137.

LIM, C. Y. & TAN, H. T. 2008. Non-audit service fees and audit quality: The impact of auditor specialization. *Journal of Accounting Research*, 46 (1), 199–246.

Louw, A. & Maroun, W. 2017. Independent monitoring and review functions in a financial reporting context. *Meditari Accountancy Research*, 25 (2), null.

Maroun, W. & Jonker, C. 2014. Critical and interpretive accounting, auditing and governance research in South Africa. *Southern African Journal of Accountability and Auditing Research*, 16 (1), 51–62.

Myers, J. N., Myers, L. A. & Omer, T. C. 2003. Exploring the term of the auditor-client relationship and the quality of earnings: A case for mandatory auditor rotation? *The Accounting Review*, 78 (3), 779–799.

Nagy, A. 2012. Audit partner specialization: the case of Andersen followers. *Managerial Auditing Journal*, 27 (3), 251–262.

Offermanns, M. & Peek, E. 2011. Investor reactions to PCAOB inspection reports.

Palmrose, Z. V. 1988. An analysis of auditor litigation and audit service quality. *The Accounting Review*, 63 (1), 55.

PCAOB. 2013. Discussion – Audit Quality Indicators. Available: https://pcaobus.org/News/ Events/Documents/05152013_SAGMeeting/Audit_Quality_Indicators.pdf [Accessed 16 October 2016].

Peecher, M. E., Schwartz, R. & Solomon, I. 2007. It's all about audit quality: Perspectives on strategic-systems auditing. *Accounting, Organizations and Society*, 32 (4–5), 463–485.

Porter, B., Simon, J. & Hatherly, D. 2014. *Principles of External Auditing*, West Suzzex, John Wiley & Sons.

Quick, R. 2012. EC green paper proposals and audit quality. *Accounting in Europe*, 9 (1), 17–38.

Shroff, N. 2015. Real effects of financial reporting quality and credibility: Evidence from the PCAOB regulatory regime.

Solomon, J. 2010. *Corporate Governance and Accountability, Third Edition,* West Susex, United Kingdom, John Wiley and Sons Ltd.

The European Commission. 2001. *European Commission* [Online]. [Accessed].

Unerman, J. & O'Dwyer, B. 2004. Enron, WorldCom, Andersen et al.: a challenge to modernity. *Critical Perspectives on Accounting,* 15 (6–7), 971–993.

Chapter 8: Professional liability

1. Introduction

The scandals faced by the auditing profession in the early part of the 21st century resulted in a new regulatory era. This era has seen a revision of existing legislation increasing auditor liability to third parties (AHL vs Deloitte, Part 30, 2004). Examples of such scandals include the corporate collapses at the start of the 21st century and in response to such scandals, the introduction of legislation such as Sarbanes-Oxley Act of 2002 (SOX) SOX requirements have increased the potential auditor liability because of the requirements imposed on auditors in identifying and reporting internal control deficiencies (Bush et al., 2007). The implementation of these is important, as it is in the best interest of the auditing profession and also protects the image of the profession (Bazerman et al., 2002). In addition, it imposes further quality controls over the profession, and these should improve audit quality.

Recent developments in the field of auditor liability include, in a South African context, KPMG which audited a company owned by politically exposed people (PEP)[1]. It is alleged that KPMG failed to identify the funds earmarked for supporting farmers in rural communities which were subsequently diverted by an audit client. KPMG's public image has been tarnished because of their association with these PEP leading to significant loss of revenue (Africa, 2018). Legal liability may also result.

The law with regards to auditor liability differ in each jurisdiction (Toda and McCarty, 2004). For example, in common law[2] countries such as the United Kingdom, United States of America, and Australia, there are legislative requirements imposed on the auditing profession. In contrast, civil law[3] countries such as Germany and France do not have legislative requirements imposed on the auditing profession (Chung et al., 2010).

The objective of this chapter is to understand what is meant by auditor liability, and how the exposure to auditor liability can vary among jurisdictions. The chapter will then include an analysis of transnational audits and the impact on auditor liability.

2. Auditor liability

There is no single definition of auditor liability. The basic premise is that auditors need to be held liable for providing sub-standard services[4] (Schwartz, 1993; Samsonova-Taddei and

---

1   Politically exposed people means individuals with significant political influence or the power to exert such influence.
2   Common law is developed from custom and case law and is used as the source of law.
3   Civil law is developed from Roman law and legislation is the primary source of law.
4   Chapter 7 explains that a good quality audit results in the correct audit opinion being issued. If an audit is not of the appropriate quality, it has not been carried out in accordance with International Standards on Auditing (ISA's) and can increase auditor liability as a sub-standard service has been provided.

Humphrey, 2015). What is common is that auditor liability can either be joint and several or proportionate (Narayanan, 1994; Palmrose, 1994).

In most jurisdictions, auditors can be held jointly and severally liable (ibid). An example of joint and several liability is when a company goes bankrupt. An auditor held jointly and severally liable must also pay damages on behalf of the bankrupt company, even if the auditor is found responsible for only a small fraction of the total liability (ibid). Even if an audit partner is not responsible for any wrongdoing, he or she will still be held liable for any liability along with the partner responsible (ibid). Empirical studies have found that 90% of the litigation cases result in auditor liability being joint and several (Palmrose, 1987). In addition, 50% of these litigation cases involve financial failure/distress of the audit client (Palmrose, 1994).

In various jurisdictions this varies as to the party who has a claim against the auditors for sub-standard service (Narayanan, 1994). The audit client is one party but there can be a multitude of possible other parties. These include potential and current investors/lenders, employees, and the public. What is common across jurisdictions is that it must be identified to whom the auditor owes a duty of care with regards to the opinion that they issue (Chung et al., 2010). If the auditor violates this duty due to negligence or malice, the auditor could be held liable for damages (Chung et al., 2010).

In order to clarify to which party or parties the auditor owes a duty of care, four standards can be applied. These need to be applied to the applicable jurisdiction's legislative requirements for auditors in order to identify to whom the auditor owes a duty of care. It must be noted that the auditor owes a duty of care to its audit client based on all four standards[5]. These four standards are the (Chung et al., 2010):

- privity rule,
- near-privity standard,
- restatement rule; and
- the reasonable foreseeability rule.

In addition to the duty of care, such duty of care must have been breached and this resulted in a loss to the parties to which this duty is owed. The loss must be a financial loss. Once the duty of care is established, one can assess whether the duty has been breached by the auditor's actions. The financial loss suffered is then defined in legal terms, where the party to which the duty of care was owed is in a less favourable position than they would have been had this breach of duty not occurred (Geiger and Raghunandan, 2002; King and de Beer, 2018). This could include the value of the investment in shares lost by shareholders

---

5   For South African students please note that only the 4th standard is applicable to contractual based claims. This is legislated by the Auditing Professions Act of 2005. For delictual based claims, all four standards apply.

or the credit risk exposure or write-off from a loan which is no longer receivable by a lender (King and de Beer, 2018).

2.1 Privity rule

Of the four rules discussed in part 2.1, 2.2, 2.3 and 2.4, this is the most restrictive in terms of auditor liability. In order for the auditor to incur legal liability, privity requires a contractual or direct relationship to exist between auditor and another party (Chung et al., 2010). The United States of America and Canada are two jurisdictions in which the privity rule is applied for determining to whom the auditor owes a duty of care. In these jurisdictions, the audit client is one part. The current shareholders can have this direct relationship (Pacini et al., 2000).

2.2 Near-privity rule

In instances where this forms the standard, three pre-requisites must be satisfied before auditors can be held liable for negligent misrepresentation to non-contractual third parties (Trakman and Trainor, 2005):

1. the auditor must have known that financial reports were to be used for a particular purpose;
2. the known party or parties were intended to be able to rely on those reports; and
3. there must have been some conduct linking the auditor to the relying party.

An example of instances where this rule may apply is when the issue of a loan is contingent on the fact that the financial statements are audited. The bank will then decide whether to grant the loan based on the fact that the audit opinion is unmodified. In obtaining an understanding of the entity, the auditors would have identified that their audit client is in the process of obtaining a loan and the audited financial statements will be used as motivation for the granting of such loan (particular purpose). The auditor would also be aware that the loan being granted will be contingent on the fact that an unmodified audit report is issued (reliance). Finally, the audit of the financial statements and the granting of the loan form a link between auditor and the bank. This is because the granting of the loan, which is the bank's operations, is linked to the outcome of the audit work performed by the auditor. This increases the auditor's liability due to the reliance by a third party of whom the auditor is aware (Palmrose, 1987; Palmrose, 1994; Pacini et al., 2000; Trakman and Trainor, 2005; Chung et al., 2010).

2.3 The restatement rule

This rule broadens the class of persons to whom the auditor owes a duty. This includes both identifiable and unidentifiable beneficiaries. The identity of the specific third parties does not need to be known, only the members of a limited group needs to be known to the auditor

(Bush et al., 2007). This group can include the current shareholders of the audit client. The shareholders are a known group, but the auditor may not know each of them specifically.

2.4 The reasonable foreseeability rule

In this instance, the auditor has a duty of care owed to all those who the auditor should reasonably foresee as receiving and relying on the audited statements. The duty only extends to those users who use the audited financial statements in the making of economic decisions. This duty also extends only to users who obtain a firm's financial statements directly from the audited entity (Bush et al., 2007).

In jurisdictions which are be regarded as having a civil-law based legal system, this rule is used to identify to whom the auditor owes a duty of care. Examples of these jurisdictions include Germany and France (Pacini et al., 2000; Trakman and Trainor, 2005; Chung et al., 2010). These jurisdictions have legislation providing for auditor contractual liability. Such liability is limited to a certain range of monetary amounts based on certain factors. These jurisdiction's auditing profession had few required changes to be made post the financial scandals of the early 21st century (Pacini et al., 2000; Trakman and Trainor, 2005; Chung et al., 2010). These jurisdiction's legal systems allowed for the identification of whom the auditor owed a duty of care to and the extent of the claim for any negligence or wrong-doing (Pacini et al., 2000; Trakman and Trainor, 2005; Chung et al., 2010).

Table 1 below summarises the jurisdictions and the standard that applies to them:

Table 1: Jurisdictions and auditor liability rules that apply				
Jurisdiction	Privity	Near-Privity	Restatement	Reasonable Foreseeability
USA	✔	✔	✔	✔
Canada		✔		
UK	✔			
Australia			✔	
New Zealand			✔	
South Africa			✔	
France				✔
Germany				✔

(Chung et al., 2010)

3. A South African context

In a South African context, auditor's liability is dealt with in ss1 and 46 of the Auditing Profession Act, No 26 of 2005 (APA) (APA2005).

3.1 Auditor liability in South Africa

In terms of the APA, the auditor has no liability to their audit client or third party unless they were negligent or malicious. If the third party can prove that the auditor knew or could reasonably have been expected to know that the opinion would be used by the audit client to induce a third party or that the third party would rely on the opinion, then the auditor can potentially be held liable. The auditor can only be held liable if such parties in fact did rely on the opinion and have sustained/suffered a financial loss (APA; S46, 2005; King and de Beer, 2018). The extent of the damages that can be claimed may be different for a contractual claim versus a delictual claim (Wainer, 2009; King and de Beer, 2018).

3.2 Expanded reporting duty

The APA requires an auditor (who would be the registered auditor responsible for the audit engagement) to report the audit client to the Independent Regulatory Board for Auditors (IRBA). Such requirement arises when 'any unlawful act or omission committed by any person responsible for the management of an entity, which:

- has caused or is likely to cause material financial loss to the entity or to any partner, member, shareholder, creditor or investor of the entity in respect of his, her or its dealings with that entity; or
- (ii) is fraudulent or amounts to theft; or
- (iii) represents a material breach of any fiduciary duty owed by such person to the entity or any partner, member, shareholder, creditor or investor of the entity under any law applying to the entity or the conduct or management thereof' (APA; S1, 2005).

This is defined as a reportable irregularity. If the auditor fails to report a reportable irregularity they may incur liability to any partner, member, shareholder, creditor or investor (APA; S46, 2005).

The issue which arises for the auditor is an ethical conundrum, where reporting a reportable irregularity will harm their relationship with the audit client and potentially lead to a loss of revenues (Maroun and Gowar, 2013). The auditor has an incentive not to report such reportable irregularity. Not reporting the reportable irregularity can give rise to greater auditor liability (Malsch and Gendron, 2011; Maroun and Atkins, 2014). This is because the South African auditor has both legislative (APA) and regulatory liability to identify and report, if necessary, non-compliance with laws and regulations to IRBA. Not doing so can result in auditor liability because of negligence. Therefore, the implementation of more legislation and regulation on the auditor increases auditor liability.

3.3 Ethical considerations

Finally the International Federation of Accountant's (IFAC) code on ethics for auditors introduces a requirement for auditors to identify and discuss non-compliance with laws and regulations committed by their audit client with those charged with governance/management of the entity (IESBA, 2016).

Section 360: Non-Compliance with Laws and Regulations (NOCLAR) of the IRBA code of Professional Conduct (CPC) requires the auditor to discuss all non-compliance with laws and regulations identified during an audit with management of the organisation (IESBA, 2016). Based on this discussion, the auditor must then assess whether further action is required. In a South African context, the auditor must assess whether there is a reportable irregularity which must be reported to IRBA (IESBA, 2016). This new ethical requirement also enhances the requirement of ISA 250 according to which the auditor needs to consider laws and regulations in the audit of a set of financial statements (ISA 250 is discussed in more detail in Chapter 8).

4. Reducing or limiting liability

The auditor can reduce their liability by means of incorporating a disclaimer in the terms of the audit engagement (such disclaimer may not be upheld in a court of law as the auditor will still owe a duty of care to the relevant parties).

It is recommended practice that audit firms make use of professional indemnity insurance. Such insurance protects the auditor/audit firm because, if the auditor does incur legal costs and costs of settlement the insurer will pay a portion (if not all) of these costs to the respective parties. This does not reduce the auditor's liability but it does reduce the impact that legal claims have on the individual auditor or audit firm (Cunningham, 2004; King and de Beer, 2018).

The auditor can also limit their liability by way of their form of incorporation. If the firm is incorporated as a partnership it will expose the respective partners to a greater level of liability as opposed to if the firm is incorporated as a limited liability company. This does depend on the relevant jurisdiction but often limited liability firms or partnerships will reduce the extent of the liability the auditor can incur. (Firth et al., 2012). This form of incorporation results in the auditor's liability being limited which means that the claimants can only claim on the audit firm's assets and not the assets held by the auditors in their own personal capacity. The liability is also joint and several, meaning that all the audit partners are liable for auditor liability. Such disbursement of risk is favourable in that overall, it reduces an individual's liability (Cunningham, 2004).

4.1 Fraud and error

An expectation gap exists as to what the auditor does by way of their audit engagement and what various stakeholders expect of the auditor (Porter, 2009). The common misconception is that an audit of financial statements is performed to detect fraud. Such misconception may result in an auditor incurring liability due to differences in expectations.

ISA 240 does require that the auditor consider the risk of fraud in the performance of their audit procedures but does not put any responsibility on the auditor to detect fraud. In addition it makes the auditor aware that as a result of their audit procedures they may detect fraud, but that is not the primary purpose of an audit (ISA 240, 2011).

For more detail on fraud and the auditor's responsibility concerning fraud, refer to Chapter 6

5. Case law related to auditor liability

In a South African context, there are cases that deal with auditor liability. Axiam Holdings Limited versus Deloitte & Touche, 2005, dealt with the limitation of an auditor's liability (2005).

The 1999 financial statements failed to present fairly the financial position of Axiam Holdings Limited (AHL) (ibid). They misrepresented AHL's nett worth — reflecting a nett profit before tax of R29 million whereas, in fact, AHL suffered a nett loss of R77 million (ibid). This inaccurate information resulted from what is set out hereafter (ibid). Deloitte failed to include a bad debt of R68 888 000 in the income statement (ibid). This amount was reflected as goodwill. In addition, non-existent income in an amount of R10.3 million was included in the financial statements as profit (ibid). Furthermore, an irrecoverable or non-existent bad debt of R28 million was incorrectly reflected as a loan to a shareholder (ibid).

It was alleged, by AHL that Deloitte, 'in conducting the audit and completing the financial statements, did not, inter alia, do so with the requisite professional and reasonable skill and care. Had Deloitte done so the 1999 statements would have accurately represented AHL's financial position, alternatively, would have contained a qualified audit opinion. Thus, Deloitte, in conducting the audit and certifying the 1999 statements, was negligent' (AHL vs Deloitte, 2005, Part 5).

During February 2000 two companies within the PSG group, one of which was the PSG bank, concluded linked agreements with AHL in terms of which shares in AHL were purchased and its business financed ('Holdings Limited versus Deloitte & Touche,' 2005). It was alleged that at that time, Deloitte was aware of the negotiations and that the 1999 statements and audit opinion would be relied on by the two companies in that process (ibid).

AHL claimed that Deloitte owed the two companies a duty, prior to 22 February 2000, to warn them that the 1999 statements and the audit opinion were incorrect, alternatively to warn them that it had not conducted the audit properly and that they should not rely on the 1999 statements and the audit opinion. Deloitte failed to issue the warnings and such failure was negligent (ibid).

The South African Supreme Court found that silence or inaction cannot constitute a misrepresentation unless there is a duty to speak or act. 'You cannot disclose what you do not know; and to hold a person liable for what that person ought to have known, is to equate constructive knowledge with actual knowledge' ('Holdings Limited versus Deloitte & Touche,' 2005 part 30).

From an international perspective, the case of *Moore Stephens vs Stone & Rolls Limited* in the United Kingdom, was a test of auditor liability (2009). Creditors of Stone & Rolls claimed that the fraud committed by the owner of Stone & Rolls should have been detected by Moore Stephens, the company's auditors (ibid). The court found and the House of Lords ratified that Stone and Rolls, owned by an individual who was a 'fraudster', found that all fraud committed was attributed to the company and that the company should have been aware of this fraud and primarily liable for it (ibid). 'The auditors owed a duty to perform their audit diligently to the company (not to individual shareholders or creditors), and so if the company tried to bring a claim for breach of that duty it would necessarily be relying on its own illegality' (ibid). Therefore, as the auditors were not negligent in their duties and the fact that detection of fraud is ancillary to the primary purpose of the audit of financial statements, they were not liable for any contractual or delictual damages (ibid).

6. Transnational audits

The Transnational Audit Committee (TAC) appointed by the International Federation of Accountants (IFAC) defines a transnational audit as:

> 'an audit of financial statements which are or may be relied upon outside the audited entity's home jurisdiction for purposes of significant lending, investment or regulatory decisions; this will include audits of all financial statements of companies with listed equity or debt and other public interest entities which attract particular public attention because of their size, products or services provided' (IFAC, TAC 1; Page 12010).

There are several issues, which arise in transnational audits. The auditor is exposed to increased auditor liability as there are more parties relying on the auditor's audit opinion (Humphrey, 2009). The auditor also has to be aware of the differences in user's language, ethical, cultural, legislative, regulatory, reporting and auditing standards (Humphrey, 2009).

An example of a transnational audit is a subsidiary of an American based parent company that complies with Sarbanes-Oxley (SOX). The jurisdiction in which the subsidiary operates is outside of America. Therefore, the company does not need to comply with SOX in its own jurisdiction. This subsidiary uses IFRS and SOX requires all subsidiaries of parent companies who must comply with SOX to use US GAAP. The subsidiary must also comply with SOX. The auditor must be aware that this is a transnational audit, as their opinion will be relied upon by regulators such as the Securities Exchange Commission (SEC). This increases audit liability. (The provisions of SOX are discussed in more detail in Chapter 2: Regulatory environment for audit and assurance).

In addition to an increase in auditor liability, the auditor has to change the nature of the audit evidence by incorporating SOX-required audit procedures. For example, an auditor will need to perform audit procedures over a reconciliation between IFRS and US GAAP accounting policies. This will require specialised knowledge by an audit team member.

In conclusion, the auditor needs to obtain an understanding of whether their engagement is a transnational audit as this has implications of the auditor's liability and audit strategy. This understanding will be obtained by performing procedures required by ISA 315: Identifying and Assessing the Risks of Material Misstatement through Obtaining an Understanding of the Entity (ISA 3152009). The auditor will also need to take the guidance in ISA 600 into account. This is discussed in more detail in Chapter 14

7. Summary

- In determining which of the standards a jurisdiction falls into is a matter of understanding the law regarding auditors in such jurisdiction.
- The basis used to develop this understanding of legislative requirements is for the auditor to identify the legal system for such jurisdiction (Chung et al., 2010).
- The legal systems are civil law, common law, statutory law, religious law or a combination of these.
- In jurisdictions where the legal system is more common law-based, the standards to identify to whom the auditor owes a duty of care are privity, near-privity or the restatement rule.
- In such jurisdictions the auditors have a lower liability to third parties as the potential parties in such standards are narrowly defined (Richard Baker et al., 2001).

- In contrast, jurisdictions where the legal system is more civil-law based, the standard applicable is the reasonable foreseeability test which identifies a broader range of third parties, meaning the auditor owes a duty of care to a broader range of parties increasing auditor liability (Richard Baker et al., 2001).

8. References

2005. *Holdings Limited versus Deloitte & Touche.* Supreme Court of Appeal, South Africa.

2009. *Moore Stephens versus Stone and Rolls Limited.* House of Lords.

Africa, Q. 2018. *KPMG's strategy to regain South Africa's trust failed before it even got started* [Online]. Johannesburg. Available: https://qz.com/africa/1255505/kpmg-loses-south-african-governments-business-after-corruption-linked-to-guptas-vbs-bank/.

Bazerman, M. H., Loewenstein, G. & Moore, D. A. 2002. Why good accountants do bad audits. *Harvard business review,* (80), 96–102, 134.

Bush, T., Sunder, S. & Fearnley, S. 2007. Auditor liability reforms in the UK and the US: A comparative review.

Chung, J., Farrar, J., Puri, P. & Thorne, L. 2010. Auditor liability to third parties after Sarbanes-Oxley: An international comparison of regulatory and legal reforms. *Journal of International Accounting, Auditing and Taxation,* 19 (1), 66–78.

Cunningham, L. A. 2004. Choosing gatekeepers: the financial statement insurance alternative to auditor liability. *UCLA L. Rev.,* 52, 413.

Firth, M., Mo, P. L. & Wong, R. M. 2012. Auditors' organizational form, legal liability, and reporting conservatism: Evidence from China. *Contemporary Accounting Research,* 29 (1), 57–93.

Geiger, M. A. & Raghunandan, K. 2002. Auditor tenure and audit reporting failures. *Auditing: A Journal of Practice & Theory,* 21 (1), 67–78.

Humphrey, C. L., Anne; Woods, Margaret 2009. The global audit profession and the international financial architecture: Understanding regulatory relationships at a time of financial crisis. *Accounting, organizations and society,* 34 (6–7), 810–825.

IAASB 2009. International Standard on Auditing 315: Identifying and Assessing the Risk of Material Misstatement. London.

IAASB 2011. International Standard on Auditing 240:The Auditor's Responsibilities Relating to Fraud in an Audit of Financial Statements. London.

IESBA 2016. Reporting Non-compliance with Laws and Regulations. London: [IESBA].

IFAC 2010. Definition of Transnational Audit. *TAC Guidance Statement 1.* New York: [IFAC].

IRBA 2005. Auditing Professions Act.

King, M. & de Beer, L. 2018. *The Auditor: Quo Vadis?,* Routledge.

Malsch, B. & Gendron, Y. 2011. Reining in auditors: On the dynamics of power surrounding an "innovation" in the regulatory space. *Accounting, Organizations and Society,* 36 (7), 456–476.

Maroun, W. & Atkins, J. 2014. Section 45 of the Auditing Profession Act: Blowing the whistle for audit quality? *The British Accounting Review,* 46 (3), 248–263.

Maroun, W. & Gowar, C. 2013. South African Auditors Blowing the Whistle without Protection: A Challenge for Trust and Legitimacy. *International Journal of Auditing,* 17 (2), 177–189.

Narayanan, V. 1994. An analysis of auditor liability rules. *Journal of Accounting Research,* 39–59.

Pacini, C., Hillison, W. & Sinason, D. 2000. Auditor liability to third parties: An international focus. *Managerial Auditing Journal,* 15 (8), 394–407.

Palmrose, Z. V. 1987. Litigation and independent auditors-the role of business failures and management fraud. *Auditing – A Journal of Practice & Theory,* 6 (2), 90–103.

Palmrose, Z. V. 1994. The Joint & (and) Several vs. Proportionate Liabilty Debate: An Empirical Investigation of Audit-Related Litigation. *Stan. JL Bus. & Fin.,* 1, 53.

Porter, B. 2009. *Report on Research Conducted in the United Kingdom and New Zealand in 2008 Investigating the Audit Expectation-performance Gap and Users' Understanding of, and Desired Improvements to, the Auditor's Report.* Citeseer.

Richard Baker, C., Mikol, A. & Quick, R. 2001. Regulation of the statutory auditor in the European Union: A comparative survey of the United Kingdom, France and Germany. *European accounting review,* 10 (4), 763–786.

Samsonova-Taddei, A. & Humphrey, C. 2015. Risk and the construction of a European audit policy agenda: The case of auditor liability. *Accounting, Organizations and Society,* 41, 55–72.

Schwartz, R. 1993. The impact of liability rules and auditing standards on audit quality. working paper, Northwestern University.

Toda, M. & McCarty, W. 2004. Corporate governance changes in the two largest economies: what's happening in the US and Japan. *Syracuse J. Int'l L. & Com.,* 32, 189.

Trakman, L. E. & Trainor, J. 2005. The rights and responsibilities of auditors to third parties: A call for a principled approach. *Queen's LJ,* 31, 148.

Wainer, H. 2009. Comments on: *Auditor Liability.*Auditor Liability – The APA and the legal consequences. STUDENTS, W. U. Johannesburg.

PART B

Chapter 9: Client acceptance and continuance

1. Introduction

Accepting and retaining audit clients are ongoing struggles for professional accountants. Regulatory, best practices and codes of governance are considered by both professional accountants and its clients (Arens, 2017). This chapter discusses the professional accountant's roles and responsibilities in terms of the tendering process, regulatory requirements and why a change of a professional service provider may take place (section 2). Section 3 and 4 deal with the client acceptance process in detail:

A review of the relevant professional standards which prescribe the minimum steps which need to be taken when accepting a new engagement, as well as applicable regulatory requirements;

The process typically followed by practitioners when tendering for new clients, including ethical considerations; and

An overview of the processes followed when deciding whether or not to continue to provide services to client.

Section 5 covers regulatory matters and codes of governance insofar of client acceptance and continuance. It will be useful to outline key definitions in this chapter detailed below:

Table 1: Definition of key terms	
Term	**Definition**
Audit[1]	An examination of the financial statements of any issuer/preparer by an independent expert[2] in accordance with generally accepted auditing standards in the prevailing jurisdiction and, where applicable, other requirements, rules or prescriptions issued by regulators/policymakers.
Assurance engagement	An engagement in which a professional accountant in public practice expresses a conclusion designed to enhance the degree of confidence of the intended users other than the responsible party about the outcome of the evaluation or measurement of a subject matter against criteria (International Ethics Standards Board for Accountants (IESBA), 2006).

▶

---

1   There is no single definition of an 'audit'. This definition is based on the guidance issued by the IAASB and contained in SOX.

2   A registered auditor or certified public accountant, depending on the jurisdiction.

Table 1: Definition of key terms	
Term	**Definition**
Professional accountant	An individual in public practice and their firms (IESBA, 2018 p.71).
IAASB	International Auditing and Assurance Standard Board
Professional services	Professional activities performed for clients (IESBA, 2018 p.243). Services requiring accountancy or related skills performed by a professional accountant include accounting, auditing, taxation, management consulting and financial management services.
IEBSA	International Ethics Standards Board for Accountants
IRBA	Independent Regulatory Board for Auditors
SAICA	South African Institute for Chartered Accountants
FRC	Financial Reporting Council

2. Tendering

Tendering for a professional appointment involves a professional accountant participating in a call for the provision of professional services to a prospective client. This may be because of a decision by the client to change a professional service provider (Fontaine et al., 2013) or mandatory rotation of the service provider (Casterella and Johnston, 2013, Jackson et al., 2008).

Before agreeing to provide a client with services, the professional accountant should be satisfied that there are no substantive reasons for refusing the requested engagement. This involves, as part of the tendering process, the execution of procedures which are designed to provide information about the client's business, the functioning of its governance structures and the overall risk environment (IAASB, 2009c, IAASB, 2009b).

Practitioners can tender for different types of professional services (Asare et al., 2005). Examples include the provision of, *inter alia,* accounting, tax or internal audit services; project management services; audit or reviews of financial statements or other types of assurance services (Hodges and Young, 2009). This section focuses on the client acceptance and continuance process for an audit of financial statements. The process, followed for other assurance or non-assurance services will be similar. This is considered in more detail in Chapter 21.

2.1 A change of a professional accountant

A change of professional accountant occurs when an organisation's professional accountant resigns or is dismissed. The facts or circumstances surrounding the change may not be public knowledge (Mande and Son, 2012) but prior research provides several examples for changing professional accountants:

- Client-service provider relationship: the perceived lack of attention received from the professional service provider in the form of not meeting deadlines, insufficient communication, unreturned telephone calls or not communicating problems (Feldman Barr and McNeilly, 2003, Addams and Davis, 1994, Beattie and Fearnley, 1995, Magri and Baldacchino, 2004, Whisenant et al., 2003, Fontaine et al., 2013);
- Perceived lack of industry knowledge by the service team (DeAngelo, 1981, Feldman Barr and McNeilly, 2003);
- Lack of involvement from senior executives from the professional service provider with the business entity (Carcello et al., 1998);
- Change as a result of a merger or acquisition in order to have a uniform professional service provider for a group of companies (Feldman Barr and McNeilly, 2003, FRC, 2013);
- High fees, an unexpected increase in fees or an inability to afford the fees for professional services (Addams and Davis, 1994, Beattie and Fearnley, 1995, Magri and Baldacchino, 2004, Whisenant et al., 2003, Fontaine et al., 2013); and
- Concern surrounding audit quality: the removal of an auditor because of an actual or perceived decline in the quality of audit services (DeAngelo, 1981, Fontaine et al., 2013).

The professional service provider may opt to resign for the following reasons:

- The risk profile of the business entity is no longer acceptable in terms of its professional firms' risk management policies (Bell et al., 2001);
- The professional service provider's ethical independence requirements cannot be maintained by the firm or network of firms (IESBA, 2018); and
- The fees generated from providing services to the client are not sufficient to cover the audit firm's risk exposure and/or costs.

The process starts when an audit firm is invited by a company to tender for an audit engagement. This process is illustrated in Figure 1.

Figure 1: Pre-engagement activities

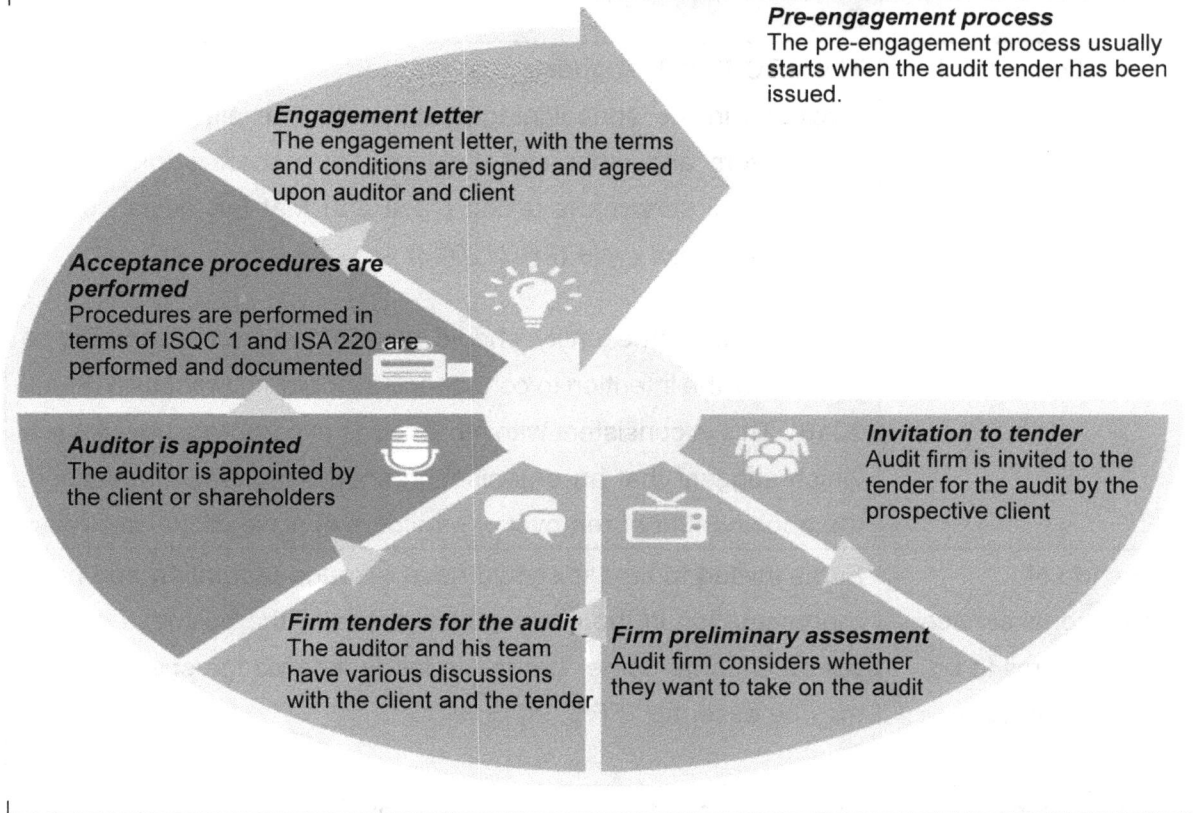

Pre-engagement process
The pre-engagement process usually starts when the audit tender has been issued.

Engagement letter
The engagement letter, with the terms and conditions are signed and agreed upon auditor and client

Acceptance procedures are performed
Procedures are performed in terms of ISQC 1 and ISA 220 are performed and documented

Auditor is appointed
The auditor is appointed by the client or shareholders

Invitation to tender
Audit firm is invited to the tender for the audit by the prospective client

Firm tenders for the audit
The auditor and his team have various discussions with the client and the tender

Firm preliminary assesment
Audit firm considers whether they want to take on the audit

When the decision is made to change the professional accountant, codes on corporate governance recommend that a company follow a formal tendering process to ensure that a suitable replacement is found (Fontaine et al., 2013). This will be discussed in the next section.

2.2 General process for appointing a professional accountant

Each jurisdiction may have specific requirements for appointing a professional accountant but a review of the prior literature reveals a general process for soliciting professional accounting services. This is summarised in Table 2.

Table 2: General tendering process

Stage	Details
Development of an initial scorecard	A workshop can assist with the development of an initial scorecard considering stakeholders, those charged with governance and management. This initial scorecard should be flexible and can be shared with invited participants (KPMG, 2018).

▶

Table 2: General tendering process	
Stage	**Details**
Notification of tender	The FRC (2013) suggests that the decision to tender should be disclosed in the annual/integrated report. The aim is to explain to investors and other stakeholders that tendering for material professional services is taking place and that this is part of the normal business cycle (FRC, 2013). As a courtesy, the entity should also inform its current service provider of the intention to commence a tendering process (KPMG, 2018). This is consistent with most codes of corporate governance which suggest that an organisation should be transparent about the appointment or removal of providers of professional services.
Selection of professional service provider firms to be invited to participate in the tender	Firms invited to tender should have a sound reputation and have representation in the geographical areas of the business entity's operations. In some cases, industry knowledge/specialisation may be essential (FRC, 2013).
Potential conflicts with codes of ethics	The rendering of non-audit services by the same firm responsible for the audit of the client's financial statements will result in a threat to the audit firm's independence. Depending on the jurisdiction, the professional accountant may also be prohibited from rendering these services to an audit client. This is discussed in more detail in Section 3.4.
Provision of information to professional service providers invited to tender	For the tendering process to be successful, the business entity should provide adequate information to its shortlist of professional service providers. The same information must be made available to all participants to the tender (FRC, 2013). This can be achieved by service providers accessing a central contact person from the business entity, or an on-line data room can be created in which all information is stored and accessed by the professional service providers. The initial scorecard can be amended during this stage (KPMG, 2018).
Format of tenders	The business entity should provide a clear guideline (as per the scorecard) on how to submit a tender and its format (KPMG, 2016). Alternatives to a formal presentation may allow for an interactive experience (KPMG, 2018).

▶

Table 2: General tendering process	
Stage	**Details**
Concluding on the outcome	Service quality (and not price) should drive the final decision (KPMG, 2018). Prospective professional service providers can demonstrate quality in the following ways: A clear understanding of the business entity, its industry, competitive position and risk profile; A detailed plan is supplied on the way in which services are to be provided, as are appropriate to the client's circumstances; A rigorous methodology/process developed by the professional accountant which should be followed for executing the services. Where applicable, this can include the use of new technologies, analytical tools or access to shared networks which may contribute to the value of the service offering; Transition plans between predecessor and incoming professional service providers; Quality of the engagement partner and experience of the audit team; The appropriateness of the planned communication with and reporting to the applicable members of management; and Any additional assurance required beyond the national statutory requirements (FRC, 2013, KPMG, 2018).
Transition	The success of the tendering process is dependent on how well the transition period is managed. From the perspective of both the business entity and the incoming professional services provider, it is best to allocate a dedicated resource to deal with transition-related issues. The incoming professional services provider should be involved in all material developments relating to the new engagement (FRC, 2013). The existing/outgoing professional accountant should provide information regarding the business entity honestly and unambiguously (KPMG, 2018, FRC, 2013).

Table 2 is prepared from the perspective of an organisation seeking to appoint a professional accountant. In order for the professional accountant to accept an invitation to provide those services, a formal client acceptance process must be followed. This is discussed in detail in Section 3.

3. Client acceptance process

The overall objective is for the auditor to establish whether or not any preconditions for an audit are present (see Section 4.1) and to confirm that the auditor and those charged with the client's governance have a common understanding of the purpose of audit engagement (IAASB, 2009a). To achieve these objectives, the IAASB outlines specific requirements for accepting (or choosing to continue with) a client engagement. These are contained in the following international standards of auditing[3] (ISA):

- ISQC 1 – International standards on quality control;
- ISQM 1(draft) – International standard on quality management; and
- ISA 220 – Quality control for an audit of financial statements.

An overview of these standards and the relevant ethical considerations pertaining to client acceptance will be provided.

3.1 ISQC 1

In summary, a firm will establish a system of quality control in order to achieve reasonable assurance that the firm and its personnel comply with professional standards and the applicable legal and regulatory requirements. Reasonable assurance should be obtained that reports issued by the firm or engagement partner are appropriate (IAASB, 2009a, IAASB, 2009c). For a detailed review of ISQC 1's control provisions, readers are referred to Chapter 7. Figure 2 summarises the main provisions of ISQC 1 dealing specifically with the decision to accept a new client or to continue providing assurance services to an existing client.

3.2 International Standard of Quality Management (ISQM) 1– exposure draft

ISQM 1 deals with an audit firm's responsibilities to design, implement and operate a system of quality management for audits, reviews of financial statements and other assurance or related services engagements. This includes the responsibility of engagement quality reviewers. The main objectives are to improve the robustness of an audit firm's systems of quality by introducing a more proactive and tailored approach to manage quality, increase in leadership responsibilities and accountability and improving firm governance. Focus is

---

3   For the purpose of this chapter, the application of these ISAs is limited to professional appointments. Quality control is discussed in more detail in Chapter 7. Reporting on the outcome of an audit engagement is dealt with in Chapter 18.

also placed on modernising the standard for the complex evolving environments, the impact of technology and the use of external service providers. The exposure draft was issued in February 2019 and was available for comment until July 2019. The finalised standard has not yet been issued by the IAASB.

Figure 2: Summary of ISQC 1's client acceptance/continuance provisions

Competence of the engagement team – (ISQC 1 para 26 (a) and para A18 & 23)

- The engagement leader has to ensure that all members of the engagement team are competent and have the requisite skills, knowledge and capabilities to deal with the intricacies of the audit.
- This includes all team members having the required level of education and appropriate experience on other audit engagements.
- Staff with suitable experience should be available to supervise less experienced team
- members.
- Where necessary, the engagement team should consider the use of experts (see also Chapter 15).

Compliance with codes of ethics – (ISQC 1 para 24 (b)

- All members of the engagement team should comply with the audit firm's ethical code of conduct and the code of conduct as issued by the IESBA. The engagement leader should remain alert to facts or circumstances which may pose a threat to the fundamental principles of integrity, objectivity, confidentiality, professional behaviour and professional competence and due care.
- This is elaborated on in Section 3.4.

Integrity of management – (ISQC 1 para 26 and para A19–20, A 23)

- The auditor should ensure that the client will not have a negative impact on the auditor's reputation.
- To assess the level of reputational risk, the auditor should consider the client's business standing, including its relationship with third parties and regulators.
- The risk assessment can also consider the nature of the entity, the members on the board of the directors, past corporate performance and management's view on internal controls.
- Where relevant, the auditor may have to consider management's attitude towards the audit fee and whether management is aggressively trying to lower the fee.

Adapted from IAASB (2009c)

3.3 ISA 220

ISA 220 deals with the specific responsibilities of the auditor regarding quality control procedures for an audit of financial statements and the responsibilities of the engagement quality control reviewer. The standard appears to be similar to ISQC 1 but, unlike the former, it applies at the engagement level rather than to the audit firm as a whole.

The engagement partner is responsible for the quality of each engagement. This requires the engagement partner to:

- Remain alert for evidence of non-compliance with relevant ethical requirements by members of the engagement team[4] (IAASB, 2009b, para 9 & 10);
- Obtain relevant information from the firm and, where necessary, network firms, to identify and evaluate circumstances and relationships which create threats to independence (IAASB, 2009b, para 11 (a));
- Evaluate information on identified breaches, if any, of the firm's independence policies and procedures to determine whether they create a threat to independence for the audit engagement (IAASB, 2009b, para 11(b));
- Take appropriate action to eliminate threats or reduce them to an acceptable level by applying safeguards (IAASB, 2009b, para 11(b)); and
- Consider, in extreme cases, if it is necessary to withdraw from the audit engagement after taking relevant regulatory issues into account (IAASB, 2009b par 11(c), IESBA, 2018 s 210.7 A2).

The timing of the engagement also needs to be considered. The firm must be able to perform and complete the engagement within the required reporting timeframe (IESBA, 2018). This will require a sufficient number of staff, as well as access to necessary resources, including the client's systems processes and staff. The engagement leader must be satisfied that there will be sufficient time to complete the required planning, execution and reporting procedures/ processes (IAASB, 2009b, IAASB, 2009c, IAASB, 2011, Sutton, 1993, Francis, 2004).

Finally, for the audits of listed entities' financial statements, the engagement quality control reviewer[5] should consider the engagement team's independence and whether or not appropriate consultation has taken place on matters involving differences of opinion and on other difficult or contentious matters (IAASB, 2009b, para 21). This is because ISA 220 should be applied together with the relevant ethical requirements (IAASB, 2009b, par 1). These are discussed in more detail below.

---

4   If non-compliance is noted, appropriate action should be taken. This is discussed in more detail in Chapter 3.

5   A partner, other person in the firm, suitably qualified external person, or a team made up of such individuals – none of whom is part of the engagement team – with sufficient and appropriate experience and authority to objectively evaluate the significant judgement the engagement team made and the conclusions it reached in formulating the auditor's report.

3.4 Ethical considerations

When deciding whether or not to tender for or accept an engagement, the professional accountant should remain alert for any material ethical issues. The code of professional ethics issued by the IESBA (the code)[6] is useful for this purpose (Jakubowski et al., 2002).

3.4.1 IESBA Code of Ethics

The IESBA Code of Ethics for Professional Accountants (2018) contains a framework to identify and manage threats to a practitioner's ethics. This is outlined in Chapter 3. The two main ethical principles for this chapter are independence and threats to objectivity. These two requirements are of great importance when dealing with acceptance or continuance of assurance engagements (IESBA, 2018).

3.4.2 Independence requirements for audit assurance engagements

Most legislation and codes of best practice require audit firms (including network firms) to be independent of their audit clients in mind and in appearance (Francis, 2004). Independence of mind is:

'the state of mind that permits the expression of a conclusion without being affected by influences that compromise professional judgment, thereby allowing an individual to act with integrity, and exercise objectivity and professional scepticism' (IESBA, 2018 p. 29).

Independence in appearance is:

'the avoidance of facts and circumstances that are so significant that a reasonable and informed third party, having knowledge of all relevant information, including safeguards applied, would reasonably conclude a firm's, or a member of the assurance team's, integrity, objectivity or professional scepticism had been compromised' (IESBA, 2018 p. 28).

Independence should be evaluated against the significance of any economic, financial and other relationship from the perspective of an informed third party. When it comes to audit engagements, members of the assurance team, the firm and network of firms are required to be independent of the financial statement audit client. Independence requirements extend to interests and relationships between members of the assurance team and directors, officers and employees of the financial statement audit client, particularly if they play a key role in

---

6   Different jurisdictions may introduce additional rules or regulations which apply when an auditor tenders for a client. It is also possible that these regulations do not require compliance with the code. Nevertheless, the code provides a broad set of principles which guide the client acceptance and continuance process and is the focal point for this chapter.

preparing the client's financial statements (IESBA, 2018). The auditor should also consider whether or not any threats to independence may be created by:

- Financial or business relationships with the audit client during or after the period covered by the financial statements but before the acceptance of the financial statement audit engagement, or
- Past services provided to the audit client (IESBA, 2018).

3.4.3 Conflict of interest

Conflict of interest creates a threat to objectivity. A registered auditor/accountant should not allow a conflict of interest to compromise professional or business judgement. IESBA (2018) lists examples where conflict of interest may arise:

- Already providing advisory services to an entity which has issued a tender for audit services;
- Advising two clients who are in competition or are bidding to acquire the same target entity;
- Providing services to both the vendor and purchaser in the same transaction;
- Determining valuations for both the buyer and seller of the same assets;
- Representing two clients on the same legal matter;
- For a licence agreement, providing an assurance report for the licensor on royalties and advising the licensee on amounts payable;
- Providing a client to invest in the business of a professional accountant;
- The professional accountant has a material financial interest in a company for which it also provides services;
- Providing strategic advice to a client on its competitive position while having a similar interest with a major competitor of the same client; and
- Advising a client on procuring a product or service while having a royalty or commission agreement with the potential seller of that product or service.

The process to identify actual or potential conflicts of interest will depend on factors such as the nature of professional services to be provided, the size and structure of the firm and the size and nature of the firm's client base (IESBA, 2018). Conflicts of interest arising from the providing of non-assurance services should also be considered.

Providing non-assurance services to an audit client usually give rises to a significant threat to independence. This is especially true if the non-assurance services are material and are used directly or indirectly to support the preparation of the financial statements (IESBA, 2018). Possible safeguards to reduce the threat to independence include:

- Discussing independence concerns with those charged with the client's governance (usually the audit committee);
- Obtaining the client's acknowledgement of responsibility for the results of the non-assurance service;
- Precluding personnel who provided the non-assurance service from participating in the financial statements' audit engagement;
- Engaging another audit firm to review the results of the non-assurance service or having another audit firm re-perform the non-assurance service to the extent necessary to enable it to take responsibility for the service (IESBA, 2018);
- Use of separate engagement teams guided by clear policies and procedures regarding confidentiality;
- Creation of separate areas of speciality within the auditing firm to limit passing of confidential client information; and
- Use of confidentiality agreements for employees and partners (IESBA, 2018).

It should be borne in mind that many jurisdictions prohibit the rendering of non-assurance services to their audit clients. This is the case, even if the auditor is of the view that the safeguards listed above can reduce any threat to independence to an acceptably low level. This is discussed in more detail in Chapter 3.

3.4.4 Contacting the outgoing auditor

Before accepting an engagement, the professional accountant will usually contact the outgoing/predecessor practitioner. The purpose of the inquiry is to ascertain if there are any reasons to refrain from accepting a proposed engagement.

The exact process to be followed will vary among jurisdictions (see section 320.7 in IESBA, 2018) but, as a general rule, the professional accountant will require the client's written permission to contact either the existing or predecessor accountant. To this end, the proposed clients should inform their current or predecessor accountant of the decision to discontinue their services and grant permission for the existing accountant to discuss the client's affairs with the proposed accountant (see section 320.A7 in IESBA (2018). In cases where the professional accountant is unable to contact the existing accountant, requests for information are refused, or the client refuses to give permission to contact the incumbent, the professional accountant should assess if this increases any risks associated with accepting the engagement (see section R320.8(b) in IESBA, 2018).

Once the professional accountant is confident that ethical requirements are not contravened, and the prescriptions of ISA 220 and ISQC 1 are satisfied, the engagement can be accepted. The predecessor accountant should promptly transfer client material in his/her possession to the incoming professional. As an exception, the predecessor accountant may refuse to transfer materials in order to exercise a lien or other security in respect of unpaid fees (IAASB, 2009b, IAASB, 2009c).

3.4.5 Long association of personnel (including partner rotation) with an audit client

Familiarity and self-interest threats might be created by long association and close personal relationships with members of senior management (see section 520.20 in IESBA, 2018). Table 3 provides details regarding 'time-on' and 'cooling-off' periods for professional accountants auditing public interest entities:

Table 3: Time on and cooling-off periods		
Role[7]	Time-on period[8] (years)	Cooling-off period (years)
Engagement partner	7	5
Engagement quality control reviewer	7	3
Key audit partner[9]	7	2
Combination of roles		
Key audit partner & engagement partner	4 or more	5
Engagement partner & engagement quality control reviewer	4 or more	3

Adapted from IESBA (2018), s540

In exceptional cases one additional year may be added to the time-on period with the concurrence of the governing body and as long as the key audit partner eliminates or reduces independence threats (IRBA, 2018 see section R540.7).

Restrictions placed on the abovementioned individuals during their cooling-off period are:

- May not be an engagement team member;
- Consult with the engagement team or the client regarding technical or industry-specific issues, transactions or events affecting the audit engagement. Discussions surrounding conclusions pertaining to the prior years' time-on period is permitted;

---

7   If key audit partner moves to another audit firm the time-on period continues if the audit client changes audit firm as well (see section R540.189 in IESBA, 2018).

8   In calculating time-on period, the number of years will not be restarted unless the individual ceases to act in any of the roles in Table 3. The minimum period is a consecutive period equal to, at least, the cooling-off period (see section R540.10 in IESBA, 2018).

9   Key audit partner can be either the engagement partner, engagement quality control reviewer or other audit partners who make key decisions or judgements on significant matters on the audit. Other auditors, for example, may be audit partners responsible for significant subsidiaries or divisions (IESBA, 2018, p241).

- Be responsible for leading or co-ordinating the professional service provided by the audit firm to the audit client;
- Overseeing the relationship between the firm and the client; and
- Undertake any role, for example, provision of non-assurance services which can result in significant and frequent interaction with the audit client or exerting direct influence on the external audit (IESBA, 2018 see section R540.20).

3.4.6 Summary of the client acceptance process

The ethical considerations discussed above should not be viewed in isolation. Collectively, they provide a basis for concluding if accepting a client creates an unacceptably high threat to compliance with the fundamental principles (IAASB, 2009b). This is illustrated in Figure 3.

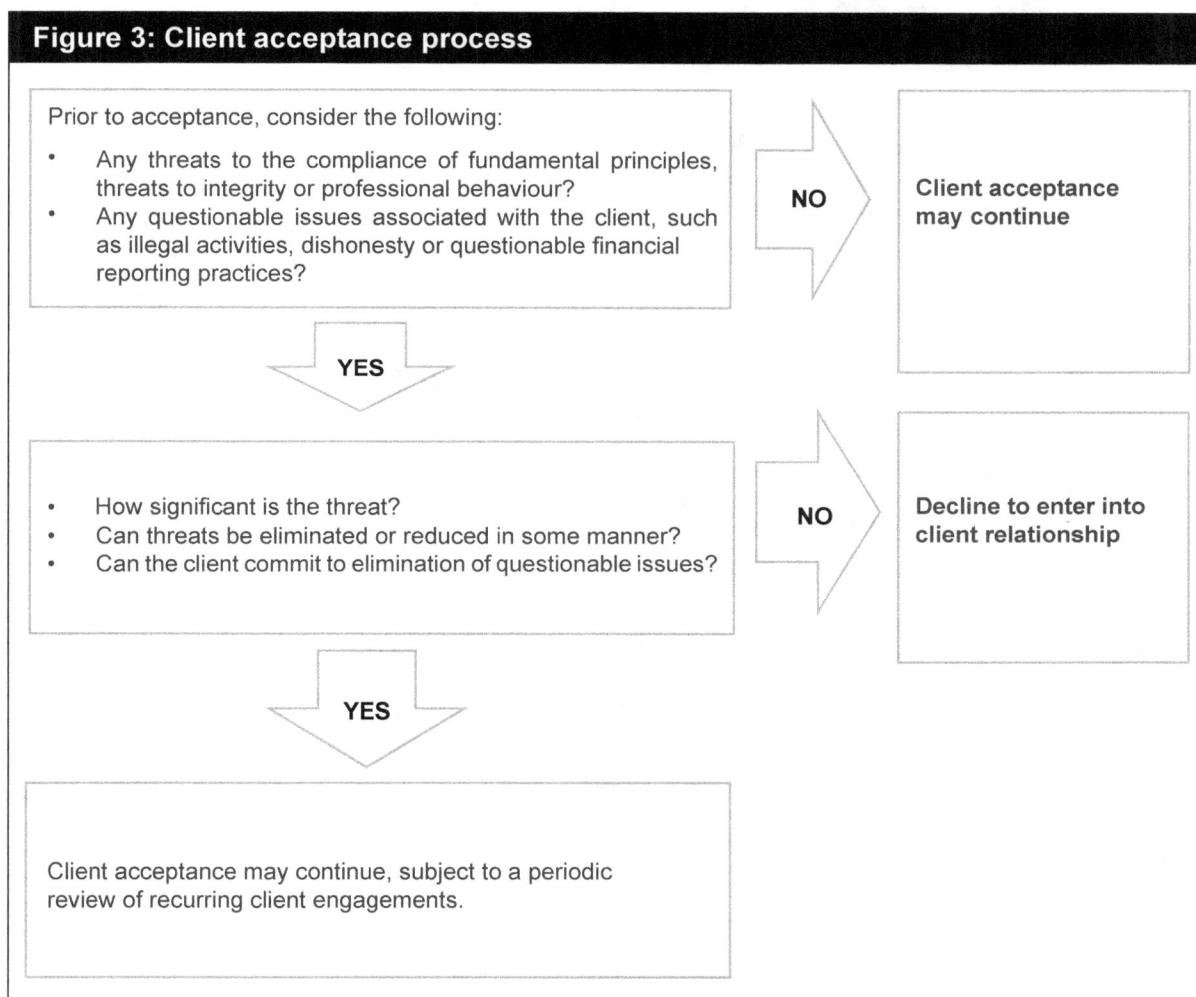

Figure 3: Client acceptance process

Prior to acceptance, consider the following:

- Any threats to the compliance of fundamental principles, threats to integrity or professional behaviour?
- Any questionable issues associated with the client, such as illegal activities, dishonesty or questionable financial reporting practices?

NO → Client acceptance may continue

YES ↓

- How significant is the threat?
- Can threats be eliminated or reduced in some manner?
- Can the client commit to elimination of questionable issues?

NO → Decline to enter into client relationship

YES ↓

Client acceptance may continue, subject to a periodic review of recurring client engagements.

If the professional accountant decides to accept the appointment, he or she still has a responsibility to revisit his/her acceptance decisions periodically. Therefore, the assessment of potential threats to independence and professional behaviour will be performed, at a minimum at the start of each recurring engagement (Johnstone, 2000, IAASB, 2009b).

4. ISA 210 – Agreeing on the terms of audit engagements

Agreeing on the terms of an audit engagement includes both acceptance of a new engagement and continuation of an existing engagement. The goal is to confirm the terms of the engagement between the auditor and management. This is dealt with by ISA 210 which addresses:

- Preconditions of an audit;
- Agreement on audit engagement terms;
- Recurring audits;
- Acceptance of a change in the terms of an audit engagement; and
- Additional considerations in engagement acceptance.

Each of the above is discussed below.

4.1 Preconditions of an audit

As a general rule, an assurance engagement can only be performed if there is an identifiable subject matter and clearly defined criteria for assessing/measuring the subject matter (IAASB, 2009d). In the context of a financial statement audit, this means that there must be:

- An acceptable financial reporting framework[10] used to ensure that the financial statements are a fair presentation of the economics of the underlying transactions and balances; and
- Agreement between the auditor and management on their responsibilities in connection with the financial statements.

Management is ultimately responsible for the preparation of financial statements and internal controls designed to safeguard the entity's assets. As per ISA 200, the auditor's objective is to express an opinion on the financial statements and not to substitute for poor performance by management. To ensure that the auditor can achieve this objective, the IAASB (2009a) states that management must provide:

- Access to all information which is relevant to the preparation of financial statements;
- Additional information which the auditor may request for the audit; and
- Unrestricted access to the organisation's employees or agents in order to obtain audit evidence.

---

10 Examples include: International Financial reporting Standards (IFRS), IFRS for Small-and Medium Sized Entities and US GAAP.

4.2 Agreement on audit engagement terms

The contract between the auditor and the client (the engagement letter) contains all pertinent terms and conditions. ISA 210 (para A22) states that it is preferred that the engagement letter is signed before the audit commences to ensure that both the engagement leader and client are aware of what is required and any possible limitations before the audit commences (IAASB, 2009a).

The form and content of the engagement letter may vary from entity to entity and may be affected by statutory requirements. IAASB (2009a) suggests that the following points should be included in the engagement letter:

- The scope of the audit, including reference to applicable legislation, regulations, ISAs and any other professional guidelines to which the auditor adheres;
- The form and timing of any communication of findings arising during the audit engagement (see also Chapter 17);
- The requirement of the auditor to report on key audit matters (see also Chapter 17);
- The fact that inherent limitations of internal controls exist and that there is an unavoidable risk that some material misstatements may not be detected, even though the audit is properly planned and performed in accordance with ISAs (see also Chapter 8);
- Audit planning and performance arrangements, including the composition of the engagement team (see also Chapter 13);
- Management's expectations and, in particular, the fact that management will provide written representations and access to all information of which management is aware and is relevant to the preparation of the financial statements (see also Chapter 13);
- The arrangements for obtaining draft financial statements, including all information relevant to their preparation and any other relevant information (see also Chapter 13);
- A request for management to acknowledge receipt of the audit engagement letter and to agree to the terms of the engagement outline; and
- Refer to Appendix 1 ISA 210 for draft engagement letter example.

4.3 Recurring audits

The IAASB (2009a) requires the auditor to revise the terms of engagement if circumstances have changed or to remind the audit client of the existing terms when:

- There is an indication that the audit client misunderstood the objectives and scope of the audit;
- There are revised or special terms in the recurring audit engagement;

- There has been a change in senior management;
- There has been a significant change in ownership of the audit client;
- There has been a significant change in the nature or size of the audit client's business;
- There has been a change in the financial reporting framework adopted in the preparation of the audit client's financial statements; or
- A change relating to other reporting requirements.

4.4 Acceptance of a change in the terms of an audit engagement

An audit client may request a material change to the terms of engagement when there has been a change in circumstances affecting the client's requirements or when there has been a misunderstanding concerning the nature of the services originally requested (IAASB, 2009a). For example, an entity which is not obligated to have its financial statements audited may request that an audit engagement be changed to a review (see Chapter 21) if contractual requirements with a third party (which originally necessitated an audit) fall away.

The auditor should not agree to change the terms of the audit engagement when there are no justifiable reasons to do so, for example, if the request for a change relates to information which is incorrect, incomplete or otherwise unsatisfactory. Similarly, a client may request an audit engagement be changed to a review or agreed-upon procedures (see Chapter 21) because there is insufficient evidence to support an unmodified audit opinion (IAASB, 2009a).

5. Regulatory requirements

In addition to the guidance provided by ISAs and codes of ethics, different jurisdictions regulate the appointment and removal of financial statement auditors. Examples include the United States of America (USA), South Africa, the United Kingdom (UK) and the European Union (EU).

5.1 United States of America (USA)

The Sarbanes–Oxley Act of 2002 (SOX) deals with the appointment of external auditors. It requires an audit committee to accept responsibility for the following:

- The appointment, compensation and monitoring of the work of any registered public accounting firm employed by an organisation;
- Pre-approval of any auditing and non-audit related services; and
- Disclosure to investors, by means of periodic reports, of non-audit services performed by the organisation's dedicated assurance firm.

SOX also introduces several mandatory requirements concerning auditor independence which need to be taken into account during the client acceptance and continuance process discussed in Section 4. These are summarised in Table 3.

Table 3: Auditor independence requirements under SOX	
Services outside the scope of practice of auditors (Section 201)	The appointed auditor may not perform the following services to the audit client: • Bookkeeping or other services related to the accounting records or financial statements of the audit client; • Financial information system design and implementation; • Appraisal or valuation services, fairness opinions, or contribution-in-kind reports; • Actuarial services; • Internal audit outsourcing services; • Management functions or human resource functions; • Broker or dealer, investment adviser, or investment banking services; • Legal services and expert services unrelated to the audit; and • Any other service which the Board determines, by regulation to be impermissible.
Pre-approval requirements (Section 202)	• A registered public accounting firm may provide non-audit related services, other than listed above if pre-approved by the audit committee. • The aggregate of non-audit services may not exceed 5% of the total revenue paid to the public accounting firm.
Audit partner rotation (Section 203)	• Both the lead partner and engagement partner can serve on the client for a maximum period of 5 years.

▶

Table 3: Auditor independence requirements under SOX	
Auditor reports to audit committees (Section 204)	The audit committee should be promptly informed of the following: • All critical accounting policies and practices to be used; • All alternate treatments of financial information within generally accepted accounting principles which have been discussed with management, ramifications of the use of such alternate disclosures and treatments, and the treatment preferred by the registered public accounting firm; and • Other material written communications between the registered public accounting firm and client management, such as any management letter or schedule of unadjusted differences.
Conflict of interest (Section 206)	A public accounting firm may not perform any audit to an audit client if either the chief executive officer, controller, chief financial officer, chief accounting officer, or any person serving in an equivalent position at the audit client, was employed by the registered independent public accounting firm and participated in any capacity in the audit of that issuer during the one year preceding the date of the initiation of the audit.

Adapted from SOX (2002)

5.2   United Kingdom (UK)

The UK Corporate Governance Code (FRC, 2016b) vests the responsibility for appointing monitoring of the services provided by an external auditor with the Board of Directors. The FRC (2016b) delegates this responsibility to an audit committee which will also take responsibility for, inter-alia:

- Approval and review of the terms of engagement or any modifications to the scope of additional work to be undertaken;
- Approval of remuneration for audit services;
- Assessing the independence of the external auditor taking into account, *inter alia,* relevant legislation, ethical standards and other professional requirements;
- Discussing threats to auditor independence and the safeguards applied to mitigate those threats;
- Developing and managing the policy for employing individuals who were previously members of the audit engagement team or the audit firm; and
- Ensuring the rotation of the engagement leader where applicable.

5.3 European Union (EU)

Within the European Union, audit committees should have primary responsibility for the appointment of the auditor. The FRC (2016a) states that the following form part of audit committees' responsibilities:

- Negotiating the fee and scope of the audit;
- Initiating a tender process;
- Influencing the selection and appointment of an engagement partner;
- Making formal recommendations to the Board of directors regarding the appointment, re-appointment and removal of the external audit provider;
- Assessing the qualifications, expertise, resources, and independence of the external audit service provider on an annual basis; and
- Commenting on the effectiveness of the audit process to stakeholders and recommending whether or not to re-appoint the incumbent auditor.

If the external audit service provider resigns, it is the responsibility of the audit committee to investigate the reasons for the resignation and to consider if any action is required (FRC, 2016a).

In line with SOX, EU legislation also limits the proportion of non-audit fees which may be incurred during a year by reference to the average audit fee. This requirement is applied at the group audit level for public interest entities. Non-audit fees may not exceed 70% of the average of a group's statutory audit fees over the previous three years (FRC, 2013).

5.4 South Africa

The audit committee's responsibilities in connection with the appointment of an external auditor are included in the Companies Act No. 71 of 2008. The Companies Act (2008) requires the audit committee to:

- Nominate an independent registered auditor for appointment by shareholders at an annual general meeting;
- Determine the fees paid to the auditor and the auditor's terms of engagement;
- Pre-approve any non-audit services rendered by the auditor and conclude that the auditor is receiving no other fees/compensation from the company;
- Disclose in the company's financial statements that the audit committee is satisfied that the auditor is independent of the company; and
- Consider if the auditor's independence has been compromised because of a previous appointment as an auditor or because of any non-audit services performed by the auditor.

The King IV Report on Corporate Governance for South Africa complements the above requirements (IOD, 2016). This suggests that the audit committee should detail disclosures in the company's integrated reports dealing with the following:

- The independence of the external auditor taking into account and providing details on:
  i. The policy and controls which address the provision of non-audit services by the external auditor and the nature and extent of services rendered during the year;
  ii. The tenure of the external audit firm, if the audit firm was involved in a merger or acquisition, the tenure of the predecessor firm;
  iii. The rotation of the designated external audit partner; and
  iv. Significant changes to management during the external audit firm's tenure which mitigate the attendant risk of familiarity between the external auditor and management.
- The audit committee's views on the quality of the external audit against audit quality indicators, including inspection reports issued by the applicable regulator.

5.4.1 Rotation of engagement partners and audit firms

South African legislation and codes of conduct addressed the rotation of engagement partners and audit firms responsible for audit and review engagements. The Companies Act (2008) requires an engagement partner not to serve as an external auditor to one audit client for more than five consecutive years. If an engagement partner has served as an external auditor for two consecutive years and then ceases to be an engagement partner on that specific audit client, this individual can only be re-appointed until the expiry of at least a further two years. For joint audit arrangements, the audit client must manage rotation insofar that both engagement partners do not rotate in the same year (Companies Act, 2008).

In 2017 the Independent Regulatory Board for Auditors (IRBA) announced mandatory audit firm rotation effective for financial years ending on or after 1 April 2023. An audit firm (including network firm) is limited to ten service years as an external auditor to a public interest entity. The same firm can only be re-appointed after the expiry of five years (IRBA, 2017). The date of audit firm rotation is determined by measuring the time for which an audit firm has been the auditor of a public interest entity as at the start of the first financial year commencing on or after 1 April 2023 (PWC, 2017).

Research findings focusing on mandatory audit firm rotation (MAFR) included the following:

- MAFR will be slowing down the rate of transformation in the audit industry as a whole;
- Big 4 and the non-Big 4 firms believe that MAFR will impose significant additional costs on the audit profession and will require a redirection of spending from areas such as training and bursaries into tendering for work;

- MAFR may increase the degree of concentration of the Big 4 firms auditing JSE listed companies;
- It is unlikely that audit committees or shareholders will recommend mid-tier firms for appointment at annual general meetings because of the lack of resources, skills, experience and international presence of the mid-tier firms in comparison to the Big 4 firms;
- Increase in audit fees;
- Loss of client-specific knowledge and expertise upon rotation; and
- Cost and disruption to both the client and audit firm are considered significant when compared to mere partner rotation.

(Kwon et al., 2014; Harber and Marx, 2019; Harber and Maroun, 2020)

6. Summary

- This chapter outlines the process usually followed by an organisation when seeking to obtain the services of a professional accountant and the professional accountant's own evaluation process before deciding to accept a proposed engagement.
- Key to deciding to accept an engagement are the provisions of ISQC 1 and ISA 220. These deal with, whether or not the engagement team has the necessary skills and resources to complete the engagement; the integrity of the client and risks posed by accepting the engagement.
- Of particular importance is the need to ensure that, by accepting the client, the professional accountant's ethical standing will not be undermined. If unacceptably high threats to compliance with the fundamental principles will result from engagement, the professional accountant should not accept the engagement.
- Once the decision has been taken to accept the engagement, ISA 210 provides guidance on formulating the terms of the engagement; circumstances in which the terms of the engagement may be modified and how to deal with recurring audit engagements.
- Finally, this chapter examines some of the regulatory provisions from the USA, the UK, the EU and South Africa, which are relevant for the appointment of auditors. These include, for example, provisions dealing with restrictions on non-audit services and responsibilities for reporting on the independence and quality of the services provided by an external auditor.

7. References

Addams, H. L. & Davis, B. 1994. Privately held companies report reasons for selecting and switching auditors. *The CPA Journal,* 64, 38.

Arens, A., Elder, RI, Beasley, MS, Hogan, CE 2017. *Auditing and Assurance Services* Essex, Pearson.

Asare, S., Cohen, J. & Trompeter, G. 2005. The effect of non-audit services on client risk, acceptance and staffing decisions. *Journal of Accounting and Public Policy,* 24, 489–520.

Beattie, V. & Fearnley, S. 1995. The importance of audit firm characteristics and the drivers of auditor change in UK listed companies. *Accounting and business research,* 25, 227–239.

Bell, T. B., Landsman, W. R. & Shackelford, D. A. 2001. Auditors' perceived business risk and audit fees: Analysis and evidence. *Journal of Accounting research,* 39, 35–43.

Carcello, J. V., Hermanson, D. R. & Hermanson, R. H. 1998. Factors associated with audit client relationships "at risk". *Journal of Customer Service in Marketing & Management,* 4, 1–14.

Casterella, J. R. & Johnston, D. 2013. Can the academic literature contribute to the debate over mandatory audit firm rotation? *Research in Accounting Regulation,* 25, 108–116.

Companies Act 2008. Companies Act No. 71 of 2008. *In:* (2008), C. A. (ed.). Republic of South Africa.

Deangelo, L. E. 1981. Auditor size and audit quality. *Journal of Accounting and Economics,* 3, 183–199.

Feldman Barr, T. & Mcneilly, K. M. 2003. Marketing: Is it still "just advertising"? The experiences of accounting firms as a guide for other professional service firms. *Journal of Services Marketing,* 17, 713–729.

Fontaine, R., Letaifa, S. B. & Herda, D. 2013. An interview study to understand the reasons clients change audit firms and the client's perceived value of the audit service. *Current Issues in Auditing,* 7, A1–A14.

Francis, J. R. 2004. What do we know about audit quality? *The British Accounting Review,* 36, 345–368.

FRC 2013. Audit Tenders *Notes on best practice* London: Financial Reporting Council Limited.

FRC 2016a. Guidance on Audit Committees *London, September.*

FRC 2016b. The UK corporate governance code. *London, September.*

Hodges, S. & Young, L. 2009. Unconsciously competent: Academia's neglect of marketing success in the professions. *Journal of Relationship Marketing,* 8, 36–49.

IAASB 2009a. ISA 210: Agreeing the terms of audit engagements In: South African Institute of Chartered Accountants (ed.) *SAICA Members' Handbook.* Pietermaritzburg: LexisNexis.

IAASB 2009b. ISA 220: Quality Control for Audits of Historical Financial Information. In: South African Institute of Chartered Accountants (ed.) *SAICA Members' Handbook.* 2009 ed. Pietermaritzburg: LexisNexis.

IAASB 2009c. ISA 330: The auditor's response to assessed risk. In: South African Institute of Chartered Accountants (ed.) *SAICA Members' Handbook.* 2009 ed. Pietermaritzburg: lexisnexis.

IAASB 2009d. ISA 330: The auditor's responses to assessed risks. In: South African Institute of Chartered Accountants (ed.) *SAICA Members' Handbook.* 2009 ed. Pietermaritzburg: lexisnexis.

IAASB 2011. Audit quality an IAASB perspective. *In:* BOARD, I. A. A. S. (ed.). IFAC.

IESBA 2006. Code of ethics for professional accountants.

IESBA 2018. Handbook of the International Code of Ethics for Professional Accountants *Including International Independence Standards* New York: International Federation of Accountants (IFAC).

IOD 2016. *King IV Report on Corporate Governance in South Africa*, Lexis Nexus South Africa, Johannesburg, South Africa.

IRBA 2017. Rule on Mandatory Audit Firm Rotation Johannesburg Independent Regulatory Board for auditors.

IRBA 2018. IRBA Code of Professional Conduct for Registered Auditors. Johannesburg Independent Regulatory Board for Auditors.

Jackson, A. B., Moldrich, M. & Roebuck, P. 2008. Mandatory audit firm rotation and audit quality. *Managerial Auditing Journal,* 23**,** 420–437.

Jakubowski, S., Chao, P., Huh, S. & Maheshwari, S. 2002. A cross-country comparison of the codes of professional conduct of certified/chartered accountants. *Journal of Business Ethics,* 35**,** 111–129.

Johnstone, K. M. 2000. Client-acceptance decisions: Simultaneous effects of client business risk, audit risk, auditor business risk, and risk adaptation. *Auditing: A Journal of Practice & Theory,* 19**,** 1–25.

KPMG 2016. Getting real value from the audit tender process.

KPMG 2018. Getting real value from the audit tender process.

Magri, J. & Baldacchino, P. J. 2004. Factors contributing to auditor-change decisions in Malta. *Managerial Auditing Journal,* 19**,** 956–968.

Mande, V. & Son, M. 2012. Do financial restatements lead to auditor changes? *Auditing: A Journal of Practice & Theory,* 32**,** 119–145.

SOX 2002. Sarbanes-Oxley Act of 2002, Pub. L. 107–204, 116 Stat. 745. *SOX.* United States of America.

Sutton, S. G. 1993. Toward an Understanding of the Factors Affecting the Quality of the Audit Process. *Decision Sciences,* 24**,** 88–105.

Whisenant, S., Sankaraguruswamy, S. & Raghunandan, K. 2003. Evidence on the joint determination of audit and non-audit fees. *Journal of accounting research,* 41, 721–744.

1.   Introduction

The objective of an audit of financial statements is for the auditor to obtain reasonable assurance about whether or not the financial statements are free from material misstatement (due either to fraud or to error). On the basis of the evidence obtained, the auditor expresses an opinion on whether or not the financial statements have been prepared, in all material respects, with the applicable financial reporting framework (IAASB, 2016a, para 11). To achieve this objective, ISA 200 requires an audit engagement to be performed to the highest ethical standards (IAASB, 2016a, para 11). This was discussed in detail in Chapter 3 which dealt with how codes of ethics form part of the broader auditing and professional accounting environment. In addition to ethical conduct, the auditor must plan and execute the engagement in order to obtain sufficient appropriate evidence to support the audit opinion, something which requires the auditor to apply professional judgment and exercise a degree of professional scepticism (IAASB, 2016a, para 11).

How an auditor plans an audit engagement is discussed below. In this chapter, we introduce the concept of business and audit risk which form the basis for what is colloquially referred to as the planning, scoping and execution of an audit engagement. Refer to Figure 1.

Figure 1: Execution and scoping

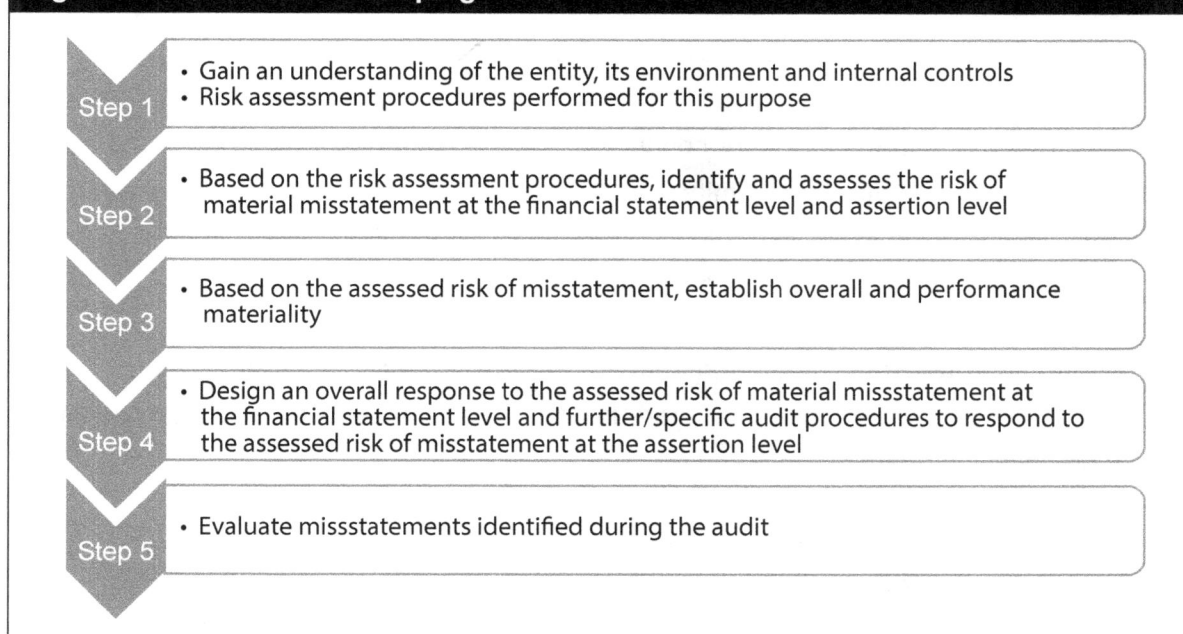

Step 1
- Gain an understanding of the entity, its environment and internal controls
- Risk assessment procedures performed for this purpose

Step 2
- Based on the risk assessment procedures, identify and assesses the risk of material misstatement at the financial statement level and assertion level

Step 3
- Based on the assessed risk of misstatement, establish overall and performance materiality

Step 4
- Design an overall response to the assessed risk of material missstatement at the financial statement level and further/specific audit procedures to respond to the assessed risk of misstatement at the assertion level

Step 5
- Evaluate missstatements identified during the audit

(IAASB, 2016b; IAASB, 2016c; IAASB, 2016d; IAASB, 2016f; IAASB, 2016e)

To correctly identify and assess relevant factors which would result in an auditor expressing an inappropriate opinion, a detailed understanding of the client, its business environment and internal controls is essential (Figure 1, Step 1). This is discussed in more detail in Chapter 11.

Once the auditor has obtained an understanding of the client, specific issues which give rise to audit risk are identified. This is done at an overall and assertion level (Figure 1, Step 2) to determine the risk of material misstatement as explained in more detail in Chapter 12. The auditor uses the assessed risk of material misstatement to calculate materiality (Figure 1, Step 3, Chapter 13) and determine an appropriate response to the risk of material misstatement. This is addressed by Step 4 which requires the auditor to design and perform audit procedures which including substantive tests and tests of controls (Chapter 13). Finally, in Step 5, the auditor evaluates any misstatements identified (Figure 1, Step 4) according to the determined materiality level and concludes on the effect of misstatements on the audit report (Chapter 17 and 18).

2. Understanding risks in the entity

As part of the process of gaining an understanding of the entity, the auditor will need to evaluate the nature of the entity, the industry in which the entity operates as well as the internal control structure and control environment (IAASB, 2016b). The objective is to form a view on the types of business risks to which the organisation is exposed and, in turn, identify risks of misstatement to the financial statements.

2.1 Business risks

Business risks result from significant conditions, events, circumstances actions or inactions which may adversely affect an entity's ability to achieve its objectives and deliver its strategies. Business risks can also result from setting inappropriate objectives and strategies (Arena et al., 2010; Jansen van Rensburg, 2013).

Risk identification requires a thorough knowledge of all aspects of the business and is the responsibility of senior management. There is no generally accepted method for identifying risks. Companies achieve this in a variety of ways:

- Interviews, surveys and staff polls;
- Stakeholder engagement;
- Business reviews, incident analysis, scenario analysis;
- Time and motion studies and process reviews (usually by internal or external experts); and
- Internal and external audits.

(Arena et al., 2010; Segal and Maroun, 2014)

To understand risk, the auditor needs to understand the different types of risk in terms of their classification and explanation. Table 1 is useful for analysis of business risks by explaining the different risks which can be faced by an organisation.

Table 1: Types of risk	
Risk classification/ category	**Explanation**
Business or operational risks	The risks which result from an entity's activities arising from its structure, operations, staff, people, products and system processes. Examples include: • System failures resulting in lost revenue and damages to brands (also a reputation risk) • Fraud • Health and safety issues, such as workplace injuries and the effects of injuries on staff morale and staff productivity • Loss of key suppliers • Faulty goods being produced and sold because of defective equipment of poor quality systems
Country risks	The risks that arise from being associated with an organisation's business and transactions or the holding of assets in a specific country. These risks may be political, economic or may arise from regulatory and policy instability and radical change. Risks are often a combination of all these elements. Examples include: • The risk of depending on a single country or region for the majority of sales (may also relate to strategic risks) • High levels of crime • General skills shortages • Complex tax regimes • Difficulties in repatriating funds to home country • Currency instability • Credit ratings • Inflation

►

Table 1: Types of risk	
Risk classification/ category	**Explanation**
Country risks (cont.)	Country risks may include political risks as a separate sub-category. These risks can include: • Political instability resulting in an uncertain business environment • Nationalisation/privatisation • Discrimination against foreign businesses
Environmental risks	The risk of environmental issues preventing the organisation from achieving its objectives. Environmental risks sometimes overlap with country risks and may occur because of political, economic, socio-cultural, technological, environmental and legal changes. Examples include: • Climate change • Natural disasters • Environmental protection laws (also a regulatory risk)
Financial risks	Risks associated with the financial operations of an entity which include factors such as: • Credit risk – losses incurred because of other parties not performing in terms of the contract • Currency risk – losses because of currency variations • Interest rate risks – interest rate changes as a result of liquidity changes
Reputational risks	Risks associated with an entity's reputation as a result of failure to manage the different risks. For example: • Producing and selling defective products is not only an immediate operational or financial risk. It can damage the reputation of the firm • Association with illegal or socially irresponsible actions • Damage to a firm's brand or image because of inappropriate policies, processes or procedures being followed

▶

Table 1: Types of risk	
Risk classification/ category	**Explanation**
Strategic risks	The risk that an entity's strategy is inappropriate for achieving its objectives. For example: • The strategy does not deal with the firm's business environment • An out-of-date strategy • Strategy overlooks key limitations or opportunities • Strategy fails to take important risks into account
Regulatory risks	Risks arising from specific laws and regulations. For example: • Criminal sanctions • Fines and penalties • Legal costs Regulatory risks will also give rise to operational, financial, and reputational risks.

(Collier and Ayei-Ampomah, 2008; Segal and Maroun, 2014; Raemaekers et al., 2016; Segal et al., 2017; IAASB, 2019)

Business risks can be framed in different ways. Risks are often seen as negative, as factors which prevent an entity from achieving its goals. Management, as a result, aims to reduce the likelihood of the risk occurring (Segal et al., 2017). Risks can also be thought of strategically(Collier and Ayei-Ampomah, 2008; Segal et al., 2017). They can highlight areas of uncertainty in a planned transaction or business model (Raemaekers et al., 2016). This allows management to think comprehensively about the risk and how best to restructure the transaction or plan the business model accordingly (Segal et al., 2017). In some cases, risk can also reveal an opportunity for the organisation (Collier and Agyei-Ampomah, 2008; Segal and Maroun, 2014).

2.2 Audit risk

Once these business risks have been thoroughly understood and fully integrated with the auditor's understanding of the entity, the auditor can make an accurate assessment of audit risk.

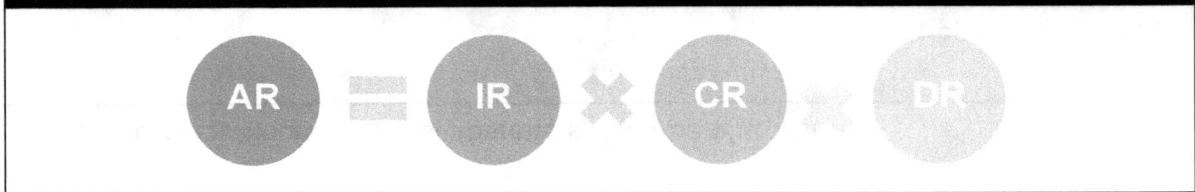

Audit risk is the risk that the auditor expresses an inappropriate audit opinion when the financial statements are materially misstated (IAASB, 2019). The auditor will need to assess audit risk as a function of risk of material misstatement and detection risk (Schultz et al., 2010).

The risk of material misstatement consists of a combination of the inherent risk that fraud or errors may occur and the risk that internal controls fail to prevent or detect the risk (Sardasht and Rashedi, 2018). Inherent and control risks are independent of the auditor and are referred to as entity risk (Sardasht and Rashedi, 2018).

Inherent risk is described as the susceptibility of an assertion about a class of transaction, account balance or disclosure to a misstatement which may be material, either individually or when aggregated with other misstatements, before consideration of any related controls (IAASB, 2019).

Control risk is described as the risk that a misstatement which may occur in an assertion about a class of transaction, account balance or disclosure and may be material, either individually or when aggregated with other misstatements, will not be prevented, or detected and corrected, on a timely basis by the entity's system of internal control (IAASB, 2019). The risk of material misstatement is the risk that the financial statements of an organisation have been misstated to a material degree (IAASB, 2019).

The risk that the auditor will fail to detect misstatements is called *detection risk* (IAASB, 2019). For a given level of audit risk the detection risk has an inverse relationship to the assessed risk of material misstatement being the combination of inherent and control risk (IAASB, 2016c). The greater the auditor's assessed risk of material misstatement, the lower the accepted detection risk can be and therefore more audit evidence is required by the auditor (IAASB, 2016c; IAASB, 2016h).

Once the accurate assessment of audit risk is performed, the auditor is able to determine significant classes of transactions, account balances and disclosures and relevant assertions which will form the basis for the audit approach, including the calculation of audit materiality (see also Chapters 12 and 13). The process followed to assess inherent, control and detection risk is discussed in more detail below.

An auditor performs a risk assessment through risk assessment procedures (Collier and Agyei-Ampomah, 2008; IAASB, 2019). Risk assessment procedures are necessary to gain an understanding of the entity which is being audited. They include enquiry, analytical procedures and observation and inspection of balances, transactions, and processes (Arena et al., 2010). Risk assessment procedures are performed with information obtained from the client's acceptance and continuance procedures, information obtained from the auditor's previous experience and other audit engagements (Wielligh et al., 2014). The risk assessment procedures are explained in Table 2.

Table 2: Risk assessment procedures and explanation	
Risk assessment procedure	Explanation
Inquiries	Inquiries involve direct inquiries from management, internal audit and those charged with governance. Inquiries can also include direct inquiries towards employees, legal counsel, sales personnel, risk management function and other personnel.
Analytical procedures	Analytical procedures may include the analysis of both financial and non-financial information. These procedures are used to identify the existence of unusual or unexpected relationships. In many instances, the result of broad analytical procedures will require further corroboration in the form of other audit procedures. For example, a decline in sales year on year will be corroborated by inspection of a decrease in customer contracts.
Observation and inspection	Observation and inspection may support inquiries of management and others and may also provide additional necessary information. These include observation and inspection of the entity's operations, plans, strategies, records and other documents, reports prepared by management, physical observation of the entity's premises and other facilities.

(IAASB, 2019)

According to (IAASB, 2019, para A127), risk assessment procedures (including evidence obtained about the design and implementation of internal controls) are used to support the assessment of the risk of material misstatement (IAASB, 2019). This will include an assessment of specific account balances and be geared through the assessment of inherent and control risk of that account balance, as well as of the likelihood and magnitude of the risk occurring (Hammersley et al., 2011).

Chapters 11 and 12 cover in more detail the process followed to gain an understanding of the audit client and to assess the risk of material misstatement. Chapter 13 details how to reduce the audit risk to an acceptable level.

4. Summary

- The auditor needs to have a thorough understanding of the business risks facing the entity.
- Business risks can include country, reputational, business, financial and strategic risks. The identification of business risks forms the starting point of identifying and quantifying audit risk.
- Audit risk is a function of inherent risk, control risk and detection risk.
- Inherent and control risks are independent of the auditor and, when combined, are referred to as risk of material misstatement. The risk that the auditor will fail to detect misstatements is called detection risk. There is an inverse relationship between risk of material misstatement and detection risk.
- To gauge audit risk, the auditor performs risk assessment procedures. These include inquiry, analytical procedures, observation and inspection. Risk assessment procedures enable the auditor to understand the various elements of the entity effectively.
- The execution of risk assessment procedures is presented separately in this chapter but, in practical terms, the procedures are executed at the same time as gaining an understanding of the client, determining materiality and concluding on the planned audit approach.

5. References

Arena, M., Arnaboldi, M. & Azzone, G. 2010. The organizational dynamics of enterprise risk management. *Accounting, Organizations and Society,* 35 (7), 659–675.

Collier & Agyei-Ampomah 2008. *Management Accounting: Risk and Control Strategy,* Oxford, CIMA Publishing.

Hammersley, J. S., Johnstone, K. M. & Kadous, K. 2011. How do audit seniors respond to heightened fraud risk? *Auditing: A Journal of Practice & Theory,* 30 (3), 81–101.

IAASB 2016a. ISA 200: Overall objectives of the Independent Auditor and the Conduct of an Audit in Accordance with International Standards on Auditing.

IAASB 2016b. ISA 315 R: Identifying and Assessing the Risks of Material Misstatment through Understanding the Entity and its Environment.

IAASB 2016c. ISA 320: Materiality in Planning and Performing an Audit.

IAASB 2016d. ISA 330: The Auditor's Responses to Assessed Risks.

IAASB 2016e. ISA 450: Evaluation of misstatemenst identified during the audit.

IAASB 2016f. ISA 500: Audit evidence.

IAASB 2019. International Standard on Auditing 315 (Revised 2019) : Identifying and assessing the risks of material misstatement. International Auditing and Assurance Standards Board.

Jansen van Rensburg, L. 2013. *Tax risk management: A framework for implementation.* University of Pretoria.

Raemaekers, K., Maroun, W. & Padia, N. 2016. Risk disclosures by South African listed companies post-King III. *South African Journal of Accounting Research,* 30 (1)**,** 41–60.

Sardasht, M. S. & Rashedi, E. 2018. Identifying Influencing Factors of Audit Risk Model: A Combined Fuzzy ANP-DEMATEL Approach. *The International Journal of Digital Accounting Research,* 18 (24)**,** 69–117.

Schultz, J. J., Bierstaker, J. L. & O'Donnell, E. 2010. Integrating business risk into auditor judgment about the risk of material misstatement: The influence of a strategic-systems-audit approach. *Accounting, Organizations and Society,* 35 (2)**,** 238–251.

Segal, T. & Maroun, W. 2014. Tax risk-management analysis: Comparison between the United States of America, the United Kingdom and South Africa. *Journal of Economic and Financial Sciences,* 7 (2)**,** 375–392.

Segal, T. G., Segal, M. & Maroun, W. 2017. The perceived relevance of tax risk-management in a South African context. *Meditari Accountancy Research,* 25 (1)**,** 82–94.

Chapter 11: Understanding the entity

1. Introduction

As discussed in Chapter 10, the purpose of risk assessment procedures is for the auditor to obtain an understanding of the entity (IAASB, 2019a). Understanding the entity involves the understanding of the entity's organisational structure, ownership, and governance, its business model, and the integrated use of information technology (IT) (Wielligh et al., 2014). The IT environment is particularly important to understand as many organisations have complex IT infrastructures (Wielligh et al., 2014). This chapter discusses the purpose of risk assessment procedures in informing the understanding of an entity (Section 2.1). This is followed by a discussion on the nature and understanding of the IT environment (Section 2.2) with a view to informing the auditors response.

2. Understanding the client

By performing risk assessment procedures (Chapter 10), the auditor obtains an understanding of:

- The control environment relevant to the preparation of the financial statements (IAASB, 2019a, para A99–A108);
- The entity's risk assessment process relevant to the preparation of the financial statements (IAASB, 2019a, para A109–A113);
- The entity's process for monitoring the system of internal control relevant to the preparation of the financial statements (IAASB, 2019a, para A114–A117); and
- The entity's information system and communication relevant to the preparation of the financial statements (IAASB, 2019a, para A132–A136) and the control activities component (IAASB, 2019a, para A147–A157).

2.1 The requirements of ISA 315 (Revised)

ISA 315 R deals with the auditor's responsibility for gaining an understanding of the entity, its environment and internal controls in order to identify and assess the risk of material misstatement in the financial statements (ISA 315, para 1–3). The standard specifies the different 'components' or aspects of the entity on which the auditor should focus.

Table 1: Obtaining an understanding of the entity	
ISA 315 R Component	**Details**
Obtain an understanding of the control environment relevant to the preparation of the financial statements (Ref: Para. A99–A108).	Understanding the set of controls, processes, and structures that address: (Ref: Para. A101–A102) (a) *How management's oversight responsibilities are carried out, such as the entity's culture and management's commitment to integrity and ethical values; whether internal or outsourced and the independence of the outsourcing;* (b) *The entity's assignment of authority and responsibility;* (c) *How the entity attracts, develops and retains competent individuals; and* (d) *How the entity holds individuals accountable for their responsibilities in the pursuit of the objectives of the system of internal control.* ***And evaluating whether the above has been created within:*** (i) A culture of honesty and ethical behaviour. (ii) A control environment that provides an appropriate foundation for other components of the entity's system of internal control. (iii) The identification of control deficiencies in the control environment which do not undermine the other components of the entity's system of internal control. (Ref: Para. A99–A100)

▶

Table 1: Obtaining an understanding of the entity	
ISA 315 R Component	**Details**
Obtain an understanding of the entity's risk assessment process relevant to the preparation of the financial statements through performing risk assessment procedures (Ref: Para. A 109–113)	Understanding the entity's process for (Ref: Para. A109–A110) (a) *Identifying business risks relevant to financial reporting objectives; assessing the significance of those risks, including the likelihood of their occurrence; and* (b) *Addressing those risks.* **And evaluating whether:** (i) The entity's risk assessment process is appropriate to the entity's circumstances considering the nature and complexity of the entity. (Ref: Para. A111–A113)
Obtain an understanding of the entity's process for monitoring the system of internal control relevant to the preparation of the financial statements, through performing risk assessment procedures (Ref: Para. A114–A117)	Understanding those aspects of the entity's process which address: (a) *Ongoing and separate evaluations for monitoring the effectiveness of controls, and the identification and remediation of control deficiencies identified and the entity's internal audit function, if any, including its nature, responsibilities, and activities; (Ref: Para. A116–A118); and* (b) *Understanding the sources of the information used in the entity's process to monitor the system of internal control, and the basis upon which management considers the information to be sufficiently reliable for the purpose; (Ref: Para. A119–A120).* **And evaluating whether:** (i) The entity's process for monitoring the system of internal control meets the needs of the entity considering the nature and complexity of the entity (Ref: Para. A121–A122).

▶

Table 1: Obtaining an understanding of the entity	
ISA 315 R Component	**Details**
Obtain an understanding of the entity's information system and communication relevant to the preparation of the financial statements, through performing risk assessment procedures (Ref: Para. A130)	Understanding the entity's information processing activities including its: (a) *Data and information, the resources to be used in such activities and the policies that define, for significant classes of transactions, account balances and disclosures:* (Ref: Para. A132– A143) *namely:* (i) How data flows through the entity's information system, including the initiation, recording, processing, and correction of information in the general ledger, financial statements as well as disclosure of these; (ii) The accounting records, specific accounts in the financial statements and other supporting records relating to the flows of information in the information system; (iii) The financial reporting process used to prepare the entity's financial statements, including disclosures and (iv) The entity's resources, including the IT environment, relevant to the above information. (b) *Understanding how the entity communicates significant matters which support the preparation of the financial statements and related reporting responsibilities in the information system and other components of the system of internal control:* (Ref: Para. A144–A145). (i) Between people within the entity, between management and those charged with governance; and with external parties, such as those with regulatory authorities.

►

Table 1: Obtaining an understanding of the entity	
ISA 315 R Component	**Details**
	And evaluating whether: (i) The entity's information system and communication sufficiently support the preparation of the entity's financial statements per the applicable financial reporting framework. (Ref: Para. A146).
Gain an understanding of the control activities component through performing risk assessment procedures (Ref: Para. A147–A157)	Identifying controls that address risks of material misstatement at the assertion level in the control activities component as follows: (a) *Significant risk controls* (Ref: Para. A158–A159); (b) *Journal entry controls (including non-standard, non-recurring, unusual, or adjusting* (Ref: Para. A160–A161); (c) *Operating effectiveness control testing in determining the nature, timing, and extent of substantive testing* (Ref: Para. A162– A164); (d) *Other appropriate risk assertion-based controls* (Ref: Para. A165); (e) *IT application controls* (A166 – A171); *and* (f) *Related IT risks and controls addressing these IT risks* (A172 – A174). ***And evaluating whether:*** (i) The controls above are designed effectively to address the risk of material misstatement at the assertion level, or effectively designed to support the operation of other controls and whether the control has been implemented by performing procedures in addition to the inquiry of the entity's personnel. (Ref: Para. A175–A181).

(Segal et al., 2017; IAASB, 2019a; Adams et al., 2020b)

To understand the entity, the auditor needs to obtain an understanding of the controls implemented by management. Controls are implemented by management to achieve management's objectives in each business process/cycle (IAASB, 2019b). The auditor obtains the understanding of the controls by performing walkthroughs of transactions in each cycle and documenting the various risks, controls and processes in an audit work paper. There may be numerous cycles at an entity ranging from the revenue cycle to the payroll cycle, however, cycles and controls are dependent on the nature of the entity and the goods and services which they supply (Adams et al., 2020a).

Technology and the use of IT in businesses occurs on a daily basis at both large and small organisations (Collier and Ayei-Ampomah, 2008; Rubino et al., 2017). Therefore, understanding the IT environment is crucial for understanding the entity. This is discussed below.

2.2 Understanding the nature of the IT environment

The starting point for obtaining an understanding of the entity's IT environment is to gain an understanding of the entity's general IT control environment.

2.2.1 General IT controls

General controls are the basic controls that can be applied to IT systems such as applications, operating systems, databases and supporting IT infrastructure (Curtis and Borthick, 1999). A description and example of general controls is summarised in Table 2.

Table 2 – General Controls		
Function	**Definition**	**Example**
Application	Application software is a program or group of programs designed for end-users	Microsoft Word Microsoft Excel SAP
Database	A database is an organised collection of structured information or data typically stored electronically.	Student database containing student number, age, gender, race, marks, etc. Customer database containing address information, sales history, etc.

▶

Table 2 – General Controls		
Function	**Definition**	**Example**
Operating System	An operating system is system software that manages computer hardware, software resources and provides common services for computer programs.	Windows Operating systems

Apple MacOS |
| Network | A network consists of two or more computers linked to share resources, exchange files or allow electronic communication. | A Local Area Network (LAN) is a network that connects devices usually in the same building or local area.
A router is often used when multiple Local Area Networks need to be connected. |

(Curtis and Borthick, 1999)

Application controls are controls operating at a business processing level and apply to the processing of transactions within specific individual applications. Application controls are both manual and computerised controls but relate to one application or transaction type (IAASB, 2019a; Adams et al., 2020b). Application controls provide comfort over transactions and ensure that transactions are valid, accurate and complete. The effective functioning of application controls is dependent on a strong general control environment (Wielligh et al., 2014). Given the increasing use of IT, the section below focuses on IT application controls.

2.2.2 IT application controls

When considering application controls it is important to understand that the system is divided into inputs, processes and outputs (Wielligh et al., 2014). Figure 1 indicates how information systems work.

Figure 1: The workings of information systems

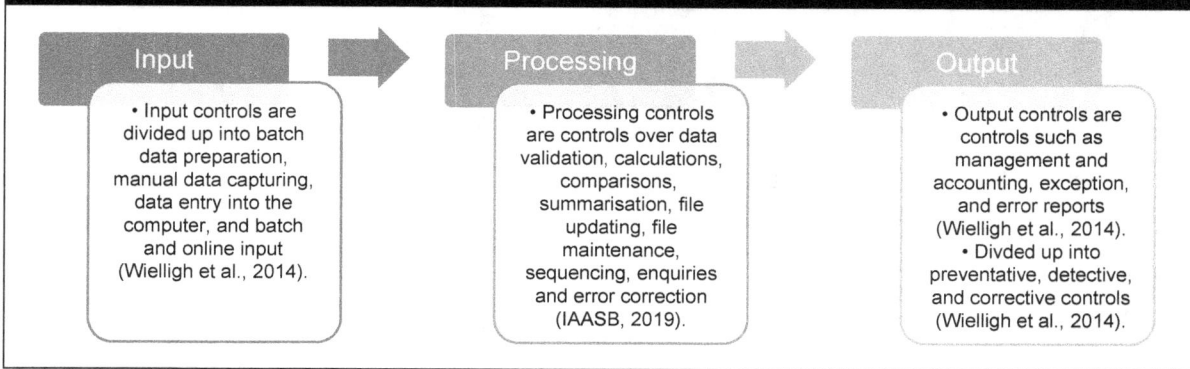

Input	Processing	Output
• Input controls are divided up into batch data preparation, manual data capturing, data entry into the computer, and batch and online input (Wielligh et al., 2014).	• Processing controls are controls over data validation, calculations, comparisons, summarisation, file updating, file maintenance, sequencing, enquiries and error correction (IAASB, 2019).	• Output controls are controls such as management and accounting, exception, and error reports (Wielligh et al., 2014). • Divded up into preventative, detective, and corrective controls (Wielligh et al., 2014).

Input Controls

Input controls can be sub-divided into batch inputs, inline inputs and online inputs. Table 3 provides an analysis of input controls.

Table 3 – Analysis of input controls

Batch input (manual)	Inline input (batching)	Online input (real-time processing)
Accumulation of several transactions that need to be captured	Online entry of individual transactions and periodic batch processing	The online entry of individual transactions which are captured and processed in real-time
Source documents for a specific period	Online entry takes place at a workstation with periodic validation and processing	Online entry takes place at a workstation with immediate validation and processing
Source documents are converted to machine-readable format and stored on a secondary storage medium	Approved transactions are stored in a transaction file/ log	If validation is not successful, an error message will appear on the screen/device
Transaction file is imported into computer and validation takes place	The transactions in the transaction file are periodically updated to the master file	Approved transactions are immediately updated to the master file

►

Table 3 – Analysis of input controls		
Batch input (manual)	**Inline input (batching)**	**Online input (real-time processing)**
Transaction file is sorted according to the master file primary keys as needed and updating of the master file takes place	A reference data file is kept until complete updating occurs	Output data is generated

(Wielligh et al., 2014; Haislip et al., 2016)

Batch input consists of the accumulation of several transactions that need to be captured. Therefore controls over source document conversion, file importation and file sorting are required (Wielligh et al., 2014). Inline input consists of online entry of individual transactions and periodic batch processing. Therefore, controls over logs and log reviews are required (Rubino et al., 2017). Online input consists of online entry of individual transactions which are captured and processed in real-time (Rubino et al., 2017). The controls over transmissions, online processing and error reports are required (Wielligh et al., 2014).

Processing controls

Processing controls establish that data are complete and accurate during updating. The common processing controls are run control totals, computer matching, and programmed edit checks (Adams et al., 2020b).

Run-to-run totals reconcile the input control totals with the totals of items that have updated the file (Wielligh et al., 2014). Updating can be controlled by generating control totals during processing (Adams et al., 2020b). The totals, such as total transactions processed or totals for critical quantities, can be compared manually or by computer (Marx et al., 2014). Discrepancies are noted for investigation (Adams et al., 2020b). Computer matching agrees the input data with information held on master or suspense files with unmatched items noted for investigation. Most matching occurs during input but, under some circumstances, it may be required to ensure completeness of updating. For example, a matching program might match employee timecards with a payroll master file and report missing or duplicate timecards (Rubino et al., 2017).

Processing controls ensure that internal and external electronically transmitted files and transactions are received from an identified source and processed accurately and completely (Rubino et al., 2017). Table 4 provides an analysis of processing controls.

Table 4: Analysis of processing controls	
Domain	**Control**
File transmission controls	Checks for completeness and validity of content, including date and time, data size, volume of records, and authentication of source.
Data transmission controls	Application of selected input controls to validate data received (eg, key fields, reasonableness, etc.).
Automated file identification and validation	Files for processing are available and complete.
Automated functionality and calculations	Specific calculations conducted on one or more inputs and stored data elements produce further data elements. Use of existing data tables (eg, master files or standing data such as rating tables).
Audit trails and overrides	Automated tracking of changes made to data, associating the change with a specific user. Automated tracking and highlighting of overrides to normal processes.
Data extraction, filtering, and reporting	Extract routine outputs are assessed for reasonableness and completeness. Automated allocation of transactions (eg, for reinsurance purposes, further actuarial processes, or fund allocation). Evaluation of data used to perform estimation for financial reporting purposes.
Interface balancing	Automated checking of data received from feeder systems (eg, payroll, claims data, etc.) into data warehouses or ledger systems. Automated checking that balances on both systems match, or if not, an exception report is generated and used.
Automated functionality and aging	Automated functionality and aging

►

Table 4: Analysis of processing controls	
Domain	**Control**
Duplicate checks	Comparison of individual transactions to previously recorded transactions to match fields. Comparison of individual files to expected dates, times, sizes.

(Wielligh et al., 2014; IAASB, 2019a)

Output controls

Output controls can be divided into preventative, detective and corrective controls (Wielligh et al., 2014). Preventive controls attempt to deter or prevent undesirable events from occurring. The distribution and transmission of reports and documentation is a critical element in implementing adequate preventative controls (Marx et al., 2014). Preventative controls include distribution checklists, transmission checks and workstation display activities (Abbott et al., 2012). Detective controls identify problems within a company's processes once they have occurred (Marx et al., 2014) Detective controls include controls over transmissions, reviews and reconciliations (IAASB, 2019a).

Detective controls include controls such as comparisons and reviews of distribution checklists. Corrective controls include any measures taken to repair the damage or restore resources and capabilities to their prior state following an unauthorised or unwanted activity (IAASB, 2019a). Examples of corrective controls include mending a system, quarantining a virus, terminating a process or rebooting a system (Collier and Ayei-Ampomah, 2008). Table 5 deals with output controls.

Table 5: Analysis of output controls		
Preventative controls	**Detective controls**	**Corrective controls**
Distribution checklists should be kept of who is permitted to receive certain reports	Comparison of transmittal sheets with output descriptions	Source errors should be returned to the user responsible for the source creation
Transmittal sheets to indicate to whom the reports were transmitted	Reviewing of the distribution checklists for timely receipt of printouts/electronic files	Processing errors should be handled by technical staff
Distribution logs of all those who received the output	Reviewing of transaction lists and comparisons to source documentation	Error logs should be kept by the control group in order to control resubmission

►

Table 5: Analysis of output controls		
Preventative controls	**Detective controls**	**Corrective controls**
Report release forms that must be signed before reports are taken	Reviewing the lists of computer generated transactions	Follow up on the review procedures over the lists
Workstation display activities	Reviewing the lists of changes made to a master file	Follow up on unauthorised changes made to a master file
Batch totals in place to batch check input to output	Reconciling batch totals per computer to the totals originally calculated	Follow up on reconciling items identified through the batch total reconciliation
Reconciliations and reveiws performed	All reconciliations and reviews should be signed by a senior as proof of review	Regular monitoring of reconciliation discrepancies should be perfromed

(Collier and Agyei-Ampomah, 2008; Rubino et al., 2017)

2.2.3 The nature and characteristics of IT applications

After obtaining an understanding of the general and application controls in an IT environment, the auditor also needs to consider various other characteristics concerning the complexity of the IT applications. The auditor needs to consider the IT environment relevant to the flows of transactions and information processing in the information system. The auditor gathers information about the nature and characteristics of the IT applications used as well as the supporting IT infrastructure (IAASB, 2019a).

Table 6 includes examples of the matters which the auditor may consider in obtaining the understanding of the IT environment and examines the complexity of IT applications used in the entity's information system.

Table 6: Matters to consider in obtaining an IT environment understanding and complexity understanding of IT application.				
#	**Matters to consider**	**Software: non-complex (simple commercial)**	**Software: mid-sise & moderate**	**Software: Large or complex**
A: The extent and manner of:				
1.	Automated procedures for processing and their complexity	Routine processes with low levels of risk	Routine processes with moderate levels of risk	Extensive and complex automated procedures

►

#	Matters to consider	Software: non-complex (simple commercial)	Software: mid-sise & moderate	Software: Large or complex
2.	The entity's reliance on system- generated reports in the processing information	Simple automated report logic	Simple relevant automated report logic	Complex automated report logic; report generators
3.	The data inputted into the system or process	Data input manual	Data input and interface: simple	Data input and interface: complex
4.	IT facilitation & communication between applications and databases through system interfaces (internal & external)	No automated interfaces	Small number of simple data inputs and interfaces	Large number of data inputs and complex interfaces
5.	The volume and complexity of data in the digital form being processed by the information system: accounting records or other information stored in digital form and the location of stored data	Low volume of data; simple locally available data (verified manually)	Low volume of data or simple data	Large volume of data or complex data; Data warehouses. Use of internal or external IT service providers (eg, third-party storage or hosting of data)

Table 6: Matters to consider in obtaining an IT environment understanding and complexity understanding of IT application.

►

#	Matters to consider	Software: non-complex (simple commercial)	Software: mid-sise & moderate	Software: Large or complex
Table 6: Matters to consider in obtaining an IT environment understanding and complexity understanding of IT application.				
B: IT applications and IT infrastructure:				
1.	The type of application	Purchased application: minimal or low customisation	Purchased application or simple legacy or low-end enterprise resource planning (ERP) applications with little or no customisation	Custom-developed applications or more complex ERPs with significant customisation
2.	The complexity of the nature of the IT applications and the underlying IT infrastructure	Small, simple laptop and client-based	Mature and stable mainframe; small or simple client-server software as a service cloud	Complex mainframe; large or complex client-server; web-facing; infrastructure as a service cloud
3.	Third-party hosting or outsourcing of IT	In the event of outsourcing: a mature, competent host	If outsourced, competent, mature, (eg a cloud provider)	Competent, mature proven provider for certain applications
4.	Emerging technologies which affect its financial reporting	No use of emerging technologies	Limited use of emerging technologies in certain applications	Mixed-use of emerging technologies across multiple platforms
C: IT Processes:				
1.	Personnel: number & skills of IT support resources managing security and changes to the IT environment	Less personnel with limited IT knowledge	Minimal personnel with IT skills	Dedicated IT departments with skilled personnel and advanced programming skills

▶

169

#	Matters to consider	Software: non-complex (simple commercial)	Software: mid-sise & moderate	Software: Large or complex
	Table 6: Matters to consider in obtaining an IT environment understanding and complexity understanding of IT application.			
2.	The complexity of processes to manage access rights	Sole personnel with administrative access manages access rights	Few individuals with administrative access manage access rights	Complex processes managed by the IT department including complex access rights
3.	The complexity of the security over the IT	Simple access	Some web-based applications	Multiple web-based platforms
4.	Whether program changes have been made to the manner in which information is processed	Commercial software with no source code installed	Some commercial applications with no source code; traditional systems development lifecycle	New or large number of complex changes, many system developments cycles annually
5.	The extent of change within the IT environment	Changes limited to version upgrades of commercial software	Changes consist of commercial software upgrades, enterprise resource planning (ERP) version upgrades, or legacy enhancements	A new or large number of complex changes, several development cycles each year, detailed ERP customisation
6.	Major data conversion during the period, the nature and significance of the changes made, and the manner of conversion	Software upgrades provided by the vendor/supplier. No data conversion features for an upgrade	Minor version upgrades for commercial software applications with limited data conversion	Major version upgrade

(Abbott et al., 2012; Wielligh et al., 2014; IAASB, 2019a)

Once the auditors have obtained an understanding of the controls, they will be able to assess the risk of material misstatement at the financial statement and assertion level. This is discussed in more detail in Chapter 12.

3. Summary

- The auditor should perform risk assessment procedures to obtain an understanding of the entity's organsational structure, ownership and governance, its business model and the integrated use of IT.
- The auditor should understand the industry, regulatory and other external factors, as well as measures used internally and externally to assess the entity's financial performance.
- The auditor must evaluate whether the entity's accounting policies are appropriate and consistent with the applicable financial reporting framework.
- The auditor should understand the components of the entity's system of internal control, control environment, the entity's risk assessment process and the entity's process to monitor the system of internal control.
- As IT is a crucial part of an organisation's environment, it is necessary for the auditor to have a comprehensive understanding of the client's general and application IT controls. The auditor gathers information about the nature and characteristics of the IT applications and infrastructure.
- The auditor's understanding of the entity will inform the assessed risk of material misstatement and the planned audit response.

4. References

Abbott, L. J., Parker, S. & Peters, G. F. 2012. Internal Audit Assistance and External Audit Timeliness. *AUDITING: A Journal of Practice & Theory,* 31 (4)**,** 3–20.

Adams, Diale & Richard 2020a. *Auditing notes for South African students,* South Africa, Lexis Nexis.

Adams, A., Richard, G. & Diale, T. 2020b. *Auditing Notes for South African Students* South Africa, Lexis Nexis.

Collier & Agyei-Ampomah 2008. *Management Accounting: Risk and Control Strategy,* Oxford, CIMA Publishing.

Collier & Ayei-Ampomah 2008. *Management Accounting Risk and Control Strategy,* Oxford, CIMA Publishing.

Curtis, M. B. & Borthick, A. F. 1999. Evaluation of internal control from a control objective narrative. *Journal of Information Systems,* 13 (1)**,** 63–81.

Haislip, J. Z., Peters, G. F. & Richardson, V. J. 2016. The effect of auditor IT expertise on internal controls. *International Journal of Accounting Information Systems,* 20**,** 1–15.

IAASB 2019a. International Standard on Auditing 315 (Revised 2019) : Identifying and assessing the risks of material misstatement. International Auditing and Assurance Standards Board.

IAASB 2019b. International Standard on Auditing 315 (Revised 2019): Identifying and assessing the risks of material misstatement. International Auditing and Assurance Standards Board.

Marx, B., Schonfeldt, N., Van Der Watt, A., Van Dyk, V. C., Mare, D. J. & Ramuedzisi , M. T. 2014. *Fundamentals of Auditing*, LexisNexis South Africa.

Rubino, M., Vitolla, F. & Garzoni, A. 2017. How IT controls improve the control environment. *Management Research Review*.

Segal, T. G., Segal, M. & Maroun, W. 2017. The perceived relevance of tax risk-management in a South African context. *Meditari Accountancy Research,* 25 (1)**,** 82–94.

Wielligh, P., Prinsloo, F., Penning, G., Butler, R., Nathan, D., Kunz, R. & Moth, V. 2014. *Auditing Fundamentals in a South African context,* South Africa, Oxford University Press.

Chapter 12: Overall and assertion level risk

1. Introduction

Risk of material misstatement can be broken down into overall financial statement level and assertion level risks (Wielligh et al., 2014b). This chapter discusses the components of audit risk (Section 2) followed by a discussion of risks at the overall financial statement level (Section 2.1). The use of assertions and their impact on risk assessment is discussed in Section 2.2. Section 3 considers the relationship between overall and assertion level risk and significant audit risk.

2. The components of audit risk

Audit risk is the risk of the auditor expressing an inappropriate audit opinion when the financial statements are materially misstated. In Chapter 10, audit risk is defined as the quotient of inherent, control and detection risk. Inherent and control risk can be combined to yield risk of material misstatement. The components of audit risk are highlighted in Figure 1:

Figure 1: The components of audit risk

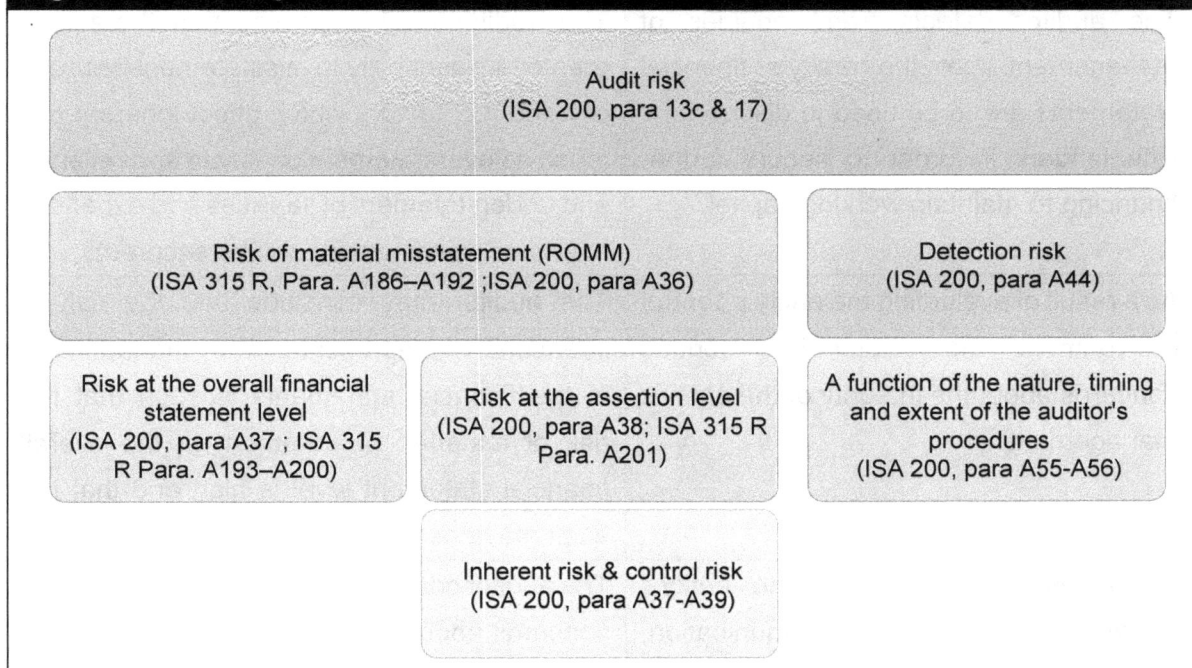

Audit risk
(ISA 200, para 13c & 17)

Risk of material misstatement (ROMM)
(ISA 315 R, Para. A186–A192 ;ISA 200, para A36)

Detection risk
(ISA 200, para A44)

Risk at the overall financial statement level
(ISA 200, para A37 ; ISA 315 R Para. A193–A200)

Risk at the assertion level
(ISA 200, para A38; ISA 315 R Para. A201)

A function of the nature, timing and extent of the auditor's procedures
(ISA 200, para A55-A56)

Inherent risk & control risk
(ISA 200, para A37-A39)

(IAASB, 2009a; IAASB, 2019)

2.1 Risk at the overall financial statement level

Risks of material misstatements at the financial statement level refer to pervasive risks which potentially affect multiple assertions relating to balances and transactions and as a result have an impact on the financial statements as a whole (IAASB, 2019). Control deficiencies, for example, not complying with the codes of good corporate governance, can give rise to the risk at the financial statement level (IAASB, 2019) as the control environment may be poor in the absence of good corporate governance. In some cases, the risk of material misstatement at the financial statement level is so high that the auditor concludes that the engagement cannot be conducted (IAASB, 2019).

Table 1 provides examples which may be relevant to the auditor's consideration of the risks of material misstatement at the overall financial statement level.

Table 1: Relevant examples of ROMM at the overall financial statement level	
Example	**Auditor's consideration**
The entity faces operating losses and liquidity problems and is reliant on funding which has not yet been secured.	The auditor may determine that the going concern basis of accounting gives rise to a risk of material misstatement at the financial statement level. The accounting framework may need to be applied using a liquidation basis which would likely affect all assertions pervasively.
The auditor detects from inquiries of management that the entity's financial statements are to be used in discussions with lenders in order to secure further financing to maintain working capital.	The auditor may determine that there is a greater susceptibility to misstatement because of fraud risk factors which affect inherent risk (such as overstatement of assets and revenue and understatement of liabilities and expenses to ensure that financing will be secured).
As a result of evaluating the entity's control environment, the auditor has serious concerns about the integrity of the entity's management.	The auditor may conclude that the risk of intentional misrepresentation by management in the financial statements is such that the risk of material misstatement at the overall financial statement level is high and that the audit may possibly not be conducted.
As a result of evaluating the entity's information system and communication, the auditor determines that significant changes in the IT environment have been poorly managed, with no oversight from management and those charged with governance.	The auditor concludes that there are significant concerns about the condition and reliability of the entity's accounting records and the risk of material misstatement at the overall financial statement level is high.

(IAASB, 2019, para A195–A198)

2.2   Risk at the assertion level

In identifying and assessing the risks of material misstatement, the auditor uses assertions (IAASB, 2019). The auditor may choose to combine assertions about classes of transactions and events and related disclosures with the assertions about account balances and related disclosure (IAASB, 2019, para A189). Classes of transactions refer to the income statement items (the transactions which move through the entity) and account balances refer to the year-end items (the final balance sheet) (Adams et al., 2020). Table 2 provides an explanation of the assertions.

Table 2: Assertions			
Classes of transactions	**Explanation**	**Account balances**	**Explanation**
Occurrence	Transactions or events that have been recorded or disclosed have in fact occurred and pertain to the entity.	Existence	Assets, liabilities and equity interests exist.
Completeness	All transactions or events which should have been recorded have been recorded and all related disclosures have been included.	Rights and obligations	The entity holds or controls the rights to assets and the entity has obligations to the liabilities.
Accuracy	Amounts related to recorded transactions and events have been recorded appropriately and related disclosures have been appropriately measured and described.	Completeness	All assets, liabilities and equity interests which should have been recorded have in fact been recorded and all related disclosures which should have been included in the financial statements have been included.

▶

175

Table 2: Assertions			
Classes of transactions	**Explanation**	**Account balances**	**Explanation**
Cut-off	Transactions and events have been recorded in the correct accounting period[1].	Accuracy, valuation and allocation	Assets, liabilities and equity interests have been included at appropriate amounts and any resulting valuation or allocation adjustments have been appropriately recorded and related disclosures have been appropriately measured and described.
Classification	Transactions and events have been recorded in the proper accounts.	Presentation	Assets, liabilities and equity interests have been recorded in the proper accounts.
Presentation	Transactions and events are appropriately aggregated or disaggregated and clearly described and related disclosures are relevant and understandable in the context of the requirements of the applicable financial reporting framework.	Presentation	Assets, liabilities and equity interests are appropriately aggregated or disaggregated and clearly described and related disclosures are relevant and understandable in the context of the requirements of the applicable financial reporting framework.

(Wielligh et al., 2014b; IAASB, 2019, para A190)

3.   Significant audit risks

As part of the process of identifying risks at the overall and assertion level, ISA 315 requires the auditor to determine if any risks are significant risks. In exercising judgment as to which

---

1   Cut-off must be considered relating to transactions and balances both before and after year-end. Transactions or events that relate to the current financial period should not be recorded in the next financial period and, similarly, transactions or events that relate to the next financial period should not be recorded in the current financial period (Wielligh et al., 2014b).

risks are significant, the auditor shall consider whether the risk is a risk of fraud; whether the risk is related to significant economic, accounting or other developments; the complexity of transactions; whether the risk involves significant transactions with related parties; the degree of subjectivity in the measurement of financial information and whether the risk involves significant transactions that are outside the normal course of business (Wielligh et al., 2014a; IAASB, 2016). Refer to Table 3.

Table 3: Increased inherent risk factors	
Factor	**Increased inherent risk**
Transactions for which there are multiple acceptable accounting treatments involving subjectivity.	✔
Accounting estimates which have high estimation uncertainty or complex models.	✔
Complexity in data collection and processing to support account balances.	✔
Account balances or quantitative disclosures which involve complex calculations.	✔
Accounting principles which may be subject to differing interpretation.	✔
Changes in the entity's business which involve changes in accounting, for example, mergers and acquisitions.	✔

(Wielligh et al., 2014b; IAASB, 2019)

For significant risks, the auditor should gain an understanding of the relevant controls which may have been in place to address the risk (ISA 315, para A137–A139) (IAASB, 2016). The identification of significant risks will also impact the nature, timing and extent of the test procedures carried out by the auditor. This is discussed in more detail in Chapter 13 (IAASB, 2016). Table 4 provides a summary of the ISAs referring to significant audit risk and their specific requirements (IAASB, 2019, para A128).

Table 4: Specific ISA responses	
Response	**ISA**
Controls that address significant risks are required to be evaluated for effective design and implementation.	315 R

Table 4: Specific ISA responses

Response	ISA
Controls that address significant risks must be tested in the period when the auditor intends to rely on the operating effectiveness of such controls and substantive procedures to be planned and performed, specifically to respond to the identified significant risk.	330
The higher the auditor's assessment of risk the more persuasive audit evidence is required.	330
The significant risk identified by the auditor must be communicated to those charged with governance.	260
The auditor must take into account significant risks when determining those matters which required significant auditor attention and are matters which may be key audit matters.	701
A timely review of audit documentation by the engagement partner at the appropriate stages during the audit allows significant risks to be resolved on a timely basis and to the engagement partner's satisfaction on or before the date of the auditor's report.	220
More involvement by the group engagement partner is required if the significant risk relates to a component in a group audit and for the group engagement team to direct the work required at the component by the component auditor.	600
When identifying and assessing the risks of material misstatement because of fraud, the auditor will, based on a presumption that there are risks of fraud in revenue recognition, evaluate which types of revenue, revenue transactions, or assertions give rise to such risks.	240

(IAASB, 2009e; 2009b; 2009f; 2009g; 2009d; 2009c; 2019)

Finally, it must be stressed that risk assessment is an iterative process which impacts planning, execution and reporting (Wielligh et al., 2014b). Throughout the audit, additional financial statement or assertion level risks may be identified resulting in additional testing (Wielligh et al., 2014b; Adams et al., 2020). The level of existing risks can also be revised as audit work is performed or when completing the audit (Refer to Chapters 13 and 17).

4. Summary

- Risks of material misstatement can be evaluated from the financial statement and the assertion level.

- Risks of material misstatements at the financial statement level refer to pervasive risks which have an impact on the financial statements as a whole. For example, the financial statements may be prepared using the incorrect basis of accounting or significant deficiencies in internal controls contribute to the financial being susceptible to pervasive fraud and error.

- Assertion-level risks are evaluated for specific balances and classes of transactions. Examples include the risk that expenses are incomplete, revenue is overstated or asset balances do not exist.

- The auditor may choose to combine assertions about classes of transactions and events and related disclosures with the assertions about account balances and related disclosures.

- The auditor is required to determine if any risks identified during the risk assessment process are significant risks. These significant risks require specific audit responses.

5. References

Adams, Diale & Richard 2020. *Auditing notes for South African students,* South Africa, Lexis Nexis.

IAASB 2009a. ISA 200: Overall objectives of the independent auditor and the conduct of an audit in accordance with international standards on auditing. *SAICA Members' Handbook.* 2009 ed. Pietermaritzburg: LexisNexis.

IAASB 2009b. ISA 220: Quality Control for Audits of Historical Financial Information. *SAICA Members' Handbook.* 2009 ed. Pietermaritzburg: LexisNexis.

IAASB 2009c. ISA 240: The auditor's responsibility realting to fraud in an audit of financial statements. *SAICA Members' Handbook.* 2009 ed. Pietermaritzburg: LexisNexis.

IAASB 2009d. ISA 260 Revised: communication with those charged with governance. *SAICA Members' Handbook.* 2009 ed. Pietermaritzburg: Lexis Nexis.

IAASB 2009e. ISA 330: The Auditor's Responses to Assessed Risks. *SAICA Members' Handbook.* 2009 ed. Pietermaritzburg: Lexis Nexis.

IAASB 2009f. ISA 600: Special considerations – Audits of Group Financial Statements (Including the work of component auditors). *SAICA Members' Handbook.* 2009 ed. Pietermaritzburg: Lexis Nexis.

IAASB 2009g. ISA 701: communicating key audit matters in the independent auditor's report. *SAICA Members' Handbook.* 2009 ed. Pietermaritzburg: Lexis Nexis.

IAASB 2016. ISA 315 R: Identifying and Assessing the Risks of Material Misstatment through Understanding the Entity and its Environment.

IAASB 2019. International Standard on Auditing 315 (Revised 2019) : Identifying and assessing the risks of material misstatement. International Auditing and Assurance Standards Board.

Wielligh, P. V., Prinsloo, F., Penning, G., Butler, R., Nathan, D., Kunz, R. & Moth, V. 2014a. *Auditing Fundamentals in a South African context,* South Africa.

Wielligh, V., Prinsloo, F., Penning, G., Butler, R., Nathan, D., Kunz, R. & Moth, V. 2014b. *Auditing Fundamentals in a South African context,* South Africa.

1. Introduction

Once the auditor has identified the risk of material misstatement, as explained in Chapter 12, the auditor is required to reduce the risk to an acceptable level. This requires the auditor to determine the value of materiality, the nature, timing and extent of the audit response and the audit evidence required. Audit evidence is obtained by way of audit procedures.

The chapter consists of three parts. Section 2 discusses materiality. This is followed by Section 3 which is the auditor's response. This includes a discussion of audit strategy, audit plan and the use of sampling. Section 4 covers audit evidence and its sufficiency and appropriateness.

2. Materiality terms and applications

Materiality is a fundamental reporting principle in the audit process (Gray and Manson, 2007; Edgley, 2014; Cerbone and Maroun, 2019). Materiality thresholds are used to determine if errors or omissions will impact stakeholders' decisions based on the financial statements (Teck-Heang and Ali, 2008). Auditors make independent decisions regarding materiality and an assessment on whether the financial statements offer a true and fair view of the financial position, performance and cash flows of the reporting entity (Gray and Manson, 2007; Edgley et al., 2015). ISA 320 deals with the determination of materiality for the purpose of planning and performing an audit engagement (IAASB, 2009b, para 1).

2.1 Understanding materiality

Materiality is comprised of planning and performance materiality (IAASB, 2009i). Planning materiality is used in the determination of the audit strategy and plan and performance materiality is used to execute the engagement (IAASB, 2009i). Performance materiality is the amount set by the auditor at less than overall materiality and is used to perform the audit work (Wielligh et al., 2014). If applicable, performance materiality also refers to the amount or amounts set by the auditor at less than the overall materiality for particular classes of transactions, account balances or disclosures (IAASB, 2009i).

2.1.1 Planning materiality

Planning an audit involves establishing the overall audit strategy for the engagement and the development of an audit plan (IAASB, 2009a). The concept of materiality is applied by the auditor both in planning and performing the audit and in evaluating the effect of identified misstatements and uncorrected misstatements on the financial statements and the audit opinion (IAASB, 2009b, para 5). The auditor uses planning materiality to determine, identify, and assess the nature, timing, and extent of risk assessment procedures (IAASB, 2009a). In practice, planning materiality is determined based on the auditor's initial understanding of the client and an interim trial balance. Several factors need to be considered when quantifying planning materiality. Refer to Table 1.

Table 1 – Factors to be considered when quantifying planning materiality		
#	**Factors to consider**	**Explanation of the factors**
1	Use of benchmarks	As materiality is relative, it is necessary to establish bases or benchmarks against which it can be measured. Example: a misstatement of CU 30 000 is material, relative to net income of CU 300 000 but not necessarily material, relative to a net income of CU 3 000 000.
2	Importance of specific information to users	If, for example, a bank or other financial institution has advanced a loan to a client based on the maintenance of certain ratios (eg maintenance of current assets to current liabilities) the auditor will assess the current assets and liabilities as important. This is also because of reliance on these amounts by the user (the bank and other financial institutions).
3	Key disclosures	This will also be industry-specific for example, directors' remuneration in listed companies is often a key disclosure because of statutory and governance considerations in different jurisdictions.
4	Legal requirements	Specific or standard legislation disclosure will need to be assessed. This is as per users' expectation of fair presentation of these amounts and disclosures.
5	Governance opinions	The governance and management concerns and risk appetite will also be considered.

Adapted from (IAASB, 2009i)

2.1.2 Performance materiality

Performance materiality must be determined for the purposes of assessing the risks of material misstatements (in classes of transactions and account balances) and for determining the nature, timing, and extent of additional further audit procedures (Section 3) (IAASB, 2009b; Adams et al., 2020b). When computing performance materiality, the auditor needs to consider that an error may not be confined to only one account balance and may, therefore, result in a material misstatement in other areas of the financial statements (IAASB, 2009b; Wielligh et al., 2014; Adams et al., 2020b).

Performance materiality levels are used when the auditor performs tests on specific account balances or classes of transactions (IAASB, 2009b, para 11). If, for example, the auditor sets planning materiality for the audit of accounts receivable at CU 200 000, the objective will be to determine *aggregate* errors for amounts above CU 200 000 (IAASB, 2009b; Adams et al., 2020b). Performance materiality will be used to assess the individual differences which in total would exceed the CU 200 000 (Adams et al., 2020b).

2.1.3 The link between planning and performance materiality

Planning materiality is based on the auditor's initial understanding of the entity. After setting planning materiality, further information may be identified by the auditor which may affect the auditor's initial planning materiality assessment. This may cause the auditor to reassess the planning materiality amount (IAASB, 2009b; Wielligh et al., 2014).

There is an inverse relationship between materiality and risks of material misstatement (Chapter 12) (IAASB, 2009i). The higher the risk of material misstatement, the lower the materiality has to be (IAASB, 2009h). The lower the risk of material misstatement, the higher the materiality must be (IAASB, 2009i; Adams et al., 2020a).

Once materiality has been established, the auditor needs to design an overall response to the assessed risk of material misstatement at the financial statement level and specific audit procedures to respond to the assessed risk of misstatement at the assertion level. This also needs to be considered in a group audit environment. Refer to Chapter 14.

3. Auditor response

The auditor's response will incorporate the overall audit strategy, as well as its expansion into the nature, timing and extent of the audit procedures, known as the audit plan (Meliyev, 2018).

3.1 Audit strategy and audit plan

As part of the planning activities, the auditor must establish an overall audit strategy which sets the scope, timing, and direction of the audit and guides the development of the audit plan (Meliyev, 2018). ISA 300 provides guidance regarding the development of an audit strategy (Meliyev, 2018). The planning of an audit has several benefits such as ensuring that time is dedicated to important areas of the audit, problems can be identified and resolved timeously and the audit can be efficiently and effectively managed in terms of the allocation of staff and responsibilities (IAASB, 2009a, para 2).

In evaluating the overall audit strategy, the auditor will consider the following:

- Identification of the characteristics of the engagement that define its scope;
- The reporting objectives of the engagement;
- The factors that are significant in directing the engagement team's efforts;
- The results of preliminary engagement activities; and
- Ascertaining the nature, timing, and extent of resources necessary to perform the engagement.

(IAASB, 2009a; Meliyev, 2018; Sardasht and Rashedi, 2018)

Table 2 guides an auditor in developing the audit strategy. This is done by illustrating factors to consider and providing specific examples of these factors.

Table 2 – Considerations when developing the audit strategy		
#	Factors to consider	Example of factors
1	Characteristics of the engagement (ISA 300, para 8(a))	• The financial reporting framework used by the company. • Industry-specific reporting requirements. • The extent to which components are audited by other auditors (Chapter 14). • The number of locations and the expected coverage at the company. • The need for specialised knowledge. • The presence of an internal audit function and whether this can be used to assist the auditors (Chapter 15). • The possibility of using computer-assisted audit techniques (CAAT's) in the audit. • Availability of client staff and information.
2	Reporting objectives, the timing of the audit and nature of communication (ISA 300, para 8(b))	• Reporting deadlines applicable to the entity. • The way meetings will be organised with management and those charged with governance. • The format in which management and those charged with governance require reports such as the audit report and management letters, as well as the timing of these reports. • The expectations from management regarding status updates from the auditor. • Nature and extent of communication with the audit team regarding team meetings and timing of the reviews of work as part of the quality control guidelines.

►

Table 2 – Considerations when developing the audit strategy		
#	Factors to consider	Example of factors
3	Significant factors, preliminary engagement activities, and knowledge gained (ISA 300, para 8(c), 8(d))	• Preliminary identification of high-risk areas. • The impact of the overall risk of material misstatement on the direction and supervision of the audit (Chapter 12). • Impact of prior year audit information such as deficiencies in internal control and management action to address the deficiencies. • Changes in the reporting framework and the impact on standards applied. • The volume of transactions as this may influence the audit plan. • Significant business developments such as changes in key processes, key management, or mergers and acquisitions. • Significant industry developments.
4	Nature, timing, and extent of resources (ISA 300, para 8(e))	• Selection of the engagement team. This includes the assignment of audit work to team members depending on the knowledge and experience of staff. • Engagement budgeting including the time set aside for areas with a higher risk of material misstatement.

(IAASB, 2009a, para 8 and Appendix)

The auditor must design and perform audit procedures to respond to the assessed risk of material misstatement at the assertion level (IAASB, 2009c, para 6). This requires the nature, timing, and extent of the procedures carried out to be appropriate for the given level of audit risk (Sardasht and Rashedi, 2018) (IAASB, 2009a, para 9). The components of an audit plan are explained in ISA 330. Table 3 lists and describes these components.

Table 3 – Nature, timing, and extent	
Term	**Meaning**
Nature (ISA 330, para A5)	Nature of the audit procedure refers to: • How the procedures are performed – A test of control or a substantive procedure; and • The method through which these procedures are performed, inspection, observation, inquiry, confirmation, recalculation, reperformance, or analytical procedure. The nature is dependent on the assessed level of control dependence and the risk assessed and is the most important factor when responding to risk (ISA 330, para A5).
Timing (ISA 330, para A6)	Timing refers to when the control tests or substantive procedures will be performed and will be dependent on whether the auditor can rely on the controls identified at the client.
Extent (ISA 330, para A7)	Extent refers to the quantity of testing or the sample sizes used in both the control tests and substantive tests.

(IAASB, 2009c)

3.1.1 Nature of the audit procedures

The auditor's procedures will consist of:

- Tests of controls (ISA 330, para 4);
- Substantive analytical review (ISA 330, para 4 & ISA 520, para 4); and
- Substantive tests of detail (ISA 330, para 4).

(IAASB, 2009c)

This is represented and explained in Figure 1.

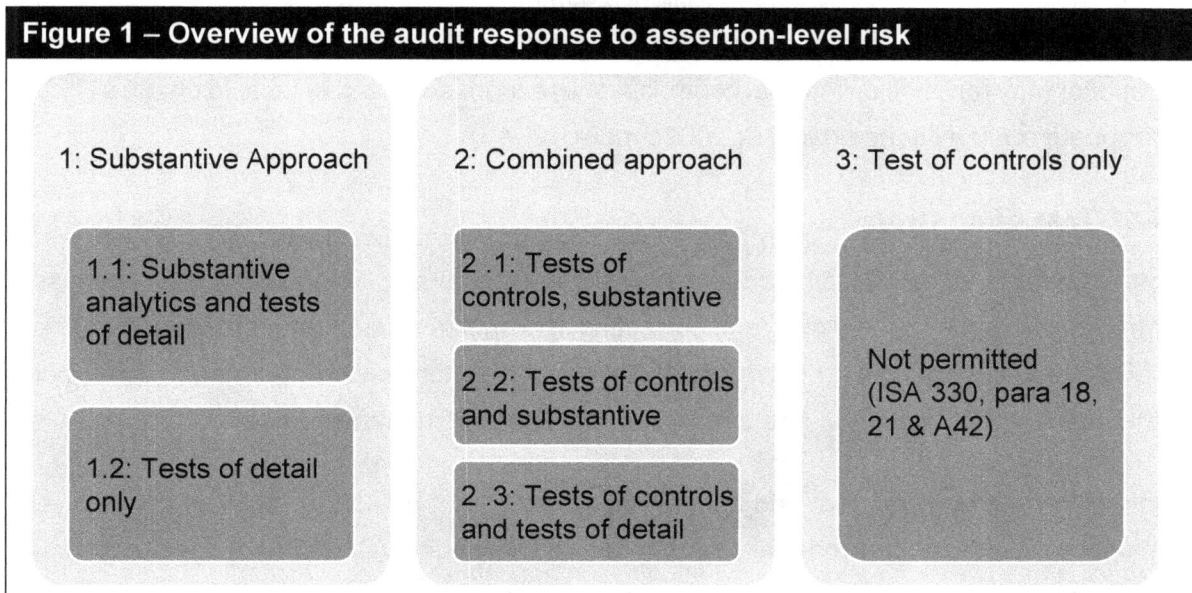

Figure 1 – Overview of the audit response to assertion-level risk

1: Substantive Approach	2: Combined approach	3: Test of controls only
1.1: Substantive analytics and tests of detail	2 .1: Tests of controls, substantive	Not permitted (ISA 330, para 18, 21 & A42)
1.2: Tests of detail only	2 .2: Tests of controls and substantive	
	2 .3: Tests of controls and tests of detail	

The nature of the audit procedures will be affected by the risk of material misstatement (IAASB, 2009c, para 7). This considers the inherent and control risk (explained in Chapter 12). A higher inherent risk may require more reliance on tests of detail focusing on the affected assertion (IAASB, 2009c, para A9). The auditor is not precluded from testing controls. In some cases, the client may have a comprehensive system of internal controls which the auditor can rely on to address the risk of material misstatement (Collier and Agyei-Ampomah, 2008). Nevertheless, as the risk of material misstatement increases, the auditor performs more substantive testing to complement any control work. For significant audit risks, at least some substantive tests of detail must be performed (Abbott et al., 2012).

In addition, a higher risk of material misstatement may lead to a change in the type of substantive procedures. The auditor needs to gain more relevant and reliable evidence to support the conclusions reached (Collier and Agyei-Ampomah, 2008). As a result, the auditor may rely less on substantive analytics and more on tests of detail. Where tests of detail are performed, the auditor will also try to obtain more persuasive evidence by, for example, using less observation and inspection and more recalculations and external confirmations (IAASB, 2009c; IAASB, 2009d). If a client has a control which addresses one or more assertions, the auditor may test that control to respond to the underlying risk of material misstatement (IAASB, 2009c, para A10 & A20). If the tests of control are effective, this can decrease the extent of tests of detail required (IAASB, 2009c, para A46). Similarly, if the test of control is not effective, the extent of substantive procedures may need to be increased (IAASB, 2009c, para A46).

If control risk is high, the auditor may carry out audit procedures (in addition to the risk assessment procedures) to identify and assess more accurately the risk of material misstatement (Collier and Agyei-Ampomah, 2008). However, as part of the overall response to audit risk, the auditor considers the client's control environment. If there is a weak control environment, evidence obtained from tests of controls may not be conclusive. In these cases, the auditor may rely less on internal controls and use more substantive tests to obtain sufficient appropriate audit evidence (IAASB, 2009c, para A2–A3).

3.1.2 Test of controls

Tests of controls refers to audit procedures designed to evaluate the operating effectiveness of controls in preventing or detecting and correcting, material misstatements at the assertion level (IAASB, 2009c, para 4(b)). In terms of ISA 315R, the auditor needs to gain an understanding of the internal control system and specifically the use of IT (Chapters 10 and 11).

Controls can be both manual and computerised (Abbott et al., 2012). Manual controls refer to those controls that are manually performed by individuals (Collier and Agyei-Ampomah, 2008). They may be solely manual where no IT generated reports are used or they may be IT-dependent where an employee is using a system-generated report to test the validity of a particular control (Collier and Ayei-Ampomah, 2008). IT controls are a significant factor in almost all organisations (Curtis and Borthick, 1999). As a result, it is necessary to understand the IT controls (Chapter 11).

Application controls must be evaluated in the context of the general control environment (Rubino et al., 2017). The general controls refer to the overarching control environment which exists. As a general rule the auditor will only rely on and test the application controls if the control environment is sound. The 'components' of the general control environment include:

- Access management;
- Program and change management; and
- Operation management.

Table 4 lists and explains these three control areas. It also provides examples of how the auditor could test these control areas.

Table 4 – Access, program and change and operation management		
Process	**Definition**	**Auditor testing**
Access		
Authentication	Controls which ensure a user accessing the IT application or other aspect of the IT environment is using the owner's log-in credentials.	Using test data to test the user access controls (ie: fake/dummy access passwords).
Authorisation	Controls which allow users to access the information necessary for their job responsibilities and nothing further, which facilitates segregation of duties.	Inspection of log reports to identify the users who did not have the authority to access information did not, in fact, access the information.
Provisioning	Controls to authorise new users and modifications to existing users' access.	Using CAATS to draw reports of instances where new users accessed information without authorisation.
Deprovisioning	Controls to remove user access upon termination or transfer.	Using test data to test that certain access rights have been removed.
Privileged access	Controls over administrative or powerful users' access.	Inspection of log reports to identify where superuser access has been superseded.
User access reviews	Controls to recertify or evaluate user access for ongoing authorisation over time.	Inquiries from management about systems utilised to evaluate user access.
Security configuration controls	Each technology generally has key configuration settings which help restrict access to the environment.	Using test data to test the key configuration settings.
Physical access	Controls over physical access to the data centre and hardware, as such access may be used to override other controls.	Physically observe the access controls in place over the data centre and hardware.

►

Table 4 – Access, program and change and operation management		
Process	**Definition**	**Auditor testing**
Program and change		
Change management process	Controls over the process to design, programme, test and migrate changes to a production (ie end-user) environment.	Inspection of minutes of meetings and IT documentation of change management processes over authorisation, implementation, testing, and post user verification.
Segregation of duties over change migration	Controls which segregate access to make and migrate changes to a production environment.	Inspect minutes/correspondence with change migration consultants to ascertain that the system has been tested and issues have been communicated with the board and management.
Systems development or acquisition or implementation	Controls over initial IT application development (or concerning other aspects of the IT environment).	Inspect contracts and minutes of meetings for authorisation over IT application development.
Data conversion	Controls over the conversion of data during development, implementation, or upgrades by the IT environment.	Inspect evidence (eg signature of the employee who performed the task) that the data from the 'old' system was thoroughly checked for accuracy before being captured onto the new system.
Job scheduling	Controls over access to schedule and initiate jobs or programs that may affect financial reporting.	Using test data verify that user access will only permit access to certain jobs and applications.
Job monitoring	Controls to monitor financial reporting jobs or programs for successful execution.	Inspect reports for signatures or digital signatures of monitoring of financial reporting jobs.

►

Table 4 – Access, program and change and operation management		
Process	**Definition**	**Auditor testing**
Backup and recovery	Controls to ensure backups of financial reporting data occurs as planned and that such data are available and can be accessed for timely recovery in the event of an outage or attack.	Inspect access controls if back-ups are kept on a cloud server, inspect for documentation, implementation, and testing of key backups.
Intrusion detection	Controls to monitor for vulnerabilities and or intrusions in the IT environment.	Inspect documentation for evidence of regular testing which is crucial in an era of ransomware attacks.

(Marx et al., 2014; IAASB, 2019)

Application controls

The first purpose of the test of controls is to reduce substantive audit procedures by relying on the client's internal controls (Knechel and Salterio, 2016). This is based on the auditors assessment that internal controls work effectively in preventing or detecting the risks of material misstatements at the assertion level (Knechel and Salterio, 2016).

Application controls provide comfort over transactions and ensure that transactions occurred and are authorised (validity), complete, and accurately recorded and processed (Marx et al., 2014). These application controls address the relevant assertions related to the various transactions (Chapter 12). Before an auditor tests the operating effectiveness of controls, the auditor will first ensure that the design of the control is appropriate and that the control has been implemented. (Chapter 11).

3.1.3 Analytical procedures

Analytical procedures are used as a substantive procedure to obtain some evidence over assertions related to account balances or classes of transactions. In some cases, analytical procedures can be more effective or efficient than tests of details for achieving particular substantive testing objectives (IAASB, 2009c; Wielligh et al., 2014).

3.1.4 Substantive procedures

A substantive procedure is a process, step or test which provides conclusive evidence regarding the assertion-level risks. The auditor will rely on different combinations of tests of detail, tests of controls and substantive analytical reviews to obtain sufficient appropriate audit evidence (IAASB, 2009c).

Table 5 provides a descriptive overview of the different types of substantive procedures which can be performed by the entity.

Table 5 – Descriptive overview of substantive procedures	
Source	**Explanation**
Inspection	Reviewing of source documents or contracts.
Observation	Physical verification of assets or a control occurring.
External confirmation	Obtaining direct written confirmation from a third party (external).
Recalculation	Verifying the mathematical accuracy of source documents or accounting records by recalculating amounts.
Re-performance	The auditor repeating the same procedure as previously performed by the entity's staff.
Analytical procedures	The use of comparisons and analyses of relationships among financial and non-financial data to assess whether account balances, totals, and disclosures appear reasonable compared to auditor's expectations.
Inquiry	Inquiry consists of obtaining information from both internally and outside the entity. Evaluating the response from inquiry forms a key part. It should be noted that it is important to obtain corroborating evidence where inquiries are completed.

Mandatory testing

Some substantive procedures always need to be performed:

- Tests over closing processes (ISA 330, para 20 & A52).
- Substantive tests of detail over significant risks (ISA 330, para 21 & A53). Note that substantive analytical procedures alone will be inappropriate.
- Presentation and disclosure (ISA 330, para 24 & A59).

3.1.5 Timing of audit procedures

In addition to affecting the nature of the audit procedure, the assessed risk of material misstatement has implications for the timing of the procedure and for the extent of audit evidence obtained (IAASB, 2009c, para 7) (Section 3.1.5 and 3.1.6).

The timing of the test of controls depends on factors such as whether or not the controls are automated or manual or if it is required to test the control at a specific period or over a period or if interim testing is possible for a specific assertion (IAASB, 2009c). In a strong control environment, the auditor can place more reliance on control testing and less on substantive testing. As a result, the auditor can perform control testing at interim periods (Wielligh et al., 2014). If the control environment is weak and cannot be relied upon, the auditor will need to perform more detailed substantive procedures (Wielligh et al., 2014). In this case, the detailed substantive procedures will need to be performed subsequent to year-end (IAASB, 2009c). Regarding substantive testing, the auditor can consider completing interim testing, provided that additional testing is completed to cover the remaining period (IAASB, 2009c, para A56). Factors which influence this decision include the control environment, the purpose of the substantive procedures, assessed risk of material misstatement and the ability to complete additional procedures to cover the remaining period (Rubino et al., 2017) (IAASB, 2009c, para A56).

3.1.6 Extent of audit testing

The extent of testing refers to the sample sizes used in both the control and substantive testing of the audit. In a strong control environment – especially with strong automated controls – the auditor will probably place reliance on automated control tests including the use of CAATS (IAASB, 2009c, para A16). Testing from prior periods will also assist the auditor in determining the extent of current year audit procedures.

Prior period testing will also help inform the auditor of the extent of the use of IT and sample sizes in an audit. In a less IT-intense environment, the auditor will use increased sample sizes to perform the detailed substantive testing to gain comfort over the audit evidence obtained (IAASB, 2009r). An increase in control comfort decreases the extent of substantive testing and a decrease in control comfort increases the extent of substantive testing (Rubino et al., 2017).

The sampling means available to the auditor are as follows:

a. *Selecting all items* : Instances where 100% testing may be applicable: tests of detail, the population comprises of a small number of large items or the use of information systems allows 100% of the population to be tested (ISA 500, para A53).

b. *Selecting specific items*: This is influenced by the auditors' understanding of the entity and the assessed risk of material misstatement. The approach is used for target testing where an auditor selects high-value items, items over a certain amount or items to obtain specific information. The results of procedures applied to items selected specifically cannot be projected to the entire population.

c. *Audit sampling*: Sampling is the application of audit procedures to less than 100% of items in a class of transactions or account balance. The sample is selected from the population which is the entire set of data (IAASB, 2009g).

(IAASB, 2009d; Jones, 2017)

When obtaining evidence, the auditor is not restricted to using only one method but a combination of methods may be used (IAASB, 2009d, para A52). There are multiple factors which the auditor needs to consider with regard to sampling. Figure 2 indicates these factors.

Figure 2 – Sampling considerations

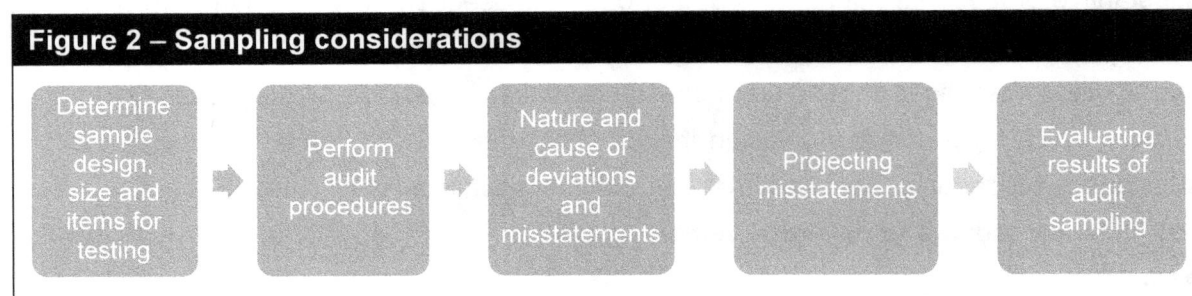

Sample design, size and selection of items for testing

ISA 530 provides guidance regarding the sample design, sample size and selection of items for testing to ensure that reasonable conclusions are reached.

- When the auditor is selecting the audit sample, the purpose of the audit procedure and the characteristics of the population from which the sample will be drawn must be considered (IAASB, 2009g, para 6). Statistical sampling is where there is a random selection of items and each item has an equal chance of being selected (Jones, 2017). Random and systematic selection are methods viewed as statistical sampling methods (IAASB, 2009g, para A20). When specific items are selected for testing, this is not considered as statistical sampling.

- The auditor will determine a sample size sufficient to reduce sampling risk to an acceptably low level (IAASB, 2009g, para 7). Sampling risk is the risk which the auditor's conclusion, based on the sample, may be different from the conclusion had the entire population been selected. There are two errors which can occur with sampling risk (Jones, 2017):

  - The tests of controls are more effective than they are or that a material misstatement does not exist when in fact it does; or
  - The test of controls is less effective than it actually is or a material misstatement exists when it actually does not.

(Srivenkataramana, 2018)

Regarding the above, the first error results in audit failure as an inappropriate audit opinion may be issued. The second error will result in an inefficient audit as unnecessary audit work will be performed (IAASB, 2009g, para 5). The lower the risk that the auditor is willing to accept, the greater the sample size will be (IAASB, 2009g, para A10). The sample size is determined by statistical means or professional judgement (IAASB, 2009g, para A11; Jones, 2017).

Performing audit procedures

When performing the audit procedures, the auditor may need to replace an item selected in the sample (IAASB, 2009g, para 10). If the auditor cannot apply the designed audit procedure or cannot apply suitable alternate procedures, the item selected will be treated as a deviation from the prescribed control where the test is a test of control or misstatement where tests of details are being performed (IAASB, 2009g).

Nature and cause of deviations and misstatements

The auditor will need to consider if the deviation or misstatement identified is an anomaly (IAASB, 2009g, para 13). This is where the deviation or misstatement is not representative of the population (IAASB, 2009g, para 5). When an anomaly is found and is established as an anomaly, it must not be projected onto the population as it is not representative of the population (Srivenkataramana, 2018).

Projecting Misstatements

Only for tests of detail will the auditor project misstatement found in the sample to the population (IAASB, 2009g, para 14). The anomalous misstatement must be added to the projected misstatement to obtain the total misstatement (IAASB, 2009g, para A19). For tests of control, the deviation is not projected as the sample deviation rate is also the projected deviation rate (IAASB, 2009g, para A20).

Evaluating the results of audit sampling

The auditor is required to evaluate the results of the sample and whether the use of audit sampling has provided a reasonable basis for concluding on the population (IAASB, 2009g, para 15). The auditor is required to determine:

- Tolerable rate of deviation: the maximum rate of deviation which the auditor is willing to accept and is still able to conclude that the control operates effectively.
- Tolerable misstatement: the maximum misstatement that the auditor is willing to accept and still conclude that the account balance/transaction is not materially misstated.

(Jones, 2017)

If there is a high sample deviation rate it may lead to a high risk of material misstatement. For tests of detail, a high misstatement amount in the sample may cause the auditor to believe that the account balance or transaction is materially misstated (IAASB, 2009g, para A21). For the test of detail, if the misstatement (projected misstatement + anomalous) exceeds the tolerable misstatement, the sample does not allow a reasonable basis for a conclusion to be reached on the population (IAASB, 2009g, para A22). If audit sampling does not provide a reasonable basis for a conclusion about the population, the auditor may:

- Request management to investigate misstatements identified and to make any necessary adjustments; or
- Amend the nature, extent, and timing of further audit procedures to achieve the required assurance (ISA 530, para A23).

4. Audit evidence

The audit strategy and audit plan will result in the designing of audit procedures to obtain sufficient and appropriate evidence to ensure that the reasonable assurance opinion provided is the correct one. Sufficient and appropriate audit evidence falls within the scope and objective of ISA 500, 501 and 505 (IAASB, 2009j).

4.1 Scope and objective of ISA 500

ISA 500 explains what constitutes audit evidence and deals with the auditor's responsibility to design and perform audit procedures to obtain sufficient appropriate audit evidence. ISA 500 applies to all audit evidence obtained during the audit. However, other ISAs (including ISA 501 and ISA 505) deals with audit evidence to be obtained concerning a particular topic and specific procedures to obtain audit evidence (IAASB, 2009d).

- ISA 501 deals with specific considerations by the auditor in obtaining sufficient appropriate audit evidence concerning inventory, litigation and claims involving the entity (IAASB, 2009e, para 1).
- ISA 505 deals with the auditor's use of external confirmation procedures to obtain audit evidence (excluding those dealt with in ISA 501) (IAASB, 2009f, para 1).

As explained in ISA 200 (para 5), reasonable assurance is obtained when the auditor has sufficient appropriate audit evidence to reduce audit risk to an acceptably low level. ISA 500 requires the auditor to perform audit procedures to obtain sufficient appropriate evidence (IAASB, 2009d, para 6). Audit procedures comprise of risk assessment procedures (Chapter 10), tests of controls and substantive tests (Section 3.1.4) (IAASB, 2009d, para A10; Lessambo, 2018).

The sufficiency (quantity) and appropriateness (quality) of audit evidence are interrelated (IAASB, 2009d, para A4). The quantity of audit evidence needed is affected by the auditor's assessment of the risks of material misstatement (IAASB, 2009d, para A4). The higher the assessed risks, the more (sufficient) and/or higher quality (appropriate) audit evidence will be required (IAASB, 2009d; Lessambo, 2018). Appropriate audit evidence measures the quality of audit evidence, that is, its relevance and its reliability in providing support for the conclusions on which the auditor's opinion is based (IAASB, 2009d, para A5).

The auditor must consider the relevance and reliability of the information used as audit evidence (IAASB, 2009d, para 8). The reliability of audit evidence is influenced by its source and nature and is dependent on the circumstances under which the evidence is obtained (IAASB, 2009d, para A5). For instance, the following may increase the reliability of audit evidence: evidence that is obtained from external sources, the controls surrounding the preparation of information are working effectively, evidence obtained directly by the auditor and evidence that is in documentary format (IAASB, 2009d, para A31). The relevance of audit evidence is influenced by the purpose of the audit evidence, the assertions addressed, and the direction of testing (IAASB, 2009d, para A27).

There are different sources of audit evidence. Typically, these include accounting records, system charts, control descriptions and third-party sources which can be used to confirm balances, transactions and representations (IAASB, 2009d, para A7–A9). Various procedures can be used to test these sources (IAASB, 2009d). The testing of the audit evidence is directly linked to the audit procedures performed (Section 2.1.1). Refer to Table 5 in Section 3.1.4.

4.2 Using information produced by the entity

In terms of ISA 500, when using information produced by the entity, the auditor must evaluate whether the information is sufficiently reliable for the auditor's purpose. This will include the accuracy and completeness of the information and whether it is precise and detailed. This may be established when performing risk assessment procedures (ISA 315) or during performing tests of detail and controls (IAASB, 2009d). In some instances, the auditor may rely on the client's expert for obtaining audit evidence. This is dealt with in Chapter 15.

4.1.1 Data CAAT's

Data CAATs use the computer to test balances and transactions either through substantive analytics or recalculations. Data CAATs include extracting reports and performing procedures such as extraction of creditors lists and debtors age analysis; stratifying balances for further testing; casting Masterfile balances and extracting reports of duplicate values (Adams et al., 2020a).

4.1.2 Concerns about the quality of audit evidence

If there are inconsistencies between two sources or the auditor has doubts about the relevance and reliability of the audit evidence obtained, additional audit procedures should be performed (IAASB, 2009d, para 11). If the auditor is unable to obtain sufficient and appropriate evidence, the auditor would need to consider the impact on the audit opinion as discussed in Chapter 18.

5. Summary

- In summary, the execution of an audit commences with a thorough understanding of the client obtained by performing risk assessment procedures (Chapter 10). The objective is to assess the risk of material misstatement at the financial statement and assertion level.

- The assessed risk of misstatement informs the planned audit approach. The auditor computes the planning and performance materiality. Once materiality has been determined the auditor decides on the nature, timing, and extent of the necessary audit procedures.

- Audit procedures include tests of controls, analytical procedures and substantive tests of detail. The objective of performing audit procedures is to ensure that sufficient and appropriate audit evidence is obtained to support the audit opinion.

6. References

Abbott, L. J., Parker, S. & Peters, G. F. 2012. Internal Audit Assistance and External Audit Timeliness. *Auditing: A Journal of Practice & Theory,* 31 (4), 3–20.

Adams, Diale & Richard 2020a. *Auditing notes for South African students,* South Africa, Lexis Nexis.

Adams, A., Richard, G. & Diale, T. 2020b. *Auditing Notes for South African Students* South Africa, Lexis Nexis.

Cerbone, D. & Maroun, W. 2019. Materiality in an integrated reporting setting: Insights using an institutional logics framework. *The British Accounting Review,* In press.

Collier & Agyei-Ampomah 2008. *Management Accounting: Risk and Control Strategy,* Oxford, CIMA Publishing.

Collier & Ayei-Ampomah 2008. *Management Accounting Risk and Control Strategy,* Oxford, CIMA Publishing.

Curtis, M. B. & Borthick, A. F. 1999. Evaluation of internal control from a control objective narrative. *Journal of Information Systems,* 13 (1), 63–81.

Edgley, C. 2014. A genealogy of accounting materiality. *Critical Perspectives on Accounting,* 25 (3), 255–271.

Edgley, C., Jones, M. J. & Atkins, J. 2015. The adoption of the materiality concept in social and environmental reporting assurance: A field study approach. *The British Accounting Review,* 47 (1), 1–18.

Gray, I. & Manson, S. 2007. *The audit process: principles, practice and cases,* Cengage learning EMEA.

IAASB 2009a. International Standard on Auditing 300: Planning an audit of financial statements. International Auditing and Assurance Standards Board.

IAASB 2009b. International Standard on Auditing 320: Materaility in planning and performing an audit. International Auditing and Assurance Standards Board.

IAASB 2009c. International Standard on Auditing 330: The auditors responsibility to assessed risks. International Auditing and Assurance Standards Board.

IAASB 2009d. International Standard on Auditing 500: Audit Evidence. International Auditing and Assurance Standards Board.

IAASB 2009e. International Standard on Auditing 501: Audit evidence – specific considerations for selected items. International Auditing and Assurance Standards Board.

IAASB 2009f. International Standard on Auditing 505: External confirmations. International Auditing and Assurance Standards Board.

IAASB 2009g. International Standard on Auditing 530: Audit Sampling. International Auditing and Assurance Standards Board.

IAASB 2009h. ISA 315 R: Identifying and Assessing the Risks of Material Misstatement. *SAICA Members' Handbook.* 2009 ed. Pietermaritzburg: LexisNexis.

IAASB 2009i. ISA 320: Materiality in planning and performing an audit. *Saica Members' Handbook.* 2009 ed. Pietermaritzburg: LexisNexis.

IAASB 2009j. ISA 500 Audit Evidence. *SAICA Members' Handbook.* 2009 ed. Pietermaritzburg: LexisNexis.

IAASB 2019. International Standard on Auditing 315 (Revised 2019): Identifying and assessing the risks of material misstatement. International Auditing and Assurance Standards Board.

Jones, P. 2017. *Statistical sampling and risk analysis in auditing,* Taylor & Francis.

Knechel, W. R. & Salterio, S. E. 2016. *Auditing: Assurance and risk,* Taylor & Francis.

Lessambo, F. I. 2018. Audit Evidence and Documentation. *Auditing, Assurance Services, and Forensics.* Springer.

Marx, B., Schonfeldt, N., Van Der Watt, A., Van Dyk, V. C., Mare, D. J. & Ramuedzisi , M. T. 2014. *Fundamentals of Auditing,* LexisNexis South Africa.

Meliyev, I. I. 2018. A Quantitative Approach to Existing Issues of Audit Planning in Appropriateness and Relevance Analysis. *International Journal of Management Science and Business Administration,* 4 (3), 15–18.

Rubino, M., Vitolla, F. & Garzoni, A. 2017. How IT controls improve the control environment. *Management Research Review.*

Sardasht, M. S. & Rashedi, E. 2018. Identifying Influencing Factors of Audit Risk Model: A Combined Fuzzy ANP-DEMATEL Approach. *The International Journal of Digital Accounting Research,* 18 (24), 69–117.

Srivenkataramana, T. 2018. Application of Statistical Sampling to Audit and Control. *DHARANA-Bhavan's International Journal of Business,* 12 (1), 14–19.

Teck-Heang, L. & Ali, A. M. 2008. The evolution of auditing: An analysis of the historical development. *Journal of Modern Accounting and Auditing,* 4 (12), 1.

Wielligh, P., Prinsloo, F., Penning, G., Butler, R., Nathan, D., Kunz, R. & Moth, V. 2014. *Auditing Fundamentals in a South African context,* South Africa, Oxford University Press.

1. Introduction

ISA 600 applies to group audits, particularly, a situation in which an auditor may need to rely on the work of one or more component auditors (IAASB, 2009d, para 1). In general, a component auditor may be required to express an audit opinion on the financial statements of a component and the group engagement team may decide to use the audit evidence gathered by the component auditor to provide audit evidence for the group audit opinion (IAASB, 2009d, para 3). For example, a component set of financial statements may make up a large portion of the group's revenues, expenses, assets, and liabilities. The component auditor will audit these elements of the financial statements. The component auditor audits a large portion of the group and their opinion covers a large part of the group. The group auditor relies on this to issue their group audit opinion. Table 1 below defines key terms referred to in ISA 600.

Table 1: Definitions	
Part	**Definitions**
Component	An entity or business activity for which group or component management prepares financial information which should be included in the group financial statements.
Component auditor	An auditor who, at the request of the group engagement team, performs work on financial information related to a component for the group audit.
Group	All the components financial information of which is included in the group financial statements. A group always has more than one component.
Group audit opinion	The audit opinion on the group financial statements. Special considerations: audits of group financial statements (including the work of component auditors).
Group financial statements	Financial statements which include the financial information of more than one component. The term 'group financial statements' also refers to combined financial statements aggregating the financial information prepared by components which have no parent but are under common control.
Group-wide controls	Controls designed, implemented and maintained by group management over group financial reporting.

▶

Table 1: Definitions	
Part	**Definitions**
Significant component	A component identified by the group engagement team: • that is of individual financial significance to the group; or • because of its specific nature or circumstances is likely to include significant risks of material misstatement of the group financial statements.

(IAASB, 2009d)

2. Group audits and audit risk

Audit risk is a function of the risk of material misstatement and the possibility that the auditor does not detect the misstatement (IAASB, 2009e). In the context of a group audit, this includes the risk of a component auditor not identifying a misstatement in the financial statements of the component and the risk that the group auditor does not detect the misstatement (IAASB, 2009d, para 6). In this context, ISA 600 deals with the following:

- How to apply *ISA 220: Quality Control for an Audit of Financial Statements* (IAASB, 2009g) to ensure that, collectively, the group engagement is carried out to high standards. The group and component auditors are required to comply with the group auditor's quality control policies and procedures. This is done by way of group instructions issued to component auditors, in which certain quality control requirements are requested to be complied with and incorporated into the planning and obtaining of audit evidence.
- The group audit team is required to perform procedures over the audit evidence gathered by component auditors. These may include analytical procedures to assess whether risks identified have been addressed by the component auditor or the group auditor obtaining their own audit evidence (IAASB, 2009d).

2.1 Additional considerations for group audits

The standard outlines two primary objectives (IAASB, 2009f) and prescribes additional considerations and procedures which are discussed in detail below on page 202:

Table 2: Steps in the audit process and ISA 600

Requirements of ISA 600	Explanation
Allocation of responsibilities (ISA 600, para 11)	The responsibility for the group audit engagement needs to be clearly defined by the group engagement leader.
Client acceptance/ continuance (ISA 600, para 12–14)	The requirements and procedures related to client acceptance and continuance remain the same as for an individual audit client. The terms of the engagement must also be established in line with the requirements of ISA 210 (IAASB, 2009f).
Audit strategy and planning (ISA 600, para 15 – 16)	The group engagement team shall develop the overall group strategy and plan per the requirements of ISA 300 which will be reviewed by the group engagement partner.
Understanding the environment – the group, the component and the environment (ISA 600, para 17–20)	The group auditor shall: • Understand the group, its components, and its environment. • Understand the component auditor.
Materiality (ISA 600, para 21–23)	The group engagement team shall determine the following: • Materiality for the overall group financial statements. • Materiality for specific group accounts or transactions which may be considered higher risk. • Component materiality for component auditors who will perform an audit or review for the group audit.
Respond to assessed risk (ISA 600, para 24 – 37)	The group auditor must consider the following when responding to the assessed risks: • Significance of components because of financial contribution or because of risk. • Audit work to be performed for components depending on the significance. • The use of component auditors. • The consolidation process.

►

Table 2: Steps in the audit process and ISA 600	
Requirements of ISA 600	**Explanation**
Communication with the component auditor (ISA 600, para 40 – 41)	The group engagement team will communicate what is required from the component auditor in terms of: • The work to be performed as well as the format; • The ethical requirements; • Component materiality where applicable; • Significant risks of material misstatements at the group level that may apply to the component; and • List of related parties. The component auditor will also be required to communicate certain matters such as compliance with ethical requirements and compliance with group engagement team requirements; identification of significant cases of non-compliance; a list of uncorrected misstatements; indicators of management bias; any significant deficiencies in internal control and the component auditors' overall findings and conclusions.
Concluding (ISA 600, para 42 – 49)	The group auditor must: • Conclude on sufficiency and appropriateness of audit evidence. • Report to management/those charged with governance in compliance with ISA 260 and ISA 265.

(IAASB, 2009d)

2.2 Responsibility, acceptance, continuance, and terms of engagement

The auditor is required to prepare the terms of engagement according to ISA 210 (IAASB, 2009f) and perform a client acceptance and continuance review per ISA 220 (IAASB, 2009g). ISA 600 complements these requirements. The group engagement partner is responsible for the direction, supervision, and performance of the group audit and whether the appropriate audit report is issued (IAASB, 2009d, para 11). As a result, ISA 600 requires the group engagement audit partner to determine if sufficient appropriate evidence can be obtained about the financial information of components and the consolidation process to support an audit opinion on the group financial statements (IAASB, 2009d, para 12). Examples of matters which will be considered include:

Table 3: Additional audit requirements for group engagements	
Elements for consideration	**Explanation**
Group structures and implications for access to information	The structure of the group to assess where the consolidation takes place and how information about the consolidation process can be obtained by the group auditor.
Business models/activities	The group audit team will need to gain an understanding of the various business models and activities of the group companies. This will assist in business risk identification which will inform the risk of material misstatement assessment across the group.
Significant components	Which components are significant and where access to information is most important concerning these components.
Consolidation mechanics and related controls	The group audit team will need to understand how the audit client consolidates the group and the controls in place over the consolidation, as well as the complexity of the consolidation.
Different audit teams, as well as component auditors which belong to a different firm from the group engagement team	The identity of the different audit teams will need to be established to ensure concise and correct communication across the component audit teams.
Legal considerations (including access to information)	In terms of ISA 250, all laws and regulations applicable to the group will need to be considered by the group and component audit teams. As the group may be spread across different jurisdictions, access to information by group and component auditors must be considered. This is important as the group auditor needs to consider if sufficient and appropriate evidence can be obtained. This becomes a concern when there are restrictions to access for a significant component as it may impact the group audit opinion.

▶

Table 3: Additional audit requirements for group engagements	
Elements for consideration	**Explanation**
Changes from the prior year	An understanding will also need to be obtained if there are changes to the client for recurring engagements. For instances: • Changes in the group structure; • Changes in significant components business activities; • Changes in the structure of the board; • Changes in the financial reporting framework; and • Changes to group-wide controls.

Additional information to be included in terms of a group audit (which complements ISA 210) are provided by ISA 600, para A21 and A22. Such information includes the communication between the group auditors and the component auditors, the identification and communication of internal control deficiencies at component entities and regulatory/legal communication by relevant bodies to the group and how it should be communicated throughout the group and any restrictions imposed on the component auditors by way of laws and regulation.

If the group engagement partner, based on professional judgement, determines that a sufficient understanding of the group and components and relevant audit evidence cannot be obtained, the group engagement partner must not accept the audit engagement or should consider issuing a disclaimer of opinion in cases where it is not possible to decline the audit engagement (IAASB, 2009d, para 13).

2.3 Planning the group audit

The development of the audit strategy and audit plan in the context of a group audit, draws on similar principles which apply to the audit of a standalone audit engagement. (These principles are discussed in Chapter 13.) In the context of a group audit, ISA 600 applies the principles in ISA 315 (IAASB, 2016) at the group audit level, requiring a robust understanding of the group activities. While the entire engagement team will be involved in the process, the ultimate responsibility for the development of the audit strategy and plan remains that of the group engagement leader (IAASB, 2009d, para 15). Table 4 demonstrates how the principles which apply to a standalone audit engagement, apply in the context of a group audit.

Table 4: Link between ISA 600 and other standards.	
General	**ISA 600 – specific considerations**

ISA 315: The auditor should obtain an understanding of the entity's structure, ownership and governance, use of information technology (IT), its business model, the industry and regulatory factors, the measures used to assess performance, the applicable financial reporting framework and the accounting policies (ISA 315R, para 19 – 20) (IAASB, 2016).	• Understand the group and its components and the group-wide controls (IAASB, 2009d, para 17). Group-wide controls are discussed in more detail in the next point.
	• Understanding the group includes an understanding of both the group and the component. Some examples are provided below.
	  – The understanding of the entity's structure is important to understand the complexity of the group in terms of the type of components held (subsidiary, joint venture, associate, or an investment), the number of components and the locations. This also assists the auditor with the identification of related parties (IAASB, 2016, para A56) and (IAASB, 2009d, para A11).
	  – The IT systems. There may be service providers used, the systems may differ across components and the integration of systems (IAASB, 2016, para A56) and (IAASB, 2009d, para A11).
	  – The governance structure applicable to the group. For instance, if there are sub-committees at the component level and the role of these sub-committees. The responsibility for the financial reporting process and the approval of financial statements also have to be determined (IAASB, 2016, para A60) and if there have been any changes to the structure (IAASB, 2009d, para A11).
	  – Understanding the industry in terms of the industry and regulatory factors. The auditor will understand the industry in which the group operates to assess the risk depending on the competitive environment, supplier and customer relationships and technological developments. In terms of regulation, the impact of laws of different jurisdictions on the group where there are multiple

▶

Table 4: Link between ISA 600 and other standards.	
General	**ISA 600 – specific considerations**
	jurisdictions and industries. An example are the changes in tax regulations and the impact on the group tax figure (IAASB, 2016, para A68 – A70). – The measures used to assess financial performance at the group and component level. This will assist with determining whether there may be pressure on group and component management to achieve certain targets (IAASB, 2016, para A74 – A75). – The financial reporting framework by the group and the component including the accounting policies used (IAASB, 2016, para A82). If there are different accounting policies, there may be adjustments required on consolidation to ensure there is uniformity applied at a group level. (Refer to Section 6.) • Understand the consolidation process, including instructions issued by group management to components (IAASB, 2009d, para 17). • Consider the risk of misstatement specifically in a group context (IAASB, 2009d, para 18). • Appendix 3 of ISA 600 presents events which may result in a risk of material misstatement for group audits. The examples mentioned in Appendix 3 are obtained when the auditor gains an understanding of the group and its components. – Some examples provided in Appendix 3 which increase risk of material misstatement include a complex group structure, poor governance structures, lack of group-wide controls, abnormal related-party transactions, incomplete and unauthorised consolidation adjustments, business activities in the group which are considered high-risk and different accounting policies and year-ends in the group.

▶

Table 4: Link between ISA 600 and other standards.	
General	**ISA 600 – specific considerations**

The auditor should obtain a detailed understanding of the entity's system of internal control (ISA 315, para 21) (IAASB, 2016).	• The auditor is required to understand the group-wide controls (IAASB, 2009d, para 17).
	• Appendix 2 of ISA 600 provides examples of different control-related issues specific to consolidation/group processes (IAASB, 2009d). This includes understanding:
	  – If group and component management meet to discuss business developments.
	  – The manner in which authority and responsibility are assigned to group management and how this is monitored.
	  – The monitoring of component management and component controls by group management.
	  – The manner in which intergroup transactions are controlled, reconciled, and eliminated on consolidation.
	  – Controls over ensuring that financial information received from components is valid, accurate and complete; and
	  – The provision of a guideline which provides information regarding policies and procedures including a group financial reporting procedures manual.
	• The auditor is required to understand the consolidation process including instructions issued by group management (IAASB, 2009d, para 18).
	• To co-ordinate the consolidation process, group instructions are issued to components dealing with operational, reporting, and practical issues relating to the group (IAASB, 2009d, para A25). The group auditor should understand these instructions and consider the implications for the group audit (IAASB, 2009d, para A26).
	• Instructions are issued by group management to ensure uniformity and comparability as it specifies instructions regarding financial information, the format, accounting

►

Table 4: Link between ISA 600 and other standards.	
General	**ISA 600 – specific considerations**
	policies, reporting deadlines, and identification of related parties and intergroup transactions (IAASB, 2009d, para A24 – A25). • The group auditor will evaluate the clarity of the instructions and whether the applicable reporting framework characteristics are described, if the disclosures required are sufficient to ensure compliance with reporting standards, the identification of intercompany transactions and if the financial information is approved by component management (IAASB, 2009d, para A26).

As part of the process of understanding the client's context and assessing the risk of misstatement, the auditor should take the risk of fraud into account (IAASB, 2016). This includes a discussion of the susceptibility of the financial statements to fraud (IAASB, 2011).	• Chapter 6 provides a detailed discussion relating to fraud.
	• ISA 600 guides the assessment of fraud risk in terms of a group. Some of the factors which can be considered by the group auditor in terms of ISA 600, para A27 are listed below:
	  – Group management's assessment of the risk of material misstatement arising from fraud, the monitoring of fraud risks, and the response to fraud risks by the group.
	  – The manner in which group management identifies and responds to fraud risks in the group.
	  – If there are components subject to a higher risk of fraud.

The group auditor is also required to understand if the component auditor can be relied on (IAASB, 2009d, para 17).	The group engagement team will need to gain an understanding of the component auditor. The items which the group audit will gain an understanding of as well as how this information can be sourced is discussed in more detail in Section 6.

▶

Table 4: Link between ISA 600 and other standards.	
General	**ISA 600 – specific considerations**
ISA 320: The auditor should determine a materiality level for planning and performing the audit (IAASB, 2009b).	• Materiality levels need to be considered for both the group and for the individual components where an audit or review will be conducted (IAASB, 2009d, para 21–23). • The materiality levels are set for planning the group audit and executing the engagement. • Group materiality is used to determine the overall group strategy whereas component materiality is used for establishing the strategy at a component level. Component materiality is also used by the component auditor to evaluate uncorrected misstatements (IAASB, 2009d, para A42–A46). • It should be noted that component materiality shall be lower than materiality for the group financial statements as a whole (IAASB, 2009d, para 21–23). There can be different materiality figures across components and they need not be allocated based on a proportion of group materiality (IAASB, 2009d, para A43).
	• When determining group and component materiality, the factors mentioned in Chapter 3 relating to materiality must be considered. This includes a consideration of the benchmark to be used at the group and component level as this will be influenced by the elements of the financial statements important to users, the nature of the entity and the volatility of the benchmark (IAASB, 2009a, para A4).

(IAASB, 2009d; IAASB, 2009a; IAASB, 2011; IAASB, 2016)

3. Understanding the component auditor

As stated above, group auditors may have to rely on the work of component auditors in cases in which the group engagement team is not auditing every entity in the group. In developing the audit strategy, the group engagement partner needs to consider if reliance can be placed on the work of the component auditor and if so, to what extent (ISA 600, para 19 – 20 and para 42–45) (IAASB, 2009d). This will require, the group engagement team to gain an understanding of the component auditor. However, this is only required where the group engagement team will require the component auditor to perform work on the financial information of a component (IAASB, 2009d, para 19). Table 5 discusses the factors to consider when gaining an understanding of the component auditor.

Table 5: Considerations when understanding the component auditor	
Issues	**Detail**
The understanding and compliance of the component auditor with ethical requirements (IAASB, 2009d, para 19(a)).	The group auditor will need to assess the component auditor's independence, which will require the group engagement team to obtain a written representation by component auditors of their independence.
The component auditor's professional competence (IAASB, 2009d, para 19(b)).	The group auditor will need to obtain evidence as to the competence of the component audit firm and team. This includes whether the component auditor understands standards applicable to the audit, if any special skills are required and if the component auditor understands the financial framework (ISA 600, para A38). Often audit firms will review the work performed by the component auditor to assess this fact.
The involvement by the group auditor in work performed by the component auditor (IAASB, 2009d, para 19(c)).	The group auditor will issue group audit instructions. Such instructions can be detailed and specify what audit procedures the component auditor must perform.
The relevance of the regulatory environment in which the component auditor is auditing (IAASB, 2009d, para 19(d)).	The group auditor and component auditor obtain this understanding as part of understanding the entity and group. This is discussed in Section 4.
The adequacy of the documentation of audit work performed by the component auditor (IAASB, 2009d, para 42–45).	The group auditor will assess the sufficiency and appropriateness of the audit evidence obtained. The group auditor may perform further audit procedures if sufficient and appropriate audit evidence has not been obtained.

(IAASB, 2009d)

The following factors will influence the understanding relating to the component auditor:

- Prior association with the component auditors;
- The existence of common policies regarding audit methodologies and quality control between the group and component auditor;
- The similarity of laws and regulations which may apply to the group or jurisdiction;

- Education and training level of the component auditor team;
- Professional organisations; and
- Language and culture of the component auditor.

(IAASB, 2009d, para A33)

ISA 600, para A35 discusses how the group auditor can gain the above information. This includes, for example, requesting the component auditor to confirm the matters per para 19, visiting the component auditor to discuss the matters in para 19, and obtaining confirmation from professional bodies (IAASB, 2009d).

If there are concerns about the independence of the component auditor and/or the quality of the work performed by the component auditor, the group auditor cannot plan to place reliance on the work of the component auditor (IAASB, 2009d, para 20).

3.1 Communication with the component auditor

The group engagement team shall communicate its requirements to the component auditor on a timely basis. This communication shall set out the work to be performed, the use to be made of that work and the form and content of the component auditor's communication with the group engagement team. The group auditor must deal with the following (IAASB, 2009d, para A57–A60):

- A request that the component auditor, knowing the context in which the group engagement team will use the work of the component auditor, confirms that the component auditor will co-operate with the group engagement team.
- The ethical requirements which are relevant to the group audit and, in particular, the independence requirements which apply to the component auditor.
- In the case of an audit or review of the financial information of the component, component materiality (and, if applicable, the materiality level or levels for particular classes of transactions, account balances or disclosures) and the threshold above which misstatements cannot be regarded as clearly trivial to the group financial statements.
- Any identified significant risks of material misstatement of the group financial statements because of fraud or error which are relevant to the work of the component auditor. The group engagement team shall request the component auditor to communicate on a timely basis any other identified significant risks of material misstatement of the group financial statements caused by fraud or error in the component and the component auditor's responses to such risks.
- A list prepared by group management of related parties and any other related parties of which the group engagement team is aware. The group engagement team shall

request the component auditor to communicate timeously with related parties not previously identified by group management or the group engagement team. The group engagement team shall determine whether to identify such additional related parties to other component auditors.

It must be noted that all written communications between the group and the component auditor should be documented (IAASB, 2009d, para 50(c)). At the conclusion of the audit, the component auditor is also required to communicate with the group auditor (IAASB, 2009d, para 41). This is discussed in Section 7.

3.2 Responding to the assessed risk of material misstatement

In line with ISA 330, the group auditor is required to respond to the assessed risk of misstatement of the financial statements (IAASB, 2009c). For this purpose, it is necessary to determine the work to be performed by the group engagement team and/or the component auditors on the financial information of the components (IAASB, 2009d, para 24). Where applicable, the group engagement team must determine the extent of its involvement in the work performed by the component auditors (IAASB, 2009d). The type of work to be performed is dependent on the significance of a component. This discussion follows in Section 5.3.

3.3 Use of a component auditor

The auditor must assess each component and obtain an understanding of whether the component is significant or not (IAASB, 2009d, para 26). Significance is either due to financial size or the nature of the component because of specific risks or circumstances, for example, a highly regulated jurisdiction (IAASB, 2009d, para 27). ISA 600, para 27 and A47 provides the following guidelines when determining the significance of a component:

- The financial significance of the component.
- The identified significant risks of material misstatement of the group financial statements.
- The understanding of the component auditor.

After the group auditor has made this assessment, there is a specific approach to be followed.

This is summarised below in Table 6:

Table 6: Summary of component auditors	
Significance of component	**Response**
Significant because of financial significance	An audit of financial information on the component, using component materiality (ISA 600, para 26).
Significant because of risks of material misstatement	In terms of ISA 600 para 26 and 27, the following can be performed: An audit of financial information on the component, using component materiality. An audit of one or more account balances, transactions of disclosures which contains significant risks of material misstatement. Detailed audit procedures relating to the likely significant risks of material misstatement.
Not significant	Analytical procedures at a group level: ISA 600, para 28 & A50. Additional assessment of the adequacy of audit work : ISA 600, para 29 & A51–53.

The group auditor is required to assess the work performed by the component auditors. This is because the group auditor needs to assess what impact the component auditor's work will have on the group audit teams' planning and gathering of audit evidence.

In terms of significant components, the group auditor must, at least, be involved in the component auditors' risk assessment process to identify significant risks which may exist at the group financial statement level (IAASB, 2009d, para 30). The nature of other involvement by the group auditor may differ, but at a minimum, it will consist of the following per ISA 600, para 30:

- Discussing with the component auditor or component management business activities significant to the group.
- Discussing with the component auditor the susceptibility of the components' financial statements to material misstatement arising from fraud or error.
- Reviewing the component auditor's documentation of significant risks of material misstatement of the group financial statements.

(IAASB, 2009d)

ISA 600 para 31 and para A55 discuss the additional types of involvement which the group auditor may consider. These include:

- Meeting with the component management or component auditors to understand the component.
- Reviewing the component auditor's strategy and plan.
- Designing and performing audit procedures which are executed by the group auditor of the component auditor.
- Participating in key meetings between the component auditors and component management.

(IAASB, 2009d)

In deciding on the nature, timing, and extent of the work done on components, group-wide/ consolidation-related controls can be taken into account (IAASB, 2009c). If substantive procedures alone are insufficient/impractical or the assessed risk of misstatement includes an expectation that the relevant controls operate effectively, these controls must be tested (IAASB, 2009d, para 25). The extent of reliance on the work of component auditors, including involvement in their work, must be documented on the audit file (IAASB, 2009d, para 50).

4. Consolidation processes

As part of the response to the assessed risk of misstatement, the group or component auditor may test controls over the consolidation processes (IAASB, 2009d, para 32–37). The following needs to be considered:

- The completeness of the consolidation process (ISA 600, para 33);
- Tests over consolidation adjustments (ISA 600, para 34);
- Consistency of accounting policies and year-ends (ISA 600, para 35 and para 37); and
- Inclusion of correct component financial information (ISA 600, para 36).

Table 7 provides more detail about the consolidation considerations.

Table 7: Consolidation considerations	
Consideration	**Explanation**
Completeness of the consolidation process (ISA 600, para 33).	The group auditor will need to consider if all components have been included in the group financial statements.
Tests over consolidation adjustments (ISA 600, para 34).	The group auditor will consider if there are fraud risk factors and if there is any indication of management bias. The group auditor will consider if the adjustments reflect the underlying events, if adjustments have been authorised and if adjustments have sufficient documentation (ISA 600, para A56).
Consistency of accounting policies and year-ends (ISA 600, para 35 and para 37).	The group auditor will need to consider if consistent accounting policies by components are applied and if the year-end of components are different. If there are differences, the group auditor will need to ensure that appropriate adjustments are made where required.
Inclusion of correct component financial information (ISA 600, para 36).	The group auditor will consider whether the financial information the component auditor has reported on is the financial information incorporated in the group financial statements.

5. Communicating and concluding

The component auditor should communicate matters which are important for forming an opinion on the group financials to the group auditor. Subsequent events should also be considered when the group audit opinion is formed and as a result subsequent events testing shall be performed by the group auditor or the component auditor where an audit of the component is completed (IAASB, 2009d, para 38–39). If an audit is not completed, the component auditor should inform the group auditor of subsequent events which may require an adjustment in the group financial statements (IAASB, 2009d, para 39).

ISA 600, para 41, provides details regarding communication by the component auditor during concluding. Communication with the auditor during concluding includes communication relating to the compliance by the component auditor with ethical requirements and the group auditors requirements, indicators of management bias, a list of uncorrected misstatements, any significant deficiencies in internal control, and the component auditors overall findings (IAASB, 2009d).

The communication from the component auditor should be evaluated by the group auditor who decides on the sufficiency of the work performed and on any other actions to be taken (IAASB, 2009d, para 42–43). This includes a consideration by the group auditor of the additional procedures to perform when the work of the component auditor is deemed insufficient (IAASB, 2009d, para 43).

The group auditor must also conclude whether there is sufficient appropriate evidence to support an opinion on the group financials (IAASB, 2009d, para 44 and para A62). This includes considering the effect of uncorrected misstatements at a consolidated level and the impact of the inability to obtain sufficient and appropriate audit evidence (IAASB, 2009d, para 45). All group and component misstatements are evaluated individually and in aggregate. Once this assessment is completed, the group auditor concludes (including discussions with component auditors) on the audit opinion to be issued.

The general principles applicable for reporting and concluding on a standard audit apply in the context of group audits:

- As part of the concluding and reporting process, the group auditor considers the guidance in ISA 265 and decides whether control deficiencies are significant and should be communicated to group management and those charged with governance.
- In particular, any fraud identified at the group or component level should be communicated on a timely basis to management or those charged with corporate governance.
- In addition to the matters listed in ISA 260, ISA 600 para 49 provides items to be communicated to those charged with governance. This includes an overview of the work to be completed on components, the group engagements team involvement regarding the component and any limitations that have been noted (IAASB, 2009d).
- Statutory reporting requirements must also be taken into account (IAASB, 2009d, para 48).

6. Summary

- The chapter focused on group audit engagements and placed the group audit partner as the responsible auditor for a group of companies.
- Topics such as client acceptance and/or continuation, audit planning, understanding the group, risk assessment, the auditor's response to risk and sufficient appropriate audit evidence remain relevant for group audits.
- A group audit requires significant co-ordination in terms of different audit teams and even different audit firms. When a different audit firm is used, consideration should be given to such a firm's audit methodology and the competence of its audit teams.

- Where a group of companies stretches beyond one jurisdiction, the group audit partner should consider as part of planning the impact of different laws and regulations.

7. References

IAASB 2009a. International Standard on Auditing 320: Materaility in planning and performing an audit. International Auditing and Assurance Standards Board.

IAASB 2009b. International Standard on Auditing 320: Materiality in Planning and Performing an Audit. 2009.

IAASB 2009c. International Standard on Auditing 330: The Auditors Responses to Assessed Risks. London.

IAASB 2009d. International Standard on Auditing 600: Group Audits. London.

IAASB 2009e. ISA 200: Objective and General Principles Governing an Audit of Financial Statements. *SAICA Members' Handbook.* 2009 ed. Pietermaritsburg: LexisNexis.

IAASB 2009f. ISA 210: Agreeing to terms of audit engagements. *SAICA Members' Handbook.* 2009 ed. Pietermaritsburg: LexisNexis.

IAASB 2009g. ISA 220: Quality Control for Audits of Historical Financial Information. *SAICA Members' Handbook.* 2009 ed. Pietermaritsburg: LexisNexis.

IAASB 2011. International Standard on Auditing 240:The Auditor's Responsibilities Relating to Fraud in an Audit of Financial Statements. London.

IAASB 2016. ISA 315 R: Identifying and Assessing the Risks of Material Misstatment through Understanding the Entity and its Environment.

Chapter 15 – Placing reliance on the work of others

1. Introduction

During the audit, an auditor may be required to rely on the work of others. Reliance on others can include the use of a prior auditor's work (ISA 510) (IAASB, 2009b), reliance on management (ISA 500) (IAASB, 2009a) or an auditors' expert (ISA 620) (IAASB, 2009d) and the use of internal audit (ISA 610) (IAASB, 2009e). Although the auditor may rely on these different parties, the auditor is still responsible for ensuring that sufficient and appropriate audit evidence is gathered to support the audit opinion; the responsibility of the auditor in this regard is not diminished by relying on the work of other parties (IAASB, 2009d).

This chapter will explain the different third parties on which the auditor can rely. The chapter begins with a discussion relating to the audit of opening balances (Section 2), followed by written representations obtained from management (Section 3). Section 4 discusses the use of both a management and auditors' expert. The chapter concludes with the reliance on internal audit (Section 5).

2. Opening balances

When testing any balance, the starting point for the auditor is the opening balance of the account. If the auditors were the same in the prior year, the procedures are simple: compare the prior year closing balance with the current years' opening balance. However, if the engagement is an initial engagement, the process requires additional procedures to be performed. ISA 510 details the requirements with which the engagement team will have to comply if the audit is an initial engagement (IAASB, 2009b, para 1).

An initial audit engagement arises in two circumstances: the financial statements of the prior period were not audited, or the financial statements were audited by a predecessor auditor (IAASB, 2009b, para 4). The auditor needs to obtain sufficient audit evidence that:

- The opening balances do not contain material misstatements; and
- The opening balances reflect appropriate and consistent accounting policies.

(IAASB, 2009b, para 3)

2.1 Specific audit procedures for opening balances

If the prior period balances have been audited by a predecessor auditor, then at a minimum, the current auditor must read and review the prior year financial statements and the predecessor's audit report for any information relating to the opening balances (IAASB, 2009b, para 6).

This will include whether the prior audit opinion was modified in relation to the opening balance being audited (IAASB, 2009b, para A3). If there is a modification noted, the current auditor shall consider the impact on the risk of material misstatement in accordance with ISA 315R (IAASB, 2019, para 13). Some considerations include the reason for the modification and whether the reason for the modification still exists in the current year or whether the issue has been resolved and whether the matter is material (IAASB, 2009b, para 13). The auditor can also review the predecessor auditors' working papers to obtain evidence regarding opening balances. The adequacy of the review will be influenced by the professional competence and independence of the predecessor auditor (IAASB, 2009b, para A4).

The auditor can also perform the following procedures to ensure that the opening balances do not contain material misstatement:

- Determine if the prior periods opening balances have been correctly brought forward from the prior year (ISA 510, para 6(c)).
- Consider if audit procedures in the current year provide evidence relating to the relevant opening balances (ISA 510, para 6(c) and para A6).
    - For certain current assets and liabilities, the auditor may be able to obtain some audit evidence during the current period's audit procedures. Examples of these may include auditing the collection of accounts receivable receipts during the current period to provide comfort over the opening accounts receivable balance (ISA 510, para A6).
- Performing specific audit procedures to obtain evidence regarding opening balances.
    - For other non-current assets and liabilities such as long-term debt and property, plant and equipment the auditor may be able to obtain third party confirmation for the opening balance (ISA 510, para A7).
- Obtain evidence that the accounting policies are consistently applied (ISA 510, para 6(b)).
- If there are changes in accounting policies, the auditor will need to obtain sufficient and appropriate evidence that the change is adequately presented and disclosed in the financial statements (ISA 510, para 8).

(IAASB, 2009b)

2.2 Impact on concluding and reporting

During the concluding stage of the audit, the auditor may conclude that sufficient evidence has not been obtained regarding the opening balances and the audit opinion may need to be modified as discussed in Chapter 18 (IAASB, 2009b, para 10). The following are instances which may require a modification of the opinion:

- If the auditor is unable to obtain sufficient and appropriate evidence regarding opening balances;
- If the auditor concludes that a material misstatement exists in the opening balance;
- If the auditor concludes that the accounting policies are not consistently applied; and
- A change in accounting policy is not appropriately accounted for or not adequately presented or disclosed in terms of the financial reporting framework.

(IAASB, 2009b, para 10–12)

3. Written representations

ISA 580 deals with the auditor's responsibility to obtain written representation from management and, where appropriate, those charged with governance. Written representations are defined as 'a written statement by management provided to the auditor to confirm certain matters or to support other audit evidence. Written representations do not include financial statements, the assertions therein, or supporting books and records' (IAASB, 2009c, para 7). Written representations are considered a necessary form of audit evidence but are not considered as 'sufficient appropriate audit evidence on their own about any matters with which they deal' ((IAASB, 2009c, para 4). The fact that management has provided a reliable representation does not impact the nature and extent of other evidence which the auditor obtains (ISA 580, para 4) (IAASB, 2009c).

The objectives for the auditor are as follows:

- To obtain written representations from management or those charged with governance that they believe that they have fulfilled their responsibility for the preparation of the financial statements and completeness of the information provided to the auditor;
- To support other audit evidence relevant to the financial statements or specific assertions; and
- To respond appropriately to written representations provided by management and those charged with governance and in circumstances where written representations were not provided to the auditor.

(IAASB, 2009c, para 6)

Table 1 provides a brief explanation of the requirements stipulated in ISA 580.

Table 1 – Requirements of ISA 580	
Requirement	**Explanation**
Management from whom written representations are requested (ISA 580, para 9).	Request written representations from management with appropriate responsibilities for the financial statements and knowledge of the matters concerned.
Written representations are obtained about management's responsibilities (ISA 580, para 10–12).	The management representation letter is obtained over the following: 1. *Preparation of financial statements (ISA 580, para 10)* • Written representation detailing the fulfilment of management's responsibility for the *preparation of the financial statements* per the applicable financial reporting framework, fair representation (where applicable) as documented in terms of the audit engagement. 2. *Information provided and completeness of transactions (ISA 580, para 11)* • Management has provided the auditor with all relevant information and access to all relevant information; and • Management confirmation that all transactions have been recorded and are reflected in the financial statements. The above responsibilities will be described in the management representation letter as per the terms of the audit engagement (ISA 580, para 12).

►

Table 1 – Requirements of ISA 580	
Requirement	**Explanation**
Written representations required by other ISAs (ISA 580, para 13).	For example: • Appropriateness of accounting policies; • Matters reported in terms of the applicable accounting framework have been recognised, measured, presented or disclosed (such as plans which may affect carrying value or classification of assets or liabilities, contingent liabilities, liens or encumbrances on assets, pledged assets); • Any deficiencies in internal control of which management is aware; and • Specific audit assertions concerning judgements; and • ISA 260 requires the auditor to communicate to those charged with governance regarding the written representations which the audit has requested from management.
Date of and period(s) covered by the written representations (ISA 580, para 14).	The date should be as near as practicable to, but not after the date of the auditor's report. The written representation shall be for all the financial statements and the period referred to in the auditor's report.
Form of written representations (ISA 580, para 15).	Written representation shall be in the form of a representation letter addressed to the auditor.

In the event of the auditor having concerns about the competence, integrity, ethical values, or diligence of management, the reliability of oral and written representations needs to be assessed. Where written representations are inconsistent with other evidence, the auditor shall attempt to resolve the matter. If this cannot be resolved, the auditor will need to consider the impact of this on the reliability of representations, as well as on other audit evidence (IAASB, 2009c, para 17). This includes a consideration whether the risk assessment is appropriate and needs to be revised (IAASB, 2009c, para A23). If the auditor concludes that the written representation is not reliable, the auditor may need to consider the impact on the audit opinion (IAASB, 2009c, para 18).

In the event of management not providing the auditor with any written representation, the auditor shall discuss the matter with management, re-evaluate the integrity of management, and the effect it may have on the reliability of both written and oral representations and audit evidence in general. Lastly, the auditor will have to determine the possible effect on the opinion of the auditor's report as per ISA 705 (IAASB, 2009c, para 19). It should be noted that if management does not provide written representation or the written representation is not reliable for the responsibilities per para 10 and 11, the auditor will need to disclaim the audit opinion.

4. Using the work of an expert

The auditor may determine it necessary that expertise in other fields is required to obtain sufficient and appropriate audit evidence (IAASB, 2009d, para 7). Similarly, management may also require an expert to assist with the preparation of financial statements (IAASB, 2009a, para A35). For instance, an expert may be required for the valuation of assets, the determination of quantities or physical condition of assets, and legal opinions (IAASB, 2009d, para A1). There are two types of experts with whom the auditor will engage – the auditor's expert and management expert. The use of an auditor's expert is covered by ISA 620, and the management expert is covered by ISA 500 para 8.

Table 2 – Use of experts	
Type of expert	Explanation
Auditor's expert	An individual or organisation with expertise in a field other than accounting or auditing, whose work is used by the auditor to obtain sufficient appropriate audit evidence. This expert may be internal or external to the audit firm.
Management's expert	An individual or organisation with expertise in a field other than accounting or auditing whose work in that field is used by the entity to assist in preparing the financial statements.

(IAASB, 2009d; IAASB, 2009a)

When determining whether the work of an expert can be relied on, the auditor will consider the following:

- Competence, capabilities, and objectivity of the expert (ISA 620, para 9 and ISA 500, para 8(a));
- Obtaining and understanding of the field of expertise of the expert (ISA 620, para 10, and ISA 500, para 8(b));
- Agreement with the expert (ISA 620, para 11); and
- Evaluating the adequacy of the expert's work (ISA 620, para 12 and ISA 500, para 8(c)).

(IAASB, 2009d; IAASB, 2009a)

In the case of a management expert, the auditor will not reach an agreement with the expert as matters such as the scope of the work and the respective responsibilities will be concluded between management and the expert. However, the auditor will still be required to review the agreement to gain an understanding of these matters (IAASB, 2009a, para A46).

4.1 Competence, capabilities, and objectivity of the expert

The auditor must evaluate whether the expert has the necessary competence, capability and objectivity for the auditors' purposes (ISA 620, para 9) (ISA 500, para 8(a)) (IAASB, 2009d; IAASB, 2009a). In order to evaluate this, the auditor will need to consider the expert's professional certification and qualifications, experience, and reputation, and published papers or books written by the expert (ISA 620, para A15) (ISA 500, para A39) (IAASB, 2009d; IAASB, 2009a; Wielligh et al., 2014). The auditor will also consider whether the expert's work is subject to technical performance standards or other regulatory or industry standards (ISA 620, par A16) (ISA 500, para A40) (IAASB, 2009d; IAASB, 2009a). When evaluating objectivity, the auditor may enquire about any known interests or relationships the client has with the expert and consider what safeguards the expert implements to reduce threats to objectivity (ISA 620, para A20) (ISA 500, para A44) (IAASB, 2009d; IAASB, 2009a).

4.2 Obtaining and understanding of the field of expertise of the expert

The auditor shall obtain a sufficient understanding of the field of expertise of the auditor's expert to determine the nature, scope and objective of the expert's work and evaluate the adequacy of the work for the auditors purpose (ISA 620, para 10) (ISA 500, para 8(b)) (IAASB, 2009d; IAASB, 2009a). This includes understanding whether the expert's field of expertise is relevant to the audit, the assumptions and methods used, the models used by the expert and the sources of information used by the expert (ISA 620, para A21) (ISA 500, para A45) (IAASB, 2009d; IAASB, 2009a).

4.3 Agreement with the auditor's expert

The auditor must agree in writing the nature, scope, and objectives of the auditors' expert work (ISA 620, para 11) (IAASB, 2009d). Written instructions cover the auditor's expert terms of reference and may cover the issues listed in Table 3.

Table 3 – Auditor's expert terms of reference	
Description	**Explanation**
Nature, objective and scope of the expert's work (ISA 620, para 11(a)).	Discussions with the expert will include a discussion on relevant technical performance standards or other professional or industry requirements which the expert will follow (ISA 620, para A27).

▶

Table 3 – Auditor's expert terms of reference	
Roles and responsibilities of the auditor and the expert (ISA 620, para 11(b)).	Agreement on the respective roles and responsibilities such as the testing of source data and consent for the auditor to discuss the findings with the entity and others (ISA 620, para A28). Access to working papers will also be discussed as the expert's working paper belongs to the expert and is not part of the audit documentation unless the expert is a member of the engagement team (ISA 620, para A29).
Nature, extent, and timing of communication between the auditor and the expert, including the report to be provided (ISA 620, para 11(c)).	Effective two-way communication ensures that the expert's procedures and the audit plan integrates and also allows for changes to the expert's objectives to be made if required. The staff that will liaise with the auditor's expert to assist with timely and effective communication will also need to be identified (ISA 620, para A30).
Need for the auditor to observe confidentiality requirements (ISA 620, para 11(d)).	It is necessary for the confidentiality requirements which apply to the auditor to apply also to the auditor's expert.

(IAASB, 2009d)

4.4 Evaluating the adequacy of the expert's work

The auditor must assess the adequacy of the auditor's expert's work for the auditor's purpose (ISA 620, para 12) (ISA 500, para 8(c)). This will include:

- Assessing the relevance and reasonableness of the expert's findings or conclusions, including the consistency with other evidence. The auditor can perform procedures such as inquiries of the expert, reviewing the expert's reports and working papers, confirmation with third parties, reperforming procedures, performing detailed analytical procedures and discussing the expert's report with management (ISA 620, para A33 – A34) (ISA 500, para A49);
- The relevance and reasonableness of assumptions and methods. The auditor will consider if the assumptions appear to be generally accepted within the field and the compliance with the applicable reporting framework (ISA 620, para A35 – A37) (ISA 500, para A49); and

- Relevance, completeness and accuracy of source data. The auditor may verify the origin of the data and review the data for completeness and consistency (ISA 620, para A38 – A39) (ISA 500, para A49).

(IAASB, 2009d; IAASB, 2009a)

If the auditor deems that the auditor's expert work is not sufficient, the auditor and expert will agree on additional work to be performed, or the auditor may be required to complete additional procedures (ISA 620, para A13) (IAASB, 2009d). If sufficient and appropriate evidence is not obtained, a modified opinion may need to be issued (ISA 620, para A40) (IAASB, 2009d).

5. Reliance on internal audit

Many entities establish internal audit functions as part of their internal control and governance structures (IAASB, 2014, para 6). The dependence on internal audit is based on the nature and structure of the entity. Internal audit must be performed by an objective and competent function which applies a systematic and disciplined approach (IAASB, 2014, para 10). The external auditor's duties and obligations are not reduced by their reliance on internal audit as the external auditor has sole responsibility for the opinion issued (IAASB, 2014, para 11). The external auditor will need to determine which elements of internal audit can be relied upon (IAASB, 2014).

The external auditor shall determine whether the work of the internal audit function can be used for purposes of the audit by evaluating the following:

- The extent to which the internal audit function's organisational status and relevant policies and procedures support the objectivity of the internal auditors;
- The level of competence of the internal audit function; and
- Whether the internal audit function applies a systematic and disciplined approach, including quality control.

5.1 Using the work of internal audit

As internal audit and external audit form part of an organisation's combined assurance framework, it is vital to have continuous interaction between the two (IoDSA, 2016). Abbott et al. (2012) indicated that increased co-ordination between these functions might reduce external audit delays. External audit fees may also reduce if an organisation invests in its internal audit (Prawitt et al., 2011). Most importantly, where internal and external auditors can co-ordinate their efforts, those charged with governance can place more reliance on the functioning of an organisation's internal controls, and the quality of financial and non-financial reporting is expected to improve (IoDSA, 2016; Maroun, 2018).

ISA 610 provides guidance where external auditors expect to use the work of internal audit. The external auditor is under no obligation to use the internal auditors as part of its audit strategy nor can the use of internal audit alter or reduce the extent of audit procedures performed by external auditors (IAASB, 2014, para 3). The nature and extent to which the external auditor may place reliance on work performed by the internal auditors is dependent on the risk associated with the auditee's accounts or transactions, inherent risk considerations and the staffing of the internal audit function[1] (Bame-Aldred et al., 2012).

There are two situations in which the internal auditors can be used by external audit. Firstly, the work already performed by internal audit can be incorporated into the external audit process and results of tests performed. Alternatively, the internal audit staff can be utilised to assist in performing predefined audit procedures (IAASB, 2014, para 13). Where the audit procedures of internal audit are directed, supervised and reviewed by the external auditor, this is referred to as direct assistance (IAASB, 2014, para 14).

ISA 610 is only applicable if the external auditor determines that the work performed by internal audit is adequate for external audit purposes. Furthermore, if the work of the internal auditors is incorporated into the work of external audit, it is the responsibility of the external auditor to provide direct assistance to the internal auditors and direct, supervise and review all work performed (IAASB, 2014, para 13).

The considerations required in terms of ISA 610 include: (1) the nature and extent of reliance on the internal auditors, (2) using the work of the internal auditors, (3) determining to what extent internal auditors can be used to provide direct assistance and (4) using internal auditors to provide direct assistance.

Extent of reliance on the internal audit function
The external auditor has three choices:
- To utilise the internal audit function to perform certain audit procedures;
- To use the work already performed by the internal auditors for external audit purposes; or
- Not to use the internal audit function at all.

(IAASB, 2014).

To make this choice, the external auditor needs to consider the internal audit function as a whole. As part of the working paper file, the external auditor shall include in its documentation an evaluation of the following:

---

1   In terms of an in-house internal audit function, outsourcing or co-sourcing arrangements.

- Internal audit's organisational status, the relevant procedures, and policies which support the objectivity of internal auditors (ISA 610, para 15(a));
- The level of competence of internal audit (ISA 610, para 15(b));
- Whether or not a systematic and disciplined approach is applied by internal audit (ISA 610, para 15(c)); and
- The nature and extent of work of the internal audit function which is relevant for the external auditor's overall audit strategy and audit plan and can be relied on by the external auditor (ISA 610, para 17 – 20).

(IAASB, 2014)

If the external auditor intends to rely on the internal auditors, the external auditor will communicate with those charged with governance about how the external auditor has plans to use the work of the internal audit function (IAASB, 2014, para 20).

The external auditor may not use the internal audit function if the organisational status and supporting policies and procedures of internal audit within the business entity do not support the objectivity of internal audit. The same is true if the function lacks sufficient competence because of, for example, a lack of resources or technical knowledge or skills. It is also not possible to rely on internal audit if the function does not apply a systematic and disciplined testing approach and/or has no quality control measures in place (IAASB, 2014, para 16).

The external auditor is required to make all significant judgements in the audit to avoid excessive use of internal audit (IAASB, 2014, para 18). External audit may not use internal audit in the following instances in terms of (ISA 610, par 30):

- Areas where internal audit is expected to apply significant judgement;
- Areas where there is a high risk of material misstatement;
- Work in which the internal auditors have been involved and the findings of which have already been communicated or will be communicated to management or those charged with governance by internal audit; and
- Certain decisions made by the external auditor in accordance with the ISA's. For instance, the external confirmation process cannot be delegated to internal auditors or the discussion surrounding fraud risks.

(IAASB, 2014)

Using the work of the internal audit function

If the external auditor decides to use the work of internal audit, ISA 610 recommends the following considerations:

- The external auditor shall discuss the planned use of the internal auditors to co-ordinate activities (ISA 610, para 21). Communication between the external auditor and internal auditors is key to ensure that relevant discussions take place throughout the process (ISA 610, para A25). This includes the timing and nature of the work, extent of coverage, sampling methods, documentation of the work to be performed and review and reporting process (ISA 610, para A24);
- Read reports issued by internal audit relating to the functional area in which internal audit will be consulted to gain an understanding of the extent of audit procedures performed and the findings (ISA 610, para 22);
- Perform sufficient audit procedures on the body of work by internal audit as a whole to determine adequacy for the purpose of external audit requirements. This includes considering if the work of the IAF is properly planned, performed, supervised, reviewed, and documented. Consideration also has to be given to whether sufficient evidence has been obtained to draw reasonable conclusions and if the conclusions reached are appropriate and consistent with work performed (ISA 610, para 23);
- The nature and extent of the external auditor's audit procedures must reflect the assessment of how much judgement is involved in the area, the risk of misstatement, the extent of the internal audit functions' organisational status to support objectivity and level of competence in the selected area (ISA 610, para 24); and
- The external auditor is also required to re-perform some of the work (ISA 610, para 25). Re-performance of the work provides more persuasive evidence regarding the adequacy of the work performed by the internal auditor (ISA 610, para A30). The external auditor is not required to re-perform every area of work completed by the internal auditors but some reperformance is required (ISA 610, para A30).

(IAASB, 2014)

Determining the extent of direct assistance

In some instances, external auditors may be prohibited by law or regulations to obtain assistance from internal auditors. If not prohibited, and the external auditor is planning to use internal audit assistance directly on the external audit, the following should be considered:

- Threats to objectivity, interest and relationships of internal auditors; and
- Level of competence of internal auditors in areas selected.

(IAASB, 2014, para 28)

If external audit decides to utilise internal audit, the following must be determined when considering the nature, timing, and extent of the direction, supervision and review by the external auditor:

- The amount of judgement involved in planning and performing the relevant procedures and evaluating the audit evidence gathered (ISA 610, para 29(a));
- The assessed risk of material misstatement (ISA 610, para 29(b)); and
- The external auditor's evaluation of existence and significance of threats to the objectivity and level of competence of the internal auditors who will be assisting (ISA 610, para 29(c)).

(IAASB, 2014)

The external auditor shall not use the IAF's direct assistance when:

- Significant judgement is required within the area (ISA 610, para 30(a));
- Higher assessed risk of misstatement where judgement is required in performing audit procedures or the gathering of evidence (ISA 610, para 30(b)); and
- The area has been reviewed already by IAF and reported to those charged with governance responsibilities (ISA 610, para 30(c)).

(IAASB, 2014)

If the external auditor intends to rely on internal audit for direct assistance, the external auditor shall communicate with those charged with governance about how the external auditor plans to use the work of the internal audit function to ensure both parties reach a mutual agreement and to ensure excessive use of internal audit is avoided (IAASB, 2014, para 30).

Using internal auditors to provide direct assistance
Before using internal audit to provide direct assistance, the external auditor shall obtain:

- A written agreement obtained from the audit client that the identified internal auditors will be allowed to follow the external auditor's instructions and the client will not intervene with the work performed by the internal auditors for the external auditor for that period (ISA 610, para 33(a)); and
- Written agreement from the involved internal auditors should be obtained that all matters will be kept confidential. In turn, the internal auditor has the responsibility to inform the external auditor of any matters which may be a threat to the internal auditor's objectivity (ISA 610, para 33(b)).

(IAASB, 2014)

The external auditor shall direct, supervise, and review the work performed by the internal auditors per ISA's. Further, the direction, supervision, and review by the external auditor shall be sufficient for the external auditor to conclude that sufficient and appropriate audit evidence has been obtained by the internal auditor to justify the conclusions reached (IAASB, 2014, para 34).

6. Summary

- The external auditor may rely on different parties while conducting the audit. However, the responsibility for the opinion on the financial statement rests with the external auditor.
- In terms of opening balances, when there is a new client or a first-time audit the auditor will need to obtain sufficient and appropriate evidence that the opening balances do not contain misstatement and that consistent accounting policies have been applied. ISA 510 guides to obtain sufficient and appropriate audit evidence regarding opening balances.
- The auditor will need to obtain a management representation letter in some instances. ISA 580 discusses the representation to obtain, from whom to obtain the representation, the date, the contents, as well as the impact when there are doubts over the representation on the audit.
- ISA 500 and ISA 620 provide guidance when an auditor is considering relying on a management expert (ISA 500) or an auditor's expert (ISA 620) to obtain evidence. The standards guide the auditor about what should be complied with before reliance can be placed.
- Lastly, ISA 610 provides the auditor with guidance regarding incorporating internal audit within the audit plan to obtain sufficient and appropriate evidence.

7. References

Abbott, L. J., Parker, S. & Peters, G. F. 2012. Internal audit assistance and external audit timeliness. *Auditing: A Journal of Practice & Theory,* 31 (4), 3–20.

Bame-Aldred, C. W., Brandon, D. M., Messier Jr, W. F., Rittenberg, L. E. & Stefaniak, C. M. 2012. A summary of research on external auditor reliance on the internal audit function. *Auditing: A Journal of Practice & Theory,* 32 (sp1), 251–286.

IAASB 2009a. International Standard on Auditing 500: Audit Evidence. International Auditing and Assurance Standards Board.

IAASB 2009b. International Standard on Auditing 510: Initial audit engagements – opening balances. International Auditing and Assurance Standards Board.

IAASB 2009c. International Standard on Auditing 600: Group Audits. London.

IAASB 2009d. International Standard on Auditing 620: Using the work of an auditor's expert.

IAASB 2009e. ISA 610 Using the Work of Internal Auditors. *SAICA Members' Handbook.* 2009 ed. Pietermaritsburg: LexisNexis.

IAASB 2014. International Standard on Auditing 610: Using the work of internal auditors. International Auditing and Assurance Standards Board.

IAASB 2019. International Standard on Auditing 315 (Revised 2019): Identifying and assessing the risks of material misstatement. International Auditing and Assurance Standards Board.

IoDSA 2016. King IV Report on Corporate Governance. The Institute of Directors in South Africa

Maroun, W. 2018. Modifying assurance practices to meet the needs of integrated reporting: The case for "interpretive assurance". *Accounting, Auditing & Accountability Journal,* 31 (2), 400–427.

Prawitt, D. F., Sharp, N. Y. & Wood, D. A. 2011. Reconciling archival and experimental research: Does internal audit contribution affect the external audit fee? *Behavioral Research in Accounting,* 23 (2), 187–206.

Wielligh, P. v., Prinsloo, F., Penning, G., Butler, R., Nathan, D., Kunz, R. & Moth, V. 2014. *Auditing Fundamentals in a South African context,* South Africa.

1. Introduction

Accounting estimates are made by management based on unobservable data resulting in inherent subjectivity. This requires management to select and apply a method using assumptions and data in the calculation of an estimate. Due to methods and assumptions selected by management, coupled with the level of complexity, inherent subjectivity and management bias may increase the risk of material misstatement. Therefore, the complexity of the estimate calculation impacts on the auditor's risk assessment procedures and the risk of material misstatement assessment (IAASB, 2018, para 2–3). ISA 540R provides the auditor with robust guidance regarding the audit of estimates to ensure audit quality is achieved (KPMG, 2018).

This chapter discusses the nature of estimates (Section 1), followed by the requirements of ISA 540R (Section 2). Section 2 looks at the risk assessment procedures to be performed by the auditor relating to estimates, the auditor's response to the risk, and the auditor's conclusion. Section 3 discusses the application of ISA 540R in the context of certain accounting standards.

2. Nature of estimates

Estimates are a monetary amount for which measurement in terms of a financial reporting framework is subject to estimation uncertainty. The estimates that an entity has to make is dependent on the nature of the entity, the environment in which an entity operates in and the transactions entered into (IAASB, 2019a). Estimates comprise three components namely, methods, assumptions, and data (IAASB, 2018, para A2 – A6). Table 1 details the components of estimates:

Table 1 – Components of estimates	
Component	**Explanation**
Methods (ISA 540R, para A2).	• A method is a measurement technique used by management to develop the accounting estimate (ISA 540R, para A2); • Management uses a model that involves assumptions and data to apply the method developed (ISA 540R, para A2); and • Consideration needs to be given as to whether methods are prescribed for example by a reporting framework (ISA 540R, para A38) or if it is self-developed and the industry norms (IAASB, 2019a).

▶

234

Table 1 – Components of estimates	
Component	**Explanation**
Assumptions (ISA 540R, para A3).	• Assumptions involve judgement regarding matters such as the use of an interest or discount rate and can be selected from a range of alternatives (ISA 540R, para A3); and • An assumption is considered to be a significant assumption if a reasonable variation in the assumption would materially affect the measurement of the assumption (ISA 540R, para A42).
Data (ISA 540R, para A4–A6).	• Data can be obtained through direct observation or from an external third-party (ISA 540R, para A4); • Data may include prices agreed in market transactions, operating quantities, or forward-looking information (ISA 540R, para A5); and • Consideration needs to be given to the nature, source, accuracy, reliability, completeness, integrity, and complexity of the data used (IAASB, 2019a).

(IAASB, 2019a, IAASB, 2018)

Tables 2 indicates the inherent risk factors which will impact the auditor's nature, timing, and extent of risk assessment and further audit procedures:

Table 2 – Inherent risk factors	
Inherent risk factors	**Explanation**
Level of uncertainty (estimation uncertainty) (ISA 540R, para 4).	• Estimation uncertainty is the susceptibility to an inherent lack of precision in measurement (ISA 540R, para 12); • This may arise because of constraints on the availability of knowledge or data (KPMG, 2018); and • The greater an estimate is subject to estimation uncertainty, the higher the risk of material misstatement and the more persuasive evidence will be required (ISA 540R, para A113).
Complexity (ISA 540R, para 4).	• The models, methods, or data, which are required for the estimates process may be complex (KPMG, 2018); and • The greater the complexity levels in the method and models, this will require higher professional scepticism and the use of experts may be required (Refer to Chapter 15) (KPMG, 2018).

▶

Table 2 – Inherent risk factors	
Inherent risk factors	**Explanation**
Subjectivity (ISA 540R, para 4).	• Subjectivity relates to inherent limitations in terms of the knowledge or data required for the estimation process (KPMG, 2018); and • The degree of subjectivity associated with an accounting estimate influences the susceptibility of the accounting estimate to misstatement due to management bias or fraud (ISA 540R, para A79).
Other inherent risk factors (ISA 540R, para 4).	• This includes, for example, the risk of material misstatement that arises due to management bias, fraud, or changes in financial reporting requirements (KPMG, 2018).

(KPMG, 2018, IAASB, 2018)

Given the judgement that management may use and the variation in terms of model complexities, estimates may require more extensive procedures from the auditor (Sharp, 2020, KPMG, 2018). There may, however, be some estimates where the estimation uncertainty, complexity, or subjectivity are not very high and therefore the procedures and level of work required may not be extensive (KPMG, 2018). Given the inherent risk factors, the auditor is required to exercise professional scepticism and as the uncertainty, complexity, and subjectivity levels increase, the auditor is required to exercise greater professional scepticism (IAASB, 2018, para 8). Professional scepticism is extremely important as the auditor is required to reflect on the audit work performed relating to estimates to ensure the risk assessment, audit evidence and conclusions reached are appropriate(Sharp, 2020).

3. Auditor's requirements in terms of ISA 540R

The objective of ISA 540R is for the auditor to obtain sufficient appropriate audit evidence whether accounting estimates and related disclosures in financial statements are reasonable in the context of the applicable financial reporting framework (IAASB, 2018, para 10–11). The auditor will gain an understanding of the entity, complete a risk assessment, conclude if there is a significant risk, test the operating effectiveness of controls if applicable, complete applicable substantive procedures, and consider the disclosure of estimates (IAASB, 2019c). This is what has been explained in Chapter 10 (Risk assessment procedures), Chapter 11 (Understanding the entity), Chapter 12 (Overall and assertion level), and Chapter 13 (Response).

ISA 540R applies to all estimates from complex estimates to simple estimates (KPMG, 2018). As a result, the concept of 'scalability' is included in ISA 540R and this considers the fact that the estimation uncertainty, subjectivity, and complexity will vary amongst estimates (KPMG, 2018). This will influence the risk assessment and the audit approach adopted for estimates (KPMG, 2018).

When obtaining audit evidence relating to estimates, the auditor is required to comply with ISA 500 (IAASB, 2018, para 30) (Refer to Chapter 13). For instance, information may have been produced by the entity, prepared by management experts, or obtained from external sources (IAASB, 2018, para A126). As mentioned in ISA 500, the auditor will need to ensure that evidence obtained is reliable which is influenced by the source, nature, and circumstances of how information is obtained (IAASB, 2018, para A127). The auditor may also need to consider if an entity uses a service organisation when making accounting estimates as consideration will be given to ISA 402 – Audit Considerations Relating to an entity using a service organisation (IAASB, 2018, para A132).

Table 3 – Table 8 includes the requirements that the auditor will consider when obtaining sufficient and appropriate audit evidence regarding estimates. Where there is a link between ISA 540R and other ISA's, the link is described in the tables as well. Figure 1 illustrates an overview of the auditor's requirements per ISA540R. Each of these aspects is addressed in more detail in the applicable table.

Figure 1 – Overview of auditor's requirements

Risk assessment procedures and related activities:
- Obtain an understanding of the entity and its environment.
- Obtain an understanding of the entity's internal control related to the entity's accounting.
- Retrospective adjustment and consideration of the use of experts.

Identifying and assessing the risks of material misstatement:
- Separate assessment of inherent and control risk completed by the auditor.
- Consider if the identified risks of material misstatement are considered significant risks.

Response to assessed risks of material misstatements:
- Test of controls & substantive procedures.
- Evaluate the sufficiency and appropriateness of audit evidence.

Concluding on the evidence obtained and impact on the audit opinion:
- Inability to obtain sufficient and appropriate audit evidence.
- Determine whether accounting estimates are misstated.

Communication:
- Written communication with those charged with governance/ management.

Table 3 describes the risk assessment procedures that the auditor will perform to gain an understanding of estimates. The risk assessment process followed is summarised in Table 3.

Table 3 – Risk assessment procedures	
ISA	**Discussion**
Risk assessment procedures and related activities (ISA 315R, para 19–27) and (ISA 540R, para 13 – 15)	
The entity and its environment (ISA 540R, para 13 (a) – (d))	
<u>Obtain an understanding of the entity and its environment</u>, including the entity's internal control related to the entity's accounting estimates (ISA 540R, para 13) (ISA 315R, para 19–20).	• The normal ISA 315R requirements apply to estimates. • The auditor needs to understand the entity's transactions, events, and conditions which may result in estimates or changes to estimates in terms of the applicable financial reporting framework (ISA 540R, para 13(a)). ISA 540R focuses on understanding the drivers of risk relating to an estimate and therefore requires the auditor to gain an understanding of the entity and its environment (KPMG, 2018). • The requirements of the applicable financial reporting framework relating to accounting estimates in terms of measurement, recognition, and disclosure and how the requirements apply to the estimates (ISA 540R, para 13(b)). The auditor will gain an understanding of the financial reporting framework that prescribes specific criteria, methods, or disclosure (ISA 540R, para A24 – A25)). • Regulatory factors relevant to the entity's accounting estimates (ISA 540R, para 13(c)). • Nature of the accounting estimates and related disclosures that the auditor expects based on the understanding of para 13(a) – 13(c) (ISA 540R, para 13(d)). • The procedures performed by the auditor to gain an understanding is influenced by the above factors. For instance, an entity may have few transactions or there may be no regulatory factors or the business may be simple. In this case, the risk assessment procedures may be less extensive (ISA 540R, para A20 – A22).

▶

Table 3 – Risk assessment procedures	
ISA	**Discussion**
The entity's internal controls (ISA 540R, para 13 (e) – (j))	

Obtain an understanding of the entity and its environment, including the entity's internal control related to the entity's accounting estimates (ISA 540R, para 13) (ISA 315R, para 21–26).	• The **nature and extent of governance** that is in place over management's process relating to estimates (ISA 540R, para 13(e)). Consideration will be given to whether those charged with governance understand the risks applicable, if they have the skills and knowledge to understand what influences the estimate and if those charged with governance oversee managements' estimate process (ISA 540R, para A28 – A30) (ISA 315R, para 21).
	• Managements identification regarding the need for specialised knowledge or skill such as the use of an expert (ISA 540R, para 13(f)).
	• **How the entity's risk assessment process identifies and responds to risks arising from estimates** (ISA 540R, para 13(g)). The auditor will consider how management addresses the susceptibility of the estimate to management bias and fraud. Factors that the auditor will consider include, the attention that management gives to the estimate, the review process relating to estimates, how management identifies incentives or motives for bias and how management monitors changes to methods, assumptions and data (ISA 540R, para A32– A33) (ISA 315R, para 22).
	• The entity's **information system related to estimates** such as:
	  – The transactions or balances that contain significant estimates (ISA 540R, para 13(h)(i)).
	  – How management **identifies and selects** the methods, assumptions, and data required for the estimates (ISA 540R, para 13(h)(ii)(a)).
	  – The auditor will consider if there is a change to these components and if this change is appropriate. Similarly, if there are no changes the auditor will consider if the current circumstances support no changes to be made (ISA 540R, para A36 – A37).

►

Table 3 – Risk assessment procedures	
ISA	**Discussion**
	– In terms of the **model selected** the auditor will need to obtain an understanding of the model used. This includes how management selected the model, the validation of the model such as the mathematical integrity, the logic of the model, the appropriateness, accuracy, and completeness of the data used, the robustness of the model to change and the documentation of the model in terms of limitations, data, assumptions, and validations performed (ISA 540R, para A39, and para A99). – Regarding the **assumptions**, the auditor will need to understand the justification for management's assumptions, management's assessment of the accuracy and completeness of assumptions, applicable financial reporting requirements, how management determines the consistency of the assumptions with each other, with the entity and with other matters such as the interest rate or regulatory factors (ISA 540R, para A40). – In terms of **inactive or illiquid markets,** the auditor will need to consider if management's adaption of the method is appropriate; if suitable skills and knowledge were used and the performance of sensitivity analysis to determine the range of outcomes (ISA 540R, para A43). – In terms of gaining an understanding of the data selected and used, the auditor will consider nature and source of the data, how management evaluates the appropriateness, accuracy, and completeness of data, the consistency of data used and how the integrity of data is maintained (ISA 540R, para A44). – The information system is discussed in ISA 315R, para 25.

▶

Table 3 – Risk assessment procedures	
ISA	**Discussion**

	– Managements **understanding of the degree of estimation uncertainty** (ISA 540R, para 13(h)(ii)(b)). The auditor will consider, if management, for instance, considered different methods, assumptions, and data inputs and if management performed a sensitivity analysis to understand the impact of different estimate components (ISA 540R, para A45). The applicable reporting framework may require specific disclosure regarding estimation uncertainty (ISA 540R, para A48–A49), which the auditor will need to consider when auditing the estimate.
	    – How management addresses the estimation uncertainty which includes **selecting a point estimate** (ISA 540R, para 13(h)(ii)(c)). The point estimate is the amount selected by management for recognition or disclosure in the financial statements (ISA 540R, para 12(e)).
	    – Refer to ISA 540R, Para 16 for the impact that the estimation uncertainty will have on the auditor's identification and assessment (Refer to Section B of the table under the heading 'Identification and assessment of risk' for a further discussion).
	• **Control activities** relevant to the audit over managements process for making accounting estimates (ISA 540R, para 13(i)) (ISA 315R, para 24).
	    – When gaining an understanding, the auditor will consider the review and approval of estimates by management, segregation of duties between those approving the estimates, and those committing the entity to the transactions and the effectiveness of the design of controls (ISA 540R, para A51).

►

Table 3 – Risk assessment procedures	
ISA	**Discussion**
	– The auditor will also need to consider if extensive information technology (IT) is used for estimates as the auditor needs to consider the general and application controls around the estimates process. This includes if the information system can process large volumes of data if the design of models are reviewed, the completeness and accurate extraction of data, managements process regarding access to change and maintenance of individual models and controls over the transfer of information as well as journal entries (ISA 540R, para A50 – A54). • How management **reviews and responds** to the outcome of previous estimates (retrospective review) (ISA 540R, para 13(j)).
Other activities when performing risk assessment procedures	
Retrospective adjustment performed by the auditor (ISA 540R, para 14).	• A retrospective review of significant accounting estimates is required in terms of ISA 240 para 33(b)(ii) (IAASB, 2009) • If management completes a retrospective review it will assist the auditor in identifying the effectiveness of management's prior estimation process, information regarding the complexity or estimation uncertainty relating to estimates and information regarding the susceptibility of the estimate to management bias (ISA 540R, para A55). • A difference between an estimate and the amount recognised does not automatically mean that a misstatement exists. The auditor will need to assess the difference to determine whether a misstatement exists or not (ISA 540R, para A60).

▶

Table 3 – Risk assessment procedures	
ISA	**Discussion**
The auditor will need to consider whether the engagement team requires specialised knowledge or skills (ISA 540R, para 15).	• The auditor will consider if specialised skills or knowledge is required to understand the estimate, identify, and assess the risks of material misstatement, respond to the risks, and conclude on the estimate (ISA 540R, para 15). • Factors that the auditor will consider include, the degree of estimation uncertainty, the complexity of the method used, the complexity of the financial reporting frameworks, the degree of judgement for data and assumptions, and the complexity of the IT system used for estimates (ISA 540R, para A61). • The auditor may require the use of an expert, for instance, estimates involving expected credit loss allowances or insurance contract liability (ISA 540R, para A62 – A63). Refer to Chapter 15 for more guidance on the use of experts.

(IAASB, 2018, IAASB, 2019b, IAASB, 2019c, KPMG, 2018, IAASB, 2019e, IAASB, 2009)

Once the auditor gains an understanding of the entity and its environment, including internal control, the auditor is required to identify and assess the risks of material misstatement, which is explained in Table 4. This is important as the auditor's response is dependent on this assessment.

Table 4 – Identifying and assessing risks of material misstatement	
ISA	**Discussion**
Identifying and assessing the risks of material misstatement (ISA 315R, para 28–37) and (ISA 540R, para 16–17)	
Identifying and assessing risks of material misstatement	
The auditor is required to make a separate assessment of inherent and control risk (ISA 540R, para 16) (ISA 315R, para 31–34).	• An important aspect of ISA 540R is that the auditor is required to conduct a separate assessment of inherent risk and control risk when assessing the risk of material misstatement (ISA 540R, para 4 and para 6).

▶

Table 4 – Identifying and assessing risks of material misstatement	
ISA	**Discussion**
	• The assessment of inherent risk depends on the extent that the inherent risk factors (Table 2) impact the likelihood and magnitude of misstatement (KPMG, 2018). Additional inherent risk factors to consider is the change in the financial reporting framework which may also cause the components of estimates to change as well as the susceptibility to misstatement due to management bias or fraud ISA 540R, para A8 – A9).
	• As this assessment will differ amongst estimates, ISA 540R includes the concept of 'the spectrum of inherent risk' (ISA 540R, para 4 and para A66) (KPMG, 2018, IAASB, 2018). As included in ISA 315R, para A220, the determination regarding the spectrum of inherent risk is a matter of professional judgement.
	• Depending on where the risk assessment falls on the spectrum, this influences the audit procedures to be completed (Sharp, 2020). The higher the inherent risk on the spectrum, the more persuasive evidence is required to conclude that the estimate is reasonable (ISA 540R, para 18, para A68 – A69) (Sharp, 2020). For estimates that fall on the higher end of the spectrum, the exercise of professional scepticism becomes even more vital (ISA 540R, para A69).
	• Events occurring after the date of financial statements may provide additional information that can impact the auditor's assessment of risk and the testing to be performed (ISA 540R, para A70). Refer to Chapter 17 for more information relating to subsequent events and the impact on the audit.
	• Considerations taken into account for the assessment of inherent risk could be:
	– The degree to which an accounting estimate is subject to estimation uncertainty (ISA 540R, para 16(a)). When considering estimation uncertainty, the auditor will consider the following (ISA 540R, para A72):

▶

Table 4 – Identifying and assessing risks of material misstatement	
ISA	**Discussion**
	– If the financial reporting framework requires a method that has a high level of estimation uncertainty, for example, if unobservable inputs are used or the use of assumptions requires forward-looking forecasts and therefore, there is a high level of estimation uncertainty.
	– The business environment may also have an impact, for instance, if the market experiences uncertainty or disruptions.
	– The possibility of management obtaining precise information relating to a present condition or about the incidence and impact of future conditions.
	– The degree to which the selection and application of the **method, model, assumptions, and data** are subjected to complexity and subjectivity (ISA 540R, para 16(b)(i)):
	▪ The auditor may consider if management used specialised skills for the model which may indicate complexity. If management developed a complex model without having sufficient experience or uses a model that is not common or established, it may indicate that the susceptibility to risk is higher (ISA 540R, para A76).
	▪ The auditor also needs to consider the complexity in terms of how complex the process is to derive the data, the reliability of the data, the complexity of maintaining the integrity of the data, and if there is a need to interpret complex contractual terms (ISA 540R, para A77).
	▪ Regarding subjectivity, if the financial reporting framework does not specify the methods, valuation approach, and concepts, this may increase subjectivity (ISA 540R, para A78).

▶

Table 4 – Identifying and assessing risks of material misstatement	
ISA	**Discussion**
	– The degree to which **management's point estimate** is subjected to complexity and subjectivity (ISA 540R, para 16(b)(ii)). If there is more subjectivity this may result in a large variety of outcomes which may result in management selecting a point estimate that is influenced by bias and is therefore misstated (ISA 540R, para A79). The auditor would need to consider such circumstances when planning the audit. • ISA 540R, para A67 provides examples that may impact the inherent risk assessment. In terms of the expected credit loss model, the model may use a complex set of data relating to historical data and future developments which may result in significant estimation uncertainty and significant judgements. Relating to the inventory obsolescence provision, there may be little subjectivity or estimation uncertainty although the systems may be complex. There may be accounting estimates that are not complex but may require significant judgement. • Control risk needs to be assessed to address the inherent risks at the assertion level. The auditor needs to consider the design of the controls that **the auditor intends to place reliance on to ensure the controls address the inherent risk** (ISA 540R, para A10) (ISA 315R, para 34). • If the auditor does not intend to rely on controls as part of the audit approach for estimates, the assessment of the risk of material misstatement for estimates will be the same as the assessment of inherent risk (ISA 315R, para 34).
Auditor to consider if the identified risks of material misstatement are considered significant risks (ISA 540R, para 17) (ISA 315R, para 32).	• The auditor will need to apply judgement to consider if the risks that have been identified and assessed for the estimate are significant risks (ISA 540R, para 17). • A significant risk may be considered where the assessed risks of material misstatement are close to the upper end of the spectrum (ISA 315R, para A220).

▶

Table 4 – Identifying and assessing risks of material misstatement	
ISA	**Discussion**
	• If the auditor considers the estimate to be **a significant risk**, the auditor is required to understand the entity's controls including control activities relevant to the risk (ISA 540R, para 17) (IAASB, 2019c)(ISA 315R, para 26(a)(i)).

(IAASB, 2019e, IAASB, 2019c, IAASB, 2019b, IAASB, 2018)

Table 5 explains the auditor's response to the assessed risk of material misstatement. The auditor will either follow a combined approach or a substantive approach as explained in ISA 330. In terms of the substantive approach, ISA 540R explains three approaches that can be followed by the auditor which are explained in the table. This includes obtaining audit evidence from events occurring up to the date of the auditor's report, testing how management made the accounting estimate and developing an auditor's point estimate or range.

Table 5 –Response to the assessed risks of material misstatement	
ISA	**Discussion**
c. Response to assessed risks of material misstatements (ROMM) (ISA 330, para) and (ISA 540R, para 16 – 17)	
Test of controls	
7. Test of controls (ISA 540R, para 19) (ISA 330, para 8). *For risks identified as significant risks and those not identified as significant risks.*	• The auditor will only design and perform tests of controls if the auditor's risk assessment includes an expectation that the controls are working effectively **or** if substantive procedures cannot provide sufficient and appropriate evidence (ISA 540R, para 19) (ISA 330, para 8). • The greater the reliance that the auditor places on the effectiveness of a control, the more persuasive evidence will be required (ISA 540R, para 19) (ISA 330, para 9). This may influence the nature and quantity of evidence that the auditor will obtain (ISA 540R, para A83). • When considering relying on controls, the auditor will consider the nature and volume of transactions, the effectiveness of the design of controls, the monitoring of controls, the competency of those involved in control activities and the evidence and frequency of the performance of control activities (ISA 540R, para A86).

►

Table 5 –Response to the assessed risks of material misstatement	
ISA	**Discussion**
8. Specific requirements for significant risks (ISA 540R, para 20) (ISA 330, para 15 and para 21).	• If an estimate is considered a significant risk, the auditor will have to **test controls in the current period,** only if reliance will be placed on the internal controls (ISA 540R, para 20) (ISA 330, para 15); and • If the procedures are only substantive procedures, **tests of details must be performed** (ISA 540R, para 20) (ISA 330, para 21). The tests of detail performed are included in ISA 540R, para 18 which is discussed next (ISA 540R, para A90).
Substantive Procedures (Tests of details) (ISA 540R, para 18)	
9. Design and perform further audit procedures (ISA 540R, para 18) (ISA 330, para 6 – para 7).	• The auditor will consider the assessed risks of material misstatement and the reason for the assessment when designing further procedures (ISA 540R, para 18) (ISA 330, para 7(a)). • The higher the risk of material misstatement, the more persuasive evidence will be obtained (ISA 540R, para 18) (ISA 330, para 7(b)). • It is important to note that irrespective of the assessed risk of material misstatement, the auditor must perform substantive procedures for each material class of transaction, account balance, and disclosure (ISA 540R, para 18) (ISA 330, para 18). • There are three testing approaches which the auditor may use to conduct further audit procedures (ISA 540R, para 18). 　1. Obtain audit evidence from events occurring up to the date of the auditor's report (ISA 540R, para 21). 　2. Test how management made the accounting estimate (ISA 540R, para 22–27). 　3. Develop an auditor's point estimate or range (ISA 540R, para 28–29). • Any of the above testing approaches can be used by the auditor either individually or in combination (ISA 540R, para A81).

▶

Table 5 –Response to the assessed risks of material misstatement	
ISA	**Discussion**
9.1 Approach 1 Obtain audit evidence from events occurring up to the date of the auditor's report (ISA 540R, para 21).	• If the audit approach includes obtaining evidence from events occurring up to the date of the auditor's report, the auditor shall evaluate whether audit evidence is sufficient and appropriate to address risks of material misstatement relating to the accounting estimates (ISA 540R, para 21). • An example of this could be where a discontinued line of inventory is sold after year-end, and this may provide information regarding the net realisable value of inventory at year-end (ISA 540R, para A91). • If the auditor does not intend on using this approach, the auditor is still required to consider if the impact of events between the date of financial statements and the date of the audit report are correctly identified and accounted for in the financial statements (ISA 560, para 6 and para 8).

9.2 Approach 2 – Test How Management Made the Accounting Estimate (ISA 540R, para 22).	• When the auditor tests how management makes the estimates, the auditor is required to obtain sufficient and appropriate audit evidence regarding the risk of material misstatement related to:
	   – The selection and application of the methods, significant assumptions, and the data (ISA 540R, para 22(a)).
	   – How management selected the point estimate and developed related disclosures about estimation uncertainty (ISA 540R, para 22(b)).
	
	• The method of testing management's process may be applicable when the auditor's review of the estimate process based on prior experience indicates the process is appropriate, the financial reporting framework specifies how management should make the estimate or the accounting estimate is derived from routine processing of data or the estimate is based on a large population of similar items (ISA 540R, para A94).

►

Table 5 –Response to the assessed risks of material misstatement	
ISA	**Discussion**

Process the auditor will follow when adopting **Approach 2**	• When adopting Approach 2 the auditor will be required to consider the components of estimates, **namely the methods, assumptions, and data**, that are used by management. The following will need to be considered by the auditor:
	  – Whether the methods, significant assumptions and data **are appropriate** in the context of the applicable financial reporting framework (ISA 540R, para 23(a), 24(a) and 25(a)).
	  – Consider and address whether judgments made in selecting methods, significant assumptions, and data give rise to **indicators of possible management bias**. (IAASB, 2019d) (ISA 540R, para 23(b), 24(b) and 25(b)).
	  – Address whether calculations are applied correctly and are accurate (ISA 540R, para 23(c)).
	  – Address whether, when complex modelling is involved, judgments have been applied consistently and model design meets the requirements of the financial reporting and if adjustments to output are consistent with the measurement objectives (ISA 540R, para. 23(d)).
	  – Address whether the integrity of significant assumptions and data are maintained in applying the method (ISA 540R, para. 23(e)).
	  – Address whether significant assumptions are consistent with each other (ISA 540R, para 24(c)). Refer to Section 9.2.4 and ISA 540R, para 24(c) for more detail.
	  – Address whether, when applicable, management has the intent to carry out specific courses of action and can do so (ISA 540R, para 24(d)).
	  – Address whether the data is relevant and reliable in the circumstances (ISA 540R, para 25(c)).
	  – Address whether the data has been appropriately understood or interpreted by management, including contractual terms (Para. 25(d)).
	• The above considerations will be discussed next.

►

Table 5 –Response to the assessed risks of material misstatement	
ISA	**Discussion**

9.2.1 Consideration of whether the **methods, significant assumptions, and data are appropriate** in the context of the applicable financial reporting framework (ISA 540R para 23(a), 24(a) and 25(a))	• When there are changes to the **methods, assumptions, and data,** the auditor needs to consider if this is justified. If the change is not justified by a change in circumstances or new information or if the auditor notes significant inconsistencies with the assumptions, the auditor will need to discuss the concerns with management (ISA 540R, para A95).
	• Arbitrary changes may result in inconsistent financial statements over time and could be an indicator of management bias or possible misstatements (ISA 540R, para A97).
	• When considering if the **method (par 23(a)), assumptions (para 24(a)) and data (par 25(a)) are appropriate** including applicable changes the auditor will consider:
	  – If managements rationale for the selection of the components is appropriate (ISA 540R, para A97, para 102, and A106).
	  – If the method is appropriate given the requirements of the financial reporting framework, industry requirements, and the environment the company operates in. If management has used different methods that result in different estimates of how these differences were reconciled (ISA 540R, para A97, para 102, and A106).
	  – If changes made to the components are based on new circumstances or new information (ISA 540R, para A97, para 102 and A106).

9.2.2 Consider and address whether judgments made in selecting methods, significant assumptions, and data give **rise to indicators of possible management bias**.	• Management bias may be difficult to detect, however, examples of management bias may be the selection of assumptions that yield a favourable estimate for management or management's selection of a point estimate that indicates patterns of optimism or pessimism (ISA 540R, para A134). • When the auditor identifies indicators of management bias, the auditor may need to have further discussions with management (ISA 540R, para A96). The auditor shall consider the impact on the audit (ISA 540R, para 32). This includes a consideration of whether the risk assessment and response remains appropriate and if the financial statements are free from material misstatement (ISA 540R, para A135).

▶

Table 5 –Response to the assessed risks of material misstatement	
ISA	**Discussion**
(IAASB, 2019c) (ISA 540R, para 23(b), 24(b) and 25(b)).	• The auditor will need to consider if sufficient and appropriate evidence has been obtained regarding the methods, assumptions, and data (ISA 540R, para A96). • If there is an intention to mislead, management bias will be considered fraudulent (ISA 540R, para 32).
9.2.3 Further considerations relating to the method are as follows: Address whether: • **Calculations** are applied in **accordance with the method and are accurate** (ISA 540R, para 23(c)). • When complex modelling is involved, **judgments have been applied consistently** and model design meets reporting requirements/adjustments to output are consistent with the measurement objective (ISA 540R, para. 23(d)). • The **integrity of significant assumptions and data** are maintained in applying the method (ISA 540R, para. 23(e)).	**Complex modelling (ISA 540R, para 23(d))** • A model may be considered complex when the method, the model design, and the use of data and assumptions require specialised skills (ISA 540R, para A98). • The auditor will need to consider if management has used appropriate skills and the policies that exist around changes of the model (ISA 540R, para A99). • The auditor will consider if the complex model is validated before use such as the soundness of the model, the mathematical integrity, accuracy and completeness of data and assumptions, and the model output compared to actual transactions (ISA 540R, para A39, and para A99). **The integrity of significant assumptions and data when applying the method (ISA 540R, para 23(e)):** • Management must ensure that the integrity of data and assumptions is maintained throughout the estimates process (input, storage, retrieval, transmission, and processing) (ISA 540R, para 101). • Corruption to assumptions and data may cause misstatements in the financial statements relating to estimates (ISA 540R, para 101). • Therefore, the auditor will need to consider if changes made are appropriately approved and there are no unintended changes during the estimates process (ISA 540R, para 101).

►

Table 5 –Response to the assessed risks of material misstatement	
ISA	**Discussion**
9.2.4 Further considerations relating to the assumptions are as follows. Address whether: • **Significant assumptions are consistent** with each other (ISA 540R, para 24(c)). • **Management has the intent to carry out specific courses** of action and can do so (ISA 540R, para 24(d)).	**Assumptions are consistent (ISA 540R, para 24(c))** • During the performance of the audit, the auditor will gain an understanding of other estimates applied by management. The auditor can use this knowledge to consider if the estimates are consistent with each other (ISA 540R, para 104). **Managements intent and ability to act (ISA 540R, para 24(d))** • Management may document certain plans relating to assets and liabilities and the appropriateness of the assumptions is dependent on management executing the plans (ISA 540R, para A105). • Some procedures that the auditor may complete could be, review of management's history in executing plans, an inspection of written documents such as approved budgets or minutes, review of subsequent events (ISA 540R, para A105). • The auditor will need to consider the requirements of the financial reporting framework because, in some instances, management's plans are not considered for determining estimates (ISA 540R, para A105).
9.2.5 Further considerations relating to the data are as follows. Address whether: • The data is relevant and reliable in the circumstances (ISA 540R, para 25(c)).	• The auditor needs to consider if the information is reliable to ensure that the information is precise and detailed to obtain audit evidence (ISA 540R, para A107). • There may be complex legal or contractual terms that are included. The auditor may need to consider if the use of specialised skills is required, the auditor may enquire from the entity's legal counsel regarding the terms and the auditor would need to consider the underlying reason for the transaction and if it makes business sense (ISA 540R, para A108).

►

Table 5 –Response to the assessed risks of material misstatement	
ISA	**Discussion**
• The data has been appropriately understood or interpreted by management, including with respect to contractual terms (Para. 25(d)).	
Additional considerations by the auditor when testing managements estimate (ISA 540R, para 26–27).	• The auditor will need to consider whether management has understood the estimation uncertainty and if this uncertainty has been addressed by management when selecting a point estimate and considering the relevant disclosures (ISA 540R, para 26). • When considering managements point estimate, the auditor will consider whether managements assumptions were selected from a range of amounts supported by relevant and reliable data, the integrity of the data, the mathematical accuracy of calculations and the if the point estimate is selected from a reasonable range of outcomes (ISA 540R, para A110). • The auditor will need to consider if the financial reporting framework prescribes the point estimate and if management has followed this guidance (ISA 540R, para A111). • Regarding the disclosure made by management, the auditor will consider the requirements of the financial reporting framework such as requirements to disclose how the estimate was determined including nature and limitations included in the process, the disclosure of significant accounting policies relating to estimates and critical judgements that were used (ISA 540R, para A112).
Auditors response when managements understanding of estimation uncertainty is not satisfactory (ISA	• The auditor will request management to perform procedures to understand and address estimation uncertainty. This includes management reconsidering the selection of the point estimate or providing additional disclosures regarding estimation uncertainty or reconsidering the estimates used (ISA 540R, para 27(a)).

▶

Table 5 –Response to the assessed risks of material misstatement	
ISA	**Discussion**
540R, para 27 and para A115 – A117).	• If the auditor is not satisfied with management's response regarding addressing the concerns surrounding estimation uncertainty, the auditor will develop an auditors point estimate or range. This is Approach 3, which is discussed next (ISA 540R, para 27(b)). • The auditor will need to determine whether a deficiency in internal control exists and needs to be reported per ISA 265 – Communicating deficiencies in internal control to those charged with governance and management.

Approach 3 – Develop an auditor's point estimate or range (ISA 540R, para 28–29).	• Approach 3 may be appropriate where, based on the auditor's prior experience, management's estimate process and the controls around the process are not effective, subsequent events have not been considered by management and management has not taken appropriate steps to understand estimation uncertainty (ISA 540R, para A118).
	
	 • The auditor's determination of whether to develop an auditor's point estimate or a range is dependent on the requirements of the financial reporting framework and the nature of the estimate, for instance, where there is less variability, a point estimate can be developed as opposed to a range (ISA 540R, para A120).
	
	 • **Methods that the auditor can follow**: The auditor can use a different model to management that is available given the industry or sector or a model that is developed by the auditor, using management's model but the auditor can use alternative data or assumptions to management and employing an auditor's expert to develop the model or provide assumptions (Refer to Chapter 15) (ISA 540R, para A121).
	
	 • Irrespective of whether the auditor uses management's or the auditor's methods, assumptions or data, the procedures that the auditor completes must complete procedures to address the matters in para 23 – para 25 relating to the:
	   – Method
	   – Significant assumptions
	   – Data

▶

Table 5 –Response to the assessed risks of material misstatement	
ISA	**Discussion**
Development of an **auditor's range** (ISA 540R, para 29)	• If the auditor develops a range, the auditor should ensure that the range only includes amounts that are supported by sufficient and appropriate audit evidence and are reasonable considering the requirements of the financial reporting framework (ISA 540R, para 29(a)).

(IAASB, 2019b, IAASB, 2019c, IAASB, 2019d, IAASB, 2018, IAASB, 2009b)

Table 6 explains the auditor's evaluation of the audit evidence to conclude if sufficient and appropriate evidence has been obtained regarding estimates.

Table 6 –Evaluation of audit evidence based on audit procedures performed	
ISA	**Discussion**
d. Overall evaluation based on audit procedures performed (ISA 330, para 24–26) and (ISA 540R, para 33)	
The auditor will need to evaluate the sufficiency and appropriateness of audit evidence (ISA 330).	• The auditor will need to evaluate based on the audit procedures performed and audit evidence obtained whether: – The assessment of the risks of material misstatement at the assertion level remains appropriate (ISA 540R, para 33(a)) *(ISA 330, para 25)*. – Management's decisions relating to the recognition, measurement, presentation, and disclosure are per the applicable financial reporting framework (ISA 540R, para 33(b)) (ISA 330, para 24–24); and – If sufficient appropriate audit evidence has been obtained. The evaluation of evidence will consider if the evidence obtained is corroborative or contradictory (ISA 540R, para 33(c) and para 34) (ISA 330, para 26). • Regarding disclosure, the auditor is required to obtain sufficient appropriate audit evidence regarding the assessed risks of material misstatement at the assertion level for disclosures (ISA 540R, para 31). When the auditor's procedures include testing how management made the accounting estimate (Approach 2) or developing an auditor's point estimate or range (Approach 3), the auditor will also obtain audit evidence regarding the disclosure that describes the estimation uncertainty (ISA 540R, para 26(b) and para 29(b)).

(IAASB, 2009b, IAASB, 2019b, IAASB, 2019c, IAASB, 2018)

Once the auditor has evaluated the sufficiency and appropriateness of the audit evidence, the auditor will conclude on the audit evidence obtained. This is explained in Table 7.

Table 7 – Conclude on the audit evidence obtained	
ISA	Discussion
e. Concluding on the evidence obtained and impact on the audit opinion (ISA 705, para 6–15) and (ISA 540R, para 34)	
Inability to obtain sufficient and appropriate audit evidence (ISA 540R, para 34).	• If unable to obtain sufficient appropriate audit evidence, the auditor will evaluate the impact on the audit and the audit opinion (ISA 540R, para 34). The auditor may need to modify the audit opinion and, as a result, consider the impact on the audit report in terms of ISA 705 (ISA 705, para 6, para 7–15 and para 16–29).
Determine whether accounting estimates are misstated (ISA 540R, para 35).	• The auditor will need to determine whether the accounting estimates and related disclosures are reasonable or if they are misstated (ISA 540R, para 35). In terms of the disclosure, the auditor will need to consider if the disclosures provided allow the fair presentation of the financial statements to be achieved (ISA 540R, para 36). • ISA 450 guides the auditor regarding misstatements and is discussed in Chapter 17. • The auditor may need to modify the audit opinion and as a result will need to consider the impact on the audit report in terms of ISA 705 (ISA 705, para 6, para 7–15 and para 16–29).

(IAASB, 2019b, IAASB, 2019c, IAASB, 2018, IAASB, 2016b)

Table 8 documents the auditor's responsibility in terms of communication as well as the audit documentation requirements.

Table 8 – Communication and documentation requirements	
Discussion	ISA
f. Communication with management and those charged with governance (ISA 580) and (ISA 540R, para 37)	
Written representation (ISA 540R, para 37).	• The auditor will request written representation from management and where appropriate those charged with governance whether the methods, assumptions, and data used to achieve the requirements of the applicable financial framework (ISA 540R, para 37) (ISA 580, para 6 and para 9).

▶

Table 8 – Communication and documentation requirements

Discussion	ISA
Communication with those charged with governance, management or other relevant parties (ISA 540R, para 38).	• The auditor will need to consider if there are any matters to communicate with regards to certain matters such as qualitative aspects of the entity's accounting practices and significant deficiencies in internal control (ISA 540R, para 38) (ISA 260, para 16 and ISA 265 para 9). • Some matters that the auditor may communicate include risks of material misstatement, the materiality of estimates to the financial statements, management's level of understanding regarding the nature and extent of the risks related to estimates, auditor's view about differences between auditor's estimate and management's estimate, indicators of management bias, if a change from the prior year in the methods or estimates was expected and if the significant assumptions are consistent with each other and with the business (Appendix 2, ISA 540R).
g. Documentation (ISA 230, para 8–11) and (ISA 540R, para 37)	
Documentation (ISA 540R, para 37).	• According to ISA 230, the auditor must prepare documentation that is sufficient to enable an experienced auditor to understand the nature, timing, and extent of audit procedures performed, results and significant matters arising. The auditor will document the following: • Key elements of the auditors understanding regarding the entity and its environment including the internal control around estimates; • The link between the assessed risk of material misstatement and the link to the audit procedures performed; • Auditor's response when management has not taken steps to understand estimation uncertainty; • Indicators of management bias, if applicable, and impact on the audit; • Significant judgements relating to the auditor's determination of whether the estimates and disclosure are reasonable if they are misstated.

(IAASB, 2019b, IAASB, 2019c, IAASB, 2018, IAASB, 2009c, IAASB, 2009a)

The section that follows will discuss the application of accounting standards when auditing estimates.

4.1 IFRS 13 – Fair value

IFRS 13 application in estimates is common for estimates. IFRS 13 defines 'fair value' (para 24). This value may be based on a directly observable price or may be estimated using a valuation technique. Also, for a non-financial asset, fair value considers the asset's highest and best use (IFRS 13, para 27).

IFRS 13 establishes a fair value hierarchy that defines three categories of valuation inputs (IFRS 13, para 72–75) (IASB, 2011):

- Level 1 inputs are unadjusted active market prices for identical assets/liabilities to those being measured (IFRS 13, para 76);
- Level 2 inputs are directly or indirectly observable inputs that are not Level 1 inputs (IFRS 13, para 81); and
- Level 3 inputs are unobservable (IFRS 13, para 86) and typically require the use of material management estimates and judgements.

(IASB, 2011)

Generally, Level 1 inputs do not pose specific challenges for the auditor. The inputs are observable and can be easily verified by the practitioner by inspection of third-party sources or confirmation (IFRS 13). As the valuation becomes more complex and subjective, the risk of material misstatement increases.

4.2 IFRS 9 – Financial instruments

Estimates may form a core part of an organisation's business model. For financial services entities, accounting for estimates can be incorporated in financial instruments and can be complex for the following reasons:

- Financial instruments are used as a core part of the entity's business model. The need to provide different levels of returns and risk exposures necessitates the use of a combination of one or more types of financial instruments (hybrid instruments) adding to the complexity of the business process;

- These firms manage macro-risk positions, with the result that multiple contracts are entered into and closed daily. The process of managing portfolios of financial instruments often involves sophisticated mathematical modelling; and
- Financial services entities operate in a highly regulated environment.

Outside of the financial services sector, financial instruments form a complementary part of the business process. For example:

- Financial instruments may be held for investment purposes such as government bonds held to maturity or investment in equity instruments which is not subject to IAS 28, IFRS 10 or IFRS 11;
- Financial instruments will almost always form part of the working capital of the organisation (trade receivables and payables) in which case they arise from the company's normal operating activities;
- Some financial instruments may be held as long-term investments for trade or other speculative purposes (IAPN 1000); and
- Financial instruments can be used to hedge exposure to risks. In some instances, these instruments form part of a designated hedging relationship with specific accounting implications (see IFRS 9, Section 6).

Lastly, IFRS 7 links to the presentation and disclosure of financial instruments in the financial statements. Its requirements included disclosure about methods, models, significant assumptions and data on which the estimates are based. Table 9 provides guidance relating to the controls around financial instruments.

Table 9 – Control environment and control testing for financial instruments	
Control	**Auditor consideration**
Commitment to competent use of financial instruments.	As financial instruments are relatively complex, only certain individuals in the entity may have a complete understanding of the financial instrument activities and have the appropriate expertise to manage the financial instruments (IAPN, App para 3).

▶

Table 9 – Control environment and control testing for financial instruments	
Control	**Auditor consideration**
Participation by those charged with governance.	An entity's policies for the purchase, sale, and holding of financial instruments are aligned with its attitude toward risk and the expertise of those involved in financial instrument activities. The entity must establish governance and control processes that: • Adequately communicate all investment decisions; and • Adequately evaluate the entity's overall risk appetite when engaging in financial instrument transactions (IAPN, App para 4).
Organisational structure.	Financial instrument activities may run on either a centralised or a decentralised basis. Such activities and related decision making depend heavily on the flow of accurate, reliable, and timely management of information. (IAPN, App para 5). If the entity has multiple locations and businesses, the difficulty of collecting and aggregating this financial instrument information is increased (IAPN, App para 5). A more centralised control structure decreases the risk of material misstatement relating to financial instruments (IAPN, App para 5).
Assignment of authority and responsibility.	Providing direction, through clearly stated policies approved by management, specifically directors, for the purchase, sale, and holding of financial instruments enables management to establish an effective approach to managing risks associated with financial instruments (IAPN, App para 6). Policies must be clear and detailed and should reflect the entity's objectives. Controls should specifically address: • The degree and level of management's expertise; • Level of sophistication of the entity's internal control and monitoring systems; • The entity's asset/liability structure;

▶

Table 9 – Control environment and control testing for financial instruments	
Control	**Auditor consideration**
	• Entity's capacity to maintain liquidity and absorb losses of capital; • Types of financial instruments the entity should be using; • Uses of financial instruments – eg speculative versus trading; and • Appropriate policies aligned with the entity's valuation capabilities. (IAPN, App para 6). Even in smaller entities, management must establish policies over financial instruments, specifically to consider whether such instruments meet the entity's objective. (IAPN, App para 6).
Human resource policies and practices.	Entities may establish policies requiring key employees, both front office and back office, to take mandatory time off from their duties to assist in the prevention and detection of fraud. (IAPN, App para 7).
Use of service organisations.	Entities may also use service organisations to initiate the purchase or sale of financial instruments, and to maintain records of transactions for the entity or to value financial instruments. Asset managers would form part of these service organisations (IAPN, App para 8). The auditor will only be able to obtain sufficient and appropriate audit evidence to rely on service organisations if management has an adequate understanding of the controls in place at these service organisations (IAPN, App para 8). The control environment at the service organisation will either strengthen or weaken the control environment over financial instruments, usually, a service organisation with a strong control environment will be positive for the entity's control evaluation of financial instruments (IAPN, App 8).

(IAASB, 2011)

5. Summary

- ISA 540R requires the auditor to gain an understanding of the entity and environment relating to estimates. Obtaining this understanding includes gaining an understanding of the internal control relating to estimates to conduct a risk assessment.
- The auditor is required to make a separate assessment of the inherent and control risk relating to an estimate. Inherent risks that apply to estimates are estimation uncertainty, subjectivity, and complexity. These factors will impact the likelihood and magnitude of the misstatement that may arise.
- The auditor is required to respond to the risk. This includes a consideration of whether the audit approach will include substantive procedures alone or a combination of tests of controls and substantive procedures.
- ISA 540R prescribes three approaches when completing substantive procedures which can be used individually or in combination. The three approaches are, obtaining audit evidence from events occurring up to the date of the auditor's report, testing how management makes the accounting estimate, or developing an auditor's estimate or range.
- Once the auditor has obtained evidence the auditor will need to conclude if sufficient and appropriate evidence has been obtained to indicate whether the financial statements are fairly presented.

6. References

IAASB 2009a. International Standard on Auditing 230: Audit documentation. *SAICA Members' Handbook.* . 2009 ed. Pietermaritsburg: LexisNexis.

IAASB 2009b. International Standard on Auditing 330: The auditors responsibility to assessed risks. *SAICA Members' Handbook.* Pietermaritsburg: LexisNexis.

IAASB 2009c. International Standard on Auditing 580: Written Representations. *SAICA Members' Handbook.* Pietermaritsburg: LexisNexis.

IAASB 2009d. ISA 265 – Communicating deficiencies in internal control to those charged with governance and management *SAICA Members' Handbook.* Pietermaritsburg: LexisNexis.

IAASB 2009 International Standard on Auditing 240: The auditor's responsibilities relating to fraud in an audit of financial statements. *SAICA Members' Handbook.* Pietermaritsburg: LexisNexis.

IAASB 2011. IAPN 1000 – Special Considerations in Auditing Financial Instruments *SAICA Members' Handbook.* Pietermaritsburg: LexisNexis.

IAASB 2016a. International Standard on Auditing 260: The Auditor's Communication with Those Charged with Governance. *SAICA Members' Handbook.* Pietermaritsburg: LexisNexis.

IAASB 2016b. International Standard on Auditing 705: Modifications to the Opinion in the Independent Auditor's Report. *SAICA Members' Handbook.* Pietermaritsburg: LexisNexis.

IAASB 2018. International Standard on Auditing 540 (Revised): Auditing accounting estimates and related disclosures. *SAICA Members' Handbook.* Pietermaritsburg: LexisNexis.

IAASB 2019a. Considerations for Management When Determining Accounting Estimates and Related Disclosures. Available: https://www.ifac.org/system/files/publications/files/ISA-540-Revised-Audit-Client-Briefing-Final-Branding.pdf [Accessed 30 June 2020].

IAASB 2019b. Flowchart: International Standard on Auditing 540 (Revised) – Linkages between ISA 540 (Revised) and Other ISAs. Available: https://www.ifac.org/system/files/publications/files/IAASB-ISA-540-Flowchart-Requirements.pdf [Accessed 30 June 2020].

IAASB 2019c. Flowchart: International Standard on Auditing 540 (Revised) – Requirements. Available: https://www.ifac.org/system/files/publications/files/IAASB-ISA-540-Flowchart-Requirements.pdf [Accessed 30 June 2020].

IAASB 2019d. Flowchart: International Standard on Auditing 540 (Revised) – Three Testing Approaches. Available: https://www.ifac.org/system/files/publications/files/IAASB-ISA-540-Flowchart-Requirements.pdf [Accessed 30 June 2020].

IAASB 2019e. International Standard on Auditing 315 (Revised 2019): Identifying and assessing the risks of material misstatement. *SAICA Members' Handbook.* Pietermaritsburg.: LexisNexis.

IASB 2011. IFRS 13 – Fair Value Measurement. United Kingdom: International Accounting Standards Board.

IASB 2014. IFRS 9 – Financial Instruments. United Kingdom: International Accounting Standards Board.

KPMG. 2018. Revision in auditing of accounting estimates. Available: https://home.kpmg/content/dam/kpmg/in/pdf/2018/10/AAU-Oct-2018-Ch2.pdf [Accessed 30 June 2020].

SHARP, L. 2020. Preparing for Changes to ISA 540 on Auditing Accounting Estimates. https://www.ifac.org/knowledge-gateway/supporting-international-standards/discussion/preparing-changes-isa-540-auditing-accounting-estimates.

PART C

Chapter 17: Completion activities

1. Introduction

During the completion stage, the auditor reviews the evidence gained during the audit and forms an opinion on the financial statements. In forming an opinion[1], the auditor will conclude whether or not the financial statements are free from material misstatement, which will need to be reported to those charged with the governance as well as to the shareholders in the audit report (IAASB, 2009a; IAASB, 2015a).

During this phase, the auditor needs to consider whether sufficient and appropriate audit evidence has been obtained (IAASB, 2009d) and whether uncorrected misstatements are material individually or in aggregate (IAASB, 2009e). The completion of the audit also requires the auditor to consider if the going concern assumption has been applied correctly (IASB, 2010; IAASB, 2016b), if there are any subsequent events which may have impacted the financial statements (IAASB, 2015b) and if the evidence supports the movements in the financial statements (IAASB, 2009b).

2. Evaluating misstatements

In Chapter 10 on assessing and Chapter 13 on responding to audit risk, you were introduced to the procedures which the auditor follows to assess the risk of misstatement of the financial statements and how the auditor responds to this assessed risk using a combination of tests of controls and substantive tests. During the course of performing risk assessment procedures or further audit procedures in response to the assessed risk of misstatement, the auditor may become aware of control deficiencies and misstatements (whether due to fraud or error) (IAASB, 2009d). These need to be carefully considered to determine the impact on the nature, timing and extent of audit work required and the implications for the audit report. IAASB (2009e) provides the applicable guidance.

A misstatement is defined as:

> 'A difference between the amount, classification, presentation, or disclosure of a reported financial statement item and the amount, classification, presentation, or disclosure that is required for the item to be in accordance with the applicable financial reporting framework.' (IAASB, 2009e, para 4).

---

1   When conducting an audit of a PCAOB public company, an external auditor is also required to form an opinion about management's assessment of the effectiveness of internal control over financial reporting (Maroun et al., 2014; PCAOB, 2017).

Management either creates or purchases information systems which are imperfect and, as a result, subject to bias and/or random processing errors. In addition, there is always the possibility that management is dishonest so there may be intentional bias, not only in management's financial statements, but also in misleading judgements and information system outputs which can dupe auditors and investors (IAASB, 2009b).

Misstatements may be factual, projected or judgemental (Ashton, 1991; IAASB, 2009e; Beasley et al., 2010; ACFE, 2016). Factual misstatements refer to misstatements made intentionally or unintentionally while projected misstatements are an extrapolation of factual misstatements over the population, a resultant of sampling techniques used (see Chapter 13). Judgemental misstatements can manifest in financial statements, especially in complex estimates (eg Peecher et al., 2010) because of phenomena such as motivated reasoning, egocentric bias and confirmation proneness by management (see Solomon and Trotman, 2003). Unlike unintentional misstatements caused by random error which tend to revert over time (eg an undetected cut-off error that overstates revenue this year will understate next year's revenue), unintentional misstatements because of bias can persist and accumulate over time.

Misstatements are identified during the execution phase of an audit engagement, detailed in Chapter 13. Lobo and Zhao (2013) find that an increase in the audit effort results in fewer misstatement and so, less restatement. Audit effort is affected by internal and external sources. Internally the resources available to perform the audit, audit fees, the experience of the audit team and term of partner involvement have been identified as factors. Externally, the complexity of the audit client including the underlying constructive transactions and the changes in the client business operations and accounting policies. Time pressure can, however, reduce the effort to identify misstatements (Braun, 2000). Other factors which may have an impact on the identification of misstatements are covered in Chapters 12 and 13.

Identified misstatements are evaluated against materiality. ISA 320 defines materiality in the same way as IFRS do and states that an item's magnitude and nature should be taken into account (IAASB, 2009c). In IFRS, materiality is defined as:

> 'Information is material if omitting it or misstating it could influence decisions that users make on the basis of financial information about a specific entity. In other words, materiality is an entity-specific aspect of relevance based on the nature or magnitude, or both, of the items to which the information relates in the context of an individual entity's financial report.' (IASB, 2010, p. A23).

Auditors set materiality to mitigate the risk of misstatement. ISA 320 states that auditors should use materiality, as described by IFRS, as a frame of reference in determining a materiality level or levels for the audit (IAASB, 2009c). In practice, however, the determination of materiality differs substantially among firms (Chewning and Higgs, 2002).

The determination of materiality is detailed in Chapter 13. Patterson and Smith (2003) note that the auditing profession sets materiality in line with the cost of audit failure. As a result, materiality is understood and computed to determine a threshold above which financial statements will not achieve fair presentation rather than according to whether or not different users of the financial statements will regard the applicable information as relevant for their decision-making processes (Edgley, 2014; 2015). During the completion of the audit, materiality is reassessed based on the final version of the financial statements. This is performed to determine whether or not there is sufficient and appropriate audit evidence to support the audit opinion (see Chapter 17).

When evaluating misstatements, the auditor sets a clearly trivial threshold which is used to identify misstatements which, in aggregate, will not result in a material misstatement. As a result, individual errors which are below the clearly trivial threshold would be considered inconsequential (IAASB, 2009e). Any other misstatements identified during the audit are assessed individually and in aggregate to determine whether the financial statements are free from material misstatement. The assessment of misstatements is performed quantitatively and qualitatively. If a misstatement is material, either quantitatively or qualitatively, the auditor has an obligation to communicate the misstatements to appropriate members of management in a timely manner. This is to allow management to correct the misstatement. Should management refuse to correct a material misstatement, the auditor may need to modify the opinion on the financial statements (see Chapter 17). The auditor must also consider if the misstatement is indicative of fraud or a systematic matter/ element (such as a breakdown in controls) and the resulting impact on the audit process (IAASB, 2009e).

2.1 Quantitative assessment

Quantitative assessment of misstatements is based on materiality and, in some cases, a materiality level determined for specific balances and transactions (IAASB, 2009e) (See also Chapter 13). Depending on the type of misstatement the evaluation approach of the auditor differs.

Projected misstatements are assessed individually against a tolerable misstatement (IAASB, 2016a). An unexpectedly high misstatement amount in a sample may cause the auditor to believe that a class of transactions or account balance is materially misstated. When the projected misstatement exceeds tolerable misstatement, the sample does not provide a reasonable basis for conclusions about the population which has been tested. The closer the projected misstatement is to tolerable misstatement, the more likely that actual misstatement in the population may exceed tolerable misstatement.

The auditor should consider other audit evidence to determine an appropriate evaluation of the projected misstatement (Felix and Grimlund, 1977; IAASB, 2016a). This includes identifying whether the misstatement is isolated or recurring. If the misstatement is isolated, it should be treated as an abnormality and would not necessarily be projected across the population (IAASB, 2016a). Should the auditor conclude that audit sampling has not provided a reasonable basis for conclusions about the tested population, the auditor should obtain further evidence from management or perform alternate audit procedures (IAASB, 2009f; Budescu et al., 2012).

Judgemental and factual misstatements are assessed individually and in aggregate. Taking into account the class of transaction, the nature of the misstatement and any specific materiality level (IAASB, 2009e). Consideration of any specific financial statement line item should be included in the evaluation as must an overall assessment on the elements of the financial statements.

2.2 Qualitative assessment

Qualitative assessments require the auditor to note if the misstatement is an isolated occurrence and evaluate the nature of the misstatement, including whether or not a misstatement is indicative of fraud (IAASB, 2009e). In other words, a misstatement which is below the quantitative materiality threshold may still be material because of its qualitative characteristics. Characteristics of the misstatement should be considered in determining whether or not a misstatement is qualitatively material. These include if each:

- Affects compliance with regulatory requirements, debt covenants or other contractual requirements;
- Masks a change in earnings or other trends, especially in the context of general economic and industry conditions;
- Affects ratios used to evaluate the entity's financial position, results of operations or cash flows;
- Affects segment information presented in the financial;
- Has the effect of increasing management compensation; and
- Is significant having regard to the auditor's understanding of known previous communications to users, for example, in relation to forecast earnings.

(IAASB, 2009e, A16)

3. The auditor's responsibilities relating to going concern

General purpose financial statements are prepared on the assumption that the entity is a going concern and will continue its operations for the foreseeable future. It is management's responsibility to assess an entity's ability to continue as a going concern. The auditors have the responsibility to obtain sufficient and appropriate audit evidence over the appropriateness of management's use of the going concern basis of accounting. In obtaining evidence the auditor should consider whether, in his or her judgment, a material uncertainty exists related to events or conditions that, individually or collectively, may cast significant doubt on the entity's ability to continue as a going concern (IAASB, 2016b, para 17–20). The auditor must also plan audit procedures and obtain evidence to address any concerns identified which includes determining whether management has already performed a preliminary assessment of the entity's ability to continue as a going concern. The assessment should be evaluated to ensure that management has identified any events or conditions which may cast significant doubt on the entity's ability to continue as a going concern and management's plans to address them (IAASB, 2016b). In accordance with IAS 1 the assessment should cover, at a minimum, twelve months from the end of the reporting period.

If a material uncertainty arises during the audit, further evidence should be obtained regarding management assessment and the feasibility of the actions taken by management to improve the entity's ability to continue as a going concern. Based on the audit evidence obtained, the auditor must conclude whether a material uncertainty exists related to events or conditions that, individually or collectively, may cast significant doubt on the entity's ability to continue as a going concern. The auditor will also communicate with those charged with governance events or conditions identified which may cast significant doubt on the entity's ability to continue as a going concern (IAASB, 2016b, para 25).

4. Subsequent events

IAASB (2015c) explains that the date of the auditor's report informs the reader that the auditor has considered the effect of events and transactions of which the auditor becomes aware, and which have occurred up to that date, referred to as 'Subsequent Events'. Subsequent events are defined in ISA 560 as events occurring between the date of the financial statements and the date of the auditor's report, as well as facts which become known to the auditor after the date of the auditor's report (IAASB, 2015b). Before issuing the audit report, the auditor performs procedures to identify events occurring after the financial year-end which may impact the financial statements. The impact on the financial statements is dependent on whether or not the event provides evidence of conditions which existed at the date of the financial statements (IAASB, 2009g). The auditor then concludes on the need to amend the financial statements and, if necessary, requests management to amend them. Any amendments not processed by management should be treated as a misstatement and evaluated as such (refer to Section 2 above).

In terms of the ISAs, an auditor has no obligation to perform procedures after the financial statements have been issued. However, in practical terms, if an auditor becomes aware of such events, appropriate action would be required to avoid an audit failure.

5. Conclusion analytics

As part of the process of concluding the audit, IAASB (2009b) requires the auditor to

> 'evaluate whether analytical procedures that are performed near the end of the audit, when forming an overall conclusion as to whether the financial statements are consistent with the auditor's understanding of the entity, indicate a previously unrecognised risk of misstatement due to fraud' (ISA 240, para 34).

The analytical procedures performed are similar to those performed during the planning phase of the audit with the intention of identifying movements in the financial statements which cannot be explained by audit evidence obtained during the audit. Conclusion analytics are done to ensure that there is sufficient and appropriate audit evidence over the financial statement from which to base an audit opinion on (IAASB, 2009f; Budescu et al., 2012).

6. Summary

- The completion of the audit requires the auditor to evaluate misstatements to assess whether the financial statements are reasonably free from material misstatement.
- During the completion of the audit the auditor will draw conclusions from the audit evidence and prepare reports to management and an audit opinion based on the evidence obtained (IAASB, 2009a; IAASB, 2015a).
- There are different types of misstatements which affect the manner in which they are evaluated (Budescu et al., 2012).
- Sufficient and appropriate audit evidence over the entity's ability to continue as a going concern and subsequent events needs to be obtained (IAASB, 2009f).
- The evidence obtained during the audit needs to explain and support the auditor's understanding of the entity and the financial statements (IAASB, 2009b).

7. References

Ashton, A. H. 1991. Experience and error frequency knowledge as potential determinants of audit expertise. *Accounting Review*, 218–239.

Beasley, M. S., Carcello, J. V., Hermanson, D. R. & Neal, T. L. 2010. *Fraudulent financial reporting: 1998–2007: An analysis of US public companies*, COSO, Committee of Sponsoring Organizations of the Treadway Commission.

Braun, R. L. 2000. The effect of time pressure on auditor attention to qualitative aspects of misstatements indicative of potential fraudulent financial reporting. *Accounting, Organizations and Society,* 25 (3), 243–259.

Budescu, D. V., Peecher, M. E. & Solomon, I. 2012. The joint influence of the extent and nature of audit evidence, materiality thresholds, and misstatement type on achieved audit risk. *Auditing: A Journal of Practice & Theory,* 31 (2), 19–41.

Chewning, E. G. & Higgs, J. L. 2002. What Does "Materiality" Really Mean? *Journal of Corporate Accounting & Finance,* 13 (4), 61–71.

Edgley, C. 2014. A genealogy of accounting materiality. *Critical Perspectives on Accounting,* 25 (3), 255–271.

Edgley, C., Jones, M. J. & Atkins, J. F. 2015. The adoption of the materiality concept in social and environmental reporting assurance: A field study approach. *The British Accounting Review,* 47 (1), 1–18.

Examiners, A. o. C. F. 2016. *Report to the nations on occupational fraud and abuse: 2016 global fraud study*, Association of Certified Fraud Examiners.

Felix, W. L. & Grimlund, R. A. 1977. A sampling model for audit tests of composite accounts. *Journal of Accounting Research,* 23–41.

IAASB 2009a. Communicating Deficiencies in Internal Control to those Charged with Governance and Management. *SAICA members' handbook. 2009.* Pietermaritsburg: LexisNexis.

IAASB 2009b. ISA 240: The auditor's responsibility realting to fraud in an audit of financial statements. *SAICA Members' Handbook.* 2009 ed. Pietermaritsburg: LexisNexis.

IAASB 2009c. ISA 320: Materiality in planning and performing an audit. *SAICA Members' Handbook.* 2009 ed. Pietermaritsburg: LexisNexis.

IAASB 2009d. ISA 330: The auditor's responses to assessed risks. *SAICA Members' Handbook.* 2009 ed. Pietermaritsburg: LexisNexis.

IAASB 2009e. ISA 450: Evaluation of misstatements identified during the audit. *SAICA Members' Handbook.* 2009 ed. Pietermaritsburg: LexisNexis.

IAASB 2009f. ISA 500 Audit Evidence. *SAICA Members' Handbook.* 2009 ed.: LexisNexis, Pietermaritzburg.

IAASB 2009g. ISA 560: Subsequent events *SAICA members' handbook. 2018.* Pietermaritsburg: LexisNexis.

IAASB 2015a. ISA 260: Communication with those Charged with Governance. *SAICA members' handbook. 2015.* Pietermaritsburg: LexisNexis.

IAASB 2015b. ISA 560: SUBSEQUENT EVENTS. *SAICA members' handbook. 2015.* Pietermaritsburg: LexisNexis.

IAASB 2015c. ISA 700: Forming an Opinion and Reporting on Financial Statements. *SAICA members' handbook. 2015.* Pietermaritsburg: LexisNexis.

IAASB 2016a. ISA 530: Audit Sampling.

IAASB 2016b. ISA 570: Going Concern. *SAICA members' handbook. 2016.* Pietermaritsburg: LexisNexis.

IASB 2010. The Conceptual Framework for Financial Reporting. International Accounting Standards Board.

International Accounting Standards Board (IASB). 2010. *The Conceptual Framework for Financial Reporting* [Online]. Available: http://eifrs.ifrs.org/eifrs/files/238/bv2012_conceptual_framework_part%20a_161.pdf [Accessed 29 January 2014].

Lobo, G. J. & Zhao, Y. 2013. Relation between audit effort and financial report misstatements: Evidence from quarterly and annual restatements. *The Accounting Review,* 88 (4), 1385–1412.

Maroun, W., Coldwell, D. & Segal, M. 2014. SOX and the Transition from Apartheid to Democracy: South African Auditing Developments through the Lens of Modernity Theory. *International Journal of Auditing,* 18 (3), 206–212.

Patterson, E. R. & Smith, R. 2003. Materiality uncertainty and earnings misstatement. *The Accounting Review,* 78 (3), 819–846.

PCAOB 2017. AS 3101: The Auditor's Report on an Audit of Financial Statements When the Auditor Expresses an Unqualified Opinion New York, NY 10036–8775: American Institute of CPAs.

Peecher, M. E., Solomon, I. & Trotman, K. T. 2010. Improving the quality of financial-statement audits by updating external auditors' accountabilities. In: Ideas, 2010. 62–64.

Solomon, I. & Trotman, K. T. 2003. Experimental judgment and decision research in auditing: the first 25 years of AOS. *Accounting, Organizations and Society,* 28 (4), 395–412.

Chapter 18: Reporting

1. Introduction

Aptly, Littleton and Zimmerman (1963) state that the financial statements are noteworthy tools for analysis and can communicate the performance of an entity to stakeholders. The reliance placed on the financial statements by stakeholders means that the financial statements must be credible and trustworthy (Prada, 2007; ACCA, 2010; Doty, 2011). As a result, external auditors are appointed to provide assurance on the financial statements and other information (see also Chapter 2). The credibility of the financial statements is achieved through the expression of an opinion by the auditor on whether or not the financial statements are prepared in accordance with an applicable financial reporting framework (IAASB, 2009a, para 3).

The audit opinion is contained in the audit report which is addressed to the company's shareholders. This is not the only communication by the external auditor. The external auditor also communicates with, *inter alia*:

- those charged with governance;
- management;
- internal auditors; and
- regulatory bodies.

This chapter focuses on the outputs of an audit, specifically, the communication with those charged with governance, the issue of the audit report to shareholders and other audit outputs. The communication among the external auditor, internal auditors and regulatory bodies are detailed in Chapter 4 and Chapter 19, respectively.

2. The different outputs of the audit process

The auditor's report on the financial statements is not the only outcome of an audit engagement. Table 1 is a non-exhaustive list of other audit outputs issued by the auditor, showing the party to whom the report is issued and the level at which the reports are issued.

Table 1: Audit outputs			
Output	**To**	**Purpose**	**Level**
Auditor's reports to users of audited financial statements (IAASB, 2015b).	The users of the financial statements.	To provide information to give users some insights about the auditor's work and findings.	Engagement level
Report to those charged with governance (IAASB, 2015a).	Those charged with governance.	To communicate the auditor's responsibilities; the planned scope and timing of the audit; information about threats to auditor objectivity and the related safeguards which have been applied and the significant findings from the audit.	Engagement level
Report on significant control deficiencies (IAASB, 2009c).	Those charged with governance.	To report significant weaknesses in controls.[1]	Engagement level
Auditor's reports to financial and prudential regulators.	Financial and prudential regulators.	• To provide assurance on aspects of the financial reporting process, for example, on internal controls. • To report matters which regulators believe are likely to be of material significance to them such as illegal acts, including suspicions of money laundering (see Chapter 5).	Engagement level

Adapted from (IAASB, 2014a)

Audit outputs are determined by various aspects for example, legislative requirements and stakeholder interests (IAASB, 2014a). The auditing profession adapts to the expectations (what the shareholder is interested in knowing) and changes to meet these expectations (Asare and Wright, 2012). As a result, each audit output has a different purpose and different target audience. (Gold et al., 2009; Gold et al., 2012; IAASB, 2014a; IAASB, 2015b).

---

1   Sarbanes Oxley Reporting is an example of this type of reporting (Refer to Chapter 2 on governance controls).

Section 3 details the auditor's responsibility for communicating with those charged with governance and Section 4 onward describes the audit report and its various components.

3. Communicating with those charged with governance

When planning an engagement, the auditor is not required to design procedures specifically to gather information to report to the governing body (IAASB, 2009c). Instead, the auditor communicates matters which come to his or her attention in the course of the engagement and which the auditor deems to be significant and relevant for the governing body's attention (IAASB, 2015a).The IAASB (2015a, para 16) identifies some of the matters which might come to the attention of the auditor and which may be of interest to the governing body in fulfilling its monitoring role. These are:

- The scope of the audit;
- Management's selection of, or changes in, significant accounting policies;
- Significant risks and exposures with a potential financial statement effect;
- Proposed and booked audit adjustments;
- Material uncertainties which may impact the going concern assumption;
- Disagreements with management;
- Expected modifications to the standard audit report;
- Material weaknesses in internal control;
- Management integrity; and
- Fraud.

(IAASB, 2015a, para 16)

3.1 Those charged with governance

As a part of the audit process, the auditor must identify and communicate with those charged with governance (Colbert, 2002; IAASB, 2015a, para 11). 'Those charged with governance' is defined by International Standards of Auditing (ISA) 260 as:

'The person(s) or organisation(s) (for example, a corporate trustee) with responsibility for overseeing the strategic direction of the entity and obligations related to the accountability of the entity. This includes overseeing the financial reporting process.'
(IAASB, 2015a, para 10(a))

Those charged with governance can be identified by their involvement in the reporting of financial performance and other information to stakeholders (Colbert, 2002).

ISA 260 makes the distinction between two-tier systems with a supervisory (wholly or mainly non-executive) board and a management (executive) board and unitary systems where both the supervision and the management function is the legal responsibility of the unitary board

(IAASB, 2015a; IOD, 2016). Regardless of the name or composition, the external auditors must establish a working relationship with those charged with governance (IAASB, 2015a).

A working relationship is important as those charged with governance can assist the auditor in obtaining sufficient and appropriate audit evidence (IAASB, 2009a, para 5). The auditor also has the obligation to communicate with those charged with governance during the completion phase of the audit. These communications include, *inter alia*, the significant findings of the audit, the significant deficiencies in internal control, key audit matters and the audit opinion (IAASB, 2009e; IAASB, 2009c; IAASB, 2015a; IAASB, 2015b).

3.2 Communication of control deficiencies

Matters identified during the performance of an audit may include the identification of control deficiencies. Deficiencies in internal controls exist when a control is designed, implemented or operated in such a way that it is unable to prevent or detect and correct misstatements in the financial statements on a timely basis; or is missing entirely.

Control deficiencies can be identified through testing of controls. However, there is no specific requirement from the ISAs to test controls for operating effectiveness (IAASB, 2009c). Control deficiencies can also be identified during the risk assessment processes, the execution phase of an audit or the completion phase.

Once a control deficiency is identified, the auditor should assess the deficiency to determine if it is a significant deficiency (IAASB, 2009c, para 2). A significant deficiency can be considered a deficiency or a combination of deficiencies in internal control over financial reporting (Ashbaugh-Skaife et al., 2007; Hogan and Wilkins, 2008; IAASB, 2009c; Jiang et al., 2010). The significance of a deficiency in internal control depends not only on whether a misstatement has actually occurred but also on the likelihood that a misstatement could occur and the potential magnitude of the misstatement (Hogan and Wilkins, 2008; Jiang et al., 2010). Significant deficiencies can exist even though the auditor has not identified misstatements during the audit (Hogan and Wilkins, 2008). If, in the auditor's professional judgement, the deficiencies are of sufficient importance, the auditor will communicate in writing the significant deficiencies in internal control to those charged with governance (IAASB, 2009c, para 7–9, A12–A18, A27).

The auditor should also ensure that matters communicated do not breach ethical principles, such as confidentiality. Confidentiality of information requires additional considerations by the auditor (IAASB, 2009h; IAASB, 2015a). IAASB (2015a) states that the confidentiality rules of accounting licensing bodies or legal requirements may restrict the external auditor's communication with those charged with governance. Therefore, the auditor's ethical responsibilities to communicate with the group may differ from its legal ones. Communicating with those charged with governance has a direct impact on the different outputs of an audit (IAASB, 2009c; IAASB, 2015a).

4. The auditor's report (ISA 700)

In order to issue an audit report, the engagement leader must follow specific regulations and guidance. Internationally, many of the accounting firms follow the ISAs as proposed by IAASB (2014b), most likely because of the convergence with IFRS (Prada, 2007). The ISAs are also widely applied in multiple jurisdictions and, as a result, the remainder of this chapter deals with auditor reporting in terms of ISAs. The following standards are relevant to the issue of the audit report: ISA 700, ISA 701, ISA 705, ISA 706, ISA 710 and ISA 720.

Users of the audit report place significant reliance on the audit report and often misinterpret an unqualified report or going concern statements to be indicative that an entity is a good investment (McEnroe and Martens, 2001). As a result, the expectations placed on auditors may not be in line with the guidance provided by the ISAs and the purpose of an audit is often misunderstood (Sikka et al., 1998; Porter, 2009). This is described as an 'expectation gap' (see Chapter 2) (Liggio, 1974; Koh and Woo, 1998; McEnroe and Martens, 2001; Schelluch and Gay, 2006; Porter, 2009; Houghton et al., 2011; Gold et al., 2012). Over time, the auditing profession has adapted and changed to reduce the expectation gap (Liggio, 1974; Koh and Woo, 1998; Sikka et al., 1998). One of the changes has been the change from a short-form audit report to a long-form audit report, referred to as 'enhanced auditor reporting' (IAASB, 2015b).

A long-form audit report prescribed by ISA 700 is intended to enhance the communicative value of the report by providing more detail on the audit work performed (IAASB, 2016b). According to the IAASB research and public consultations, enhanced auditor reporting is critical in influencing the perceived value of the financial statement audit (IAASB, 2015b). The IAASB (2015b) suggests that the intended benefits of enhanced auditor reporting include the following:

- Enhanced communication among auditors and investors, as well as those charged with corporate governance;
- Increased user confidence in auditor's reports and financial statements;
- Increased transparency, audit quality, and enhanced information value;
- Increased attention by management and financial statement preparers to disclosures referencing the auditor's report;

- Renewed auditor focus on matters to be reported which may result in increased professional scepticism; and
- Enhanced financial reporting in the public interest.

The long-form audit report is largely focused on the improvement in communication between the auditor and the shareholders (Porter, 2009; IAASB, 2016b). The following characteristics of the auditor's report can be fundamental to reducing the expectation gap:

- Title and addressee (ISA 700 para 21–22, A20–A21);
- Auditor's opinion (ISA 700 para 23–27);
- Basis for opinion (ISA 700 para 28);
- If the opinion is modified, ISA 705 para 20–28 is applicable;
- Going concern disclosure (ISA 700 para 29), if applicable, per ISA 570;
- Key audit matters (ISA 700 para 30, A40–A42, ISA 701) – if applicable (Refer to section 7);
- If an Emphasis of Matter/Other Matter paragraph is included and is applicable, ISA 706 para 8–11;
- Other Information (ISA 700 para 31, ISA 720);
- Management's responsibilities for the financial statements (ISA 700 para 33–36, A44–A49);
- Responsibilities of the auditor (ISA 700 para 37–40, A 50–A53);
- Location of the description of the auditor's responsibility (ISA 700 para 41 – 42, A54 – A56);
- Other legal and regulatory requirements (if applicable);
- Name of the engagement partner (ISA 700 para 46, A61–A63);
- Signature of the auditor (ISA 700 para 47, A64–A65);
- Auditor's address (ISA 700 para 48); and
- Date of the auditor's report (ISA 700 para 49, A60–A69).

An illustration of an audit report containing the above characteristics has been included in Appendix A. The overall structure of the audit report places more emphasis on the auditor's opinion. The purpose of the audit report is still, however, to communicate the auditor's opinion (IAASB, 2015b). The formulation of the opinion remains important and shareholders utilise the opinion as a binary finding that either the financial statements are faithfully presented or not (Francis, 2011). The forming of the audit opinion is discussed in Section 5.

5. The opinion on financial statements

The auditor forms an audit opinion on whether the financial statements are prepared, in all material respects, in accordance with the applicable financial reporting framework (IAASB, 2015b, para 10).

During the formation of an opinion, an audit firm needs to consider whether sufficient appropriate audit evidence has been obtained (IAASB, 2009d) and whether uncorrected misstatements are material, individually or in aggregate (IAASB, 2009e; Maroun and Wainer, 2014; Sultanoglu et al., 2018). The auditor must also consider whether the financial statements are prepared, in all material respects, in accordance with the applicable financial reporting framework (refer to Chapter 16).

The evaluation of whether the financial statements are prepared, in all material respects in accordance with the applicable financial reporting framework considers not only quantitative disclosures but also qualitative disclosures and aspects (IAASB, 2015b, para 12). In forming the opinion on the financial statements IAASB (2015b, Para 12–15) states that the following characteristics must be evident:

- Adequate disclosure of significant accounting policies selected and applied;
- Accounting policies selected and applied are consistent with the applicable financial reporting framework and are appropriate;
- Accounting estimates made by management are reasonable;
- Information presented in the financial statements is relevant, reliable, comparable, and understandable;
- Adequate disclosures to enable the intended users to understand the effect of material transactions and events on the information conveyed in the financial statements;
- Terminology used in the financial statements, including the title of each financial statement, is appropriate; and
- Whether the financial statements adequately refer to or describe the applicable financial reporting framework.

(IAASB, 2015b, Para 12–15)

5.1 Comparative information

Comparative information forms a key part of financial statements. Under IAS 1, an entity must disclose comparative information in respect of the previous period for all amounts reported in the current period's financial statements (International Accounting Standards Board (IASB), 2014, IAS 1 para 38). From an auditing perspective, comparative information refers to corresponding figures and comparative financial statements (IAASB, 2018, para 6). The audit opinion is on the financial statements as a whole (IAASB, 2015b).

The auditor should determine whether the financial statements include the comparative information required by the applicable financial reporting framework and whether or not this information is appropriately classified (IAASB, 2018, para 7 – 9). It is not necessary to amend the auditor's opinion with respect to prior period information except in the circumstances detailed below:

- If the auditor's report on the prior period includes a qualified opinion, a disclaimer of opinion or an adverse opinion and the matter which gave rise to the qualification remains unresolved, the auditor should modify the opinion on the current period's financial statements (IAASB, 2018, para 11).
- If the auditor obtains evidence that a material misstatement exists in the prior period financial statements on which an unmodified opinion has been issued previously and the corresponding figures have not been properly restated or appropriate disclosures have not been made, the auditor should modify the opinion in accordance with (IAASB, 2018, para 12).
- If the prior financial statements were not audited, or if a predecessor auditor audited them, an 'Other Matter paragraph' should be included in the auditor's report as detailed in Section 6 (IAASB, 2018, para 13–14).

5.2 Other information

Other information refers to financial or non-financial information included in the entity's annual report (IAASB, 2015e). It is important to note that the auditor's opinion does not cover the other information included in the annual report (IAASB, 2015b) but the auditor is still required to read and consider the other information for consistency (IAASB, 2015e). Other information poses an additional risk to the auditor. If it is materially inconsistent with the financial statements, it may indicate that there is a material misstatement in the financial statements or a material misstatement of the other information. This may undermine the credibility of the financial statements and the auditor's report (Johnstone, 2000; IAASB, 2015c). These material misstatements may also influence the economic decisions of the user of the financial statements (Houghton, 1983; Bessell et al., 2003; Francis, 2011; Maroun and Wainer, 2014).

It is important for the auditor to read the other information and to consider whether or not there is a material inconsistency between the other information and the financial statements and between the other information and the auditor's knowledge obtained in the audit. In assessing the other information, the auditor should consider whether there is a material inconsistency between the other information and the financial statements and/or the auditor's knowledge obtained during the audit (IAASB, 2015c, para 14–20). The auditor is also required to remain alert to any indications that the other information may be materially misstated, including differences between the other information and the general knowledge of the auditor and other internal inconsistencies (IAASB, 2015e).

If the auditor identifies material inconsistencies, the auditor is required to respond appropriately and consider the impact on the audit report (IAASB, 2015c). The auditor should discuss the matter with management (IAASB, 2015c, para 16) and ascertain whether there is a material inconsistency, a material misstatement of the financial statements and/or if the auditor's understanding of the entity and its environment needs to be updated. If there is an inconsistency, management should make the correction (IAASB, 2015c, para 17–19). However, if management refuses to make the correction, the auditor should discuss the matter with those charged with governance as discussed above. The information should be corrected after which the auditor should perform additional procedures to obtain comfort over the changes made. If the information was not corrected, the appropriate action would be dependent on whether or not the audit report has been issued. If the audit report has not been issued, the auditor may want to consider withdrawing from the engagement and if the report has been issued the auditors are required to take appropriate action to bring the inconsistency to the attention of the user (IAASB, 2015e). The decision tree regarding other information has been included in Appendix B.

5.3 The validity of the application of the going concern assumption

Comparative information and other information are not the only matters that an auditor should take into consideration when evaluating disclosures in terms of an applicable framework (IAASB, 2015b, para 12). The auditor should also consider whether, in his/her judgement, a material uncertainty exists which relates to events or conditions that, individually or collectively, may cast significant doubt on the entity's ability to continue as a going concern (IAASB, 2009g, para 17–20; Sultanoglu et al., 2018) (see Chapter 16).

By their very nature, these issues are likely to be considered a critical/ key audit matter (discussed in Section 7) and need to be communicated in the auditor's report. Where the auditor has identified conditions which cast doubt on the going concern assumption, but audit evidence confirms that no material uncertainty exists, the auditor's description of key audit matters in the auditor's report may include aspects of the identified events or conditions disclosed in the financial statements (IAASB, 2016b, A41). This is because, while the auditor may conclude that no material uncertainty exists, he/she may determine that one or more matters relating to this conclusion are critical/ key audit matters.

The auditor will assess the impact of the going concern assessment on the auditor's report. Appendix C illustrates the effect of that and auditors' going concern assessment on the audit report. The auditor will also communicate with those charged with governance events or conditions identified which may cast significant doubt on the entity's ability to continue as a going concern (IAASB, 2009g, para 25).

5.4 Concluding and forming an audit opinion

An opinion is issued after consideration of the comparative information, misstatements identified, other information and the validity of the going concern assumption (see also Chapter 16). Should the auditor find no evidence of material misstatement, an unqualified opinion will be issued. However, if there are material misstatements in the comparative information, financial statements or other information the auditor will have to modify the opinion accordingly (IAASB, 2015b; Sultanoglu et al., 2018). The opinion would also have to be modified if the going concern assumption is incorrectly applied (see Appendix C).

The decision regarding which type of modified opinion is appropriate depends on the nature of the matter giving rise to the modification and the auditor's judgement about the pervasiveness of the effects or possible effects of the matter on the financial statements (IAASB, 2015c, Para A1). Table 2 summarises the modifications made to the audit opinion dependent on the pervasiveness of the material issue.

Table 2: Modification to audit opinion		
Nature of matter giving rise to the modification	**Auditor's judgement about the pervasiveness of the effects or possible effects on the financial statements**	
	Material but not pervasive	**Material and pervasive**
Financial statements are materially misstated	Qualified	Adverse
Inability to obtain sufficient appropriate audit evidence	Qualified	Disclaimer

(IAASB, 2015c, Para A1)

The above table shows what type of audit opinion is applicable given the nature of the material issue and the pervasiveness of the issue on the financial statements. From the above it can be ascertained that material issues which are pervasive result either in an adverse or a disclaimer of opinion. Pervasive effects on the financial statements are those that, in the auditor's judgment are not confined to specific elements, accounts or items of the financial statements or are confined but represent a substantial proportion of the financial statements (IAASB, 2015c). Pervasiveness may also refer to disclosures which are fundamental to users' understanding of the financial statements or matters which are of a legal nature (Palmrose and Scholz, 2004; IAASB, 2015c).

The IAASB and the PCAOB[2] have similar definitions for a qualified, adverse and disclaimer of opinion. These are defined by IAASB (2015c) and PCAOB (2017b) below:

- A qualified opinion states that, except for the effects of the matter(s) to which the qualification relates, the financial statements present fairly in all material respects, the financial position, results of operations and cash flows of the entity in conformity with the relevant financial standards;
- An adverse opinion states that the financial statements do not present fairly the financial position, results of operations, or cash flows of the entity in conformity with the relevant financial standards; and
- A disclaimer of opinion states that the auditor does not express an opinion on the financial statements.

The diagram below illustrates the auditor's choices based on the material issue[3] and the assessment of the nature of the item.

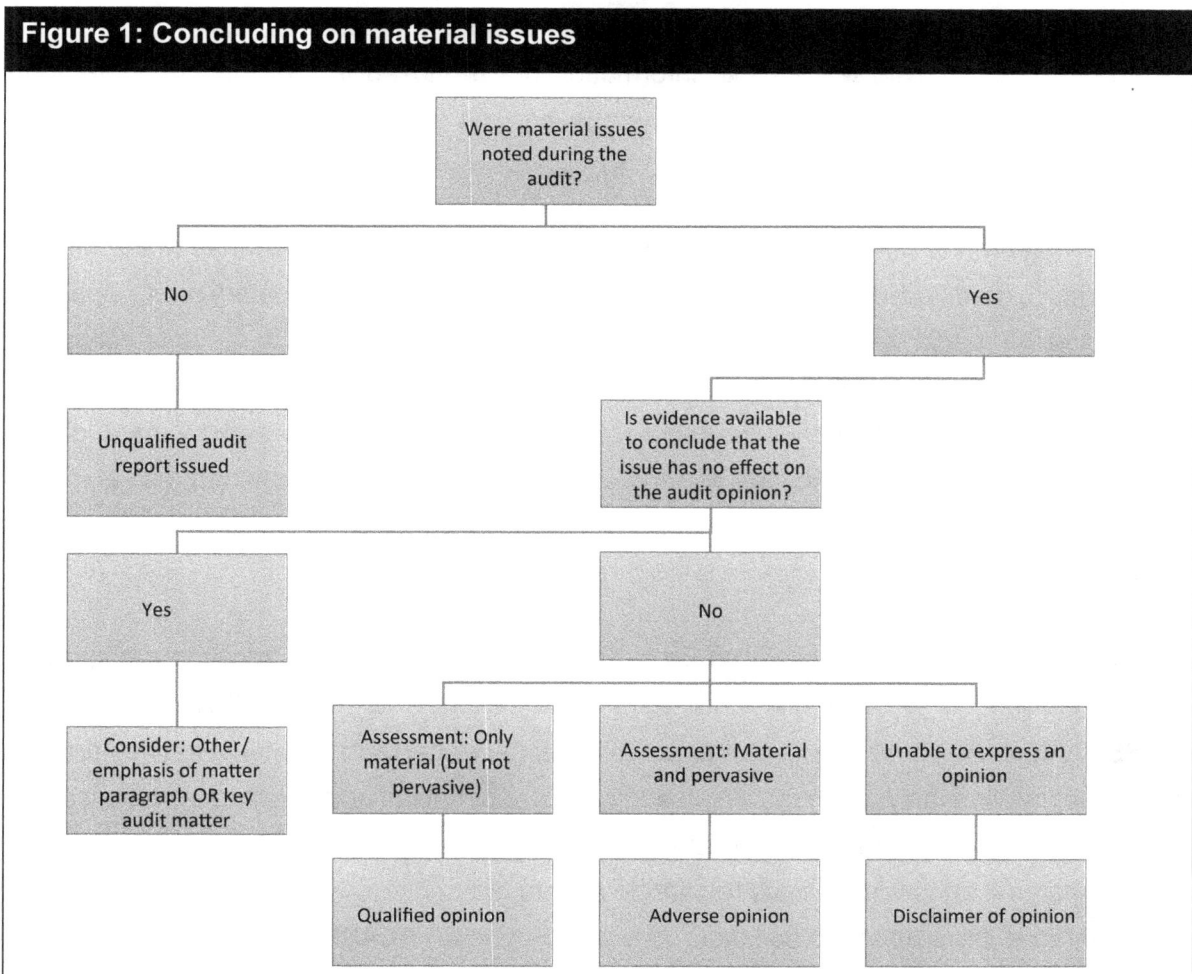

Figure 1: Concluding on material issues

Were material issues noted during the audit?

No → Unqualified audit report issued → Yes → Consider: Other/ emphasis of matter paragraph OR key audit matter

Yes → Is evidence available to conclude that the issue has no effect on the audit opinion?

No → Assessment: Only material (but not pervasive) → Qualified opinion

Assessment: Material and pervasive → Adverse opinion

Unable to express an opinion → Disclaimer of opinion

(adapted from IAASB, 2015b; IAASB, 2015c; IAASB, 2015d)

---

2   Public Company Accounting Oversight Board (PCAOB) is a non-profit corporation created by the Sarbanes–Oxley Act of 2002 to oversee the audits of public companies and other issuers.
3   Material issues refer to material misstatements or the inability to obtain sufficient and appropriate audit evidence.

The opinion is the first item in the audit report placing emphasis on whether or not the financial statements are faithfully represented. Although a modification of an opinion is only applicable if there is a material issue, there are other means of communicating issues which arose during the audit with shareholders such as an Emphasis of Matter or Other paragraph (IAASB, 2015d). There are also consequences for the audit firm releasing a report with the incorrect opinion as this is considered an audit failure (Francis, 2011). An audit failure can permanently damage a firm's reputation, leading to the closure of an audit firm. The demise of Arthur Anderson after the Enron scandal surfaced is an excellent example (Chaney and Philipich, 2002).

6. Other modifications to the audit report (ISA 706)

The inclusion of other explanatory paragraphs is said to be to draw the attention of the reader to specific matters considered to be fundamental to users' understanding of the financial statements or the audit (IAASB, 2015d). An Emphasis of Matter paragraph is used to draw users' attention to information disclosed in the financial statements while an 'Other Matter paragraph' is used to draw users to information not disclosed in the financial statements (IAASB, 2015d). These additional paragraphs can be seen to be addressing both the information gap and the expectation gap (Vanstraelen et al., 2011; Asare and Wright, 2012).

The prior research concludes that, once the information is disclosed in the notes to the financial statements, a modification to the auditor's report in the form of an explanatory paragraph does not provide the reader with incremental information and does not alter the reader's perception of the entity (Houghton, 1983; Bessell et al., 2003). The Emphasis of Matter paragraphs, therefore, have little value to the users and can rather be seen as an attempt by the auditor to limit liability through communication with the users (Chung et al., 2010). In contrast, an 'Other Matter paragraph' is likely to influence readers' perceptions as it brings to light information not disclosed in the financial statements (Houghton, 1983).

In light of these research findings, an Emphasis of Matter or Other Matter paragraph should only be included when necessary and should not mislead the reader (Chung et al., 2010; IAASB, 2015d). An Emphasis of Matter or Other Matter paragraph is not a suitable substitute for a description of individual critical/key audit matters or critical audit matters as discussed in Section 7. In accordance with IAASB (2015d) is also not a substitute for the reporting required when a material uncertainty exists relating to events or conditions which may cast significant doubt on an entity's ability to continue as a going concern (IAASB, 2009g). Please refer to Appendix A for an illustration of an auditor's report.

Table 3 details possible situations involving the inclusion of either an Emphasis of Matter or Other Matter paragraph included in the auditor's report.

Table 3: Scenarios and appropriate inclusions in the audit report	
Scenario	**Type of paragraph to be included in the auditor's report**
To alert users that the financial statements are prepared in accordance with a special purpose framework (IAASB, 2016c, para 14).	Emphasis of Matter
If there is a restriction on the entity regarding the amendment of financial statements to the effects of subsequent events and there is a note in the financial statements (IAASB, 2009f, para 12).	Emphasis of Matter
If there is an amendment to the previous financial statements and there is a note in the financial statements regarding the reason for the amendment (IAASB, 2009f, para 16).	Emphasis of Matter
If there is a circumstance in which the auditor disagrees with the framework applied; however the entity is required by law to prepare their financial statements in accordance with that framework (IAASB, 2009b. Para 19).	Emphasis of Matter
If there is a restriction on the entity regarding the amendment of financial statements to the effects of subsequent events and there is no note in the financial statements (IAASB, 2009f, para 12).	Other Matter
If there is an amendment to the previous financial statements and there is no note in the financial statements regarding the reason for the amendment (IAASB, 2009f, para 16).	Other Matter
If the prior period financial statements have been audited by another auditor or never audited before (IAASB, 2018, para 19).	Other Matter
If an inconsistency arises after reporting date regarding other information and is not corrected by management (IAASB, 2015e, para 19).	Other Matter

The inclusion of an Emphasis of Matter or Other Matter paragraph/s and does not modify the audit opinion as discussed in Section 5 (IAASB, 2015d). ISA 706 results in a modification of the audit report, and not a modification of the audit opinion.

7. Critical/key audit matters (KAM)[4] (ISA 710)

In terms of the ISAs, Registered Auditors are required to communicate KAMs in auditors' reports issued on listed entities, as well as when the auditor is required by law or regulation to communicate KAM in the auditor's report (IAASB, 2018). The description of KAMs in the revised auditor's report is intended to be specific to the entity and to provide useful and relevant information about the audit of an entity to the user of the auditor's report. IAASB (2016b, para 8) defines critical/ key audit matters (KAMs) as:

'... those matters that, in the auditor's professional judgement, were of most significance in the audit of the financial statements; KAMs are, in all cases, a selection of matters communicated with those charged with governance.'

Significance is described by IAASB (2016b, para A2) as the relative importance of a matter, seen in context of both qualitative and quantitative factors. In accordance with IAASB (2016b, para 9) three main areas are identified namely: areas of significant auditor attention, significant auditor judgements relating to areas in the financial statements and the effect on the audit of significant events.

KAMs must be communicated in a separate section of the auditor's report under a separate heading as required by IAASB (2016b, para 11) including an explanation of why the auditor considered the matter to be a KAM and a reference to the related disclosure in the financial statements. In communicating KAMs, the following process is suggested (Cordos and Fülöpa, 2015):

- Describe the matters in the key audit matters section of the report using appropriate subheadings for each;
- Include the reasons the auditor considers the matter to be one of most significance in the audit, its effect on the audit and how it was addressed during the audit;
- Refer to a statement regarding the management's disclosure about the matter, if applicable;
- Include standard wording about key audit matters;
- When applicable, add an explicit statement that the auditor determined there were no key audit matters to report; and
- Explain the requirement to determine and communicate key audit matters for a qualified or adverse opinion, prohibited for disclaimer of opinion.

---

4   The PCAOB and the IAASB have aligned reporting requirements with respect to key audit matters (KAMs). The PCAOB refer to KAMs as critical audit matters (CAM) in terms of their reporting standard: *AS 3101, The Auditor's Report on an Audit of Financial Statements When the Auditor Expresses an Unqualified Opinion*. This book uses the approach emerging in practice to refer simply to KAMs. A review of the differences between guidance issued by the IAASB and the PCAOB is beyond the scope of this book.

KAMs are not a substitute for expressing a modified opinion. Matters giving rise to a qualified audit opinion or an adverse opinion (see Section 5.4) are not intended to be replaced by KAMs as the intention is not to provide a separate opinion on individual KAMs (IAASB, 2016b). If the auditor determines that there are no KAMs, this should be disclosed in the auditor's report (IAASB, 2016b, para 16).

The number of matters to be included in the auditor's report differs from case to case (Cordos and Fülöpa, 2015). KAMs are dependent on the size and complexity of the analysed entity, the nature and conditions of its business and 'the facts and circumstances of the audit engagement' (IAASB, 2016b, para A1). An illustration of an audit report including the KAM paragraph has been included in Appendix A.

The communication of KAM provides additional information to users of the financial statements to assist them to understand the matters which, in the auditor's opinion, are of most significance in the audit of the financial statement (IAASB, 2016b). The amendments and adoption of new standards, including the extended reporting on KAM, by both the International Auditing and Assurance Standards (IAASB) and the Public Company Accounting Oversight Board (PCAOB) was in direct response to the demand for more information on matters important to users' understanding of audited financial statements and the audit (IAASB, 2016b; PCAOB, 2017a; Sirois et al., 2018).

Following a consultation process, the IAASB and the PCAOB propose requiring the communication of KAM in the auditor's report. These additional communications are expected to enhance the value of the auditor's report by:

> 'helping investors and other financial statement users focus on aspects of the company's financial statements that the auditor also found to be challenging' (PCAOB, 2017a) and providing a '(...) roadmap to help users better navigate complex financial reports and focus them on matters likely to be important to their decision-making' (IAASB2011, para 36).

The increase in the value of the audit report is yet to be proven. Research on the impact of additional disclosures is inconclusive with the majority concluding that there is no significant impact on the user (Chong and Pflugrath, 2008; Gold et al., 2012; Mock et al., 2012). Other concerns are also raised regarding the perceptions and expectations created by including additional information in audit reports (Vanstraelen et al., 2012). These include:

- Users may inappropriately rely on an auditor's disclosures as a 'substitute for reading the financial statements' (IAASB, 2012, para. 63);

- The additional disclosures may diminish the overall effectiveness of the auditor's communication on key matters (IAASB, 2016b); and
- The auditor's commentary may unintentionally bias users' reading of an entity's financial statements, leading users to discard otherwise useful information (Sirois et al., 2018).

Sirois et al. (2018) noted that the addition of KAM to the audit report has resulted in changes to users' perceptions as well as users assessing the related financial statements disclosure in less detail. This diminishes the usefulness of the financial statements. However, KAM can provide users with information relevant for deciding if disclosures provided by the management are biased or not (Vanstraelen et al., 2012; Cordos and Fülöpa, 2015).

8. Summary

- Audit outputs are a direct result of the procedures performed during the audit and the subsequent communication with those charged with governance. Of particular importance is the need for the auditor to build rapport with those charged with governance to ensure the timely completion of the audit.
- Upon completion of the audit, an auditor's report which provides an opinion on the client's financial statements is issued. The audit opinion indicates whether or not the financial statements achieve fair presentation in accordance with the applicable financial reporting framework. Key to the formulation of the audit opinion are the provisions of ISA 450, ISA 705, ISA 710 and ISA 720. These deal with the evaluation of misstatements, comparative and other information, and the assessment of the entity's ability to continue as a going concern.
- Guidance on the structure of the auditor's report is provided in ISA 700 which prescribes specific paragraphs detailing management and the auditor's responsibilities.
- Finally, this chapter examines other modifications to the auditor's report prescribed by ISA 701 and ISA 706. These require the inclusion of separate sections detailing KAMs, specifically for listed entities, and either an Emphasis of Matter or Other Matter paragraph depending on the nature of the matter identified.

Appendix A

INDEPENDENT AUDITOR'S REPORT (IAASB, 2015b, para 21)

To the Shareholders of ABC Company [or Other Appropriate Addressee] (IAASB, 2015b, para 22)

Report on the Audit of the Financial Statements[5]

Opinion (IAASB, 2015b, para 23–27)

In our opinion, the accompanying financial statements present fairly, in all material respects, (or give a true and fair view of) the financial position of ABC Company (the Company) as at December 31, 20X1, and (of) its financial performance and its cash flows for the year then ended in accordance with International Financial Reporting Standards (IFRSs).

We have audited the financial statements of the Company, which comprise the statement of financial position as at December 31, 20X1, and the statement of comprehensive income, statement of changes in equity and statement of cash flows for the year then ended, and notes to the financial statements, including a summary of significant accounting policies.

Basis for Opinion (IAASB, 2015b, para 28)

We conducted our audit in accordance with International Standards on Auditing (ISAs). Our responsibilities under those standards are further described in the Auditor's Responsibilities for the Audit of the Financial Statements section of our report. We are independent of the Company within the meaning of [indicate relevant ethical requirements or applicable law or regulation] and have fulfilled our other responsibilities under those ethical requirements. We believe that the audit evidence we have obtained is sufficient and appropriate to provide a basis for our opinion.

Key Audit Matters (IAASB, 2016b, para 9–11)

Key audit matters are those matters that, in our professional judgment, were of most significance in our audit of the financial statements. Key audit matters are selected from the matters communicated with [those charged with governance], but are not intended to represent all matters that were discussed with them. Our audit procedures relating to these matters were designed in the context of our audit of the financial statements as a whole. Our opinion on the financial statements is not modified with respect to any of the key audit matters described below, and we do not express an opinion on these individual matters.

This section would be tailored to the facts and circumstances of the individual audit engagement and the entity.

Going Concern (IAASB, 2009g, para 19–25)

---

5   The sub-title 'Report on the Audit of the Financial Statements' is unnecessary in circumstances when the second sub-title 'Report on Other Legal and Regulatory Requirements' is not applicable.

The Company's financial statements have been prepared using the going concern basis of accounting. The use of this basis of accounting is appropriate unless management either intends to liquidate the Company or to cease operations, or has no realistic alternative but to do so. As part of our audit of the financial statements, we have concluded that management's use of the going concern basis of accounting in the preparation of the Company's financial statements is appropriate.

Management has not identified a material uncertainty that may cast significant doubt on the entity's ability to continue as a going concern, and accordingly none is disclosed in the financial statements. Based on our audit of the financial statements, we also have not identified such a material uncertainty. However, neither management nor the auditor can guarantee the Company's ability to continue as a going concern.

Other Information (IAASB, 2015b, para 31)

The content of this section may include, among other matters: (a) a description of the auditor's responsibilities with respect to other information; (b) identification of the document(s) available at the date of the auditor's report that contain the other information to which the auditor's responsibilities apply; (c) a statement addressing the outcome of the auditor's work on the other information; and (d) a statement that the auditor has not audited or reviewed the other information and, accordingly, does not express an audit opinion or a review conclusion on it.

Responsibilities of [Management[6] and Those Charged with Governance or other appropriate terms for the Financial Statements (IAASB, 2015b, para 32–34).

Management is responsible for the preparation and fair presentation of these financial statements in accordance with IFRSs[7], and for such internal control as management determines is necessary to enable the preparation of financial statements that are free from material misstatement, whether due to fraud or error. Those charged with governance are responsible for overseeing the Company's financial reporting process.

Auditor's Responsibilities for the Audit of the Financial Statements (IAASB, 2015b, para 35–40)

The objectives of our audit are to obtain reasonable assurance about whether the financial statements as a whole are free from material misstatement, whether due to fraud or error,

---

6   Throughout the illustrative auditor's reports in the Proposed ISAs, the term management may need to be replaced by another term that is appropriate in the context of the legal framework in the particular jurisdiction. For example, those charged with governance, rather than management, may have these responsibilities.

7   Where management's responsibility is to prepare financial statements that give a true and fair view, this may read: 'Management is responsible for the preparation of financial statements that give a true and fair view in accordance with IFRSs, and for such ...'

and to issue an auditor's report that includes our opinion. Reasonable assurance is a high level of assurance, but is not a guarantee that an audit conducted in accordance with ISAs will always detect a material misstatement when it exists. Misstatements can arise from fraud or error and are considered material if, individually or in the aggregate, they could reasonably be expected to influence the economic decisions of users taken on the basis of these financial statements.

Report on Other Legal and Regulatory Requirements (IAASB, 2015b, para 41)

[The form and content of this section of the auditor's report would vary depending on the nature of the auditor's other reporting responsibilities prescribed by local law, regulation, or national auditing standards. Depending on the matters addressed by other law, regulation or national auditing standards, national standard setters may choose to combine reporting on these matters with reporting as required by the ISAs (shown in the Report on the Audit of the Financial Statements section), with wording in the auditor's report that clearly distinguishes between reporting required by the ISAs and other reporting required by law or regulation.]

The engagement partner responsible for the audit resulting in this independent auditor's report is [name]. (IAASB, 2015b, para 42)

[Signature in the name of the audit firm, the personal name of the auditor, or both, as appropriate for the particular jurisdiction] (IAASB, 2015b, para 43)

[Auditor Address] (IAASB, 2015b, para 44)

[Date] (IAASB, 2015b, para 45)

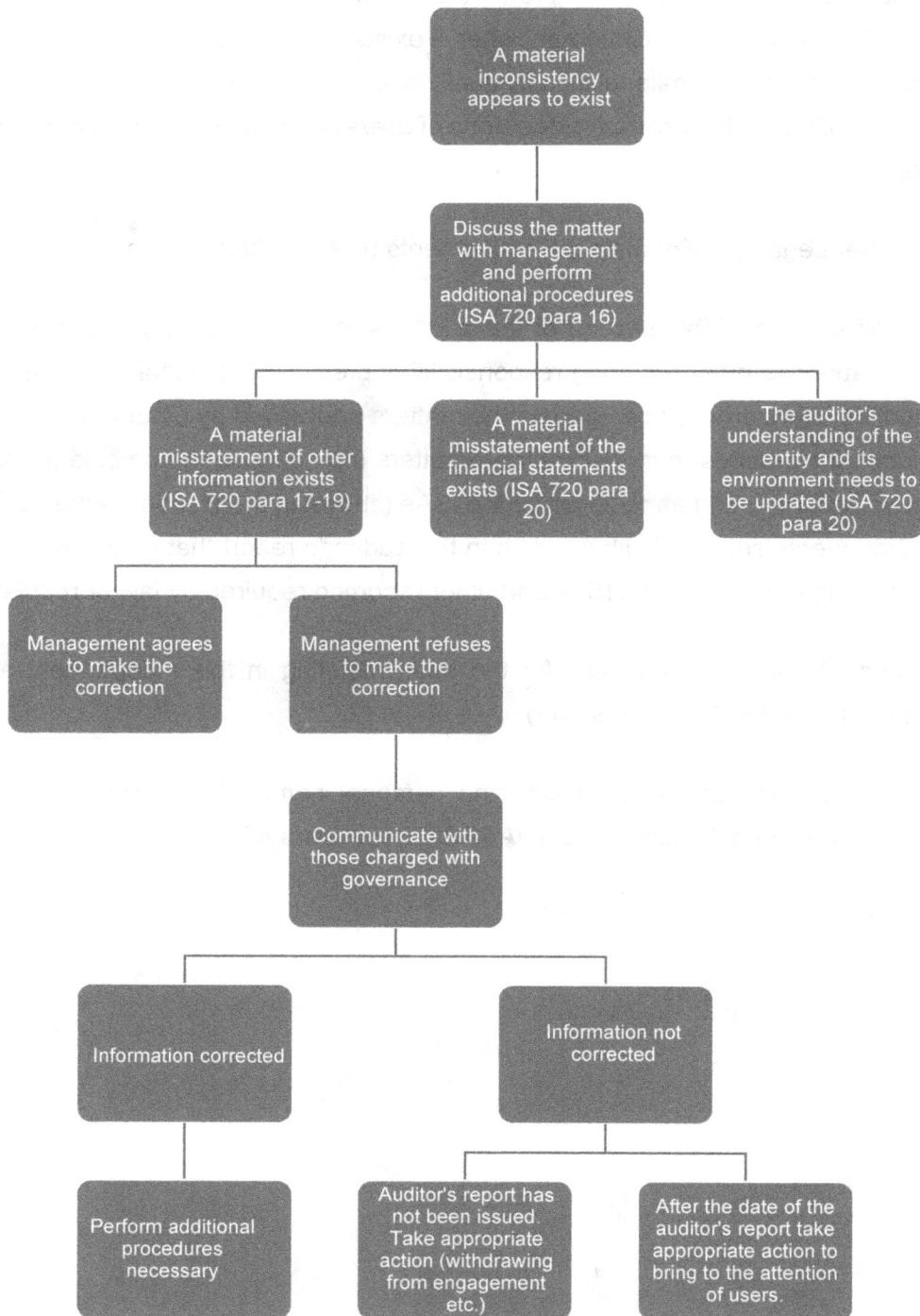

A material inconsistency appears to exist

Discuss the matter with management and perform additional procedures (ISA 720 para 16)

A material misstatement of other information exists (ISA 720 para 17-19)

A material misstatement of the financial statements exists (ISA 720 para 20)

The auditor's understanding of the entity and its environment needs to be updated (ISA 720 para 20)

Management agrees to make the correction

Management refuses to make the correction

Communicate with those charged with governance

Information corrected

Information not corrected

Perform additional procedures necessary

Auditor's report has not been issued. Take appropriate action (withdrawing from engagement etc.)

After the date of the auditor's report take appropriate action to bring to the attention of users.

Appendix C

```
                          ┌─────────────┐
                          │ Audit report │
                          └──────┬──────┘
          ┌──────────────────────┼──────────────────────────┐
  ┌───────────────┐    ┌────────────────┐        ┌──────────────────────┐
  │ Going concern │    │  Not going     │        │  Going concern       │
  │ baisis of     │    │  concern and   │        │  appropriate         │
  │ accounting is │    │  liquidation   │        │  but material        │
  │ inappropriate │    │  basis used    │        │  uncertainy          │
  │               │    │  by entity     │        │  exists              │
  └───────┬───────┘    └───────┬────────┘        └──────────┬───────────┘
  ┌───────────────┐    ┌────────────────┐      ┌─────────────┴─────────────┐
  │   Adverse     │    │  Emphasis of   │  ┌────────────────┐   ┌────────────────┐
  │   opinion     │    │  matter        │  │ Matter is      │   │ Matter is not  │
  └───────────────┘    └────────────────┘  │ appropriately  │   │ disclosed      │
                                           │ dislosed       │   └───────┬────────┘
                                           └───────┬────────┘   ┌────────────────┐
                                       ┌────────────────┐       │ Qualified or   │
                                       │ Section titled │       │ adverse        │
                                       │ 'Material      │       │ opinion        │
                                       │ uncertainty    │       └────────────────┘
                                       │ related to     │
                                       │ Going Concern' │
                                       └────────────────┘
```

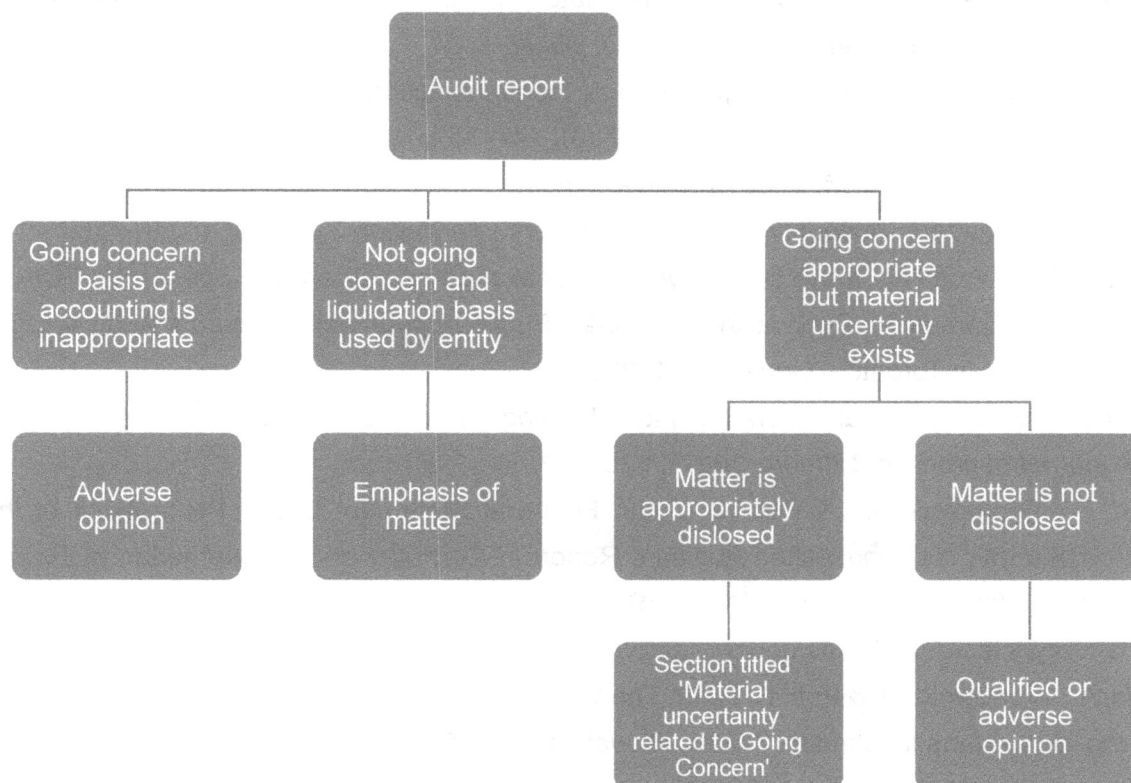

(adapted from IAASB, 2015b; IAASB, 2016a)

9. References

ACCA 2010. Reshaping the audit for the new global economy. *Accountancy Futures,* 1, 68–70.

Asare, S. K. & Wright, A. M. 2012. Investors', auditors', and lenders' understanding of the message conveyed by the standard audit report on the financial statements. *Accounting Horizons,* 26 (2), 193–217.

Ashbaugh-Skaife, H., Collins, D. W. & Kinney Jr, W. R. 2007. The discovery and reporting of internal control deficiencies prior to SOX-mandated audits. *Journal of accounting and economics,* 44 (1–2), 166–192.

Bessell, M., Anandarajan, A. & Umar, A. 2003. Information content, audit reports and going-concern: an Australian study. *Accounting & Finance,* 43 (3), 261–282.

Chaney, P. K. & Philipich, K. L. 2002. Shredded reputation: The cost of audit failure. *Journal of accounting research,* 40 (4), 1221–1245.

Chong, K. M. & Pflugrath, G. 2008. Do different audit report formats affect shareholders' and auditors' perceptions? *International Journal of Auditing,* 12 (3), 221–241.

Chung, J., Farrar, J., Puri, P. & Thorne, L. 2010. Auditor liability to third parties after Sarbanes-Oxley: An international comparison of regulatory and legal reforms. *Journal of International Accounting, Auditing and Taxation,* 19 (1), 66–78.

Colbert, J. L. 2002. Corporate governance: communications from internal and external auditors. *Managerial Auditing Journal,* 17 (3), 147–152.

Cordos, G. S. & Fülöpa, M. T. 2015. Understanding audit reporting changes: introduction of Key Audit Matters. *Accounting and Management Information Systems,* 14 (1), 128.

Doty, J. 2011. Auditing in the Decade Ahead: Challange and Change – Speech by PCAOB Chairman James R. Doty at the Canadian Public Accountability Board's Audit Quaility Symposium in Toronto – December 1, 2011.

Francis, J. R. 2011. A framework for understanding and researching audit quality. *Auditing: A journal of practice & theory,* 30 (2), 125–152.

Gold, A., Gronewold, U. & Pott, C. 2009. Financial Statement Users' Perceptions of the IAASB's ISA 700 Unqualified Auditor's Report in Germany and the Netherlands. Report Prepared for the AICPA's and IAASB.(September). New York, NY. Available at: http://www. ifac. org/sites/default/files/downloads/Study_4_ASB_ResearchReport. pdf.

Gold, A., Gronewold, U. & Pott, C. 2012. The ISA 700 auditor's report and the audit expectation gap–do explanations matter? *International Journal of Auditing,* 16 (3), 286–307.

Hogan, C. E. & Wilkins, M. S. 2008. Evidence on the audit risk model: Do auditors increase audit fees in the presence of internal control deficiencies? *Contemporary Accounting Research,* 25 (1), 219–242.

Houghton, K. A. 1983. Audit reports: Their Impact on the loan decision process and outcome: An experiment. *Accounting and business research,* 14 (53), 15–20.

Houghton, K. A., Jubb, C. & Kend, M. 2011. Materiality in the context of audit: the real expectations gap. *Managerial Auditing Journal,* 26 (6), 482–500.

IAASB 2009a. ISA 200: Overall objectives of the independent auditor and the conduct of an audit in accordance with international standards on auditing. *SAICA Members' Handbook.* 2009 ed. Pietermaritsburg: LexisNexis.

IAASB 2009b. ISA 210: Agreeing the terms of audit engagements. *SAICA Members' Handbook.* Pietermaritsburg: LexisNexis.

IAASB 2009c. ISA 265: Communicating Deficiencies in Internal Control to Those Charged with Governance and Management. New York: International Federation of Accountants.

IAASB 2009d. ISA 330: The auditor's responses to assessed risks. *SAICA Members' Handbook.* 2009 ed. Pietermaritsburg: LexisNexis.

IAASB 2009e. ISA 450: Evaluation of misstatements identified during the audit. *SAICA Members' Handbook.* 2009 ed. Pietermaritsburg: LexisNexis.

IAASB 2009f. ISA 560: Subsequent events *SAICA members' handbook. 2018.* Pietermaritsburg: LexisNexis.

IAASB 2009g. ISA 570: Going Concern. *SAICA members' handbook.* Pietermaritsburg: LexisNexis.

IAASB 2009h. ISA 610: Using the work of internal auditors. *SAICA members' handbook.* Pietermaritsburg: LexisNexis.

IAASB 2011. Enhancing the value of auditor reporting: Exploring options for change. *Consultation paper.*

IAASB 2012. Invitation to Comment: Improving the Auditor's Report. International Federation of Accountants New York, NY.

IAASB 2014a. Framework for Audit Quality: Key Elements that Create an Environment for Audit Quality.

IAASB 2014b. *Handbook of International Quality Control, Auditing, Review, Other Assurance, and Related Services Pronouncements*, International Federation of Accountants.

IAASB 2015a. ISA 260: Communication with those Charged with Governance. *SAICA members' handbook. 2015.* Pietermaritsburg: LexisNexis.

IAASB 2015b. ISA 700: Forming an Opinion and Reporting on Financial Statements. *SAICA members' handbook. 2015.* Pietermaritsburg: LexisNexis.

IAASB 2015c. ISA 705:Modifications to the Opinion in the Independent Auditor's Report. *SAICA members' handbook. 2015.* Pietermaritsburg: LexisNexis.

IAASB 2015d. ISA 706: Emphasis of Matter Paragraphs and Other Matter Paragraphs in the Independent Auditor's Report. *SAICA members' handbook. 2015.* Pietermaritsburg: LexisNexis.

IAASB 2015e. ISA 720: The Auditor's Responsibilities Relating to Other Information in Documents Containing Audited Financial Statements. *SAICA members' handbook. 2015.* Pietermaritsburg: LexisNexis.

IAASB 2016a. ISA 570: Going Concern. *SAICA members' handbook. 2016.* Pietermaritsburg: LexisNexis.

IAASB 2016b. ISA 701: Communicating Key Audit Matters in the Independent Auditor's Report. *SAICA Members' Handbook.* Pietermaritsburg: LexisNexis.

IAASB 2016c. ISA 800: Special considerations – Audits of financial statements prepared in accordance with special purpose frameworks. *SAICA members' handbook. 2018.* Pietermaritsburg: LexisNexis.

IAASB 2018. ISA 710: Comparative information corresponding figures and comparative financial statements. *SAICA members' handbook. 2018.* Pietermaritsburg: LexisNexis.

International Accounting Standards Board (IASB) 2014. *A Guide through IFRS,* London, IFRS Foundation.

IOD 2016. *King IV Report on Corporate Governance in South Africa*, Lexis Nexus South Africa, Johannesburg, South Africa.

Jiang, W., Rupley, K. H. & Wu, J. 2010. Internal control deficiencies and the issuance of going concern opinions. *Research in Accounting Regulation,* 22 (1), 40–46.

Johnstone, K. M. 2000. Client-acceptance decisions: Simultaneous effects of client business risk, audit risk, auditor business risk, and risk adaptation. *Auditing: A Journal of Practice & Theory*, 19 (1), 1–25.

Koh, H. C. & Woo, E. S. 1998. The expectation gap in auditing. *Managerial Auditing Journal*, 13 (3), 147–154.

Liggio, C. D. 1974. Expectation gap-accountants legal Waterloo. *Journal of contemporary business*, 3 (3), 27–44.

Littleton, A. C. & Zimmerman, V. K. 1963. Accounting Theory: Continuity and Change. *Prentice-Hall*.

Maroun, W. & Wainer, H. 2014. A critical review of South African Audit Practice Statement 3. *Southern African Journal of Accountability and Auditing Research*, 16, 15–21.

McEnroe, J. E. & Martens, S. C. 2001. Auditors' and investors' perceptions of the "expectation gap". *Accounting Horizons*, 15 (4), 345–358.

Mock, T. J., Bédard, J., Coram, P. J., Davis, S. M., Espahbodi, R. & Warne, R. C. 2012. The audit reporting model: Current research synthesis and implications. *Auditing: A Journal of Practice & Theory*, 32 (sp1), 323–351.

Palmrose, Z. V. & Scholz, S. 2004. The circumstances and legal consequences of non-GAAP reporting: Evidence from restatements. *Contemporary Accounting Research*, 21 (1), 139–180.

PCAOB 2017a. AS 3101: The Auditor's Report on an Audit of Financial Statements When the Auditor Expresses an Unqualified Opinion New York, NY 10036–8775: American Institute of CPAs.

PCAOB 2017b. AS 3105: Departures from Unqualified Opinions and Other Reporting Circumstances. New York, NY 10036–8775: American Institute of CPAs.

Porter, B. 2009. Report on Research Conducted in the United Kingdom and New Zealand in 2008 Investigating the Audit Expectation Performance Gap and Users' Understanding of, and Desired Improvements to, the Auditor's Report. Citeseer.

Prada, M. 2007. Transcript: Quality of public company audits from a regulatory perspective. International Organization of Securities Commission.

Schelluch, P. & Gay, G. 2006. Assurance provided by auditors' reports on prospective financial information: implications for the expectation gap. *Accounting & Finance*, 46 (4), 653–676.

Sikka, P., Puxty, A., Willmott, H. & Cooper, C. 1998. The impossibility of eliminating the expectations gap: Some theory and evidence. *Critical Perspectives on Accounting*, 9 (3), 299–330.

Sirois, L. P., Bédard, J. & Bera, P. 2018. The informational value of key audit matters in the auditor's report: Evidence from an eye-tracking study. *Accounting Horizons*.

Sultanoglu, B., Mugan, C. S., Sekerdag, U. & Oran, A. 2018. The auditor's opinion modifications around domestic and global financial crises. *Meditari Accountancy Research*.

Vanstraelen, A., Schelleman, C., IMBA, I. H. & RA, R. M. 2011. A Framework for Extended Audit Reporting.

Vanstraelen, A., Schelleman, C., Meuwissen, R. & Hofmann, I. 2012. The audit reporting debate: Seemingly intractable problems and feasible solutions. *European Accounting Review,* 21 (2), 193–215.

PART D

Chapter 19: Outsourcing

1. Introduction

Outsourcing commences with the development of a business case for moving internally completed processes or tasks to an external service provider. This includes an analysis of the existing internal function, the desired outcomes for the function and the assessment of the capabilities required by the service provider (Bielski, 2006).

According to Desai et al. (2011) an organisation has three options when considering the funding and functioning of any of its business functions, namely:

- In-house maintenance of the function;
- Outsourcing of the function to a third party; or
- Co-sourcing of the function, where the organisation partners with an outside service provider.

If a decision is made to outsource a function, an organisation must also decide with whom to enter into such an arrangement. Options available are:

- An independent non-assurance related service provider, eg information technology (IT) processes;
- Its current assurance service provider; or
- An alternate assurance provider, independent from the organisation.

(Abbott et al., 2007)

This chapter focuses on the outsourcing of internal audit services and information technology services, regulatory requirements and corporate governance practices. The independence requirements of the assurance provider in context of outsourcing of these functions are discussed in detail. The decision to outsource, for example, internal functions[1] is dependent on the combined assurance model implemented by the organisation (IoD, 2016). An organisation's audit committee[2] plays an important role in the assessment of decisions surrounding outsourcing pertaining to non-audit related services (IoD, 2016). The audit committee should take into consideration the level of assurance required (where applicable), the cost of the service vs the benefit obtained and the appointment of a 'caretaker' of the relationship with the contracting entity (Bielski, 2006; IoD, 2016). In particular, issues such as

---

1   Examples include IT related processes, valuation services, forensic investigation or internal audit.
2   The terms 'audit committee', 'board of directors' and 'those charged with governance' are used interchangeably in this chapter.

independence, regulatory requirements and service quality need to be considered (Abbot et al., 2007). Outsourcing by means of an entity using a service organisation is also included in the scope of this chapter and discusses the responsibility of the assurance provider to obtain sufficient appropriate audit evidence pertaining to the audit client.

2. Definitions

Outsourcing is not defined in the International Federations for Accountants Code of Ethics (2006) so a definition is obtained from the prior academic research. Outsourcing is defined as devising a contract with an external organisation to take primary responsibility for providing business processes to the primary organisation (Yang et al., 2007). Loh and Venkatraman (1992, p. 9) define outsourcing as the significant contribution by external vendors in the physical and/or human resources associated with the entire or specific components of the IT infrastructure in the user organisation. Outsourcing can also be defined as products supplied to the multinational firm by independent suppliers from around the world (Kotabe, 1992: p. 103, cited in Gilley and Rasheed, 2000). IESBA (2018) defines professional services as services performed for clients.

For purposes of this chapter, outsourcing is defined as a contractual relationship entered into with an external and independent third party to provide services to the organisation which would usually be provided internally by the organisation (Loh and Venkatraman, 1992; Gilley and Rasheed, 2000; Yang et al., 2007).

3. Regulatory requirements, codes of best practice and code of ethics

Regulatory requirements and codes of best practice are primarily concerned with independence of the current assurance service provider when engaging in non-audit related services to its audit client (Knechel et al., 2012). This is within the context of outsourcing of services, such as internal audit, to a current assurance provider. This section will compare the requirements in the United States of America, United Kingdom and South Africa. Lastly, the limitations of the International Ethics Standards Board for Accountants (IESBA) (2018) on the current assurance service provider will be briefly discussed.

3.1 United States of America

Organisations within the ambit of the Sarbanes Oxley Act (SOX, 2002) have specific limitations when considering outsourcing arrangements to an organisation's current assurance service provider. In terms of s201 of SOX, the following services are *prohibited* as they are seen as having a material adverse impact on the independence of the current assurance service provider:

- 'bookkeeping or other services related to the accounting records or financial statements of the audit client;
- financial IT design and implementation;
- appraisal or valuation services, fairness opinions, or contribution-in-kind reports;
- actuarial services;
- internal audit outsourcing services;
- management functions or human resources;
- broker or dealer, investment adviser, or investment banking services;
- legal services and expert services unrelated to the audit; and
- any other service which the Board determines, by regulation, is impermissible'.

Services other than those listed above, such as taxation services, may be provided by the current assurance service provider if the audit committee pre-approves the expenditure. In addition, the total cost of the non-audit services must not exceed 5% of the total revenue paid by the organisation to the current assurance service provider (SOX, 2002). SOX (2002) does not distinguish between routine and non-routine outsourced internal assurance function (IAF), possibly because it may have negative connotations for both auditor independence and audit quality (Abbot et al., 2007).

3.2 United Kingdom

The United Kingdom's requirements are documented in their Audit Regulations in which te appropriateness of the provision of non-audit services by a current assurance service provider must be monitored for any independence concerns. Audit committees are entrusted the following responsibilities (Financial Reporting Council, 2016 (hereafter referred to as the FRC):
- To review the assurance service provider in terms of independence, objectivity and the effectiveness of the audit process;
- Disclosure by means of an explanation of how the current assurance providers' objectivity and independence have been safeguarded; and
- Development and implementation of a policy on the engagement of the assurance service provider to supply non-audit services. This extends to continuous monitoring and reporting to the board of directors to address concerns relating to the assurance service provider discussed above.

3.3 South Africa

The South African Companies Act (2008) contains certain limitations pertaining to the appointment of a registered auditor. The focus of relevance is whether the registered auditor *previously* provided other services to the same company.

S90 prohibits the appointment of a registered auditor where a professional accountant maintained any of the company's financial records or prepared any of the financial statements or habitually performed the duties of an accountant or bookkeepers or related secretarial work for the company. This restriction is valid for the five years prior to the appointment as a registered auditor (Republic of South Africa, 2008).

S94 deals with audit committee composition and responsibilities. For non-audit related services the audit committee has the following duties:

- Determining the nature and extent of any non-audit services that the registered auditor may or may not provide;
- Pre-approving of any proposed agreement with the registered auditor for the provision of non-audit services to the company; and
- Ascertaining that the registered auditor does not receive any direct or indirect remuneration or other benefit from the organisation, except as auditor or for rendering of other permitted services (Republic of South Africa, 2008).

These sections are relevant as audit committees are required to make submissions to the board of directors on any matters concerning the company's accounting policies, financial control, records and reporting (Republic of South Africa, 2008) which can possibly be affected by an outsourcing arrangement.

In terms of King IV, outsourcing is not limited to only internal audit services. King IV refers to a number of possible outsourced functions, such as (IoD, 2016):

- provision of professional corporate governance services, performed by either a juristic person or a full or part time individual;
- an outsource service provider arrangement within the IT sphere;
- investment activities and decisions;
- employee retirement fund administration; and
- internal audit services.

The responsibility for approval and overseeing of outsourcing arrangements lies with the governing body or any committee to which the responsibility has been delegated. With regards to outsourcing of internal audit services, King IV emphasises that the role and responsibility of the Chief Audit Executive must be clear (IoD, 2016). In terms of the Auditing Profession Act (2005) s44 requires disclosure where a registered auditor, or any other member of the registered auditor's firm, is responsible for keeping records or accounts of an audit client. Responsibility for keeping records extends to the continuous update of financial information during the year and not to year-end closing entries, adjusting entries or framing financial statements from existing records (The Republic of South Africa, 2005).

3.4 Code of Ethics

Audit committees must be alert when considering or approving the appointment of professional service providers for taxation, internal audit or accounting services. Likewise, the assurance service providers should be aware of potential threats to independence when an additional appointment over and above the audit of the financial statements is accepted (IoD, 2016). The threats to the independence of the service providers are usually self-review threats, especially in the case when the service provided fulfills a managerial role within the contracting company (IESBA, 2018). It is not possible to reduce the threat through the implementation of any safeguards and, for this reason, service providers of IAF should not assume any managerial responsibility (IESBA, 2018).

Section 604 of the IESBA (2018) lists the following examples which involve assuming management responsibilities pertaining to internal audit services:

- Setting internal audit policies or the strategic direction of internal audit activities;
- Directing and taking responsibility for the actions of the entity's internal audit employees;
- Deciding which recommendations resulting from internal audit activities will be implemented;
- Reporting the results of the internal audit activities to those charged with governance on behalf of management;
- Performing procedures which form part of the internal control, such as reviewing and approving changes to employee data access privileges; and
- Taking responsibility for designing, implementing and maintaining internal control.

Section 606 of the IESBA (2018) lists the following examples which do not involve assuming management responsibilities pertaining to IT system services:

- Designing or implementing IT systems which are unrelated to internal control over financial reporting;
- Designing and implementing IT systems which do not generate financial information which forms a significant part of the accounting records or financial statements;
- Implementing 'off-the-shelf' accounting or financial information reporting software that was not developed by the assurance provider; and
- Evaluating and making recommendations about an IT system's design, implementation or operations by another service provider or the client.

The golden rule for both section 604 and 606 is that management acknowledges their responsibility, ensures that the non-audit service delivery does not significantly impact on internal controls relating to the audit client's financial reporting, forms a significant part of the preparation of the financial statements, takes responsibility for all managerial decisions and evaluates the adequacy of outsourced services (IESBA, 2018).

4. Requirements for entering into an outsourcing arrangement

At the outset, the organisation should have a documented mandate for the proposed outsourcing arrangement. The board of directors, or, if delegated, another board appointed committee, should pre-approve such a relationship (Institute of Directors Southern Africa, 2016; IESBA, 2018). A proper business case should be developed which will include (Bielski, 2006):

- Analysis of the current function;
- Detailing the desired outcomes;
- Assessment of the current capabilities available to the organisation; and
- Cost versus benefit analysis.

5. Advantages and disadvantages

This section compares the advantages and disadvantages of an in-house, an outsourced and a co-sourced IAF.

5.1 In-house IAF

Figure 1 illustrates the advantages and disadvantages of an in-house IAF.

Figure 1: Advantages and disadvantages of an in-house IAF

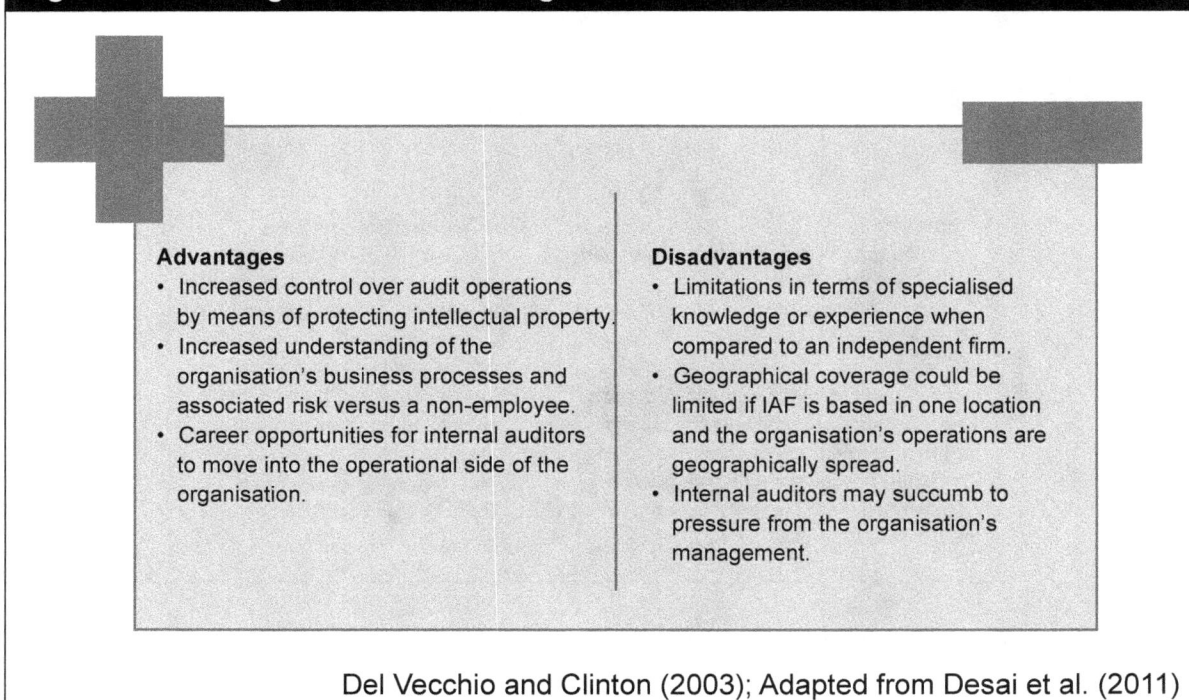

Advantages
- Increased control over audit operations by means of protecting intellectual property.
- Increased understanding of the organisation's business processes and associated risk versus a non-employee.
- Career opportunities for internal auditors to move into the operational side of the organisation.

Disadvantages
- Limitations in terms of specialised knowledge or experience when compared to an independent firm.
- Geographical coverage could be limited if IAF is based in one location and the organisation's operations are geographically spread.
- Internal auditors may succumb to pressure from the organisation's management.

Del Vecchio and Clinton (2003); Adapted from Desai et al. (2011)

5.2 Outsourced IAF

The outsourcing of an IAF to an external assurance service provider can have the following advantages and disadvantages:

Figure 2: Advantages and disadvantages of outsourcing the IAF

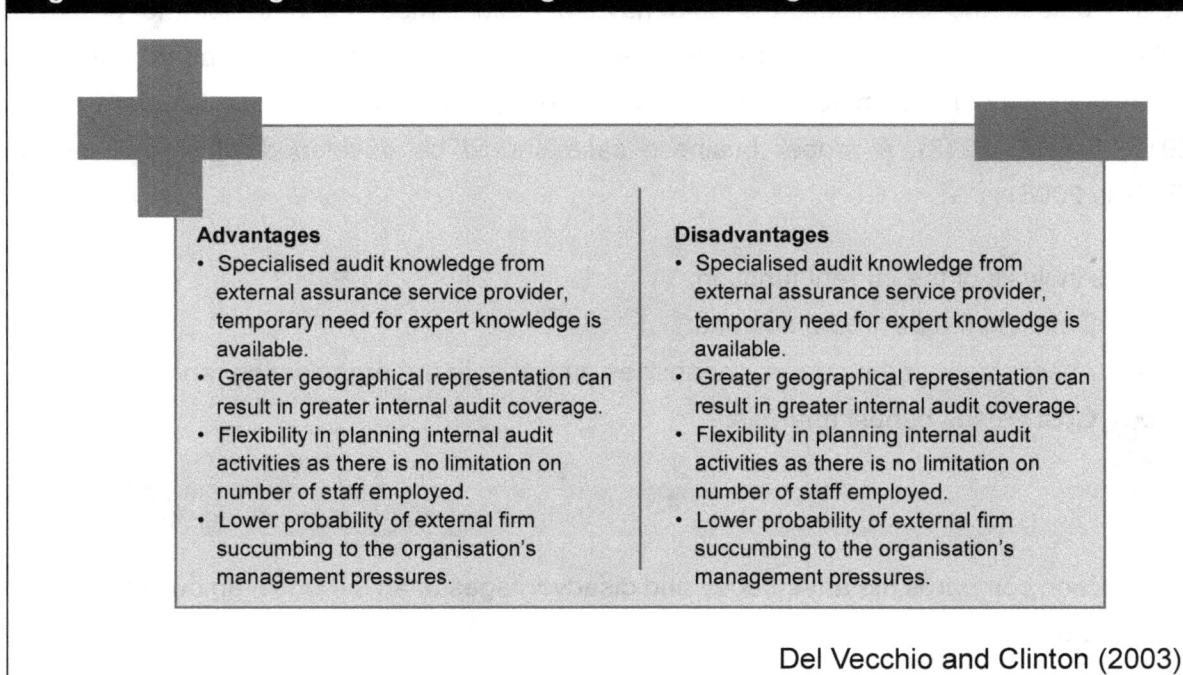

Advantages
- Specialised audit knowledge from external assurance service provider, temporary need for expert knowledge is available.
- Greater geographical representation can result in greater internal audit coverage.
- Flexibility in planning internal audit activities as there is no limitation on number of staff employed.
- Lower probability of external firm succumbing to the organisation's management pressures.

Disadvantages
- Specialised audit knowledge from external assurance service provider, temporary need for expert knowledge is available.
- Greater geographical representation can result in greater internal audit coverage.
- Flexibility in planning internal audit activities as there is no limitation on number of staff employed.
- Lower probability of external firm succumbing to the organisation's management pressures.

Del Vecchio and Clinton (2003)

5.3 Co-sourcing of IAF

Figure 3: Advantages and disadvantages of co-outsourcing the IAF

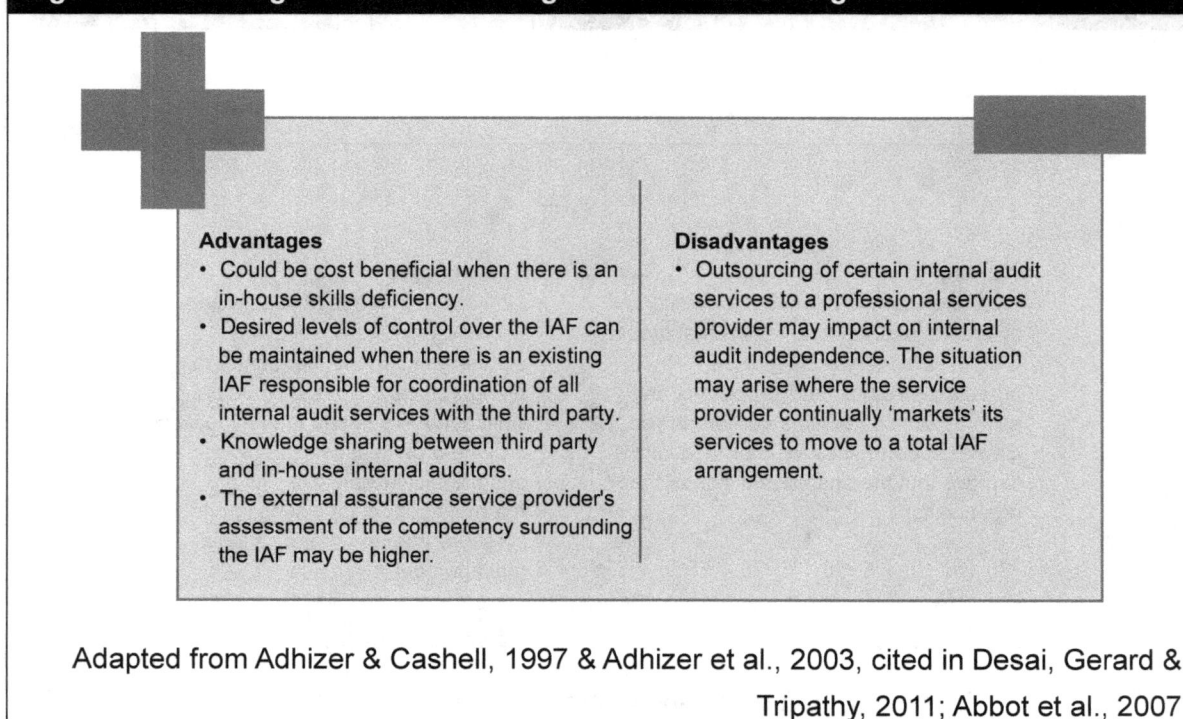

Advantages
- Could be cost beneficial when there is an in-house skills deficiency.
- Desired levels of control over the IAF can be maintained when there is an existing IAF responsible for coordination of all internal audit services with the third party.
- Knowledge sharing between third party and in-house internal auditors.
- The external assurance service provider's assessment of the competency surrounding the IAF may be higher.

Disadvantages
- Outsourcing of certain internal audit services to a professional services provider may impact on internal audit independence. The situation may arise where the service provider continually 'markets' its services to move to a total IAF arrangement.

Adapted from Adhizer & Cashell, 1997 & Adhizer et al., 2003, cited in Desai, Gerard & Tripathy, 2011; Abbot et al., 2007

6. Outsourcing of IT functions

It is generally accepted that IT strategies help to drive organisational objectives (Bart and Turel, 2010) and are part of the corporate DNA of an organisation (IoD, 2016, p6). For this reason, technology governance should address both the organisation's strategic use of IT and the need for IT reliability. IT governance encompass strategic, planning, risk management, financial reporting and regulatory compliance (Bart and Turel, 2010).

There are many IT functions or processes which can be outsourced, for example, a company may outsource processing functionality, assistance with disaster recovery, storage of data or specialised projects (Bielski, 2006). As for all outsourcing arrangements, there will be a transitional period during which the organisation and the IT service provider are experiencing initial 'teething' problems. For an IT outsourcing arrangement to be successful, a strong approach to performance management needs to be in place (Bielski, 2006). Even in the sphere of IT, certain internal audit review functions over electronic data processing (EDP) or special projects can be outsourced (if this is more efficient and cost effective than acquiring or developing the skills in-house) (Abbot et al., 2007).

The allocation of an EDP review to an organisation's existing external assurance service provider has certain advantages:

- The audit committee may gain confidence that there is a transfer of existing knowledge and the review of EDP, resulting in a more comprehensive financial statement audit;
- The external assurance provider is already familiar with the organisation's corporate culture;
- Possible reduction in the risk of budget overruns (Krishnan & Zhou, 1997, cited in Abbot et al. (2007); and
- Audit efficiencies may be achieved when there is co-ordination among the external assurance service providers and the IAF (Smith 2002, cited in (Abbot et al., 2007)).

Outsourcing of certain non-routine or specialised engagements do not impact negatively on auditor independence (Abbott et al., 2007). Both the organisation and the assurance provider will, however, have to take the applicable regulatory restrictions on rendering non-audit services to an audit client and codes of ethics (see section 3.4) into account before concluding an outsourcing agreement. The requirements of relevant codes of corporate governance should not be overlooked.

6.1 Corporate governance implications on technology and information

The board of directors should govern technology and information in such a way to support the organisation's objectives and strategies (see, for example, IoD, 2016). To give effect to this responsibility, King IV (IoD, 2016) recommends the following practices:

- The board of directors should create a policy detailing the structure on how technology and information should be approached and directed in the organisation;
- Delegate to management the responsibility to implement and manage technology and information;
- Exercise ongoing overseeing technology and information insofar as integration of people, processes, arrangements for business resilience, monitoring of incidents, performance of outsourcing services providers, identification and responsible disposal of obsolete technology, the ethical and responsible use and compliance with laws and regulations;
- Ongoing overseeing of the management of information insofar as leveraging and enhancing an organisations' intellectual capital, confidentiality, integrity and availability of information, the protection of privacy of information and the continuous monitoring of securing surrounding information;
- Oversight over technology architecture, management of the risks pertaining to sourcing technology and monitoring of responses to developments in technology; and
- Consider the need for periodic independent assurance as to the effectiveness of the organisation's technology and information arrangements (including outsourced services).

7. Implications of outsourcing for an external audit engagement

7.1 ISA 610: Use of the work of an internal auditor

Assurance service providers are required to assess the effectiveness of internal audit during an assurance engagement. Based on the results of their assessment, they may choose to utilise the work performed by the IAF, use some the internal auditors as part of their assurance review or not place any reliance on internal audit at all (IAASB, 2009b).

External auditors' evaluation will include an assessment of the objectivity of the IAF, whether in-house or outsourced. Research on the external auditor's assessment of the quality of an outsourced or in-house IAFs varies. In-house internal auditors may not be as independent as outsourced IAFs. Caplan & Emby (2005) conclude that outsourced or in-house IAFs' provide similar quality or equally competent work when considering control evaluation activities. More recent research indicates that external auditors assess the quality of outsourced or co-sourced internal audit activities to be better than those of the in-house IAF (Desai et al., 2011).

On average, external auditors assessed the outsourced IAF's objectivity more highly than an in-house function (Glover et al., 2007). Even in the case of co-sourcing arrangements pertaining to the IAF and the areas considered to be high risk, external auditors assess the quality of outsourced or co-sourced IAFs higher than in-house IAF. This is attributed to the presence of an independent presence outside the organisation (Desai et al., 2011). The result is that external auditors may be more inclined to place reliance on an outsourced IAF for dealing with a high risk area of an audit engagement than an in-house IAF (Desai et al., 2011).

7.2   ISA 402: Use of service organisations

A service organisation is a third party organisation which provides services to a user entity (an external auditor's auditee) which forms part of, or impact on the user entity's information system relevant to financial reporting (IAASB, 2009a, par 8(e)). Examples of a service organisation can be the maintenance of the user entity's accounting records, management of assets and the initiating, recording or processing transactions as an agent of the user entity. Smaller entities usually use service organisations to assist with the administration of employee tax (IAASB, 2009a, par A4 & A5). It is important to remember that a relationship with a financial institution, normal bank account operation, is not within the scope of ISA 402 (IAASB, 2009a, par 5).

ISA 402 applies when an audit client utilises a service organisation. The application of ISA 402 must be considered in terms of ISA 315[3] and ISA 330[4] to determine the internal control structure relevant to such an arrangement and the risk of material misstatement (IAASB, 2009a, par 1).

7.2.1 Parties involved

There are two sets of auditors involved, namely, a service auditor and a user auditor. A *service auditor* is defined as an auditor who, at the request of the service organisation, will provide an assurance report on the controls of a service organisation (IAASB, 2009a, par d). A *user auditor* is an auditor who audits and reports on the financial statements of a user entity *(IAASB, 2009a, par 8(h))*.

A service organisation is a third-party organisation (or segment of a third party organisation) which provides services to user entities which are part of those entities' information systems, relevant to financial reporting (IAASB, 2009a, par 8(e)). In some instances, a subservice organisation may also be present. *A subservice organisation* is a service organisation used

---

3   Identifying and assessing the risks of material misstatement through understanding the entity and its environment.
4   The auditor's responses to assessed risks.

by another service organisation to perform some of the services provided to user entities which are part of those user entities' information systems relevant to financial reporting (IAASB, 2009a, par 8(g)).

Finally the *user entity* is the entity which uses a service organisation and the financial statements of which are being audited (IAASB, 2009a, par 8(i)).

7.2.2 Relevance of ISA 402

The user auditor is required to obtain sufficient audit evidence when a user entity uses the services of one or more service organisations (IAASB, 2009a, par 1). The services provided by a service organisation are relevant to the audit of a user entity's financial statements when those services and the controls over them are part of the user entity's information system, including related business processes, relevant to financial reporting (IAASB, 2009a, par 5).

The use of a service organisation by a user entity may affect either financial reporting and/or business processes in the following ways:

- Classes of transactions in the user entity's operations which are significant to the user entity's financial statements (IAASB, 2009a, par 3(a));
- Procedures within both IT and manual systems by which the user entity's transactions are initiated, recorded, processed, corrected as necessary, transferred to the general ledger and reported in the financial statements (IAASB, 2009a, par 3(b));
- Related accounting records, either in electronic or manual form, supporting information and specific accounts in the user entity's financial statements which are used to initiate, record, process and report the user entity's transactions (this includes the correction of incorrect information and how information is transferred to the general ledger (IAASB, 2009a, par 3(c));
- How the user entity's information system captures events and conditions (other than transactions), which are significant to the financial statements (IAASB, 2009a, par 3(d));
- The financial reporting process used to prepare the user entity's financial statements, including significant accounting estimates and disclosures (IAASB, 2009a, par 3(e)); and
- Controls surrounding journal entries including non-standard journal entries used to record non-recurring unusual transactions or adjustments (IAASB, 2009a).

When a user entity uses a service organisation to perform, for example, IT related services, such a relationship introduces new IT architecture. The new IT architecture creates its own complexities and transforms the user entity's accounting and business processes. As a result, additional risks are introduced in the user entity's system of internal control which may require the user auditor to focus on the processes involved. In addition the user auditor should ensure that the required competency and capabilities are present to audit or enlist the use of an expert in the auditing of a service organisation environment (Butler, 2008).

7.2.3 Nature and extent of work performed by the user auditor

The nature and extent of work to be performed by the user auditor is dependent on the nature and services provided by the service organisation to the user entity and the relevance of such services to the audit of the user entity (IAASB, 2009a, par 4).

7.2.4 Requirements of the user auditor

ISA 315R provides guidance on which aspects of the service organisation need to be understood, especially how they relate to the entity's system of internal controls. The user auditor should understand:

- the type of services in terms of their nature, the significance of such service;
- the materiality of transactions processed and accounts affected by such a service;
- the degree of interaction between the user entity and the service organisation; and
- the relevance of contractual terms negotiated between the parties (IAASB, 2009a, par A1–11).

When assessing the systems of internal control, the user auditor will evaluate the design and implementation of relevant controls at the user entity which relate to the services provided by the service organisation, including those which are applied to the transactions processed by the service organisation (IAASB, 2009a, par 10).

The user auditor will test the effectiveness of controls introduced over the relationship with the service organisation. For example, for payroll transactions, the user entity may establish controls over the submission and receipt of payroll information which may prevent or detect material misstatements. Such controls can be a comparison of data submitted to the service organisation with the processed information received from the service organisation to address completeness of processing or the recalculation of a sample of payroll amounts for clerical accuracy and the review of the total amount of the payroll for reasonableness (IAASB, 2009a, par A12–A14).

A sufficient understanding is required of the nature and significance of the services provided by the service organisation and the effect on the user internal control relevant to the audit as a basis for the identification and assessment of risks of material misstatement (IAASB, 2009a, par 11).

Sources of information can be the contract and/or service level agreements, user manuals, system overviews, technical manuals, reports by service organisations, reports from an internal auditor or any regulatory authorities on controls at the service organisations, management letters or reports from the service auditors. (IAASB, 2009a, par A1).

If the user auditor cannot obtain a sufficient understanding of the relationship between the user entity and the service organisation, additional procedures are required. These procedures can extend to the following:

- Obtaining a type 1[5] or type 2[6] report, if available (IAASB, 2009a, 12(a)). In some instances type 1 or 2 reports may be made available to user entities (IAASB, 2009a, par A17);
- Contacting the service organisation through the user entity to obtain specific information (IAASB, 2009a, 12(b));
- Visiting the service organisation and performing procedures which will provide the necessary information about the relevant controls at the service organisation (IAASB, 2009a, 12(c)); or
- Using another auditor to perform procedures which will provide the necessary information about the relevant controls at the service organisation (IAASB, 2009a, 12(d)).

Type 1 or type 2 reports are used to support the auditor's understanding of the service organisation. The sufficiency and appropriateness of audit evidence of such reports should be evaluated against the following (IAASB, 2009a, par 13):

- Service auditor's professional competence and independence from the service organisation; and
- The adequacy of the standards under which the type 1 or type 2 report was issued.

If the user auditor plans to use one of these reports as evidence for understanding the design and implementation of controls at the service organisation, then the following procedures will be required (IAASB, 2009a, par 14(a-c)):

- Evaluate whether the description and design of controls at the service organisation is at a specified point in time (date) or for a period appropriate for the user auditor's purposes;

---

5   A report from a service auditor on the description and design of the service organisation's controls (IAASB, 2009a, par A12).

6   A report from a service auditor on the description and design of a service organisation's controls and their operating effectiveness (IAASB, 2009a, par A12).

- Evaluate the sufficiency and appropriateness of the evidence provided by the report for the understanding of the user entity's internal control relevant to the audit; and
- Determine whether complementary user entity controls identified by the service organisation are relevant to the user entity and, if so, obtain an understanding of whether the user entity has designed and implemented such controls.

A type 1 or type 2 report, supported with information about the user entity, may assist the user auditor in obtaining an understanding of (IAASB, 2009a, par A22(a-d)):

- The aspects of controls at the service organisation which may affect the processing of the user entity's transactions, including the use of subservice organisations;
- The flow of significant transactions through the service organisation to determine the points in the transaction flow where material misstatements in the user entity's financial statements may occur;
- The control objectives at the service organisation which are relevant to the user entity's financial statement assertions; and
- Whether controls at the service organisation are suitably designed and implemented to prevent or detect and correct processing errors which may result in material misstatements in the user entity's financial statements.

A type 1 or type 2 report may assist the user auditor in obtaining a sufficient understanding to identify and assess the risks of material misstatement. However, a type 1 does not provide any evidence of the operating effectiveness of the relevant controls (IAASB, 2009a, par A22). This is because of the limitations inherent in type 1 and type 2 reports.

If either of the reports is dated to a period which precedes the beginning of the period under review (of the user entity), the user auditor should discuss changes at the service organisation with a suitable and knowledgeable representative of the service organisation. In addition the user auditor should review current documentation and correspondence issued by the service organisation (IAASB, 2009a, par A23).

7.3 Assurance reports on controls at a service organisation

ISAE 3402 deals with assurance engagements undertaken by external auditors to provide reports which are relevant to user entities' internal control as it relates to financial reporting. ISA 3402 complements ISA 402 in terms of appropriate audit evidence (IAASB, 2013, par 1).

The objectives of the service auditor will be to obtain reasonable assurance in all material aspects which relate:

- that the service organisation's description of its system fairly represents the system as designed and implemented throughout the specified period (or as a type 1 report as at specific date);
- the controls related to the control objectives stated in the description of the service organisation system have been suitably designed throughout the period under review; and
- that included in the scope of the engagement, the controls operated effectively to provide reasonable assurance that the control objectives were achieved throughout the period.

The service auditor will consider the following prior to acceptance or continuance of an engagement at a service organisation (IAASB, 2013, par 13(a)):

- Capabilities and competence of the service auditor to perform the engagement;
- Criteria to be applied by the service organisation to prepare the description of its system is suitable and available to user entities and user auditors; and
- The scope of the engagement and the service organisation description of its system is not limited but will be useful to both user entity and user auditor.

The service auditor will obtain agreement of the service organisation in which management acknowledges its understanding and responsibility for (IAASB, 2013, par 13(b)):

- The preparation of the description of its system and accompanying service assertions (completeness, accuracy, method of presentation);
- Having a reasonable basis for the above assertions accompanying the description of its system;
- Stating the criteria used in the preparation of the system description (system description should start with a control objective followed by any legal or regulation requirement);
- Identifying risks for each control objective; and
- Providing the service auditor with access to all information (records, documentation, service level agreements and other matters), any additional information requested for the purpose of the engagement and unrestricted access to persons within the service organisation in order to obtain evidence.

The service auditor will address usual audit planning and execution principles such as determination of materiality (based on the fair presentation of the system description and the suitability of the design of controls), obtain an understanding of the service organisation systems of controls, obtain evidence relating to the system description and design of controls, test the operating effectiveness of controls and subsequent events (IAASB, 2013, par 19–26 & 43–44).

In the event that the service organisation has an IAF, the service auditor will obtain an understanding of the nature of the responsibilities of internal audit activities performed. Considerations will be whether the work by the IAF is adequate for the purpose of the engagement, taking into account the nature, timing and extent of the service auditor's procedures. Objectivity, technical competence, professionalism and the likelihood of effective communication between the IAF and the service auditor should be evaluated (IAASB, 2013).

8. Summary

- This chapter discusses the issue of outsourcing and the considerations which management need to take into account when deciding to outsource non-audit services.
- Section 3 discusses the regulatory requirements which apply in the USA, UK and South Africa where non-audit services are provided by current external assurance providers. This section discusses how legislation and corporate governance requirements (in each respective jurisdiction) require the service provider to be independent, with organisations being required to create mechanisms to ensure the independence of the service provider.
- The main focus of the Code of Ethics is for the external auditor to avoid any managerial responsibilities associated with outsourcing internal assurance services.
- The advantages and disadvantages of an in-house IAF, outsourcing the IAF and of co-sourcing the IAF are also discussed in section 5.
- The implication for using external service providers is discussed with focus on the use of a service organisation. In particular, the process to gather sufficient reliable audit evidence relating to the service organisation is discussed and how assurance over these organisations can be achieved by the auditor.

9. References

Abbot, L. J., Parker, S., Peters, G. F. & Rama, D. V. 2007. Corporate Governance, Audit Quality, and the Sarbanes-Oxley Act: Evidence from Internal Auditing Outsourcing. *The Accounting Review*, 803–835.

Abbott, L. J., Parker, S., Peters, G. F. & Rama, D. V. 2007. Corporate governance, audit quality, and the Sarbanes-Oxley Act: Evidence from internal audit outsourcing. *The Accounting Review*, 82 (4), 803–835.

Bart, C. & Turel, O. 2010. IT and the board of directors: An empirical investigation into the "governance questions" Canadian board members ask about IT. *Journal of Information Systems*, 24 (2), 147–172.

Bielski, L. 2006. Outsourcing success It's all in the Governance. *American Bankers Association. ABA Banking Journal,* 98 (7), 38.

Butler, R. 2008. An analysis of service-oriented architecture (SOA) to determine the impact on the activities performed by the external auditor of a SOA service consumer. *Meditari Accountancy Research,* 16 (2), 13–30.

Del Vecchio, S. & Clinton, B. D. 2003. Co-sourcing and other alternatives in acquiring internal audit services. *Internal Auditing,* 33–39.

Desai, N. K., Gerard, G. J. & Tripathy, A. 2011. Internal audit sourcing arrangements and reliance by external auditors. *Auditing: A Journal of Practice & Theory,* 30 (1), 149–171.

Financial Reporting Council 2016. The UK Corporate Governance Code. London: Financial Reporting Council Limited

Gilley, K. M. & Rasheed, A. 2000. Making more by doing less: an analysis of outsourcing and its effects on firm performance. *Journal of management,* 26 (4), 763–790.

Glover, S. M., Prawit, D. F. & Wood, D. A. 2007. Internal Audit Sourcing Arranagment and the External Auditor's Reliance Decision. *http://ssrn.com* [Online]. Available: http://ssrn.com/abstract=898800.

IAASB 2009a. ISA 402: Audit considerations relating to an entity using a service organisation. *SAICA Members' Handbook.* 2009 ed. Pietermaritsburg: LexisNexis.

IAASB 2009b. ISA 610 Using the Work of Internal Auditors. *SAICA Members' Handbook.* 2009 ed. Pietermaritsburg: LexisNexis.

IAASB 2013. ISAE 3402: Assurance reports on controls at a service organisation. *SAICA Members' Handbook.* 2009 ed. Pietermaritsburg: LexisNexis.

IESBA 2018. Handbook of the International Code of Ethics for Professional Accountants *Including International Independence Standards* New York: International Federation of Accountants (IFAC).

Institute of Directors Southern Africa 2016. Report on Corporate Governance South Africa *King IV.* Johannesburg Institute of Directors.

IoD 2016. King IV Report on Governance for South Africa 2016. Institure of Directors Southern Africa.

Knechel, W. R., Sharma, D. S. & Sharma, V. D. 2012. Non-audit services and knowledge spillovers: Evidence from New Zealand. *Journal of Business Finance & Accounting,* 39 (1–2), 60–81.

Loh, L. & Venkatraman, N. 1992. Determinants of information technology outsourcing: a cross-sectional analysis. *Journal of management information systems,* 9 (1), 7–24.

Republic of South Africa 2008. Companies Act, No. 71 of 2008.

The Republic of South Africa 2005. The Auditing Profession Act No. 26 of 2005

Yang, D. H., S., K., Nam, C. & J.W., M. 2007. Developing a Decision Model for Business Process Outsourcing. *Computers and Operations Research* 3769–3778.

1. Introduction

The objectives, scope and nature of internal audit are dependent on the size and structure of the organisation (Reding et al., 2013; Cascarino, 2015). The requirements of management and those charged with governance will determine the organisational standing and status of the internal audit function (IAF).

Together with external audit and the finance function, internal audit forms part of an organisation's assurance framework and is considered to be a 'trusted advisor' about the organisation's activities. A successful IAF requires:

- a control environment which is grounded in integrity;
- adequate resources and skills;
- risk-based approach based on the organisation's risk profile;
- an awareness of risk management and internal control; and
- support by senior management (Picket, 2010; Sarens and Abdolmohammadi, 2011; Coetzee et al., 2017).

This chapter discusses how the role of internal audit has evolved and what role regulators and international practice have had on the development of the internal audit function (section 2). This is followed by a discussion of the type of internal audit services (section 3). The role of internal audit in the broader corporate governance structure of an organisation is discussed in Section 4 and 5. Section 6 reviews the characteristics of an effective IAF. Section 7 briefly outlines the internal audit process.

2. Evolution of internal audit

Prior to 1941, accounting systems were manual, resulting in human error. Internal audit was regarded as an administrative function ensuring that the accounting records did not contain errors (Picket, 2012). As accounting systems became more complex and automated, the role of internal audit changed. At first, internal audit was regarded as an extension of the external audit function, assisting with the audit of financial statements or performing accounting-related functions. This view was maintained even after the establishment of the Institute of Internal Auditors (IIA). With more instances of corporate failure and fraud, stakeholders started paying more attention to the control environments of organisations. Global corporate scandals led to investigations and inquiries and the release of the Treadway Commission reports[1] and new statutory requirements for listed entities. A significant change required listed entities to establish audit committees.

Coupled with the Treadway Commission, reports placing more emphasis on internal controls and Sarbanes-Oxley (2002) requiring listed entities to design, implement and maintain proper controls, the role of the IAF changed. The scope of the IAF was expanded to include monitoring, testing and reviewing of financial and operational areas of an organisation, as well as environmental and social performance (Ramamoorti, 2003). Internal audit also became more formal with the IAF being headed by a dedicated practitioner or chief audit executive (CAE[2]). The result is that the role of the IAF, as part of an organisation's assurance strategy, has since been elevated (Picket, 2010, pp. 8–10).

2.1   The Institute of Internal Auditors (IIA)

In 1941 the Institute for Internal Auditors (IIA) was established because of the expansion of internal audit in many jurisdictions. By 1960 the IIA was recognised as an international leader in the internal auditing profession (Cascarino, 2015). Today, the IIA's headquarters are in Florida in the United States of America and it is considered to be the global voice of the profession (Cascarino, 2015). The mission of the IIA is to 'enhance and protect organisational value by providing risk-based and objective assurance, advice and insight' (Coetzee et al., 2017, p. 22). The IIA offers a range of certifications and qualifications which are at present (IIA, 2017c):

- Certified Internal Auditor;
- Certified Government Auditing Professional;
- Certified Financial Services Auditor;
- Certification in Control Self-Assessment;
- Certifications in Risk Management Assurance;
- Qualification in Internal Audit Leadership; and
- Certifications for Environmental, Health and Safety Auditors.

The IIA relies on a framework of principles and standards to help internal auditors achieve the IIA's stated mission. The IIA last revised its International Professional Practices Framework (IPPF) in 2017. An overview of the current guidelines included in the IPPF is discussed in section 2.2.

---

1   The Committee of Sponsoring Organisations of the Treadway Commission (COSO) formed in 1985 is a joint initiative to combat corporate fraud. It was established in the United States by five private sector organisations, dedicated to guide executive management and governance entities on relevant aspects of organisational governance, business ethics, internal control, enterprise risk management, fraud, and financial reporting. COSO has established a common internal control model against which companies and organisations may assess their control systems.

2   The terms 'Chief Audit Executive' and 'Chief Internal Auditor' are used interchangeably.

2.2 International Professional Practices Framework (IPPF)

The IPPF consists of the following six types of guidance:

Figure 1: IIA's International Professional Practises Framework (IPPF)

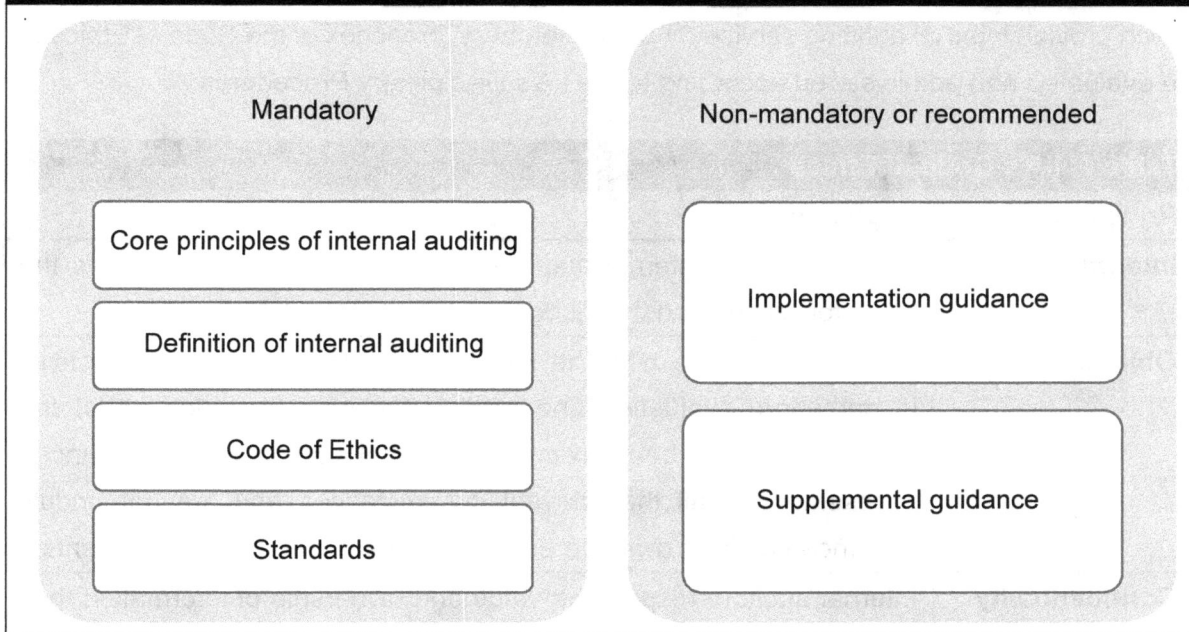

Mandatory	Non-mandatory or recommended
Core principles of internal auditing	Implementation guidance
Definition of internal auditing	
Code of Ethics	Supplemental guidance
Standards	

adapted from Coetzee et al. (2017)

2.2.1 Core principles for internal auditing

These core principles articulate internal audit effectiveness and assist an IAF to achieve internal audit's mission. There are ten principles (IIA, 2015):

- demonstrates integrity;
- demonstrates competence and due professional care;
- is objective and free from undue influence (independent);
- aligns with the strategies, objectives, and risks of the organisation;
- is appropriately positioned and adequately resourced;
- demonstrates quality and continuous improvement;
- communicates effectively;
- provides risk-based assurance;
- is insightful, proactive and future-focused; and
- promotes organisational improvement.

2.2.2 Definition of internal auditing

Internal auditing is an independent, objective assurance and consulting activity designed to add value and improve an organisation's operations. It helps an organisation to accomplish its objectives by bringing a systematic, disciplined approach to evaluate and improve the effectiveness of risk management, control and governance processes (Coetzee et al., 2017, p. 23).

2.2.3 Code of Ethics

The IIA Code of Ethics is based on four principles which apply to all individuals and entities which provide internal auditing services. For IIA members, breaches of the Code of Ethics will be evaluated and administered according to the IIA's Disciplinary Procedures.

Table 1: IIA's Code of Ethics	
Principle	**Explanation**
Integrity	The integrity of internal auditors establishes trust and provides the basis for reliance on their judgement.
Objectivity	Internal auditors exhibit the highest level of professional objectivity in gathering, evaluating and communicating information about the activity or process being examined. Internal auditors make a balanced assessment of all the relevant circumstances and are not unduly influenced by their own interests or by others in forming judgements.
Confidentiality	Internal auditors respect the value and ownership of information they are given and do not disclose this without appropriate authority unless there is a legal or professional obligation to do so.
Competency	Internal auditors apply knowledge, skills, and experience needed in the performance of internal audit services.

Adapted from IIA (2009)

The Code of Ethics includes rules of conduct for each principle in Table 1. These are summarised in Table 2:

Table 2: IIA's Rules of conduct relating to principles	
Principle	**Internal auditor will:**
Integrity	• perform their work with honesty, diligence, and responsibility; • observe the law and make disclosures expected by the law and the profession; • not knowingly be a party to any illegal activity, or engage in acts which discredit the profession or the organisation; and • respect and contribute to the legitimate and ethical objectives of the organisation.

►

Table 2: IIA's Rules of conduct relating to principles	
Principle	**Internal auditor will:**
Objectivity	• not participate in any activity or relationship which may impair or be presumed to impair their unbiased assessment. This participation includes those activities or relationships which may be in conflict with the interests of the organisation; • not accept anything which may impair or be presumed to impair their professional judgment; and • disclose all material facts known to them which, if not disclosed, may distort the reporting of activities under review.
Confidentiality	• be prudent in the use and protection of information acquired in the course of their duties; and • not use information for any personal gain or in any manner which may be contrary to the law or detrimental to the legitimate and ethical objectives of the organisation.
Competency	• engage only in those services for which they have the necessary knowledge, skills and experience; • perform internal audit services in accordance with the International Standards for the Professional Practice of Internal Auditing; and • continually improve their proficiency and the effectiveness and quality of their services.

(IIA, 2009)

2.2.4 International Standards for the Professional Practice of Internal Auditing

The IIA's Standards (the Standards) have been developed to meet the responsibilities of internal auditors and the IAF, no matter the size, complexity or structure of the organisation. In the event that any part of the standards is in contravention of law, conformance to all other parts of the standards will be expected (IIA, 2017c).

The purpose of the IIA Standards (IIA, 2017c) is to:

• define the basic principles of internal auditing;
• provide a framework for performing and promoting a broad range of value-added internal auditing;
• establish the basis for the evaluation of internal audit performance; and
• foster improved organisational processes and operations.

The IIA Standards are principles-focused, mandatory requirements made up of basic requirements for professional practice of internal auditing and interpretations which clarify terms or concepts within the standard. The Standards are divided between Attribute (1000 series) and Performance standards (2000 series). Attribute standards relate to the attributes of the organisations' internal audit activity *and* to internal auditors. Performance standards describe the nature of internal auditing and provide criteria against which performance of the IAF and internal auditors can be measured (IIA, 2017c). The standards are further divided to address both assurance services and consulting services. For example, 1000. **A**1 and 1000. **C**1 (Coetzee et al., 2017).

Table 3: Overview of the Standards		
Attribute Standards		
Number	**Title**	**Brief overview**
1000	Purpose, authority and responsibility	Internal audit charter details the responsibility of the IAF and should be consistent with the mission of internal audit and the mandatory elements of the IPPF framework (refer section 2.1). The nature of assurance and consulting services must be defined in the internal audit charter (IIA, 2016a).
1010	Recognising mandatory guidance in the internal audit charter	The internal audit charter must recognise the IIA's core principles, code of ethics, standards and the definition of internal auditing (IIA, 2016b).
1100	Independence & objectivity	The IAF must be independent and the internal auditors must be objective in performing their work (IIA, 2016c).
1110	Organisational independence	CAE reports to a level which allows the IAF to fulfil its duties (eg audit committee or board of directors). The CAE must confirm to the board, at least annually, the status of the IAF independence (IIA, 2016d).
1111	Direct interaction with the board	CAE must communicate and interact directly with the board of directors (IIA, 2016e).
1112	Chief Audit Executive roles beyond internal auditing	If the CAE have responsibilities outside the ambit of internal audit, adequate safeguards must be put in place to limit impairments to independence or objectivity (IIA, 2016f).

▶

Table 3: Overview of the Standards		
Attribute Standards		
Number	**Title**	**Brief overview**
1120	Individual objectivity	Internal auditors must have an impartial, unbiased attitude. Conflict of interest must be avoided (IIA, 2016g).
1130	Impairment to independence or objectivity	Details of any impairment (in fact or appearance) must be disclosed to appropriate parties (IIA, 2016h).
1200, 1210 & 1220	Proficiency and due professional care	Internal auditors must possess the knowledge, skills and other competencies required to perform their individual responsibilities (IIA, 2016i). Collectively the IAF must possess or obtain knowledge, skills and other competencies to perform its responsibilities (IIA, 2016j). CAE must gain competent advice and assistance if the internal auditors lack the knowledge, skills or other competencies needed to perform all or part of the engagement (IIA, 2016k).
1230	Continuing professional development (CPD)	Internal auditors must enhance their knowledge, skills, and other competencies through CPD (IIA, 2016l) .
1300	Quality Assurance and Improvement Program (QAIP)	CAE must develop and maintain a QAIP which covers all aspects of the IAF (IIA, 2016m).
1310, 1311 & 1312	Requirements of the QAIP	The QAIP must include both internal and external assessments. Internal assessment: ongoing monitoring & periodic self-assessments by persons within the organisation. External assessments: at least once every 5 years by a qualified, independent assessor/assessment team **outside** the organisation (IIA, 2016n; IIA, 2016o; IIA, 2016p).

►

Table 3: Overview of the Standards		
Attribute Standards		
Number	**Title**	**Brief overview**
1320	Reporting on the QAIP	CAE to communicate the results of the QAIP to senior management and the board of directors (IIA, 2016p).
1321	Use of 'conforms to the International Standards for the Professional Practice of Internal Auditing'	This wording can only be used by the IAF if supported by the results of the QAIP (IIA, 2016r).
1322	Disclosure of non-conformance	The CAE must disclose to senior management and the board of directors any instances of non-conformance relating to the code of ethics or standards (IIA, 2016s).
Performance Standards		
2000	Managing the internal audit activity	The CAE must effectively manage the IAF to ensure it adds value to the organisation (IIA, 2016t).
2010	Planning	The CAE must establish a risk-based plan to determine the priorities of the IAF, consistent with the organisation's goals (IIA, 2016u).
2020	Communication and approval	The CAE must communicate the IAF's plans and resource requirements, including the impact of resource limitations, to senior management and the board of directors for review and approval (IIA, 2016v).
2030	Resource management	The CAE must ensure that internal audit resources are appropriate, sufficient and effectively deployed to achieve the approved plan (IIA, 2016w).
2040	Policies and procedures	The CAE must establish policies and procedures to guide the IAF (IIA, 2016x).

▶

Table 3: Overview of the Standards		
Attribute Standards		
Number	**Title**	**Brief overview**
2050	Co-ordination and reliance	The CAE should share information, co-ordinate activities and consider relying on the work performed by other internal or external assurance and consulting service providers in order to achieve proper coverage and limit duplication (IIA, 2016y).
2060	Reporting to senior management and the board	The CAE must report periodically to senior management and the board of the IAF's purpose, authority, responsibility and performance relative to its plan and on its conformance with the code of ethics and the standards. The report should include significant risk and control issues, fraud risks, governance issues and other matters which may require the attention of senior management and the board (IIA, 2016z).
2070	External service provider and organisational responsibility for internal auditing	Where an organisation utilises an external service provider as its IAF, the provider must inform the organisation of the board's responsibility to maintain an effective IAF (IIA, 2016aa).
2100	Nature of work	Internal audit must evaluate and contribute to the improvement of **governance, risk management and control processes**. Specific responsibilities are highlighted individually for governance, risk management and control (IIA, 2016ba; IIA, 2016ac; IIA, 2016ad; IIA, 2016ae).
2110	Governance	
2120	Risk management	
2130	Control	

▶

Table 3: Overview of the Standards		
Attribute Standards		
Number	**Title**	**Brief overview**
2200	Engagement planning	**Planning** considerations entail the development of a formalised planning document detailing engagement objectives, scope, timing, resource allocations and engagement work program (IIA, 2016af; IIA, 2016ah; IIA, 2016ai; IIA, 2016aj; IIA, 2016ak).
2201	Engagement considerations	
2210	Engagement objectives	
2220	Engagement scope	
2230	Engagement resource allocation	
2240	Engagement work program	
2300	Performing the engagement	**Execution of the audit** Includes the identification, analysis, evaluation and documentation of sufficient information to achieve the engagement objectives (IIA, 2016al).
2310	Identifying information	Internal auditors must identify sufficient, reliable, relevant and useful information to achieve the engagement's objectives as per Standard 2210 (IIA, 2016am).
2320	Analysis and evaluation	
2340	Engagement supervision	Conclusions must be based on engagement results on appropriate analyses and evaluations (IIA, 2016an). Engagements must be properly supervised to ensure objectives are achieved, quality is assured and staff is developed (IIA, 2016ak).

►

Table 3: Overview of the Standards		
Attribute Standards		
Number	**Title**	**Brief overview**
2400	Communicating results	**Reporting of results**
2410	Criteria for communications	Results from all reviews must be communicated. The communication must include engagement objectives, scope and results. Communications should be accurate, objective, clear, concise, constructive, complete and timely (IIA, 2016aq; IIA, 2016ap; IIA, 2016ar).
2420	Quality of communications	
2421	Errors and omissions	If a final communication contains a significant error or omission the CAE must communicate the correct information to all parties who received the original communication / report (IIA, 2016as).
2430	Use of conducted in conformance with the standards	Final report may only include such statement if the results of the QAIP supports conformance (IIA, 2016at).
2431	Engagement disclosure for non-conformance	Non-conformance with either the Code of Ethics or the Standards must be disclosed (IIA, 2016au).
2440	Disseminating results	Results (report) must be communicated to all appropriate parties (IIA, 2016av).
2450	Overall opinions	Overall opinion issued by the internal auditor must take into account the strategies, objectives, and risks of the organisation, the expectations of senior management, the board of directors and other stakeholders (IIA, 2016aw).
2500	Monitoring process	CAE must establish and maintain a system to monitor the disposition of results communicated to management (IIA, 2016ax).
2600	Communicating the acceptance of risk	When the CAE concludes that management has accepted a level of risk which is unacceptable to the organisation, the matter must be discussed with senior management. If not resolved with senior management, the CAE must communicate the matter to the board of directors (IIA, 2016ay).

▶

The Standards referred to in Table 2 above are discussed in more detail in the internal audit process (see Section 7).

2.2.5 Implementation guidance

Implementation guidance assists internal auditors in applying the definition of internal auditing, the Code of Ethics and the Standards. Collectively it addresses the internal audit approach and methodologies (IIA, 2017a).

For example, Standard 1310 – Requirements of the Quality Assurance and Improvement Program (QAIP), requires both internal and external assessments of the internal audit activity (IIA, 2016n). The implementation guidance suggests the establishment of key performance indicators for the internal audit activity, establishment of ongoing monitoring procedures over planning, supervision, standardisation of working practices and working papers. It also recommends measures on how conformance to the standard can be demonstrated, for example, minutes from board meetings referring to a QAIP project and outcomes will be a method to demonstrate compliance (IIA, 2017b).

2.2.6 Supplemental guidance

Supplemental guidance provides guidance for conducting internal audit activities in specific sectors. These include topical areas, sector-specific issues, as well as processes and procedures, tools and techniques, programs, step-by-step approaches and examples of deliverables (IIA, 2017d). For example (IIA, 2017d):
- Assessing the adequacy of risk management using ISO 31000;
- Auditing external business relationships;
- Evaluating corporate social responsibility/sustainable development;
- Auditing capital adequacy and stress testing for banks; and
- Auditing grants in the public sector.

3. Audit services and types of reviews

The definition of internal audit makes reference to 'assurance' and 'consulting'. In an assurance engagement, the nature and scope of the engagement is determined by the IAF and takes place in accordance with an approved annual or cyclical audit plan (Coetzee et al., 2017). In a consulting engagement, the nature and scope of the services provided are advisory in nature and are performed at the request of management.

The IAF participation in a consulting engagement will be to provide an independent opinion or conclusion on a predetermined subject by performing predetermined procedures (also known as agreed upon procedures) determined by management. The distinction between assurance and consulting services will be determined during the annual audit planning, taking into account requests from management and those charged with governance. The scope of the engagement, being either assurance or consulting, will determine its classification (Cascarino, 2015). The risk-based internal audit plan should cater for consulting engagement insofar as management has requested it but should constitute an insignificant part of the total internal audit effort (Coetzee et al., 2017).

In particular, internal audit aims to assist the organisation with the improvement of risk management, control and governance processes (IIA, 2016ab). Standard 1000 requires an organisation to define the nature of assurance and consulting services performed by internal audit (IIA, 2016az). The work undertaken should add value to an organisation as illustrated by the following table of examples of possible audit or consulting services on offer by the IAF:

Table 4: Types of internal audit services and engagements	
Type of engagements	**Explanation**
Compliance audit engagements ✓ *Assurance* ✓ *Consulting*	Review of: • the internal control structure in terms of test of controls; or • adherence to relevant laws and regulations (Coetzee et al., 2017).
Information technology engagements ✓ *Assurance* ✓ *Consulting*	Evaluation of: • internal controls related to management information technology environments; • related infrastructure; • applications; and • data.
Financial audit engagements ✓ *Assurance* ✓ *Consulting*	Review the reasonableness of financial information by applying substantive procedures addressing assertions (existence, occurrence, completeness, cut-off, accuracy, rights & obligations, classification & allocation, valuation and presentation & disclosure) (Coetzee et al., 2017).
Operational audit engagements ✓ *Assurance* ✓ *Consulting*	Assessment or evaluation on economy, efficiency and effectiveness of operations.

▶

Table 4: Types of internal audit services and engagements	
Type of engagements	**Explanation**
Review of governance processes ✓ *Assurance* ✗ *Consulting*	Standard 2110 defines this review as an assessment of an organisation's governance processes for: • making strategic and operational decisions, overseeing risk management and control; • promoting of appropriate ethics and values within the organisation; • ensuring effective organisational performance management and accountability; • communicating risk and control information to appropriate areas within the organisation; and • coordinating the activities and communication information among board of directors, internal audit, external audit, other assurance providers and management (IIA, 2016ac).
Risk management ✓ *Assurance* ✓ *Consulting*	Standard 2120 requires internal audit to review the effectiveness and contribute to the improvement of risk management processes insofar as: • organisation's objectives support and align with the organisation's mission; • significant risks are identified and assessed; • appropriate risk responses are selected which are alignment with the organisation's risk appetite; and • relevant risk information is captured and communicated in order for the staff, management and board of directors to fulfil their responsibilities (IIA, 2016ad).
Fraud investigations/Acting as a contact point for alleged fraud reporting ✗ *Assurance* ✗ *Consulting*	Internal auditors can be formally requested to assist with fraud investigations when an organisation does not have a dedicated fraud and forensic unit. See Part A, Chapter 6 for the process to be followed if a forensic investigation takes place.
Responding to requests from management ✓ *Assurance* ✓ *Consulting*	Any special requests not included on the internal audit plan should be discussed with and approved by the board of directors or audit committee.

►

Table 4: Types of internal audit services and engagements	
Type of engagements	**Explanation**
Staff training × *Assurance* ✓ *Consulting*	Internal audit may be used in a consulting capacity to perform staff training from time to time.
Assistance with developing and drafting polices × *Assurance* ✓ *Consulting*	Management may request internal audit in a consulting capacity only to assist with drafting of policies. Internal audit cannot be involved in the implementation or monitoring of such policies as this may negatively influence objectivity.
Control-self assessment facilitations × *Assurance* ✓ *Consulting*	Internal auditors facilitate the introduction of the COSO control framework in organisations (Reding et al., 2013; Cascarino, 2015).

4. The need for an IAF

4.1 Organisational perspective

The organisational need for internal audit is best described in the IIA's *Performance Standard 2100 – Nature of Work* which refers to internal audit's responsibility to evaluate and contribute to the improvement of governance, risk management and control processes using a systematic and disciplined approach (IIA, 2016ba). The following table summarises the governance, risk and control responsibility of the IAF.

Table 5: Internal audit's responsibility for governance, risk and control	
2110	**Governance**
	'The Internal Audit Activity must assess and make appropriate recommendations to improve the organisation's governance processes for: • Making strategic and operational decisions; • Overseeing risk management and control; • Promoting appropriate ethics and values within the organisation; • Ensuring effective organisational performance management and accountability; • Communicating risk and control information to appropriate areas of the organisation; and • Co-ordinating the activities of, and communicating information among, the board, external and internal auditors, other assurance providers and management.' (IIA, 2016ac)

▶

Table 5: Internal audit's responsibility for governance, risk and control	
2120	**Risk Management**
	'The Internal Audit Activity must evaluate the effectiveness and contribute to the improvement of risk management processes'. (IIA, 2016ad)
2130	**Control**
	'The Internal Audit Activity must assist the organisation in maintaining effective controls by evaluating their effectiveness and efficiency and by promoting continuous improvement. Control processes aim to support the organisation in the management of risks that threaten the achievement of its objectives and should amongst others, ensure: • Financial and operational information is reliable and possesses integrity; • Operations are performed efficiently and achieve established objectives; and • Actions and decisions of the organisation are in compliance with laws, regulations and contracts'. (IIA, 2016ae)

From an operational perspective it is not uncommon for an organisation to use internal audit as a training ground for its future managers. Employing a person in the position of an internal auditor with the intention of moving into operational management at a later stage can impact the internal auditor's objectivity (Rose et al., 2013). It does, however, provide an effective way for companies to develop their human capital.

4.2   Regulatory and governance perspective

Internal audit is a recognised component of an organisation's control environment. This is evidenced by the Committee of Sponsoring Organisations of the Treadway Commission (COSO) which issued *Internal Control — Integrated Framework* in 1992 (subsequently updated in 2013 and 2017). The issue of the COSO report highlighted the purpose of internal auditors (Rezaee, 1995). In summary COSO (1992) defines the role of internal audit to:

• Provide support to management in both assurance and advisory capacities;
• Evaluate the adequacy and effectiveness of controls in response to risks within an organisation's oversight, operations and information systems; and
• Assist the organisation to maintain effective control by evaluating control efficiency and effectiveness through continual improvements.

The COSO report (1992) underlines the importance of both management *and* internal auditors to be actively involved in the understanding of internal control and establishing an effective internal control system (Rezaee, 1995). This responsibility is formalised in Standard 2130 dealing with the internal audit activities responsibility towards an organisation's control environment (IIA, 2016ae).

The United States Securities and Exchange Commission (SEC) designated the COSO framework as an adequate regulatory criterion for the evaluation of an organisation's internal control over financial reporting activities (United States Securities and Exchange Commission, 2003). Section 404 of the Sarbanes-Oxley Act (SOX) requires management to evaluate, document and report on the design and operation of its internal control over financial reporting[3]. The internal control report must be incorporated in the organisation's annual report (Sarbanes-Oxley Act (SOX), 2002). This report must address the following (Sarbanes-Oxley Act (SOX), 2002):

- management's recognition of its responsibility for establishing and maintaining adequate internal controls and procedures for financial reporting;
- the framework used by management in its evaluation of internal control;
- management's assessment of the effectiveness of the company's internal control over financial reporting. This requires disclosure of any material weaknesses identified by management in the organisation's internal control over financial reporting processes; and
- a statement indicating that the organisations' external auditors have issued a report on management's assessment of effectiveness of internal control over financial reporting.

The background, profile and independence of board members, coupled with their willingness to work with internal audit, impacts the effectiveness of an IAF (Lenz and Hahn, 2015, p. 8). Where audit committee members are independent and are considered to have sufficient accounting and finance background, more active monitoring of the IAF will be expected in terms of review of the annual internal audit plan and the results communicated by the IAF (Goodwin, 2003). The roles of the board of directors and the audit committee will be briefly discussed below.

---

3   SOX applies to publicly traded companies in the United States of America including wholly owned subsidiaries and foreign companies which are publicly traded and conduct business in the USA.

4.2.1 South Africa

In South Africa, the King IV Report on Corporate Governance for South Africa 2016 (King IV Report), issued by the Institute of Directors Southern Africa, states that internal audit is pivotal to corporate governance (IOD, 2016b, p. 31). The board of directors are entrusted the following responsibilities (IOD, 2016b):

- ensure that the audit committee oversee the IAF;
- ensure that the audit committee review the effectiveness of the IAF and the CAE on an annual basis;
- set the direction for arrangements pertaining to internal audit;
- approve the internal audit charter which is in line with IIA Standards and addressing the organisation's combined assurance requirements;
- address the skills requirements of the IAF;
- ensure that the CAE position is independent from management;
- clarify the role of the CAE where the IAF is either outsourced or co-sourced;
- monitor the risk-based internal audit plan;
- ensure that the IAF regularly reviews the organisation's risk profile and adjusts the internal audit plan accordingly;
- ensure internal audit provides an annual statement regarding the effectiveness of the organisation's governance, risk and control processes;
- ensure an external assessment of the IAF takes place at least every five years; and
- obtain confirmation from the CAE that the IAF conforms to the IIA's Code of Ethics.

In South Africa, the IAF may form part of a combined assurance model. A combined assurance model 'incorporates and optimises all assurance services and functions so that, taken as a whole, these enable an effective control environment, support the integrity of information used for internal decision-making by management, the governing body and its committees, and support the integrity of the organisation's external reports' (IOD, 2016b).

The audit committee is responsible for ensuring that a combined assurance model is implemented in a company (IOD (2016b). The King IV Report also requires the following from audit committees:

- to ensure that there is independent oversight of the IAF;
- to meet independently with internal (and external audit) to facilitate an exchange of views and concern that may not be appropriate for discussion in normal meeting proceedings; and
- to determine and ensure the effectiveness of the CAE and the internal audit arrangements.

Lastly, the South African Companies Act (2008) requires audit committees to receive and deal appropriately with any concerns or complaints, whether from within or outside the company, or on its own initiative, relating to an organisation's accounting practices and internal audit.

4.2.2 United Kingdom

The Financial Conduct Authority (FCA) Handbook lists the following requirements pertaining to internal audit (FCA, 2018):

- companies are required to establish and maintain an IAF separate and independent from the other functions and activities of the organisation;
- specific responsibilities should be assigned, such as the development of an audit plan which examines and evaluates the adequacy and effectiveness of an organisation's systems of internal control mechanisms and arrangements;
- to issue recommendations based on work performed in accordance to the internal audit plan;
- to follow up on the organisation's compliance with recommendations; and
- to report internal audit matters.

The FRC (2016) recommends that audit committees have the following responsibilities with regard to the IAF:

- the monitoring and review of the effectiveness of an organisation's IAF and its activities;
- specific monitoring of internal audit activities pertaining to risk and control of management system; and
- in the event of an organisation not having an IAF, annually assessing the need for an IAF and disclose reasons for its absence in the organisation's annual report.

The FRC has taken note of the important role which the IAF of a company can play. In their *Guidance on Board Effectiveness* (2018), the FRC highlighted the importance of independence of the IAF. This is because the IAF plays a vital role in monitoring the behaviour and culture of employees as these actions can affect the organisation. The board of directors must take into account internal audit when developing human resource policies to ensure the development of multi-disciplinary teams. The IAF is regarded as a key part of an organisation in the UK and board committees are expected to ensure the effective functioning of the IAF (FRC, 2018).

4.2.3 USA

The introduction of the Sarbanes-Oxley Act (SOX) (2002) created the need for more effective and better documented systems of internal control of financial reporting for listed companies. As a result, the Public Accounting Oversight Board (PCAOB) was established in 2004 to reform the way in which internal control systems and financial reporting systems were assured. This resulted in an increased IAF role in the development of control documentation and compliance-based auditing relating to financial reporting (Hass et al., 2006).

Under SOX (2002), the requirements relating to internal audit for an audit committee included the following new roles:

- Pre-approval of non-audit services (which includes internal audit services); and
- Disclosure to investors of the nature of any non-audit services performed by the organisation's external auditor.

By analysing the role of the IAF in South Africa, the UK and the USA, it is evident that internal audit plays a key role in organisations, assuring internal information and assisting with compliance. The audit committee has to ensure that the independence of the IAF is not impaired. This is done by ensuring that they approve the services the IAF has to provide. The audit committee has to include internal audit as part of its broader assurance model. One of the key roles of the IAF is to provide assurance to management on the effectiveness of risk management.

5. The role of internal audit in enterprise risk management (ERM)

Enterprise risk management is the responsibility of the organisation's management. As an independent assurance and consulting function, internal audit activities are pivotal in risk management (Cascarino, 2015). This is supported by the IIA Standards which require the internal audit to follow a risk-based audit methodology in developing their audit plan (IIA, 2016az) and an evaluation of the effectiveness of an organisation's risk management process (IIA, 2016ad). Internal audit's evaluation must contribute to the improvement of an organisation's risk management processes. In essence, internal audit should ensure the following (IIA, 2016ad):

- the organisation's objectives support and determine whether objectives are aligned with the organisation's mission;
- risks which have been identified have been assessed as normal to significant;
- appropriate risk responses are selected which align risks with the organisation's risk appetite; and
- relevant risk information is captured and communicated in a timely manner across the organisation, enabling staff, management and the board to carry out their responsibilities.

The IAF involvement in risk management may extend to both assurance and consulting engagements. For assurance engagements, the adequacy and effectiveness of controls in place to respond to risks within an organisation's governance, operations and information systems must be reviewed in line with taking into account the following (IIA, 2016ad):

- achievement of the organisation's strategic objectives;
- reliability and integrity of financial and operational information;
- effectiveness and reliability of operations and programs;
- safeguarding of assets; and
- compliance with laws, regulations, policies, procedures and contracts.

Furthermore, the potential for the occurrence of fraud and how an organisation manages fraud risks should be assessed.

For consultation engagements, internal auditors must address whether risks are consistent with the consulting engagement and the internal auditors should be alert to the existence of other significant risks. Internal auditors must incorporate their knowledge of risks gained during consulting engagements to evaluate an organisation's risk management process. In particular, the IAF must never assume responsibility for risk management within an organisation (IIA, 2016ad).

The role of internal audit in ERM can be in one of three forms: first is an assurance role where operational management have implemented ERM. If this is the case internal audit will fulfil a more advisory role in one or more of the following areas (Cascarino, 2015):

- reviewing the management of key risks;
- evaluation the reporting of key risks;
- evaluation the ERM process;
- providing assurance in areas audited if risks have been correctly evaluated; and
- providing assurance on the overall ERM process.

The second is more of an advisory role, even acting as the ERM co-ordinator, where internal audit assists in the ERM process by (Cascarino, 2015):

- identify and evaluate risks;
- consolidate reporting on risks;
- development of ERM framework for board approval;
- management with the development of responses to risk issues; and
- co-ordination of risk management activities.

The third is where the organisation has no measure of ERM. This is most difficult as the IAF is obligated to have a risk-based audit plan. The IAF will be required to perform a risk assessment on all areas of the business in order to develop a risk-based audit plan. Note that this will be a continuing process as business processes and systems evolve over time (Cascarino, 2015). Internal auditors must be aware of an organisation's significant risks, potentially affecting its objectives, operations or resources (Picket, 2010).

It is inappropriate for the IAF to be accountable for risk management, setting the risk appetite for the organisation, implementing the risk management processes and making decisions on appropriate responses to risk (Reding et al., 2013; Cascarino, 2015). De Zwaan et al. (2011) found that the IAF is less willing to report breakdown in risk procedures where the IAF is actively involved which, in turn, impacts negatively on internal audit's objectivity. This means that, should internal audit be held accountable for risk management, their objectivity (and independence) is impaired. Therefore, it is important to state that the responsibility remains with management to ensure that a risk management process is implemented and monitored, with internal audit ensuring that it operates and is managed effectively (FRC, 2016; IoD, 2016a).

6. Characteristics of an effective IAF

As a result of international regulatory changes (for example, SOX) and increased governance practices focusing on the profile of internal audit and its interaction with the audit committee (Barua et al., 2010), it is important for IAFs to be effective (Soh and Martinov-Bennie, 2011). This section details some characteristics of an effective IAF in support the IIA's core principles (see section 2.2.1).

6.1 Effective management of the IAF

The IIA's performance standards list the following as examples of evidence of an effectively managed IAF (IIA, 2016t):

- The purpose and responsibility of the IAF is included in the internal audit charter;
- The statement which indicates that the internal auditors conform with the Code of Ethics and the Standards; and
- The IAF considers trends and emerging issues which could impact the organisation.

At the outset the IAF must establish policies and procedures to guide all its activities (IIA, 2016x). This will be dependent on the size, complexity and risk profile of the organisation. The CAE should co-ordinate the IAF's efforts with those of external audit, other assurance providers and other external consulting services if utilised (IIA, 2016y). The nature of work performed by the IAF must contribute to the improvement of governance processes by playing an active role (IIA, 2016ab).

6.2 Organisational independence

The role of the CAE should be separate from the role of the executive management who are responsible for the design and implementation of controls (Reding et al., 2013). Therefore, the CAE should not be a member of executive management but should attend executive management meetings to stay informed of executive and strategic decisions within the organisation (Reding et al., 2013; IoD, 2016a; Coetzee et al., 2017). The IAF's independence is achieved when the CAE has free access to the chairperson of the audit committee and the board of directors (Coetzee et al., 2017). In turn, the board of directors, supported by the audit committee is responsible for the appointment, dismissal, evaluation and remuneration of the CAE (IIA, 2016d; IoD, 2016a). The CAE should report to the chair of the audit committee on the performance of duties and functions that relate to internal audit. On other duties and administrative matters, the CAE should report the member of executive management designated as appropriate for the organisation (IIA, 2016e; IoD, 2016a). It is the responsibility of the audit committee to ensure the organisational independence of the IAF (IoD, 2016a).

The CAE must manage the IAF to ensure that it adds value to the organisation. In consultation with senior management, the CAE must develop a risk-based audit plan which addresses the organisation's strategic objectives, key business objectives, associated risks and risk management plans (IIA, 2016u). When changes to the organisation's strategic objectives and business processes take place, the risk-based audit plan needs to be adjusted. The CAE must ensure that internal auditors have the necessary competency and skill to perform engagements or part of engagements (IIA, 2016j). In the event the IAF does not have the necessary skills or training to perform a certain aspect of a review, the CAE should consider outsourcing that part of the review (Coetzee et al., 2017).

6.3 Formal internal audit charter

The purpose, authority and responsibility of an IAF must be formally defined in an internal charter document. The internal charter should be reviewed by senior management and the board of directors for final approval (IIA, 2016a; IoD, 2016a).

The internal audit charter must establish the IAF's position within the organisation. Reference must be made to following (IIA, 2016a):

- the nature of the CAE's functional reporting relationship with the board (or audit committee);
- authorisation for access to records, personnel, and physical properties relevant to the performance of engagements; and
- the definition of the scope of internal audit activities.

In summary the internal audit charter must contain the following in relation to the IAF (Reding et al., 2013; IIA, 2016a):

- its purpose, authority and responsibility with reference to the definition of internal audit;
- note compliance with the IIA's IPPF (see Section 2.2);
- acknowledgement of emerging practices regarding best practices within the fields of internal audit and governance;
- organisational independence within the organisation in terms of unrestricted access to records, personnel and physical properties relevant to the performance of duties;
- functional reporting line of the CAE;
- reference to a quality assurance and improvement program for the IAF; and
- reference to a risk-based audit plan.

The internal audit charter should be reviewed on an annual basis by the board of directors, supported by the recommendation of the audit committee (IIA, 2016a; IoD, 2016a).

6.4   Continuous quality assessment and improvement program

The audit committee is responsible for the implementation of a continuous quality assessment and improvement program of the IAF and full disclosure should be made available to the board of directors (IIA, 2016q; IoD, 2016a). The quality assurance and improvement program includes internal quality review on an ongoing basis and periodic self-assessments by other persons (with sufficient knowledge and skill or internal audit practices) within the organisation (IIA, 2016o). External assessments should be conducted at least every five years by qualified independent assessors outside the organisation (IIA, 2016p). The CAE must communicate the results of both internal and external quality assurance reviews to senior management and the board of directors. The CAE should disclose the following (IIA, 2016q):

- the scope and frequency of both internal and external assessments;
- the qualifications and independence of the assessor or assessment team;
- conclusions of the assessors; and
- corrective action plans.

6.5   Continuous professional development

In terms of the IIA's attribute standards, internal auditors are required to develop themselves continuously to ensure they have the required knowledge, skills and competencies (IIA, 2016l). This can be by means of furthering academic studies or staying up to date with latest developments in internal audit standards, procedures, techniques and best practices.

The competency framework for internal auditors includes both cognitive and behavioural skills. It is important for an internal auditor to be technical, analytical and appreciative in performing his/her role. As internal auditors are interacting with human beings on a continuous basis interpersonal skills, communication and people skills are important (Picket, 2012).

6.6 Professionalism

A professional discipline is based on training, a common body of knowledge, a code of ethics, sanctions, control over services, morality, compliance with the rules and service to society (Picket, 2010). The IIA Standards deal with professionalism in several of its standards. Independence and objectivity are key to the internal auditor when performing work. Independence is the freedom from conditions which threaten the ability of the IAF or CAE to carry out responsibilities in an unbiased manner. Objectivity is an unbiased mental attitude which allows the internal auditor to perform his/her work in such a manner that no quality compromises have been made during the execution and reporting of the assignment (Picket, 2012).

A conflict of interest may arise when an internal auditor finds it difficult to fulfil his/her responsibility. Any matters regarding a conflict of interest must be reported to the CAE and to the audit committee. Impairment to organisational independence and individual objectivity may include personal conflict of interest, scope limitations, restriction on access to records, personnel and properties and internal audit related resource limitations. Impairment to independence or objectivity should similarly be disclosed to both CAE and the audit committee, depending on the nature of the impairments (Picket, 2012).

The IIA's Research Foundation published seven threats to internal auditor independence and objectivity, these are (IIA, 2003):

- self-review threat as the internal auditor reviews his/her own work;
- social pressures experienced by internal auditors;
- economic interest, as internal auditors (employed as part of an in-house IAF) are dependent on their employer for remuneration and other incentive payments;
- personal relationships between an auditee and an internal auditor;
- familiarity threat due to a possible long-term relationship between the auditee and the internal auditor;
- cultural, racial and gender bias due to lack of understanding of local culture and customs; and
- cognitive biases stemming from preconceived notions or the adoption of a particular psychological perspective when performing an audit.

For internal audit assurance engagement, the following objectives are the basis of each review:

- Reliability and integrity of information;
- Compliance with laws, policies and procedures;
- Safeguarding of assets; and
- Economy, efficiency and effectiveness of operations.

Figure 2 summarises the 'elements' of an internal audit engagement.

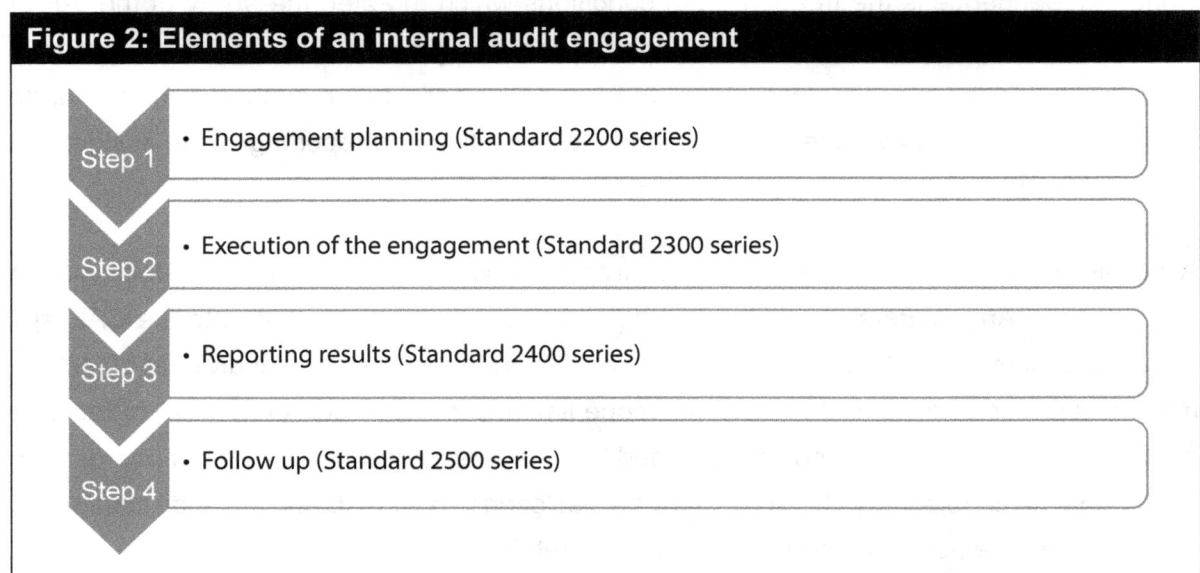

Figure 2: Elements of an internal audit engagement

Step 1
- Engagement planning (Standard 2200 series)

Step 2
- Execution of the engagement (Standard 2300 series)

Step 3
- Reporting results (Standard 2400 series)

Step 4
- Follow up (Standard 2500 series)

7.1   Engagement planning

The annual internal audit plan will include high-risk areas within an organisation which will receive internal audit coverage during a 12-month period or up to a five-year period. Prior to the start of a scheduled engagement, the CAE should ensure that human resources are committed to the planned review and that the engagement planning has been completed. Internal audit staff allocated to the engagement should be competent in the areas to be reviewed (Reding et al., 2013). During engagement planning, background information of the area to be audited must be gained. The following should be established during the planning phase (IIA, 2016af):

- documenting the procedures for the collecting, analysing, interpreting and documenting information during the engagement;
- objectives of the engagement;

- identify the technical aspects, risks, processes and transactions which should be examined; and
- the nature and extent of testing required.

The planning stage is seen as a preliminary review to achieve an understanding of the business processes and risks (IIA, 2016ag). The risks can be based on the ERM processes introduced by management or an assessment of risk done by internal audit (Cascarino, 2015; Coetzee et al., 2017). The internal auditor must gain an understanding of the operational systems and the information systems utilised by the auditee. Once an understanding of all systems is gained, the key control objectives, as determined by management, can be evaluated. The audit objectives will be derived from the assessment of the key control objectives. Once the key control objectives have been established, the internal audit will formulate a draft audit program (referred to as an engagement work program). The audit program identifies, analyses and evaluates information collated during the execution of the engagement. It defines the various tasks which need to be performed and the extent of work (IIA, 2016ak). The content of audit programs varies in form and content depending on the nature and scope of the review engagements (Picket, 2010).

Administrative tasks also need to be addressed. Time is a key factor for any IAF so budgeted hours for the review should be realistic and achievable. The extent of the work to be done and the skill sets of the individual internal auditors need to be considered. The time spent on planning an engagement will depend on the scope and complexity of the review (Cascarino, 2015; Coetzee et al., 2017) .

A formal planning document should be prepared, detailing the following (IIA, 2016af):

- engagement objectives (IIA, 2016ah);
- established criteria for the review (IIA, 2016ah);
- scope of the engagement, such as systems, records, personnel (IIA, 2016ai);
- internal audit resource allocation (IIA, 2016aj);
- review arrangements with the auditee; and
- specific guidance required (this can be a request from management or consultation provided by specialists not within the IAF) (Picket, 2010; IIA, 2016af).

7.2 Execution of the engagement

If the systems within the auditee have not been documented during the audit planning phase, the execution of the engagement will start with evaluating the systems of risk management and systems of internal control relating to the operational objectives of the auditee. This documentation can take the form of block diagrams, and flowcharts of internal control questionnaires (Picket, 2010).

The execution of the audit program defined during the planning stage represents a significant portion of the execution of the engagement. It may happen during this stage that the audit program or procedures do not satisfactorily address a control objective. In such an instance the audit program will be adjusted during the execution stages. If any adjustment takes place, the adjusted audit program should be approved by the CAE (IIA, 2016ak).

Normal testing techniques employed in external audit are also valid for internal audit such as re-performance, observation, analytical review, inspection, reconciliation and independent confirmation to name a few (Reding et al., 2013). During the execution of the audit, internal audit can apply computer assisted audit techniques to cut down on time (Cascarino, 2015).

Evidence gathered and working papers must include conclusions and engagement results. Internal auditors are required to document sufficient, reliable, relevant and useful information to support the engagement results and conclusions (IIA, 2016am). Access to engagement records must be restricted and the approval of senior management and/or legal council should be obtained prior to releasing it to external parties. Internal audit records are subject to the same retention requirements as applicable to the organisation (IIA, 2016ao). The CAE should develop and implement policies governing the custody and retention of consulting engagements (Picket, 2010; IIA, 2016ao; Coetzee et al., 2017).

The success of an engagement is dependent on the level of supervision during the review. The extent of supervision is dependent on the proficiency and experience of internal auditors allocated to the engagement.

7.3 Reporting of results

Internal auditors must communicate the results of engagements in an accurate, objective, clear, concise, constructive, complete and timely manner. The communication must include the engagement's objectives, scope and results (IIA, 2016ap). The finalisation of any audit report is a time-consuming process. The core in any audit reporting is to ensure the audit working papers and evidence gathered support the audit opinion.

Normal report compilation processes apply in that draft versions of the report need to be reviewed by the auditee to allow for comment and final review by the CAE (Coetzee et al., 2017).

In summary the audit reports should include the following (Reding et al., 2013):

- scope and objectives of the review;
- internal auditors involved;

- period of the review;
- criteria used as a measurement;
- findings;
- recommendations; and
- responses from auditees.

When including individual findings in a report, the following is a useful structure (Cascarino, 2015):

- condition;
- criteria;
- cause; and
- effect.
- The recipients of the final report must include the line manager of the area reviewed, senior management and audit committee. The format of reporting results of a review will differ from organisation to organisation. Some audit committees appreciate receiving the full report, whilst others are happy with an executive summary of the main findings.

7.4 Follow up

The CAE must establish and maintain a system to monitor audit findings communicated to management to determine if effective action has been taken to address reported matters (IIA, 2016ay). Management may also opt to accept the risk and if so, no action will be taken. The acceptance of risk by management (non-implementation of internal audit's recommendations) must be communicated to the board of directors (IIA, 2016ay).

8. Summary

- The formalisation of governance principles over the last three decades has raised the profile of internal audit.
- Today internal audit forms part of an organisation's combined assurance framework. The main focus of the internal audit process are governance, risk and control.
- The IPPF provides a theoretical framework according to which internal auditors and IAF's should operate. Core principles, the standards, the definition of internal auditing and the code of ethics are the key elements of this framework.
- The objectives, scope and nature of an IAF's responsibilities and organisational status are dependent on the size, structure and risk profile of the organisation (Reding et al., 2013; Cascarino, 2015). Ultimately, the standing of internal audit in an organisation will be dependent on the board of directors' attitude towards corporate governance principles.

- When applied effectively, internal audit can contribute positively to the organisation's operational and financial performance. This makes internal audit a key part of the overall corporate governance system and an area of growing interest for practitioners, investors and academics.

9. References

Barua, A., Rama, D. V. & Sharma, V. 2010. Audit committee characteristics and investment in internal auditing. *Journal of Accounting and Public Policy,* 29 (5), 503–513.

Cascarino, R. 2015. *Internal Auditing: An Integrated Approach*, Juta adn Company (Pty) Ltd

Coetzee, G. P., du Bruyn, R., Fourie, H. & Plant, K. 2017. *Internal Auditing: An Introduction,* Johannesburg, LexisNexis.

COSO 1992. Internal Control, Integrated Framework. New York.

De Zwaan, L., Stewart, J. & Subramaniam, N. 2011. Internal audit involvement in enterprise risk management. *Managerial auditing journal,* 26 (7), 586–604.

FCA. 2018. *Financial Conduct Authority Handbook* [Online]. Available: https://www.handbook.fca.org.uk/handbook/SYSC/6/2.html [Accessed 27 July 2018].

FRC 2016. UK Code of Corporate Governance.

FRC 2018. Guidance on Board Effectiveness. London: Financial Reporting Council.

Goodwin, J. 2003. The relationship between the audit committee and the internal audit function: Evidence from Australia and New Zealand. *International Journal of Auditing,* 7 (3), 263–278.

Hass, S., Abdolmohammadi, M. J. & Burnaby, P. 2006. The Americas literature review on internal auditing. *Managerial Auditing Journal,* 21 (8), 835–844.

IIA 2003. Independence and Objectivity: A Framework for research opportunities in Internal Auditing. *Chapter 7.* Florida: The Institute of Internal Auditors.

IIA. 2009. *Code of Ethics* [Online]. London: The Institute of Internal Auditors Available: https://na.theiia.org/standards-guidance/mandatory-guidance/Pages/Code-of-Ethics.aspx [Accessed 24 May 2018].

IIA. 2015. *The Core Principles for the Professional Practice of Internal Auditing* [Online]. Florida: The Institute of Internal Auditors. Available: https://na.theiia.org/standards-guidance/mandatory-guidance/Pages/Core-Principles-for-the-Professional-Practice-of-Internal-Auditing.aspx [Accessed].

IIA 2016a. International Standards for the Professional Practice of Internal Auditing – Standard 1000 Purpose, Authority and Responsibility. Florida: The Institute of Internal Auditors.

IIA 2016b. International Standards for the Professional Practice of Internal Auditing – Standard 1010 Recognising Mandatory Guidance in the Internal Audit Charter. Florida: The Institute of Internal Auditors.

IIA 2016c. International Standards for the Professional Practice of Internal Auditing – Standard 1100 Independence and Objectivity. Florida: The Institute of Internal Auditors.

IIA 2016d. International Standards for the Professional Practice of Internal Auditing – Standard 1110 Organisational Independence. Florida: The Institute of Internal Auditors.

IIA 2016e. International Standards for the Professional Practice of Internal Auditing – Standard 1111 Direct Interaction with the Board Florida The Institute of Internal Auditors.

IIA 2016f. International Standards for the Professional Practice of Internal Auditing – Standard 1112 Chief Audit Executive Roles beyond internal auditing Florida The Institute of Internal Auditors.

IIA 2016g. International Standards for the Professional Practice of Internal Auditing – Standard 1120 Individual Objectivity. Florida The Institute of Internal Auditors.

IIA 2016h. International Standards for the Professional Practice of Internal Auditing – Standard 1130 Impairment to Independence or Objectivity. Florida: The Institute of Internal Auditors.

IIA 2016i. International Standards for the Professional Practice of Internal Auditing – Standard 1200 Proficiency and Due Professional Care. Florida: The Institute of Internal Auditors.

IIA 2016j. International Standards for the Professional Practice of Internal Auditing – Standard 1210 Proficiency. Florida The Institute of Internal Auditors.

IIA 2016k. International Standards for the Professional Practice of Internal Auditing – Standard 1220 Due Professional Care. Florida The Institute of Internal Auditors.

IIA 2016l. International Standards for the Professional Practice of Internal Auditing – Standard 1230 Continuing Professional Development (CPD). Florida The Institute of Internal Auditors.

IIA 2016m. International Standards for the Professional Practice of Internal Auditing – Standard 1300 Quality Assurance and Improvement Program (QAIP) Florida The Institute of Internal Auditors.

IIA 2016n. International Standards for the Professional Practice of Internal Auditing – Standard 1310 Requirements of the Quality Assurance and Improvement Program. Florida The Institute of Internal Auditors.

IIA 2016o. International Standards for the Professional Practice of Internal Auditing – Standard 1311 Internal Assessments. Florida: The Institute for Internal Auditors.

IIA 2016p. International Standards for the Professional Practice of Internal Auditing – Standard 1312 External Assessments. Florida: The Institute of Internal Auditors.

IIA 2016q. International Standards for the Professional Practice of Internal Auditing – Standard 1320 Reporting on the Quality Assurance and Improvement Program. Florida: The Institute of Internal Auditors.

IIA 2016r. International Standards for the Professional Practice of Internal Auditing – Standard 1321 Use of "Conforms to the International Standards for the Professional Practice of Internal Auditing". Florida The Institute of Internal Auditors.

IIA 2016s. International Standards for the Professional Practice of Internal Auditing – Standard 1322 Disclosure of Non-conformance. Florida: The Institute of Internal Auditors.

IIA 2016t. International Standards for the Professional Practice of Internal Auditing – Standard 2000 Managing the Internal Audit Activity. Florida: The Institute of Internal Auditors.

IIA 2016u. International Standards for the Professional Practice of Internal Auditing – Standard 2010 Planning. Florida.

IIA 2016v. International Standards for the Professional Practice of Internal Auditing – Standard 2020 Communication and Approval. Florida: The Institute of Internal Auditors.

IIA 2016w. International Standards for the Professional Practice of Internal Auditing – Standard 2030 Resource Management. Florida: The Institute of Internal Auditors.

IIA 2016x. International Standards for the Professional Practice of Internal Auditing – Standard 2040 Policies and Procedures. Florida The Institute for Internal Auditors.

IIA 2016y. International Standards for the Professional Practice of Internal Auditing – Standard 2050 Coordination and Reliance Florida The Institute of Internal Auditors.

IIA 2016z. International Standards for the Professional Practice of Internal Auditing – Standard 2060 Reporting to Management and the Board Florida: The Institute of Internal Auditors.

IIA 2016aa. International Standards for the Professional Practice of Internal Auditing – Standard 2070 External Service Provider and Organizational Responsibility for Internal Auditing. Florida: The Institute of Internal Auditors.

IIA 2016ab. International Standards for the Professional Practice of Internal Auditing – Standard 2100 Nature of Work. Florida The Institute of Internal Auditors.

IIA 2016ac. International Standards for the Professional Practice of Internal Auditing – Standard 2110 Governance. Florida: The Institute of Internal Auditors.

IIA 2016ad. International Standards for the Professional Practice of Internal Auditing – Standard 2120 Risk Management. Florida: The Institute of Internal Auditors.

IIA 2016ae. International Standards for the Professional Practice of Internal Auditing – Standard 2130 Control. Florida The Institute of Internal Auditors.

IIA 2016af. International Standards for the Professional Practice of Internal Auditing – Standard 2200 Engagement Planning. Florida The Institute of Internal Auditors.

IIA 2016ag. International Standards for the Professional Practice of Internal Auditing – Standard 2201 Planning Considerations. Florida: The Institute of Internal Auditors.

IIA 2016ah. International Standards for the Professional Practice of Internal Auditing – Standard 2210 Engagement Objectives. Florida The Institute of Internal Auditors.

IIA 2016ai. International Standards for the Professional Practice of Internal Auditing – Standard 2220 Engagement Scope. Florida The Institute of Internal Auditors.

IIA 2016aj. International Standards for the Professional Practice of Internal Auditing – Standard 2230 Engagement Resource Allocation. Florida The Institute of Internal Auditors.

IIA 2016ak. International Standards for the Professional Practice of Internal Auditing – Standard 2240 Engagement Work Program. Florida The Institute of Internal Auditors.

IIA 2016al. International Standards for the Professional Practice of Internal Auditing – Standard 2300 Performing the Engagement. Florida: The Institute of Internal Auditors.

IIA 2016am. International Standards for the Professional Practice of Internal Auditing – Standard 2310 Identifying Information. Florida: The Institute of Internal Auditors.

IIA 2016an. International Standards for the Professional Practice of Internal Auditing – Standard 2320 Analysis and Evaluation. Florida The Institute of Internal Auditors.

IIA 2016ao. International Standards for the Professional Practice of Internal Auditing – Standard 2330 Documenting Information. Florida: The Institute of Internal Auditors.

IIA 2016ap. International Standards for the Professional Practice of Internal Auditing – Standard 2400 Communicating Results Florida: The Institute of Internal Auditors.

IIA 2016aq. International Standards for the Professional Practice of Internal Auditing – Standard 2410 Criteria For Communicating. Florida The Institute of Internal Auditors.

IIA 2016ar. International Standards for the Professional Practice of Internal Auditing – Standard 2420 Quality of Communications. Florida The Institute of Internal Auditors.

IIA 2016as. International Standards for the Professional Practice of Internal Auditing – Standard 2421 Errors and Omissions. Florida The Institute of Internal Auditors.

IIA 2016at. International Standards for the Professional Practice of Internal Auditing – Standard 2430 Use of "*Conducted in conformance with the International standards for the Professional Practice of Internal Auditing*". Florida The Institute of Internal Auditors.

IIA 2016au. International Standards for the Professional Practice of Internal Auditing – Standard 2431 Engagement Disclosure of Non-conformance. Florida The Institute of Internal Auditing.

IIA 2016av. International Standards for the Professional Practice of Internal Auditing – Standard 2440 Dissemenating Results. Florida The Institute of Internal Auditors.

IIA 2016aw. International Standards for the Professional Practice of Internal Auditing – Standard 2450 Overall Opinions. Florida: The Institute of Internal Auditors.

IIA 2016ax. International Standards for the Professional Practice of Internal Auditing – Standard 2500 Monitoring Progress. Florida The Institute of Internal Auditors.

IIA 2016ay. International Standards for the Professional Practice of Internal Auditing – Standard 2600 – Communicating the Acceptance of Risks. Florida The Institute of Internal Auditors.

IIA 2016az. International Standards for the Professional Practices of Internal Auditing – Standard 1000 Purpose, Authority and Responsibility. Florida: The Institute of Internal Auditors.

IIA 2016ba. International Standards for the Professional Practices of Internal Auditing – Standard 2100 Nature of Work. Florida The Institute of Internal Auditing.

IIA 2017a. Implementation Guidance New York: The Institute of Internal Auditors.

IIA. 2017b. Implementation Guide 1310: Standard 1310 – Requirements of the Quality Assurance and Improvement Program. Available: http://iia.org.au/sf_docs/default-source/quality/pdf-toolkit/implementation-guide-standard-1310.pdf?sfvrsn=2 [Accessed 26 July 2018].

IIA. 2017c. *International Standards for the Professional Practice of Internal Auditing (Standards)* [Online]. The Institute of Internal Auditors Available: https://na.theiia.org/certification/Pages/Certification.aspx [Accessed 25 May 2018].

IIA. 2017d. *Supplemental Guidance* [Online]. Florida: The Institute of Internal Auditors Available: https://na.theiia.org/standards-guidance/recommended-guidance/practice-guides/Pages/Practice-Guides.aspx [Accessed 28 May 2018].

IoD 2016a. King IV Report on Governance for South Africa 2016. Institure of Directors Southern Africa.

IOD 2016b. Report on Corporate Governance South Africa *King IV.* Johannesburg Institute of Directors

Lenz, R. & Hahn, U. 2015. A synthesis of empirical internal audit effectiveness literature pointing to new research opportunities. *Managerial Auditing Journal,* 30 (1), 5–33.

Picket, K. S. S. 2010. *The Internal Audit Handbook,* West Sussex, John Wiley & Sons Ltd

Ramamoorti, S. 2003. Internal auditing: history, evolution, and prospects. *Research opportunities in internal auditing,* 1–23.

Reding, K. F., Sobel, P. J., Anderson, U. L., Head, M. J., Ramamoorti, S., Salamasick, M. & Riddle, C. 2013. *Internal auditing: assurance & advisory services,* Institute of Internal Auditors Research Foundation.

Rezaee, Z. 1995. What the COSO report means for internal auditors. *Managerial Auditing Journal,* 10 (6), 5–9.

Rose, A. M., Rose, J. M. & Norman, C. S. 2013. Is the objectivity of internal audit compromised when the internal audit function is a management training ground? *Accounting & Finance,* 53 (4), 1001–1019.

Sarbanes-Oxley Act (SOX) 2002. Sarbanes-Oxley Act. *Washington DC.*

Sarens, J. & Abdolmohammadi, M. J. 2011. Monitoring Effects of the Internal. *International Journal of Auditing* 1–20.

Soh, D. S. & Martinov-Bennie, N. 2011. The internal audit function: Perceptions of internal audit roles, effectiveness and evaluation. *Managerial Auditing Journal,* 26 (7), 605–622.

United States Securities and Exchange Commission. 2003. Final rule: Management's report on internal control over financial reporting and certification of disclosure in exchange act periodic report Available: https://www.sec.gov/rules/final/33-8545.pdf [Accessed 24 July 2018].

1. Introduction

Auditors offer different services to their clients. Some of these will provide assurance in the sense that the auditor attests to the accuracy, fair presentation or compliance of subject matter with defined criteria (IAASB, 2013a). Other engagements may entail the auditor producing a report on factual findings (where no assurance is given) or compiling financial and other information (IAASB, 2013c; IAASB, 2013d).

The above services can be thought of as part of the broader corporate governance system. In terms of most codes of corporate governance[1] (Solomon, 2010; IOD, 2016), an organisation's governing body[2] is required to ensure that different types of assurance services are utilized to ensure an effective control environment, the integrity of data used for internal decision making and the reliability of the organisation's external reports (see, for example, IOD, 2016). In addition to the audit of financial statements (refer to Parts A, B and C of this book) an organisation will rely on different types of assurance services which form part of a combined assurance model (for details see Decaux and Sarens, 2015; Forte and Barac, 2015; IOD, 2016; Mubako, 2019; Prinsloo and Maroun, 2020). Refer to Figure 1 for on outline of key assurance-related considerations[3].

This chapter explores the different types of assurance and non-assurance services which an auditor or practitioner may render to a client. The chapter starts by defining key principles and definitions (Section 2). This is followed by a discussion of the different type of assurance engagements, including the levels of assurance provided by each (Section 3). For each assurance service type, the acceptance and continuance, planning and execution of the respective engagements are briefly discussed (Section 4). Non-assurance engagements are dealt with in Section 5. Examples of reporting for assurance engagements are discussed in Section 6.

---

1   King-IV in South Africa is an example.
2   'Governing body', 'board of directors' and 'those charged with governance' are used interchangeably.
3   Examples of principles and practices are obtained from King-IV. It is submitted that these will apply equally to most codes of corporate governance using a stakeholder-centric model. King IV is focused on because it is widely regarded as one of the most comprehensive (and current) codes of corporate governance.

Figure 1: Assurance-related practices

Assumption of assurance responsibilities

- The audit committee, as a sub committee of the governing body, is responsible for setting the direction of all material assurance services and functions, taking into account legal requirements and data integrity (of data or the report or both), the nature, scope and extent of assurance provided for reports, and the external opinions obtained.
- The audit committee should actively monitor the combined assurance functions, ensuring quality assurance services are obtained to ensure the effective functioning of internal controls and reporting functions of the organisation.
- The governing body and its committees should assess the output of the organisation's combined assurance with objectivity and professional scepticism, and by applying an enquiring mind to form their own opinion on the integrity of information and reports, and the degree to which an effective control environment has been achieved.

Relevance and implementation of combined assurance

- A combined assurance should address the organisation's significant risks and other material issues.
- Combined assurance should assist in managing the risks of the organisation at the operational, compliance and reporting level. Combined assurance will usually incorporate an organisation's internal controls and management systems, internal audit functions and independent external assurance.

Assurance of external reports

- External assurance providers are an integral part of the combined assurance process. In addition to the audit of financial statements, they can test management systems, internal controls and the disclosures found in integrated and sustainaability reports.

The role of internal audit

- The internal audit function should be directed by the audit committee, who should also approve the internal audit charter and ensure that internal audit has the required resources to fulfil its mandate.

(per IOD, 2016, pp 68–70).

2. Key definitions

Key terms used in this chapter are defined in Table 1 below (IAASB, 2017a, pp. 12–42)

Table 1: Definition of key terms	
Term	**Definition**
Underlying subject matter	The phenomenon or information which is measured or evaluated by applying criteria.
Criteria	The benchmarks used to measure or assess the underlying subject matter. The 'applicable criteria' are the criteria used for the engagement to evaluate the respective subject matter.
Practitioner	A professional accountant in public practice who performs an assurance, review or compilation engagement.
Prospective financial information	Financial information based on forecasts and projections using hypothetical assumptions about future events, management actions not yet to take place or best estimates. The information can be in the form of a forecast, projection or a combination of both.
Subject matter information	The outcome of the measurement or evaluation of the underlying subject matter against the criteria, that is, the information which results from applying the criteria to the underlying subject matter.

(IAASB, 2009a; 2013h; 2015a)

3. Types of assurance

According to the IAASB (2009a, p. 6), an 'assurance engagement' means:

> 'an engagement in which a practitioner expresses a conclusion designed to enhance the degree of confidence of the intended users other than the responsible party about the outcome of the evaluation or measurement of a subject matter against criteria'.

Assurance can cover more than just an audit of the financial statements which has led to accountants often debating the definition of assurance (Knechel and Salterio, 2016). Knechel and Salterio (2016) point out that accountants and auditors (practitioners)[4] render a variety of services to their clients (in addition to the audit of financial statements) which enhance the credibility and reliability of the underlying information. By its nature, assurance excludes consulting services because the objective of assurance is not to provide information for the

---

4   This chapter refers to a 'practitioner' rather than an 'auditor' because an audit (performed by an auditor) is only an example of a type of assurance engagement.

benefit of the organisation only or to make recommendations to management (Knechel and Salterio, 2016).

3.1 Classification of assurance services

Assurance engagements are evaluated according to two characteristics: the level of assurance provided and the role of the practitioner. In the first instance, an assurance engagement can be structured to provide either reasonable or limited assurance. For reasonable assurance:

'the practitioner reduces engagement risk to an acceptably low level...the practitioner's conclusion is expressed in a form that conveys the practitioner's opinion on the outcome of the measurement or evaluation of the underlying subject matter against the criteria' (IAASB, 2017b, para 14).

Although not referred to in the *International Framework for Assurance Engagements* (the Framework), the prior research usually characterises a reasonable assurance engagement as one providing a high (but not absolute) level of assurance (see, for example, Hodge et. al, 2009; Farooq and De Villiers, 2017). The assurance conclusion (opinion) is expressed in a positive form. In other words, the practitioner concludes on whether or not the subject matter conforms to the applicable criteria (see also Section 5).

In a limited assurance engagement, the nature, timing and extent of the procedures performed are 'limited, compared with that necessary in a reasonable assurance engagement' (IAASB, 2017b, para 15). (This is illustrated in more detail in Section 4). As a result, the practitioner provides a lower level of assurance than for a reasonable assurance engagement. Some of the academic research refers to moderate assurance to distinguish between the level of assurance provided in a limited assurance engagement and the high level of assurance in a reasonable assurance engagement (see, for example, Farooq and De Villiers, 2018; Maroun, 2019). To signal the fact that the level of assurance is lower for a limited assurance engagement than it is for a reasonable assurance engagement, the assurance opinion states whether or not anything has come to the practitioner's attention to suggest that the respective subject matter does not conform to the applicable criteria (IAASB, 2017b). This is sometimes referred to as a conclusion expressed in a negative form (see also Section 5).

Assurance engagements can also be categorised as attest or direct engagements (IAASB, 2017b). An attest engagement involves a party, not the practitioner, measuring or evaluating the subject matter against the applicable criteria. The practitioner's assurance opinion deals with whether or not the subject matter is free from material misstatement (IAASB, 2017b, para 12). In a direct engagement, the practitioner measures or evaluates the subject matter against the criteria. The practitioner's report deals with the outcome of the test procedures

(IAASB, 2017b, para 13). The services which the auditor can provide are summarised in Figure 2 below:

Figure 2: Types of assurance engagements

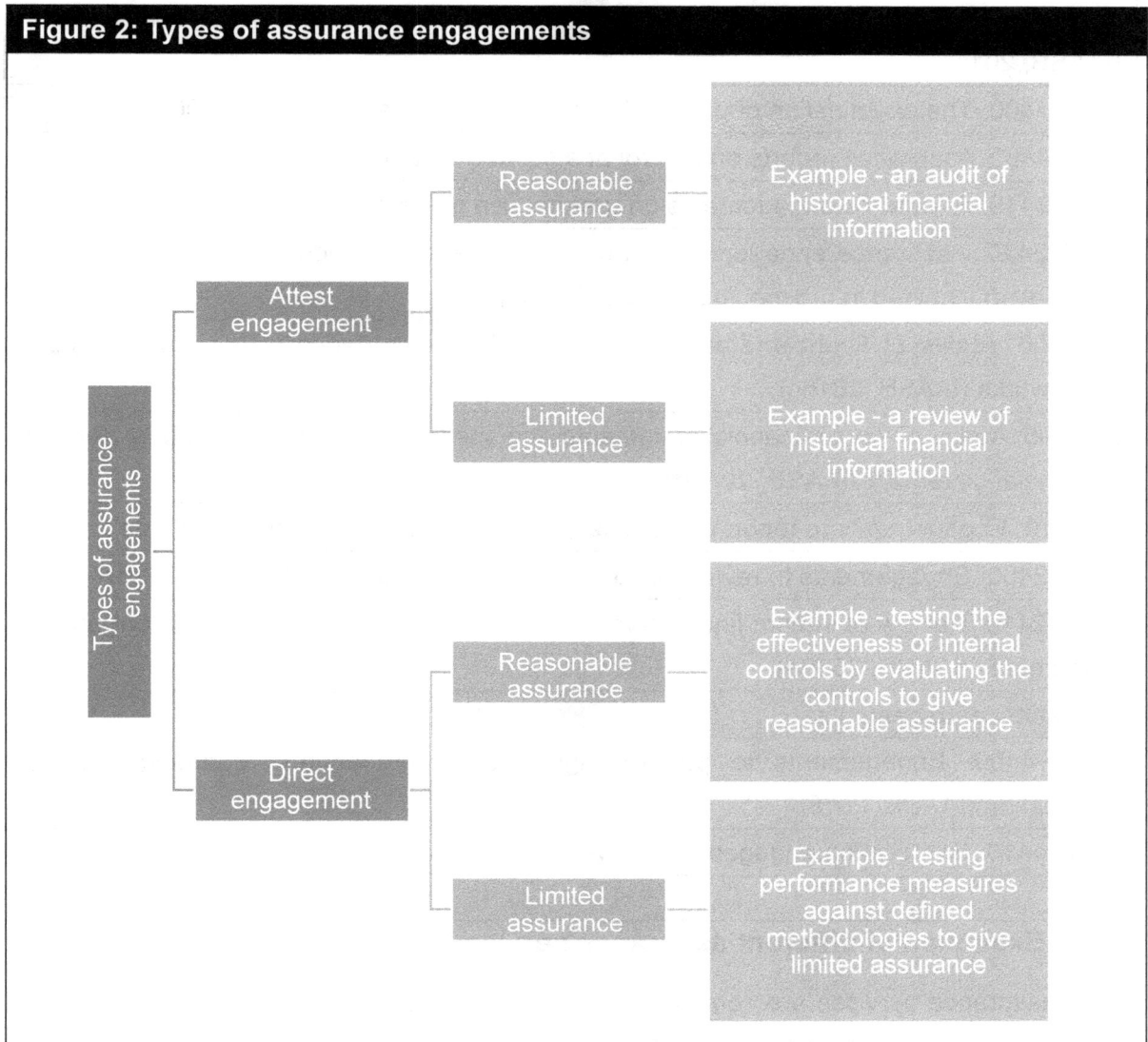

The International Auditing and Assurance Standards Board (IAASB) provides guidance on assurance and non-assurance engagements. Table 2 details the standards applicable for different engagements. These engagements have been grouped as attest (providing assurance) or non-attest (not providing assurance). For brevity, Table 2 does not distinguish between a direct or attest assurance engagement. It is submitted that the standards below could be used to structure an engagement as either a direct or attest engagement where the objective is to provide, at least, some level of assurance.

Table 2: Standards applicable for assurance and non-assurance engagements
Attest engagements
ISAE 3000: Assurance engagements other than audits or reviews of historical information (IAASB, 2015b)
ISAE 3400: The examination of prospective financial information (IAASB, 2009c)
ISAE 3402: Assurance reports on control at a service organisation (IAASB, 2013e)
ISAE 3410: Assurance engagements on greenhouse gas statements (IAASB, 2013f)
ISAE 3420: Assurance engagements to report on the compilation of pro forma financial information included in prospectus (IAASB, 2013g)
ISA 800: Audits of financial statements prepared in accordance with special purpose frameworks (IAASB, 2016c)
ISA 805: Audits of single financial statements and specific elements, accounts or items in a financial statement (IAASB, 2016d)
ISA 810: Engagements to report on summary financial statements (IAASB, 2016e)
ISRE 2400: Engagements to review historical financial statements (IAASB, 2009d)
ISRE 2410: Review of interim financial information performed by the independent auditor of the entity (IAASB, 2009e)
Non-attest engagements
ISRS 4400: Engagements to perform agreed-upon procedures regarding financial information (IAASB, 2018b)
ISRS 4410: Compilation engagements (IAASB, 2013i)

3.2 Examples of different assurance services in practice

Other assurance services are commonly encountered when dealing with information found in annual, sustainability and integrated reports, and so, information other than the annual financial statements (Ackers and Eccles, 2015; Hassan et al., 2020). Farooq and De Villiers (2017) provide a summary of the drivers of the demand for different assurance services (Simnett et al., 2009; Steinmeier and Stich, 2017; Maroun, 2020). These include:

- The growing expectation from stakeholders for companies to ensure the accuracy and reliability of the disclosures found in an integrated or a sustainability report;
- The impact which a company has on society and the environment (usually indicated by its size, listing status and the industry in which it operates);
- The legal environment in which a company operates;
- Whether or not a company operates according to codes of corporate governance which recommend or require the assurance of disclosures found in annual, integrated or sustainability reports; and

- The potential for external assurance to highlight errors or deficiencies in a company's reports to stakeholders and areas where internal controls or management systems can be improved.

In addition to the above drivers, both the Global Reporting Initiative (GRI, 2016) and the International Integrated Reporting Council (IIRC, 2013) recommend the use of external assurance services to strengthen the reliability and quality of sustainability and integrated reports respectively. There is, however, no single standard or set of professional guidelines which identify an integrated or sustainability report in its entirety as the subject matter of an assurance engagement. (For details on the reason for this, readers are referred to Cohen and Simnett (2015), Maroun and Atkins (2015), Simnett and Huggins (2015) and Maroun (2017)). As a result, companies – in consultation with their external assurance provider – will select different parts of their integrated or sustainability report for testing[5]. Table 3 summarises some of the commonly encountered external assurance engagements dealing with non-financial information included in integrated or sustainability reports.

Table 3: Other engagements		
Engagement	**Objective & assurance type**	**Examples**
ISAE 3000	• To obtain **reasonable or limited assurance** about whether the subject matter information is free from material misstatements and to report on the conclusions reached (ISAE300.10).	• Sustainability reports – compliance with GRI disclosure requirements and specific non-financial disclosures, such as number of employees, CO_2 emissions and corporate social responsibility spends. • Integrated reports – specific non-financial disclosures, aspects of key performance measures and levels of compliance with codes on corporate governance. • Effectiveness of internal controls used to collect data included in integrated or sustainability reports.

▶

---

5   For this chapter, the focus is on external assurance. An organisation will, however, seek assurance in terms of its combined assurance model of which external is only a part. A detailed review of how combined assurance is applied in an integrated reporting context is beyond the scope of this chapter.

Table 3: Other engagements		
Engagement	**Objective & assurance type**	**Examples**
AA1000AS	In a Type-1 engagement, the practitioner issues a report which concludes on the extent of adherence to the AA1000 Accountability principles of inclusivity, materiality and responsiveness: • Inclusivity: stakeholders are included in the process of developing a strategic response to sustainability and management accepts that it is accountable to a broad group of stakeholders for its sustainability performance. • Materiality: the reporting entity assesses the relevance and significance of issue for its long-term sustainability • Responsiveness: the organisation responds reasonably to stakeholders' concerns about sustainability performance. A Type-2 engagement is the same as a Type-1 engagement but in addition includes a conclusion on the reliability of sustainability performance information. Type-1 and Type-2 engagements can be structured to provide a **high or moderate level of assurance**. For further details, see AccountAbility (2008)	• These engagements are common for environmental, social and governance disclosures in integrated or sustainability reports. • The engagements are similar to those performed according to ISAE 3000 but will also include conclusions on inclusivity, materiality and responsiveness. • AA1000AS also caters for the provision of recommendations in the assurance report.

►

Table 3: Other engagements		
Engagement	**Objective & assurance type**	**Examples**
ISAE 3400	• To establish standards and provide guidance on engagements to examine and report on prospective financial information including the examination of best-estimates and hypothetical assumptions. • **Moderate assurance** is provided (ISAE3400.8–9).	• Limited assurance engagements on prospectus. • Normally applicable to the accuracy of any mathematical analysis/models. • Would support prospective information or a prospectus which may be issued separately or which accompanies an annual, sustainability or integrated report.
ISAE 3402	• To obtain **reasonable assurance** of which the controls implemented at a service organisation are designed as reported, operated effectively throughout the period and that the system description reported by the entity fairly presents the system as designed and implemented through the period (ISAE3402.8).	• Testing the controls for a service organisation which performs the payroll function of the company. • These assurance services are used to provide financial statement auditors with audit evidence. • The engagements can also be used by those charged with governance to discharge their responsibility for ensuring the integrity of an organisation's internal controls. • The results of these engagements are often not included in an annual, integrated or sustainability report.

▶

Table 3: Other engagements		
Engagement	**Objective & assurance type**	**Examples**
ISAE 3410	• To provide assurance on the greenhouse gas emissions statements and to report that the statements are free from material misstatement. • Can provide **reasonable or limited assurance** (ISAE3410.6–8).	• This type of assurance is common for disclosures dealing with greenhouse gas emissions in integrated or sustainability reports. • Assurance on greenhouse gas statements may also be required for submissions to the Carbon Disclosure Project (see CDP, 2017) or to tax authorities/environmental agencies.
ISAE 3420	• The objective in terms of the standard is to provide **reasonable assurance** about whether the pro forma financial information in a prospectus complies, in all material aspects, with the applicable criteria and to report on the findings (ISAE3420.10).	• Auditor/practitioner can be asked to report on the information contained in a prospectus when a new share issue is to take place or when the company is about to list (for example, in an Initial Public Offering).

ISA 800	• The standard is applied when the auditing a set of financial statements which have been prepared on a special purpose framework (in terms of regulations or according to the needs of the intended users).
	• The objective of the auditor is to address appropriately the special considerations relevant to:
	  – The acceptance of the engagement;
	  – The planning and performance of the engagement; and
		• Audit of financial statements prepared on a tax basis of accounting for a set of financial statements accompanying an annual or integrated report.
		• Audit of financial statements prepared on the cash receipts and disbursements basis of accounting for cash flow information which an entity may have been requested to prepare for creditors or other stakeholders. This can be presented separately or

▶

358

Table 3: Other engagements		
Engagement	**Objective & assurance type**	**Examples**
ISA 800 (cont.)	– Forming an opinion and reporting on the financial statements (IAS800.5) • The report provides **reasonable assurance.**	as part of the integrated or sustainability report. • Audit of financial statements prepared based on the provisions established by a regulator to meet the requirements of the regulator. • Audit of financial statements prepared based on the financial reporting provisions of a contract, such as, bond indenture, a loan agreement or a project grant (ISA800.A1).
ISA 805	• This ISA deals with special considerations in the application of ISA's (100–700) to an audit of a single financial statement or a specific element, account or item of a financial statement, in which the single financial statement or specific element may be prepared in accordance with a general or special purpose framework (ISA805.1). • The objective of the auditor is to address appropriately the special considerations relevant to: • The acceptance of the engagement; • The planning and performance of the engagement; and • Forming an opinion and reporting on the financial statements (IAS805.5).	• Audit of a balance sheet prepared on a liquidation basis for a bank loan agreement to prove solvency. • Audit of disclosure required in terms of regulation regarding the bonus structures, employee remuneration packages, and share options etc, otherwise not required by IFRS.

►

Table 3: Other engagements		
Engagement	**Objective & assurance type**	**Examples**
	• Report provides **reasonable assurance.**	

ISA 810	• This standard will apply when the auditor issues an opinion on a set of summarised financial statements (ISA810.1).
	• The objectives of the auditor are to:
	  – Determine whether it is appropriate to accept the engagement to report on summary financial statements;
	  – To form an opinion on the summary financial statements based on an evaluation of the conclusions drawn from the evidence obtained; and
	  – To express clearly that opinion through a written report which also describes the basis for the opinion.
	• Report provides **reasonable assurance.**
		• Summary financial statements reported in the newspapers as part of the entity's annual results or are included in an integrated report.

4. Assurance provided by different assurance services

The following are examples of services provided by independent practitioners which can be included as part of a combined assurance model:

1. Due diligence services;
2. Assurance over prospective financial information;
3. Review of interim financial information; and
4. Forensic audits.

The scope of each engagement, nature of services provided, and level of assurance are summarised in Table 4.

Table 4: Scope, nature and level of assurance provided by practitioners			
Engagement	**Scope**	**Nature of service**	**Level of assurance**
Due diligence services	Compliance with laws and regulations, financial reporting standards and valuation services related to mergers and acquisitions.	Dependent on the brief from the client.	No assurance or limited assurance (in the case of review engagements).
Assurance over prospective financial information	Procedures are limited to any prospective information related to assumptions.	Review engagement	Moderate assurance
Review of interim financial information	A review of the interim financial statements.	Review engagement	Limited assurance

Each of these engagements is discussed in more detail below.

4.1 Due diligence services

Spedding (2009, p. 3) defines due diligence as 'a process of discovery that is relevant in key business transactions and operations.' Due diligence services include objective and independent examinations which focus on legal compliance, financial compliance, tax compliance, asset valuation and operations (including environmental, social and governance matters). A due diligence is usually performed during a merger or acquisition (Angwin, 2001). Maxwell Locke & Ritter (2017) add that, in a financial due diligence, the practitioner obtains evidence on, *inter alia,* the following (Maxwell Locke & Ritter, 2017):

- Sustainable earnings potential of the potential acquiree;
- Past sales and operating expenses and trends;
- Working capital requirements of the company;
- Management forecasts and assumptions used in the forecasts; and
- Key personnel and accounting information systems.

A due diligence is not a financial statement audit but it can provide a level of assurance to the users of the report (Eilifsen et al., 2018). The objective is not to provide an opinion on whether or not the financial statements are free from material misstatement but to provide a report on findings which may be relevant to a buyer or seller of a company (Maxwell Locke & Ritter, 2017). The scope of due diligence is, limited to the type of engagement which is rendered and is dependent on the needs of the client (Spedding, 2009). Should a practitioner be required to structure the due diligence as an assurance engagement, the Framework (IAASB, 2017b) can be used as guidance. In terms of the *Framework*, the engagement can only be accepted if certain conditions have been met. The conditions described in the *Framework* are similar to those which will apply in a financial statement audit (refer to Parts B and C of this book).

After the engagement has been accepted, the practitioner will have to plan the engagement. The planning procedures depend on the scope and nature of the due diligence engagement. If the nature of the engagement is a review of historical information, the planning procedures will be similar to those of a review (see Section 4.3 below). If the due diligence is structured as a reasonable assurance engagement (including, for example, a full scope financial statement audit), then the planning procedures for a financial statement audit have to be performed (see Part B of this book for more information).

The procedures which have to be performed in the instance of a review engagement will be limited to observation, enquiries and analytical procedures. This is discussed in Part B of this book and remain the same for a due diligence review engagement. In the case of the client requiring a full audit to be performed, audit procedures in terms of ISA 500 can be performed (see Chapter 13).

4.2 Assurance over prospective financial information

Prospective financial information refers to financial information which is forward-looking or which takes into account events which are expected to take place (IAASB, 2013b). In providing assurance over prospective information, the auditor tests the forecasts made by management, based on management's assumptions regarding future events or conditions (IAASB, 2013b). Prospective financial information can include financial statements or parts of the financial statements which may be used as an internal management tool or for distribution to third parties (IAASB, 2013b).

Given the speculative nature of prospective financial information (and the nature of the assumption made by management) the auditor might not be able to perform sufficient procedures to support a reasonable assurance opinion. As a result, the practitioner will usually only provide a moderate assurance[6] (IAASB, 2013b). However, ISAE 3400 (para 9) allows for the auditor to give reasonable assurance regarding the assumption used if, in the auditor's

---

6   ISAE 3400 refers specifically to moderate assurance. Based on the nature of the procedures performed and opinion provided on the subject matter per ISAE 3400, it is submitted that this means limited assurance.

judgement, sufficient and appropriate evidence exists to support the assurance statement.

4.2.1 Accepting the engagement

In terms of ISAE 3400 (para 11), auditors should not accept such an engagement if the prospective information will be inappropriate in light of the planned use of the information (IAASB, 2013b). Auditors are, therefore, required to consider the following before accepting an engagement to test prospective information:

- How the client intends to use the information;
- Whether or not the information will be distributed to a limited number of parties or will be widely distributed;
- How management made assumptions (ie based upon accepted practice or hypothetical scenarios);
- The number and nature of elements to be included in the information; and
- The period to be covered by the information.

The terms of the engagement have to be documented in an engagement letter which should be signed by both parties as evidence of a mutual understanding of the scope and objectives of the engagement (see ISAE 3400 para 12 in IAASB, 2013b). The engagement letter should also set out the responsibilities of management and the auditor to ensure that there are no disputes or ambiguity regarding each party's responsibilities (see ISAE 3400 para 12 in IAASB, 2013b).

4.2.2 Planning considerations

The auditor should understand the client's business environment in order to gain an understanding of the significant assumptions required for the preparation of the prospective information (see ISAE 3400 para 13 in IAASB, 2013b). This requires the auditor to perform risk assessment procedures to understand fully the process followed by the entity to ensure the accuracy of the data, the assumptions used and the internal controls of the company (ibid). The process followed to gain this understanding is similar to the process followed by an auditor in planning for an audit engagement, including understanding the estimates (in terms of ISA 540). Refer to Part B of this book for additional information.

4.2.3 Period covered by the procedures

The auditor should determine the period to be covered by the prospective information as the length of time covered by the prospective information can negatively affect the accuracy of assumptions used by management (see ISAE 3400 para 14 in IAASB, 2013b). The following factors must be taken into account when determining the period of time covered:

- The economic life cycle (operating cycle) of projects;
- The reliability of the assumptions used in the models given to management; or
- The information needs of the users and stakeholders.

The above is not a complete list of factors to be considered and will depend on the company and by the information being disclosed to stakeholders.

4.2.4 Executing the plan

Execution is concerned with the nature, timing and the extent of procedures to be performed to address the risk of material misstatement in the prospective information (see ISAE 3400 para 17 in IAASB, 2013b). This is affected by the following factors:

- The probability of material misstatements in the information;
- The understanding obtained about the entity and its environment;
- The competence of management personnel who prepared the prospective information;
- The degree of judgement involved in preparing the prospective information; and
- The reliability, accuracy and integrity of the data underlying the assumptions.

In performing procedures for purposes of ISAE 3400[7], the auditor can use the principles of ISA 540 in testing estimates. This has been discussed in Chapter 16 and the same guidance can be followed. The auditor needs to obtain a written management representation letter to confirm the completeness of significant judgement areas and assumptions used in the preparation of the prospective information (see ISAE 3400 para 25 in IAASB, 2013b).

4.2.5 Presentation and disclosure

The auditor should assess the presentation and disclosure of the prospective information. The assessment should include:

- Whether the presentation of the information contains relevant information which is not misleading;
- Whether the accounting policies are disclosed, together with the prospective information, or not[8];
- Whether or not the assumptions used by management are appropriately disclosed, indicating which assumptions are hypothetical and which are best estimates; and

---

7   Para18–25 discuss the procedures which the auditor can follow in testing the assumptions used by management. The procedures are aimed at testing the estimates made by management, which include the assumptions and modes used. The auditor is, as a result, testing accounting estimates.

8   This includes if there have been any changes to the accounting policy during the period.

- The date on which information used to develop the prospective information was sourced.

(IAASB, 2013b)

4.3 Review of interim financial information

Interim financial information is any financial information which is reported according to an applicable accounting framework, either in complete or in a condensed form, for a period shorter than a company's year-end (IAASB, 2006). For example, according to IAS 34:

'Interim financial report means a financial report containing either a complete set of financial statements [as defined by IFRS] or a set of condensed financial statements for an interim period meaning 'a financial reporting period shorter than a full financial year'' (IAASB, 2018a).

The purpose of the review engagement is for the practitioner to conclude whether or not the interim financial statements are free from material misstatement and comply with the applicable accounting reporting framework (IAASB, 2006). The review procedures are limited to enquiries, analytical procedures and observations. As a result, only limited assurance is provided over the financial statements (IAASB, 2006; IAASB, 2009d; Bédard and Courteau, 2015). The scope of the review is less than that of an audit as the purpose is not to express an opinion but to conclude whether there is anything which can indicate material misstatements (IAASB, 2006).

A review of interim financial information takes place in accordance with ISRE 2410 (IAASB, 2006). ISRE 2410 only applies when the person doing the review is the entity's external auditor and can apply for any other review engagement[9] (IAASB, 2006). The purpose of the engagement is to express a conclusion about whether or not anything has come to the auditor's attention which can cause the auditor to believe that the interim financial statements are materially misstated (see ISRE 2410 para 7 in IAASB, 2006). As a result, an engagement conducted according to ISRE240 provides limited rather than reasonable assurance (see ISRE 2410 para 9 in IAASB, 2006).

The general principles which apply to this type of review engagement are presented in Table 5 below:

---

9   ISRE 2400 is issued for any person who is performing a review who is not an auditor. The procedures described in ISRE 2400 are more detailed as the practitioner performing the review might not have the required in-depth understanding of the entity as the practitioner is not the external auditor. In this case, more procedures need to be performed.

Table 5: Auditor responsibilities related to a review engagement	
Review process	**Requirements**
Acceptance and continuance	The acceptance and continuance process which the auditor needs to follow is similar to that of an audit. Before an engagement can be accepted or continued, the following must be determined: • Whether the auditor has enough resources and competence to accept the engagement; • The integrity of management; and • The ability of the auditor to comply with ethical requirements. The factors above have been discussed in detail in Part B of this book. The terms of the review engagement should be documented and agreed to in an engagement letter which is signed by the auditor and management (see ISRE 2410 para 10 in IAASB, 2009e).
Planning	Planning procedures are similar to those followed for a full scope audit. The auditor is expected to obtain an understanding of the entity and its internal control environment[10] to identify possible risks of material misstatement, evaluate the likelihood of their occurrence and to plan how to respond to the risks.[11] The procedures which have to be followed for gaining an understanding of the entity and its control environment are discussed in Chapter 8.
Execution	Auditors are required to make inquiries and perform analytical procedures over the financial statements. Information obtained does not need to be corroborated by, for example, inspecting applicable source documents or using confirmations. In the interest of efficiency, the auditor may gather audit evidence for the purposes of the year end audit while collecting evidence for the review engagement (see ISRE 2410 para 20 and 23 in IAASB, 2009e). The auditor should make inquiries regarding the existence and disclosure of subsequent events and management's assessment regarding the entity's ability to continue as a going concern (see ISRE 2410 para 26 in IAASB, 2009e).

▶

---

10   The auditor is required to understand the internal controls for the preparation of both the annual and the interim financial statements.

11   The responses to risks are limited to inquiries, analytical procedures and other review procedures which will provide the auditor with a basis for the conclusion reached.

Table 5: Auditor responsibilities related to a review engagement	
Review process	**Requirements**
Completion	Should misstatements be identified during the review, the auditor should evaluate the misstatements to determine if any uncorrected misstatements, whether individually or in aggregate, can lead to the interim results being materially misstated (see ISRE 2410 para 30 in IAASB, 2009e).
Communications	A management representation letter should be obtained from the client. The letter confirms management's roles and responsibilities and any other matters the auditor requires. The following issues should be communicated to those charged with the client's governance as soon as possible (see ISRE 2400 para 38–42 in IAASB, 2009e): • Misstatements which are material in the judgement of the auditor; • Possible frauds which have been identified; and • Significant control weaknesses or deficiencies identified, including those related to corporate governance. Should management not respond adequately or in a timeous manner, the auditor should consider the following (see ISRE 2400 para 38–42 in IAASB, 2009e): • Modifying the report, • Withdrawing from the engagement; or • Resigning from the audit of the financial statements.

Adapted from IAASB (2009e)

5. Non-assurance services

5.1 Agreed-upon procedures (AUP's)

AUP's are engagements in which the auditor performs procedures and presents a factual findings report to management (IAASB, 2013c). The planned procedures are approved by management before the auditor performs the procedures. In addition, management or the users of the report have to draw their own conclusions (IAASB, 2013c). For these reasons, AUP's provide no assurance.

AUP's may relate to financial or non-financial information. For example, they can include procedures which the practitioners complete to assist management with reaching a conclusion on:

- Compliance with external regulations or contract;
- Compliance with internal standards/processes; or
- Social or environmental performance measures.

It must be stressed that the practitioner does not draw any inferences from the procedures performed. The report issued deals only with factual findings. Management must reach its own conclusions.

5.2 Compilation engagements

In a compilation engagement, the practitioner assists management in preparing financial information (such as financial statements, summarised financial reports or special purpose accounts) without obtaining any corroborating evidence for the amounts to be presented (IAASB, 2013d). In a compilation engagement, the practitioner does not issue an opinion on the material being compiled and no assurance is provided.

5.3 Forensic services[12]

Forensic auditing (or investigation), as opposed to a financial statement audit, aims to determine the probability of fraud occurring or impact of fraud at an entity (Golden et al., 2011). The purpose of a forensic audit is not to provide an opinion on the financial statements or internal financial controls and, for this reason, a forensic engagement does not have to be structured as an assurance engagement (Golden et al., 2011). The timing of forensic services also differs in that forensic services are usually required when a suspected fraud has been detected (Kranacher et al., 2010) while a financial statement audit is an annual service which is normally mandated by statute .

A forensic engagement adds value to an organisation in that it investigates suspect/suspicious accounting transactions, determines the facts and reports on the findings (Golden et al., 2011). The nature or structure of forensic audits (or investigations) will differ significantly based on the circumstances of each investigation (Singleton et al., 2006; Kranacher et al., 2010; Manning and CFE, 2010; Singleton and Singleton, 2010; Golden et al., 2011). The prior research does, however, show a common framework which can be applied (at a broad level) for the purpose of conducting a forensic audit (also referred to as accountants) (Singleton et al., 2006; Kranacher et al., 2010; Manning and CFE, 2010; Singleton and Singleton, 2010;

---

12   These services can be structured as assurance engagements but, to the authors' best knowledge, are normally structured as non-assurance services because of their complexity and the difficulty of reaching a definitive conclusion.

Golden et al., 2011). This framework requires the following process to be followed (Canadian Institute of Chartered Accountants (CICA, 2006)):

- accepting the engagement;
- planning and scope of work;
- information collection and analysis;
- file documentation; and
- reporting.

5.3.1 Accepting the engagement

The forensic auditor may only accept an engagement if the following conditions have been met (CICA, 2006):

- The forensic auditor is independent from the client; and
- The forensic auditor has sufficient knowledge and skills to perform the investigation based upon the scope and purpose of the investigation.

It is essential for the forensic auditor to understand the scope of the engagement and the circumstances which led to the engagement (CICA, 2006). The forensic auditor should also determine the context in which the engagement should take place, for example, if the engagement and final report will be used in litigation, fraud risks assessments or contract negotiations (CICA, 2006). As part of understanding the scope and the context of the engagement, the forensic auditor should determine if there is any limitation on the scope of the engagement (CICA, 2006).

Once the above issues have been considered, the forensic auditor should determine whether sufficient staff are available to perform the engagement. An engagement letter setting out the scope, nature and purpose should accompany each investigation. The engagement letter should be prepared by the forensic auditor and should be signed by the client to ensure that the scope and nature of the investigation is correct and understood by the client (CICA, 2006; Kranacher et al., 2010; Manning and CFE, 2010). These requirements are similar to those applying to the audit of financial statements. For more details, refer to Part B of this book.

5.3.2 Planning and scope of work

With each investigation being unique (Kranacher et al., 2010; Singleton and Singleton, 2010), the forensic auditor has to be meticulous when planning the engagement. The plan must be flexible enough to accommodate any new information or problems identified during the audit. To enable the forensic auditor to plan for the engagement, the following procedures can be performed (CICA, 2006; Kranacher et al., 2010; Wells, 2017):

- The engagement leader should develop a hypothesis, based on the facts and circumstances to better plan for the audit;
- After the hypothesis has been developed, the engagement leader should determine what type of investigation techniques can be used to determine if the hypothesis is sound, taking into account time and other resources required;
- The information required to address the hypothesis should be identified and a strategy to obtain the information should be finalised; and
- The nature and timing of the procedures which have to be performed, together with the nature and timing of the reporting requirements, should be determined.

Careful planning will allow the forensic auditor to identify additional assistance which might be required from legal or other experts (CICA, 2006; Kranacher et al., 2010; Golden et al., 2011). The planning process should be supervised and reviewed by experienced staff to ensure compliance with codes of best practice (CICA, 2006).

5.3.3 Information collection and analysis

During the information collection and analysis phase of an investigation, the forensic auditor should apply a high level of scepticism (CICA, 2006). This will require the forensic auditor to determine whether the information or data collected are biased, fictitious and/or incomplete (CICA, 2006). The forensic auditor can use information obtained from the client, as well as from other sources, and should analyse all data collected, assessing the substance – and not just the form – of the information collected (CICA, 2006). The practitioner cannot assume that information is complete and accurate.

The forensic auditor should have strict controls over the handling of any information obtained ensuring the chain of custody is never broken (CICA, 2006). The controls should ensure that data integrity is maintained and that all evidence is kept confidential and preserved (CICA, 2006; Kranacher et al., 2010; Manning and CFE, 2010; Singleton and Singleton, 2010; Golden et al., 2011).

As each investigation will be unique, it is not possible to provide a list of procedures which can be performed in all situations. However, a forensic auditor can use procedures performed by external auditors, which includes relying on the work performed by others (CICA, 2006). The procedures to rely on the work of an expert are similar to the procedures required by ISA 620. Please refer to Chapter 16 for more detail on the process to be followed by the forensic auditor when relying on the work of the expert.

5.3.4 Documentation of the work performed

The form of documentation is influenced by the scope and nature of the investigation, however, a few basic principles apply to documentation (CICA, 2006; Kranacher et al., 2010; Manning and CFE, 2010; Singleton and Singleton, 2010; Golden et al., 2011; Gerson et al., 2012):

- The working papers should be kept in an organised manner;
- The work performed by the forensic auditor should be documented in a clear and concise manner to ensure any other reasonable person who performs the same procedures will come to the same conclusion;
- Information, observations and considerations should be documented in as much detail as is, in practical terms, possible; and
- Given the often confidential nature of the investigations, the working papers and accompanying documentation should be stored safely.

The retention period is determined by the nature and scope of the engagement (Golden et al., 2011). Where the forensic auditor is unsure of the documentation standards which apply, the principles followed in ISA 230 can provide guidance. However, where statute or common law principles specify documentation standards, the forensic auditor must comply with these requirements.

6. Reporting on assurance (attest and direct) engagements

The report on an assurance attestation or direct engagement should clearly and objectively state the main findings and conclusions (IAASB, 2016a; IAASB, 2016b). The reader should be able to ascertain the nature and the extent of the procedures performed. Additionally, the report should enable the reader to identify whether an attest engagement, direct engagement or non-attest engagement was performed (IAASB, 2009d; IAASB, 2013i).

The report is the product of the entire assurance process (European Court of Auditors, 2007; IAASB, 2009d; IAASB, 2016b). Properly planned and performed procedures provide the basis for a good report. The converse is also true (IAASB, 2009b). Reporting in the correct manner assists in reducing the 'expectation gap'[13]; failing to do so can result in an audit failure or additional liability (Vanstraelen et al., 2011; Asare and Wright, 2012; Gold et al., 2012).

Reports should be objective, complete, clear, convincing, relevant, accurate, constructive, and concise (INTOSAI, 2004). Assurance reports, which include audit reports, need to be written from an independent unbiased viewpoint, with actual performance judged against objective criteria. The report should be balanced in content and neutral in tone, be fair and

---

13   'Expectation gap' refers to the difference in expected performance (Liggio, 1974).

avoid misleading the reader (INTOSAI, 2004; Australian Auditing Standards Board, 2008; IAASB, 2009d; IAASB, 2013i; IAASB, 2016b).

The elements of an assurance report are summarised in Table 6. Please note that Table 6 is not a complete list of requirements per the different assurance standards and these should be referenced for further details.

Table 6: Report format for assurance and non-assurance engagements	
Requirement for attest engagements	**Requirement for non-attest engagements**
Title	Title
Addressee	Addressee
An identification and description of the subject matter information and, when appropriate, the subject matter. Depending on the engagement, specific criteria and, where applicable, a description of inherent limitations. Other information may be required to assist the reader in determining the nature and extent of the procedures performed.	Identification of specific financial or non-financial information to which the agreed-upon procedures have been applied.
A statement of the responsibility of the entity's management and the responsibility of the practitioner.	A statement that the procedures performed were those agreed upon with the recipient.
Scope paragraph describing the nature of the engagement, including a reference to the applicable standard or to relevant national standards or practices.	A statement that the engagement was performed in accordance with the International Standard on Related Services applicable to agreed-upon procedures, engagements or with relevant national standards or practices. When relevant, a statement that the auditor is not independent of the entity should be included in the report.
A statement or summary of the work performed. Additional information may be required for engagements where there is an inherent limitation (IAASB, 2009c).	Identification of the purpose for which the agreed-upon procedures were performed. A listing of the specific procedures performed

►

Table 6: Report format for assurance and non-assurance engagements	
Requirement for attest engagements	**Requirement for non-attest engagements**
A statement pertaining to the type of assurance provided.	Statement that the procedures performed do not constitute either an audit or a review and as a result, no assurance is expressed
The practitioner's conclusion, expressed in the positive form in the case of a reasonable assurance engagement or in the negative form in the case of a limited assurance engagement (see details below).	A statement that, had the auditor performed additional procedures, an audit or a review, other matters might have come to light which would have been reported. A statement that the report is restricted to those parties who have agreed to the procedures being performed. A statement (when applicable) that the report relates only to the elements, accounts, items or financial and non-financial information specified and that it does not extend to the entity's financial statements taken as a whole.
Date of the report	Date of the report
Practitioner's address	Practitioner's address
Practitioner's signature	Practitioner's signature

6.1 Positive versus negative assurance conclusions

As explained in Section 3.1, assurance conclusions can be expressed in a positive or negative form. For example, reviews in terms of ISRE 2400 provide the user of the report with limited assurance (IAASB, 2009d) while audits in terms of the International Standards of Auditing (ISA) provide the user of the report with reasonable assurance (IAASB, 2016b).

Except for instances where material issues are noted, review engagements in terms of ISRE 2400, require the practitioner's report to state the following:

'Nothing has come to the practitioner's attention based on the review that causes the practitioner to believe the financial statements do not give a true and fair view (or are not presented fairly, in all material respects) in accordance with the applicable financial reporting framework'. (IAASB, 2009d, para 27(a), emphasis added).

This provides the user with limited assurance in a negative assurance form. The different types of assurance can affect the users' perceptions of the credibility of information in the financial statements being assured (Schelluch and Gay, 2006; Hodge et al., 2009). Additionally, the report is noted to have a conclusion drawn from the procedures performed as opposed to an opinion (IAASB, 2009d).

If material issues[14] have come to the practitioner's attention, the assurance conclusion is qualified or modified accordingly (IAASB, 2009c; IAASB, 2009d; IAASB, 2011; IAASB, 2013e; IAASB, 2013f; IAASB, 2013g; IAASB, 2015b; IAASB, 2016b). The qualifications are similar to those discussed for the audit of financial statements in Chapter 17.

Non-assurance engagements, such as agreed-upon procedures, result in no conclusion being expressed because the engagements are not assurance engagements (IAASB, 2013i). As a result, these engagement reports are based solely on the factual outcomes of the procedures performed (The American Assembly, 2003; Prada, 2007; IAASB, 2013i).

6.2   Reporting on prospective information and forensic services

The format and type of reports which a practitioner issues on prospective information (Section 6.2.1) and forensic services performed (Section 6.2.2) are discussed below.

6.2.1   Reporting on prospective information

The practitioner is exposed to the risk of litigation when expressing an opinion on prospective information because of the subjective nature of the subject matter (The American Assembly, 2003; ACCA, 2010). The audit evidence obtained will not be sufficient to provide reasonable assurance and can only provide limited comfort on prospective information because of the inherent unpredictability of prospective data (ACCA, 2010). The practitioner will issue a negative assurance opinion as only a moderate level assurance can be provided (The American Assembly, 2003; Prada, 2007; IAASB, 2009c).

In addition to the negative assurance ISAE 3400 suggests that the report also include the following (IAASB, 2009c para 27):

1. Title;
2. Addressee;
3. Identification of the prospective financial information;
4. A reference to the ISAE or relevant national standards or practices applicable to the examination of prospective financial information;

---

14   Material issues refer to instances where there are misstatements or an inability to obtain sufficient and appropriate audit evidence to conclude.

5. A statement that management is responsible for the prospective financial information including the assumptions on which it is based;

6. When applicable, a reference to the purpose and/or restricted distribution of the prospective financial information;

7. A statement of negative assurance as to whether the assumptions provide a reasonable basis for the prospective financial information;

8. An opinion as to whether the prospective financial information is properly prepared on the basis of the assumptions and is presented in accordance with the relevant financial reporting framework;

9. Appropriate caveats concerning the achievability of the results indicated by the prospective financial information;

10. Date of the report which should be the date on which procedures have been completed;

11. Auditor's address; and

12. Signature.

The assurance report will state whether, based on the examination of the evidence supporting the assumptions, anything has come to the auditor's attention which causes the auditor to believe that the assumptions do not provide a reasonable basis for the prospective financial information (IAASB, 2009c).

When the auditor believes that the presentation and disclosure of the prospective financial information is not adequate, or believes that one or more significant assumptions do not provide a reasonable basis for the prospective financial information, the auditor should express a qualified or adverse opinion or withdraw from the engagement as appropriate. In some cases, a disclaimer of opinion may be required (IAASB, 2009c).

6.2.2 Reporting on forensic services

There are various ways in which the finding of the investigation can be reported but this is ultimately determined by the scope, nature and purpose of the engagement. The report can either be a written report or an oral report. It should be clear if the report is an interim, draft or final report (CICA, 2006). The tone of the report should be objective and should refer to facts (CICA, 2006). The following elements should be present in the report (CICA, 2006):

1. Names and designation of all those involved in the report or the firm;

2. The name of the client and designated person and title of the person to whom the report should be directed;

3. The date of the report;

4. The scope, objective and purpose of the engagement;

5. The information used during the investigation to substantiate findings;

6. The extent to which reliance was placed on the work performed by independent third parties;

7. The techniques used and approach followed during the engagement;

8. An explanation of the practitioner's material assumptions;

9. Definitions and explanations of key terms used in the report;

10. Findings and conclusions supported by visuals and detailed analysis to enable the user of the report to reconcile the findings to the objective, scope and purpose of the engagement;

11. Any limitations on how the report can be used or how the findings can be interpreted; and

12. Any scope limitations which may apply.

Please note that any conclusion in the report will consider whether or not the engagement has been structured to provide assurance. As explained in Section 5.3, forensic services often take the form of AUPs in which case no conclusion or opinion will be provided.

7. Summary

The audit of financial statements is not the only type of assurance service which companies can use to ensure accurate and reliable reporting to stakeholders. As more emphasis is placed on integrated and sustainability reporting, companies can be expected to use a range of internal and external sources of assurance which focus on different aspects of an organisation's internal controls, management systems, internal decision making and external reporting.

An organisation's governing body will be responsible for providing direction on the development and operation of this combined approach to, and strategy for, assurance. Part B and C of this book deal with one part of combined assurance model: the audit of financial statements. Chapter 20 discusses how the work performed by internal auditors contributes to combined assurance. This chapter focuses specifically on engagements completed by independent practitioners.

Engagements completed by an external party can deal with different subject matter including, for example, internal controls, specific disclosures in sustainability or integrated reports and prospective financial information. The engagements can be designed to provide either reasonable or limited levels of assurance. In some cases, the practitioner does not issue a conclusion or opinion and no assurance is provided. Compilations and agreed-upon procedures are examples. These engagements contribute indirectly to the operation of the broader combined assurance model because management and stakeholders rely on the fact that the respective services were completed by an expert exercising due care and skill.

8. References

ACCA 2010. Reshaping the audit for the new global economy. *Accountancy Futures,* 1, 68–70.

AccountAbility. 2008. AA1000 Assurance Standard 2008. Available: http://www.accountability. org/standards/aa1000as/index.html [Accessed 20 July].

Ackers, B. & Eccles, N. S. 2015. Mandatory corporate social responsibility assurance practices: The case of King III in South Africa. *Accounting, Auditing & Accountability Journal,* 28 (4), 515–550.

Angwin, D. 2001. Mergers and acquisitions across European borders: National perspectives on preacquisition due diligence and the use of professional advisers. *Journal of World Business,* 36 (1), 32–57.

Asare, S. K. & Wright, A. M. 2012. Investors', auditors', and lenders' understanding of the message conveyed by the standard audit report on the financial statements. *Accounting Horizons,* 26 (2), 193–217.

Australian Auditing Standards Board 2008. Australian Standard on Assurance Engagements ASAE 3500 Performance Engagements. Australia: Pearson Education Australia and CPA Australia.

Bédard, J. & Courteau, L. 2015. Benefits and costs of auditor's assurance: Evidence from the review of quarterly financial statements. *Contemporary Accounting Research,* 32 (1), 308–335.

CDP. 2017. *Climate Change* [Online]. CDP. Available: https://www.cdp.net/en/climate [Accessed 10 December 2017].

CICA 2006. Standard Practices for Investigative and Forensic Accounting Engagements.

Cohen, J. R. & Simnett, R. 2015. CSR and Assurance Services: A Research Agenda. *AUDITING: A Journal of Practice & Theory,* 34 (1), 59–74.

Decaux, L. & Sarens, G. 2015. Implementing combined assurance: insights from multiple case studies. *Managerial Auditing Journal,* 30 (1), 56–79.

Eilifsen, A., Quick, R., Schmidt, F. & Umlauf, S. 2018. Investors' perceptions of nonaudit services and their type in Germany: The financial crisis as a turning point. *International Journal of Auditing,* 22 (2), 298–316.

European Court of Auditors 2007. Performance audit manual.

Farooq, B. & De Villiers, C. 2018. Assurance of sustainability and integrated reports. *In:* DE VILLIERS, C. J. (ed.) *Sustainability Accounting and Integrated Reporting.* Oxfordshire, UK: Taylor & Francis.

Farooq, M. B. & De Villiers, C. 2017. The market for sustainability assurance services: A comprehensive literature review and future avenues for research. *Pacific Accounting Review,* 29 (1), 79–106.

Forte, J. & Barac, K. 2015. Combined assurance: A systematic process. *Southern African Journal of Accountability and Auditing Research,* 17 (2), 71–83.

Gerson, J. S., Brolly, J. P. & Skalak, S. L. 2012. The roles of the auditor and the forensic accounting investigator. *A guide to forensic accounting investigation,* 37–61.

Gold, A., Gronewold, U. & Pott, C. 2012. The ISA 700 auditor's report and the audit expectation gap–do explanations matter? *International Journal of Auditing,* 16 (3), 286–307.

Golden, T. W., Skalak, S. L., Clayton, M. M. & Pill, J. S. 2011. *A guide to forensic accounting investigation,* John Wiley & Sons.

GRI. 2016. Consolidated set of GRI sustainability reporting standards (2016). Available: https://www.globalreporting.org/standards/gri-standards-download-center/?g=ae2e23b8-4958-455c-a9df-ac372d6ed9a8

https://www.globalreporting.org/reporting/g4/Pages/default.aspx [Accessed 10 February 2017].

Hassan, A., Elamer Ahmed, A., Fletcher, M. & Sobhan, N. 2020. Voluntary assurance of sustainability reporting: evidence from an emerging economy. *Accountability Research Journal,* In Press.

Hodge, K., Subramaniam, N. & Stewart, J. 2009. Assurance of Sustainability Reports: Impact on Report Users' Confidence and Perceptions of Information Credibility. *Australian Accounting Review,* 19 (3), 178–194.

IAASB 2006. ISRE 2410: Review of interim financial information performed by the independent auditor of the entity. *SAICA Members' Handbook.* Pietermaritsburg: LexisNexis.

IAASB 2009a. FRAME : International Framework for Assurance Engagements, 2009 Edition, Volume 2A. *SAICA Members' Handbook.* 2009 ed. Pietermaritzburg: LexisNexis.

IAASB 2009b. ISA 330: The auditor's responses to assessed risks. *SAICA Members' Handbook.* 2009 ed. Pietermaritsburg: LexisNexis.

IAASB 2009c. ISAE 3400: The Examination of Prospective Financial Information. *SAICA Members' Handbook.* 2018 ed. Pietermaritsburg: LexisNexis.

IAASB 2009d. ISRE 2400: Engagements to review financial statements. *SAICA Members' Handbook.* 2009 ed. Pietermaritsburg: LexisNexis.

IAASB 2009e. ISRE 2410: Review of interim financial information performed by the independent auditor of the entity. *SAICA Members' Handbook.* 2009 ed. Pietermaritsburg: LexisNexis.

IAASB 2011. ISAE 3402: Assurance reports on controls at a service organisation: conforming amendements. *SAICA Members' Handbook.* 2011 ed. Pietermaritsburg: LexisNexis.

IAASB 2013a. Assurance Engagements Other than Audits or Reviews of Historical Financial Information. *ISAE3000.*

IAASB 2013b. International Standard on Assurance engagements 3400: The examination of prospective financial information. *ISAE3400.*

IAASB 2013c. International Standard on Related Services 4400: Engagements to perform agreed-upon procedures regarding financial information. *ISRS4400.* London: IFAC.

IAASB 2013d. International Standard on Related Services 4410 (Revised). *ISRS 4410.*

London: IFAC.

IAASB 2013e. ISAE 3402: Assurance reports on controls at a service organisation. *SAICA Members' Handbook.* 2009 ed. Pietermaritsburg: LexisNexis.

IAASB 2013f. ISAE 3410: Aurance engagements on greenhouse gas statements. *SAICA Members' Handbook.* 2009 ed. Pietermaritsburg: LexisNexis.

IAASB 2013g. ISAE 3420: Aurance engagements to report on the compilation of pro forma financial information included in a prospectus. *SAICA Members' Handbook.* 2009 ed. Pietermaritsburg: LexisNexis.

IAASB 2013h. ISRE 2400: Engagements to review financial statements. *SAICA Members' Handbook.* 2018 ed. Pietermaritsburg: LexisNexis.

IAASB 2013i. ISRS 4410: Compilation Engagements. *SAICA Members' Handbook.* 2018 ed. Pietermaritsburg: LexisNexis.

IAASB 2015a. ISAE 3000: Assurance engagements other than audits or reviews of historical financial statements. *SAICA Members' Handbook.* Pietermaritzburg: LexisNexis.

IAASB 2015b. ISAE 3000: Assurance engagements other than audits or reviews of historical financial statements. *SAICA members' handbook. 2018.* Pietermaritsburg: LexisNexis.

IAASB 2016a. ISA 260: Communication to those charged with corporate governance. *SAICA members' handbook. 2015.* Pietermaritsburg: LexisNexis.

IAASB 2016b. ISA 700: Forming an Opinion and Reporting on Financial Statements. *SAICA members' handbook. 2015.* Pietermaritsburg: LexisNexis.

IAASB 2016c. ISA 800: Special considerations – Audits of financial statements prepared in accordance with special purpose frameworks. *SAICA members' handbook. 2018.* Pietermaritsburg: LexisNexis.

IAASB 2016d. ISA 805: Special considerations – audit of single financial statements and specific elements, accounts or items of a financial statement. *SAICA Members' Handbook.* 2009 ed. Pietermaritsburg: LexisNexis.

IAASB 2016e. ISA 810: Engagements to report on summary financial statements. *SAICA Members' Handbook.* 2009 ed. Pietermaritsburg: LexisNexis.

IAASB 2017a. Glossary. *Handbook of International Quality Control , Auditing, Review, Other Assurance , and Related Services Pronouncements.*

IAASB 2017b. International Framework for assurance engagements.

IAASB 2018a. International Standard on Accounting 34: Interim financial reporting. *IAS 34.*

IAASB 2018b. ISRS 4400: Engagements to perform agreed-upon procedures regarding financial information. *SAICA Members' Handbook.* 2018 ed. Pietermaritsburg: LexisNexis.

IIRC. 2013. The International Framework: Integrated Reporting. Available: http://www.theiirc.org/wp-content/uploads/2013/12/13-12-08-THE-INTERNATIONAL-IR-FRAMEWORK-2-1.pdf [Accessed 1 October 2013].

INTOSAI 2004. Implementation guidelines for performance auditing–standards and guidelines for performance auditing based on INTOSAI's auditing standards and practical experience. Stockholm.

IOD 2016. *King IV Report on Governance for South Africa,* Johannesburg, South Africa, Lexis Nexus.

Knechel, W. R. & Salterio, S. E. 2016. *Auditing: Assurance and risk*, Taylor & Francis.

Kranacher, M. J., Riley, R. & Wells, J. T. 2010. *Forensic accounting and fraud examination*, John Wiley & Sons.

Manning, G. A. & CFE, E. 2010. *Financial investigation and forensic accounting*, CRC Press.

Maroun, W. 2017. Assuring the integrated report: Insights and recommendations from auditors and preparers. *The British Accounting Review,* 49 (3), 329–346.

Maroun, W. 2019. Does external assurance contribute to higher quality integrated reports? *Journal of Accounting and Public Policy,* 38 (4), 106670.

Maroun, W. 2020. A Conceptual Model for Understanding Corporate Social Responsibility Assurance Practice. *Journal of Business Ethics,* 161, 187–209.

Maroun, W. & Atkins, J. 2015. The Challenges of Assuring Integrated Reports: Views from the South African Auditing Community. London: The Association of Chartered Certified Accountants.

Maxwell Locke & Ritter. 2017. *Understanding the differences between an audit and financial due diligence* [Online]. Available: https://www.mlrpc.com/articles/understanding-the-differences-between-an-audit-and-financial-due-diligence/ [Accessed 31 July 2018].

Mubako, G. 2019. Interaction between internal and external auditors – insights from a developing country. *Meditari Accountancy Research,* 27 (6), 840–861.

Prada, M. 2007. Transcript: Quality of public company audits from a regulatory perspective. International Organization of Securities Commission.

Prinsloo, A. & Maroun, W. 2020. An exploratory study on the components and quality of combined assurance in an integrated or a sustainability reporting setting. *Sustainability Accounting, Management and Policy Journal,* In press.

Schelluch, P. & Gay, G. 2006. Assurance provided by auditors' reports on prospective financial information: implications for the expectation gap. *Accounting & Finance,* 46 (4), 653–676.

Simnett, R. & Huggins, A. L. 2015. Integrated reporting and assurance: where can research add value? *Sustainability Accounting, Management and Policy Journal,* 6 (1), 29–53.

Simnett, R., Vanstraelen, A. & Chua, W. F. 2009. Assurance on Sustainability Reports: An International Comparison. *The Accounting Review,* 84 (3), 937–967.

Singleton, T. W. & Singleton, A. J. 2010. *Fraud auditing and forensic accounting*, John Wiley & Sons.

Singleton, T. W., Singleton, A. J., Bologna, G. J. & Lindquist, R. J. 2006. *Fraud auditing and forensic accounting*, John Wiley & Sons.

Solomon, J. 2010. *Corporate Governance and Accountability, Third Edition,* West Susex,

United Kingdom, John Wiley and Sons Ltd.

Spedding, L. S. 2009. *The due diligence handbook: corporate governance, risk management and business planning*, Elsevier.

Steinmeier, M. & Stich, M. 2017. Does Sustainability Assurance Improve Managerial Investment Decisions? *European Accounting Review*, 1–33.

The American Assembly 2003. *The Future of the Accounting Profession,* Lansdowne Resort, Leesburg, Virginia, The American Assembly Columbia University.

Vanstraelen, A., Schelleman, C., IMBA, I. H. & RA, R. M. 2011. A Framework for Extended Audit Reporting.

Wells, J. T. 2017. *Corporate fraud handbook: Prevention and detection*, John Wiley & Sons.

1. Introduction

Public sector organisations around the world are funded wholly or partly by the government and by taxpayers (Van Thiel and Leeuw, 2002; Maroun and Lodhia, 2018). The public sector is usually larger than the private sector in size, influence and economic activity (Ball et al., 2014). The public sector usually comprises of organisations which are owned and operated by the government and exist to provide services for its citizens, as well as public goods and services. Similar to the voluntary sector, organisations in the public sector do not seek to generate a profit (Salamon and Anheier, 1998; Keating and Frumkin, 2000; Maroun and Lodhia, 2018). Public sector organisations[1] may include healthcare facilities, education (both secondary and tertiary), utilities, transport and logistical enterprises (Ball et al., 2014).

Public sector organisations are subject to audit regimes which may involve the audit of their performance, in addition to an audit of their financial statements. The difference between the public sector and private sector is that profit is not a measure of performance for public sector entities (IOD, 2016). An income statement and balance sheet does not indicate the extent to which these government entities have met their objectives (Guthrie and English, 1997; Vivian and Maroun, 2018).

In the private sector, the measurement of objectives is in terms of profit, market share and return on equity and assets. These performance measures constitute the mark against which a business is measured. Conversely, in the public sector, conventional financial reporting mechanisms may not easily capture performance measurement. This is because the objectives for government programmes are stated frequently in non-financial terms and the nature of the activities undertaken. Since effectiveness information is crucial for managing these activities, other forms of measurement and reporting are needed (Ball et al., 2014).

Performance information is defined as 'evidence which is collected and used systematically to judge the performance of a program'; performance measurement as 'the assessment of the extent to which, and the efficiency with which, objectives are being achieved' (Guthrie and English, 1997, p. 3). Performance measurement ranges from quantitative data about specific variables to assess performance to verifiable descriptive, narrative or subjective information. Performance information published by these public sector organisations detail their operational objectives as well as their performance in relation to the achievement of their objectives. An example of performance information may include a customer satisfaction index or hectares of land rehabilitated (see Büchling and Maroun, 2018; SANParks, 2018).

---

1   In a South African context, a public sector organisation refers to any state-owned entity as defined in the Companies Act of 2008 and any entity as defined in Schedule 3D of the Public Finance and Administration Act of 1999.

Stakeholder groups such as taxpayers, unions and the government will pay close attention to the performance of these organisations to evaluate whether public funds are being used appropriately and effectively (Maroun and Lodhia, 2018).

Although the financial performance and information of these entities are also audited, the focus of the entities' public accountability is on operational performance and is usually examined in terms of specified quantitative and qualitative measures and key performance indicators (KPIs) (Van Thiel and Leeuw, 2002). These public organisations should, therefore, aim to demonstrate that public money allocated to them is being used effectively, that specific targets are being met and that appropriate decisions are being made in respect of long-term planning (Maroun and Lodhia, 2018). If a public sector organisation is not performing well, its funding may be cut, its key staff replaced and in extreme situations, the organisation may even be discontinued (Marx and van Dyk, 2011).

It is important to note the distinction between an audit of performance information and the term 'performance audit'. The latter refers to the audit of value-for-money, ie whether an organisation is economical, efficient and effective (Van Thiel and Leeuw, 2002; IAASB, 2009a). Conversely, the audit of performance information is not concerned with whether the entity is economical, efficient and effective but rather focuses on the entity's statements made regarding its KPIs. In practise, the terms are often used loosely. An audit of performance information may be conducted alongside a value for money audit; on the contrary, the audit of performance information is usually performed against the following predetermined objectives: credibility, usefulness and accuracy of the reported performance (Van Thiel and Leeuw, 2002).

This chapter will discuss the assurance of performance information in the public sector. The remaining structure of this chapter is as follows. Section 2 will discuss how performance information is measured: this will be followed by how the performance information is audited, in Section 3. Section 4 will discuss how the results of the testing can be reported and Section 5 will discuss how integrated reports in the public sector are assured.

2. Measuring performance information

Public sector entities should be accountable to stakeholders for their mandate. The disclosures made by a public sector entity should be a means of expressing their public-interest mandates (Farneti and Guthrie, 2009; IOD, 2016). In this regard, measurement indices can be used. KPIs are widely used by both private and public organisations in relation to non-financial information such as social and environmental reporting. These are established as a performance objective and the organisation's performance against the target KPIs will be measured (Van Thiel and Leeuw, 2002).

Those charged with governance should ensure that they approve the policies and operational plans developed by management to give effect to the approved strategy. These should include the key performance measures and targets for assessing the achievement of strategic objectives and positive outcomes over the short, medium and long term (IOD, 2016). Public sector organisations should ensure that policies and procedures are put in place to ensure the sustainability of the organisation, both in terms of operations and finances. Those charged with governance, therefore, have the difficult task of balancing the financial needs of the organisation with the mandate they are required to fulfil (Van Thiel and Leeuw, 2002; IOD, 2016).

To balance the mandate with the sustainability of the operations, those charged with governance should ensure that performance measures are measurable and relevant. Performance measures should be captured and reported consistently to ensure that they are measurable and relevant. The measures also should be clearly defined and unambiguous. Sometimes the measurability of performance measures is difficult where the subject matter of the performance information is subjective in nature (Guthrie and English, 1997; Ball et al., 2014).

A problem often faced by preparers of annual reports is the existence of data to generate the performance information. The completeness, validity and accuracy of the supporting performance information is of vital importance to ensure the integrity of the data used in reporting. Accordingly, relevant and reliable information must be used which is also measurable and useful (Guthrie and English, 1997; Ball et al., 2014). To ensure that the disclosures in reports are relevant, performance information should take into consideration valid concerns of the public and address the specific needs of their stakeholders (Christensen and Skaerbaek, 2007).

Measuring performance is a complex exercise. Measuring and reporting the overall performance of public sector entities is more difficult to measure when compared to financial performance. This difficulty is partially resolved by the form of report that is issued. By producing an integrated report, it is possible to combine quantitative measures (such as KPIs) with qualitative verbal explanations of the entity's performance. This is in line with King IV's assertion that performance encompasses both an organisation's achievements relative to its strategic objectives, and positive outcomes in terms of its effects on the capitals and the triple context in which it operates (IOD, 2016). Specific reference is made to Part 6.2 for Municipalities and 6.6 for State Owned Entities.

Given the complexity and subjectivity involved in measuring performance, an opportunity exists to manipulate performance measurements. Manipulation can include actions where reported figures are changed or the quality of performance information is foregone in order to change the performance measure (known as the problem of perverse incentives) (Van Thiel and Leeuw, 2002).

Those charged with governance have an important role to play in the setting and achievement of performance measures (Van Thiel and Leeuw, 2002; Maroun and Lodhia, 2018). All objectives should be pre-approved and if the objectives and indicators are vague and/or open for manipulation, the document must be sent back to management for revision (Van Thiel and Leeuw, 2002; Maroun and Lodhia, 2018). At year end those charged with governance must ensure that they report the same objectives that had been pre-approved at the beginning of the year (Van Thiel and Leeuw, 2002; Maroun and Lodhia, 2018). This reduces the opportunity for management to adjust or remove objectives when they realise such objectives will not be met (Van Thiel and Leeuw, 2002; Maroun and Lodhia, 2018). Without these measures the reliability of performance measurements of public sector entities will be reduced (Van Thiel and Leeuw, 2002).

Another aspect to consider as auditors is the existence of information which may not be available at all (a scope limitation). To enhance the reliability of performance measurements, Guthrie and English (1997) recommend that performance information be audited to ensure that the underlying data is accurate, valid and complete. An audit of the performance measures will include the analysis of the performance information in its raw form in order to measure performance against the specified objectives (AccountAbility, 2008).

3. The audit of performance information

The International Organisation of Supreme Audit Institutions (INTOSAI) describes performance audit as:

> 'An independent, objective and reliable examination of whether government undertakings, systems, operations, programmes, activities or organisations are operating in accordance with the principles of economy, efficiency and effectiveness and whether there is room for improvement' (INTOSAI, 2004).

Performance auditing is, therefore, related to the evaluation of how the public sector body is utilising resources and often focuses on determining how the public sector body is achieving economy, efficiency and effectiveness, sometimes referred to as value for money auditing (INTOSAI, 2004). The auditors' role therefore includes reporting on the credibility, usefulness and accuracy of the reported performance encapsulated in the financial statements (IAASB, 2016).

Where external auditors are used to assist in the auditing of performance information, the principles of *ISAE 3000 Assurance Engagements other than Audits or Reviews of Historical Financial Information* can provide a useful framework for planning and performing assurance engagements on performance information.

3.1 The applicability of ISAE 3000

IAASB (2015) states that the ISAE 3000 is applicable to all professional accountants in the public sector who are independent of the entity for which they perform assurance engagements. As a requirement, ISAE 3000 requires the practitioner to be independent from the intended users and the responsible party. As the practitioner is performing a quasi-public function, independence is still considered a key characteristic (Pany and Reckers, 1983). In order to ensure independence, the practitioner should still comply with Parts A and B of the Code of Ethics for Professional Accountants as discussed in Chapter 3 (IAASB, 2015).

ISAE 3000 requires that the practitioner gains an understanding of the organisation and the measures to be reported on (the subject matter) to identify any possible risks of material misstatements. This allows the practitioner to design and perform evidence-gathering activities (IAASB, 2015).

When designing evidence-gathering activities the practitioner will also need to understand the rationale behind the measures that are being reported on; considering the relevance and suitability of them in terms of the objectives of the public sector organisation in order to help assess the usefulness of the information being provided. This would require the practitioner to identify the objectives against which the performance of the public sector organisation is to be evaluated. These should have been determined by the organisation itself (or by a higher level of government) (Van Thiel and Leeuw, 2002). The organisation itself may already have determined its own specific numerical KPIs. Ensuring that the evidence-gathering activities are correct will allow the practitioners to obtain sufficient and appropriate evidence to support their conclusion (IAASB, 2009b; IAASB, 2015).

3.2 Approach to performance engagements

Performance auditors can be faced with considerable variety and ambiguity in their work (INTOSAI, 2004; European Court of Auditors, 2007). As mentioned above, they need to understand the entity and the environment that requires the practitioner to become familiar with a wide range of organisational contexts and subject matters (IAASB, 2015). Table 1 contains a non-exhaustive list of different frameworks, standards and guidelines which can inform how a practitioner completes a performance audit as well as the applicable jurisdictions.

Table 1: Standards and guidelines for public sector organisation audits	
Framework/ Standard	**Jurisdiction**
ISAE 3000	International
ISSAI 3000; ISAAI 3010 and the Fundamental Principles of Performance Auditing	International
Performance Auditing: A Measurement Approach	International
Performance Auditing, Contributing to Accountability in Democratic Government	International
Accountability AA1000	International
Performance Audit Manual	European Union
Internal audit conferences Performance Audit	European Union
Literature on performance auditing and Supreme Audit Institution	European Union
L'audit (de performance) dans les secteurs public et non marchand	France
Advanced: Audit performance dans les secteurs public et non marchand (14–118f)	France
Toiminnantarkastuksen ohje	Finland
The German Court of Audit ('Bundesrechnungshof')	Germany
Regional Audit institutions (Landesrechnungshöfe)	Germany
Guidance on evaluating value for money (VFM) of PFI/PPP projects (dating from 2007)	United Kingdom
Performance Auditing: The Experiences of the United States Government Accountability Office	United States
Auditing Standard on Assurance Engagements ASAE 3500 – Performance Engagements	Australia
Técnicas de Entrevista para Auditorias	Portugal
Manual de Auditoría de Rendimiento	Spain

As shown in Table 1, jurisdictions can suggest different approaches for assuring performance information and practitioners should use the applicable guidance or framework when performing a performance audit. The remainder of this section uses the following five frameworks to provide a broad outline of performance audits:

- The Performance Audit Guidelines: International Standards of Supreme Audit Institutions (ISSAI) 3000 – 3100 issued by INTOSAI.
- ASAE 3500 issued by The Auditing and Assurance Standards Board (AUASB).
- The Performance Audit Manual issued by the European Court of Auditors.

- ISAE 3000 issued by the International Auditing and Assurance Standards Board.
- AS1000 Assurance Standard issued by Accountability.

The aforementioned frameworks place emphasis on the performance of a public entity relative to the economy, efficiency and effectiveness. This is due to the complexity in measuring performance as well as reporting on performance information (INTOSAI, 2004; European Court of Auditors, 2007; Australian Auditing Standards Board, 2008).

Economy is defined as minimising the cost of resources used for an activity. Efficiency is related to economy, which however, relates to the organisation's ability to optimally utilise resources. Effectiveness refers to the ability of an organisation to meet goals or objectives (INTOSAI, 2004; European Court of Auditors, 2007; Australian Auditing Standards Board, 2008). As illustrated by Figure 1, placing emphasis on the economy, efficiency and effectiveness can assist the audit in identifying the socio-economic needs to be addressed by the organisation through intervention.

Figure 1: Factors impacting the socio-economic needs

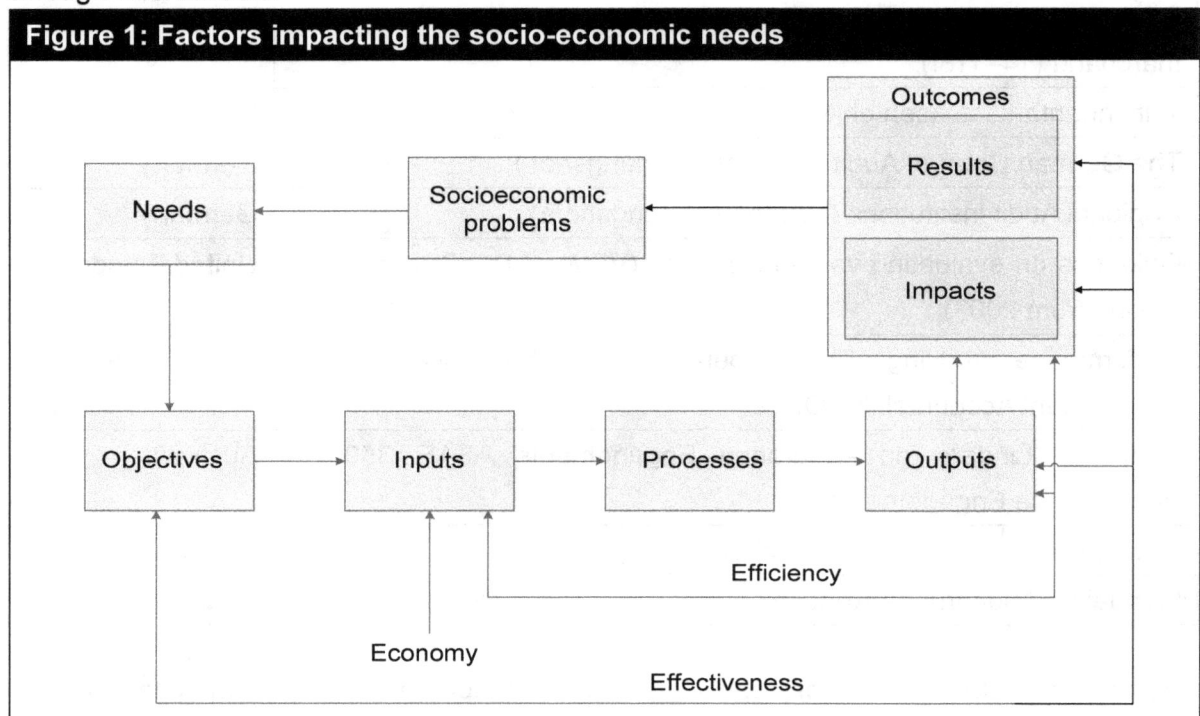

Adapted from European Court of Auditors (2007).

Performance audits can combine a 'performance directly approach' and a 'control systems approach' with a different emphasis placed on one or the other depending on the specific circumstances. A 'performance directly approach' focuses directly on the performance achieved and concentrates on inputs, outputs and outcomes (as depicted in Figure 1). The assumption adopted is that, if the performance achieved is satisfactory, there is a low risk of significant deficiencies in the design or implementation of activity or control systems (European Court of Auditors, 2007). An example of such an audit may be to assess whether the adopted policies have been suitably implemented and whether they have achieved the intended objectives (Daujotaite and Macerinskiene, 2008).

A performance directly approach is appropriate where there are suitable criteria to measure quantity, quality and cost of inputs, output and outcomes (European Court of Auditors, 2007; Australian Auditing Standards Board, 2008, IAASB, 2018 #472).

A control systems approach is designed to determine whether the audited entities have designed and implemented management and monitoring systems so as to optimise economy, efficiency and effectiveness of the entity as a whole (European Court of Auditors, 2007). The audit work will involve analysing, reviewing and testing the key components of such systems. Additionally, this approach should also consider whether systems in place produce relevant, reliable and timely information on the development of inputs (such as financial, human and other resources), processes and the delivery of the outputs, which should be compared with the operational objectives by way of performance indicators (Daujotaite and Macerinskiene, 2008).

In order to report on the engagement, the practitioner ought to have sufficient evidence to draw conclusions and to support his conclusion (AccountAbility, 2008; Australian Auditing Standards Board, 2008; IAASB, 2015). There is no specific format or wording that is prescribed by international regulations for reporting on public sector performance information (European Court of Auditors, 2007; AccountAbility, 2008; Australian Auditing Standards Board, 2008; IAASB, 2015). In some jurisdictions, however, the national regulator may issue country-specific requirements. The conclusion can provide reasonable to limited assurance dependent on the evidence obtained (AccountAbility, 2008; Australian Auditing Standards Board, 2008; IAASB, 2015).

4. Reporting on performance information

The reporting phase of a performance audit commences with the drafting of the preliminary observations and ends with a report, issued by the practitioner, containing the opinion on the performance information (European Court of Auditors, 2007; AccountAbility, 2008; Australian Auditing Standards Board, 2008; IAASB, 2015). The assurance practitioner is required to determine whether sufficient appropriate evidence has been obtained to support the conclusions expressed in the assurance report (Australian Auditing Standards Board, 2008; IAASB, 2015). The report issued should have the characteristics of reports detailed in Chapter 17

An audit report is not a record of all the audit findings; that is the purpose of the audit files (IAASB, 2009c). The report must set out the material and relevant observations and conclusions, with a clear link between the two (Australian Auditing Standards Board, 2008; IAASB, 2015). This requires structuring the report around the audit questions (or sub-questions, if one main audit question was identified) to provide a logical thread between the audit purpose, observations and conclusions. In accordance with the principles detailed in Chapter 17 there should be a logical progression of the argument, which is clearly signposted by means of the appropriate use of headings and sub-headings. The European Court of Auditors (2007) suggest five main sections for the audit reports prepared. These are summarised in Table 2:

Table 2: Main sections for the audit reports	
Element of report	**Key characteristics**
Executive summary	Should reflect accurately and comprehensively what is in the report and guide the reader to the significance of the audit questions and the answers.
Introduction	Should contain the following: A description of the audit area; objectives of the intervention and its main characteristics; principal regulations; budgetary arrangements and impact; main systems and processes; and description of the types of projects or programmes financed.
Audit scope and approach	Should set out the following: the audit subject; reasons for the audit; the audit questions to be answered; audit scope; audit criteria; audit methodology and approach; sources of data; and any limitation to the data used.
Observations	The observations section represents the main body of the report, containing the audit findings and audit evidence. This section should be structured around the audit questions, as this provides the focus for the audit and its conclusions.
Conclusions and recommendations	The primary purpose of this section is to provide clear answers to the audit questions, and to make related recommendations on how to improve. As such, the conclusions, based on the material observations, should be presented on the audit questions. The conclusions should provide answers to the questions set, rather than simply summarising the observations.

Adapted from European Court of Auditors (2007).

Often the performance information is provided as part of the public sector organisation's integrated report (IIRC, 2013), in which case the auditor's conclusion will be included within the integrated report. Such a report would present the auditor's conclusion alongside the performance information itself. The audit of performance information in public sector organisations can be approached in a similar way to the audit of KPIs in private sector organisations, and conventional audit techniques can be employed, though they will need to be tailored to the specific measures that are subject to audit (AccountAbility, 2008; Australian Auditing Standards Board, 2008; IAASB, 2015).

5. Integrated report of performance

Integrated reporting is the most recent corporate reporting innovation designed to provide a comprehensive account of how an organisation is creating value (IIRC, 2013; Stubbs and Higgins, 2014; King, 2016). The integrated report is considered a more comprehensive report which aims to address the lack of sustainability issues addressed by conventional accounting[2] (Burritt and Schaltegger, 2010; IIRC, 2011). There is only limited guidance to aid preparers when creating an integrated report which has added to the challenges experienced by preparers (IIRC, 2013; McNally et al., 2017).

The integrated report should be a concise document which explains clearly the inter-connection between material financial and non-financial performance measures (IIRC, 2013; King, 2016). It follows that the public sector and other not for profit organisations should utilise the integrated report as a means of explaining to stakeholders how they meet their objectives (Adams and Simnett, 2011; IIRC, 2013; GRI, 2016; IOD, 2016; LODHIA and MAROUN, 2017). This is in accordance with the Global Reporting Initiative (GRI) that states:

'Public agencies have a civic responsibility to properly manage public goods, resources and/or facilities in a way that supports sustainable development objectives and promotes the public interest. Public agencies are expected to lead by example in reporting publicly and transparently on their activities to promote sustainability.'
(GRI, 2005, pp. 7–8)

The International Integrated Reporting Council (IIRC) issued its 'International IR Framework' in 2013, which aims to encourage the adoption of integrated reporting across the world. The Framework is intended to be for profit-orientated entities, but it could also be adapted for public sector or not for profit organisations. The Framework refers to an organisation's resources as 'capitals' (IIRC, 2013). Capitals are used to assess value creation. Increases

---

2   The difference between an integrated report and financial statements is the non-financial disclosures made. These non-financial disclosures are utilised to assess risks and sustainability of entities. These disclosures have gained popularity and are increasingly important to stakeholders and institutional investors (Dawkins & Ngunjiri, 2008).

or decreases in these capitals indicate the level of value created or lost over a period. As an example:

Table 3: Main sections for the audit reports	
Financial	The pool of funds that is:
	• Available for use in the production of goods/the provision of services;
	• Obtained through financing or generated through operations/ investments.
Manufactured	Manufactured physical objects, including:
	• Buildings;
	• Equipment;
	• Infrastructure (eg roads, ports, bridges and waste and water treatment plants).
	Manufactured capital is often created by other organisations, but includes assets manufactured by the reporting organisation for sale or when they are retained for its own use.
Intellectual	Organisational knowledge-based intangibles, including:
	• Intellectual property, eg patents, copyrights, software, rights and licences;
	• 'Organisational capital' eg tacit knowledge, systems, procedures and protocols.
Human	People's competencies, capabilities and experience, and their motivations to innovate, including their:
	• Alignment with and support for an organisation's governance framework, risk management approach and ethical values;
	• Ability to understand, develop and implement an organisation's strategy;
	• Loyalties and motivations for improving processes, goods and services, including their ability to lead, manage and collaborate.
Natural	All environmental resources and processes that support the prosperity of an organisation, including:
	• Water, land, minerals and forests;
	• Biodiversity and ecosystem health.

►

Table 3: Main sections for the audit reports	
Social and relationship	The institutions and the relationships within and between communities, groups of stakeholders and other networks, and the ability to share information to enhance individual and collective wellbeing.
	Social and relationship capital includes:
	• Shared norms and common values and behaviours;
	• Key stakeholder relationships and the trust and willingness to engage that an organisation has developed and strives to build and protect with external stakeholders;
	• Intangibles associated with the brand and reputation that an organisation has developed;
	• An organisation's social licence to operate.

Adapted from IIRC (2013).

An integrated report is inherently subjective. Unlike financial statements, the document contains both historical and prospective qualitative and quantitative data which gives rise to concerns about the validity and reliability of the report (IIRC, 2014; Atkins and Maroun, 2015; Cohen and Simnett, 2015). Practitioners may be engaged to produce an independent verification statement on an integrated report.

Assuring reports adds to the credibility of financial statements and can enhance the degree of confidence in a report (Unerman and O'Dwyer, 2004; IIRC, 2014; IOD, 2016). Similarly, research has found that attest functions[3] have the same effect on integrated reports as well as sustainability reports (O'Dwyer et al., 2011; Maroun and Atkins, 2015; Maroun, 2018). However, there is little guidance on how an integrated report could be subject to formal assurance procedures (Maroun, 2017). Maroun (2018) states that the existing auditing standards should stand as a base for assuring the integrated report. This chapter does not address the assurance of the integrated report in its entirety but rather the assurance on performance information contained within the integrated report. The assurance approach suggested would, therefore, be to follow the guidance provided by existing standards, detailed in Section 3.

Existing standards and guidance mentioned in Section 3 do provide guidance on other engagements, however, they provide an approach rather than explicit instruction on how to perform an assurance engagement on other information (European Court of Auditors, 2007; AccountAbility, 2008; Australian Auditing Standards Board, 2008; IAASB, 2015).

---

3   The attest function is the process of conducting an examination of an entity's financial statements by a third party, where the outcome is the third party's formal certification that the financial statements fairly present the entity's financial results and financial position.

The procedures that result from each engagement are, therefore, likely to vary dependent on circumstances, the nature of the item tested and the extent to which professional judgement is applied (AccountAbility, 2008a; Australian Auditing Standards Board, 2008; European Court of Auditors, 2007; IAASB, 2018b).

6. Summary

- Often the performance information is included as part of the public sector organisation's integrated report (IIRC, 2013) (for examples see SANParks, 2017; Büchling and Maroun, 2018; SANParks, 2018). The performance information published by the public sector details their operational objectives as well as their performance in relation to the achievement of their objectives. The information is often of a different nature when compared to traditional financial information. This makes the measurement and reporting of performance information difficult and subjective (Van Thiel and Leeuw, 2002).

- Given the complexity and subjectivity involved in measuring performance, an opportunity exists to manipulate performance measurements. This will reduce the reliability of performance information of public sector entities (Van Thiel and Leeuw, 2002). As such, it is necessary to audit performance information (Guthrie and English, 1997).

- The audit of performance information in public sector organisations can be approached in a similar way to the audit of KPIs in private sector organisations, and conventional audit techniques can be employed but they will need to be tailored to the specific measures that are subject to audit (AccountAbility, 2008; Australian Auditing Standards Board, 2008; IAASB, 2015). The auditors can tailor their procedures by focusing on the economy, efficiency and effectiveness. This approach would allow a performance audit to scrutinise all performance measures (European Court of Auditors, 2007).

7. References

AccountAbility 2008. AA1000 assurance standard. London.

Adams, S. & Simnett, R. 2011. Integrated Reporting: An opportunity for Australia's not-for-profit sector. *Australian Accounting Review,* 21 (3), 292–301.

Atkins, J. F. & Maroun, W. 2015. Integrated reporting in South Africa in 2012. *Meditari Accountancy Research,* 23 (2), 197–221.

Australian Auditing Standards Board 2008. Australian Standard on Assurance Engagements ASAE 3500 Performance Engagements. Australia: Pearson Education Australia and CPA Australia.

Ball, A., Grubnic, S. & Birchall, J. 2014. 11 Sustainability accounting and accountability in the public sector. *Sustainability accounting and accountability,* 176.

Büchling, M. C. & Maroun, W. 2018. Extinction Accounting by the Public Sector – South African National Parks (SANParks). *In:* JILL ATKINS & ATKINS, B. (eds.) *Around the World in 80 Species: Exploring the Business of Extinction.*

Burritt, R. L. & Schaltegger, S. 2010. Sustainability accounting and reporting: fad or trend? *Accounting, Auditing & Accountability Journal,* 23 (7)**,** 829–846.

Christensen, M. & Skaerbaek, P. 2007. Framing and overflowing of public sector accountability innovations: A comparative study of reporting practices. *Accounting, Auditing & Accountability Journal,* 20 (1)**,** 101–132.

Cohen, J. R. & Simnett, R. 2015. CSR and Assurance Services: A Research Agenda. *AUDITING: A Journal of Practice & Theory,* 34 (1)**,** 59–74.

Daujotaite, D. & Macerinskiene, I. 2008. Development of performance audit in public sector. *In:* 5th International Scientific Conference, Business and Management, 2008.

Dawkins, C. & Ngunjiri, F. W. 2008. Corporate Social Responsibility Reporting in South Africa A Descriptive and Comparative Analysis. *Journal of Business Communication,* 45 (3)**,** 286–307.

European Court of Auditors 2007. Performance audit manual.

Farneti, F. & Guthrie, J. 2009. Sustainability reporting by Australian public sector organisations: Why they report. *In:* Accounting forum, 2009. Elsevier, 89–98.

GRI. 2005. Sector Supplement for Public Agencies. [Accessed 10 February 2017].

GRI. 2016. Consolidated set of GRI sustainability reporting standards (2016). Available: https://www.globalreporting.org/standards/gri-standards-download-center/?g=ae2e23b8-4958-455c-a9df-ac372d6ed9a8.

https://www.globalreporting.org/reporting/g4/Pages/default.aspx [Accessed 10 February 2017].

Guthrie, J. & English, L. 1997. Performance information and programme evaluation in the Australian public sector. *International Journal of Public Sector Management,* 10 (3)**,** 154–164.

IAASB 2009a. ISA 200: Overall objectives of the independent auditor and the conduct of an audit in accordance with international standards on auditing. *SAICA Members' Handbook.* 2009 ed. Pietermaritsburg: LexisNexis.

IAASB 2009b. ISA 330: The auditor's responses to assessed risks. *SAICA Members' Handbook.* 2009 ed. Pietermaritsburg: LexisNexis.

IAASB 2009c. PREF1: Preface to the International Standards on Quality Control, Auditing, Review, Other Assurance and Related Services. *SAICA Members' Handbook.* 2009 ed. Pietermaritsburg: LexisNexis.

IAASB 2015. ISAE 3000: Assurance engagements other than audits or reviews of historical financial statements. *SAICA Members' Handbook.* Pietermaritzburg: LexisNexis.

IAASB 2016. ISA 700: Forming an Opinion and Reporting on Financial Statements. *SAICA Members' Handbook.* Pietermaritsburg: LexisNexis.

IIRC 2011. Framework for Integrated Reporting and the Integrated Report.

IIRC 2013. The International Integrated Reporting Framework. 08/12/2013 ed.

IIRC. 2014. IIRC Stakeholder Feedback Survey. Available: http://integratedreporting. org/wp-content/uploads/2016/12/IIRC-Stakeholder-Survey-Report-Findings.pdf [Accessed 15 August 2016].

INTOSAI 2004. Implementation guidelines for performance auditing–standards and guidelines for performance auditing based on INTOSAI's auditing standards and practical experience. Stockholm.

IOD 2016. *King IV Report on Corporate Governance in South Africa*, Lexis Nexus South Africa, Johannesburg, South Africa.

Keating, K. E. & Frumkin, P. 2000. Reengineering Nonprofit. Available: http://citeseerx.ist. psu.edu/viewdoc/download?doi=10.1.1.200.9151&rep=rep1&type=pdf.

King, M. 2016. Comments on: *Integrated reporting*, GARI Conference, Henley on Thames, United Kingdom. 23 October.

Lodhia, S. & Maroun, W. 2017. Sustainability and integrated reporting by the public sector and not-for-profit organizations. *Sustainability Accounting and Integrated Reporting.* Routledge.

Maroun, W. 2017. Assuring the integrated report: Insights and recommendations from auditors and preparers *British Accounting Review,* Forthcoming.

Maroun, W. 2018. A Conceptual Model for Understanding Corporate Social Responsibility Assurance Practice. *Journal of Business Ethics,* In press.

Maroun, W. & Atkins, J. F. 2015. The Challenges of Assuring Integrated Reports: Views from the South African Auditing Community. 19 Nov 2015 ed.: ACCA.

Maroun, W. & Lodhia, S. 2018. Sustainability and integrated reporting by the public sector and not-for-profit organizations. *In:* MAROUN, W. & DE VILLIERS, C. (eds.) *Sustainability Accounting.*

Marx, B. & van Dyk, V. 2011. Sustainability reporting at large public sector entities in South Africa. *South African Journal of Accounting Research,* 25 (1), 103–127.

McNally, M. A., Cerbone, D. & Maroun, W. 2017. Exploring the challenges of preparing an integrated report. *Meditari Accountancy Research,* 25 (4), Forthcoming.

O'Dwyer, B. O., Owen, D. & Unerman, J. 2011. Seeking legitimacy for new assurance forms: the case of assurance on sustainability reporting. *Accounting, Organizations and Society,* 36, 31–52.

Pany, K. & Reckers, P. M. 1983. Auditor independence and nonaudit services: Director views and their policy implications. *Journal of Accounting and Public Policy,* 2 (1), 43–62.

Salamon, L. M. & Anheier, H. K. 1998. Social origins of civil society: Explaining the nonprofit sector cross-nationally. *Voluntas: International journal of voluntary and nonprofit organizations,* 9 (3), 213–248.

SANParks 2017. SANParks Annual Report 2016/2017.

SANParks 2018. SANParks Annual Report 2017/2018.

Stubbs, W. & Higgins, C. 2014. Integrated Reporting and internal mechanisms of change. *Accounting, Auditing & Accountability Journal,* 27 (7)**,** 1068–1089.

Unerman, J. & O'Dwyer, B. 2004. Enron, WorldCom, Andersen et al.: A challenge to modernity. *Critical Perspectives on Accounting,* 15 (6–7)**,** 971–993.

Van Thiel, S. & Leeuw, F. L. 2002. The performance paradox in the public sector. *Public Performance & Management Review,* 25 (3)**,** 267–281.

Vivian, B. & Maroun, W. 2018. Progressive public administration and new public management in public sector accountancy: An international review. *Meditari Accountancy Research,* 26 (1)**,** 44–69.

Chapter 23: The future of the audit profession

1. External regulation of the profession and recent technical developments

A defining feature of the audit profession is the confidence vested in it by non-expert stakeholders (Power, 1994). Codes of professional ethics, claims to technical expertise and the codification of minimum standards for executing an audit engagement have bolstered this trust and negated the need for external regulation (Chandler et al., 1993; Edwards, 2001; Zeff, 2003). This has changed since several high profile corporate failures during the 1990s and early 2000s. Laws were introduced to prohibit, for example, the rendering of non-audit services or to mandate rotation of audit partners to safeguard auditor independence and improve the quality of audit engagements (Francis, 2004; Malsch and Gendron, 2011). Independent regulators – such as the Public Company Accounting Oversight Board (PCAOB) in the USA – were tasked with monitoring audit practice and sanctioning deficient performance (Bishop et al., 2013; Löhlein, 2016). At the same time, regulators and standard-setters have attempted to define minimum standards of audit quality more clearly and expand the scope of the auditor's reporting responsibilities to increase the information being communicated to stakeholders, to enhance the transparency of the audit process and to enable higher levels of accountability by companies and their auditors (Humphrey et al., 2011; Maroun, 2014; Hay, 2015). The actual impact which these measures have had on audit quality is, however, debatable.

Regulating audit practice can have a positive effect on audit quality (Francis, 2004; Malsch and Gendron, 2011) but there is no guarantee that accountants and auditors will internalise and apply prescriptions as intended by policy-makers (van Zijl and Maroun, 2017). Legislation can also have unintended consequences (Vakkur et al., 2010). As a result, common regulatory measures have not always resulted in an increase in audit quality (see, for example, Myers et al., 2003; Carcello et al., 2011; Humphrey et al., 2011; Maroun and Gowar, 2013). Where audit engagements involve multi-national corporations or cross-jurisdiction engagements, differences in what constitutes acceptable audit practice will also be encountered, adding to the complxity of holding auditors accountable for the quality of their engagements (Hay, 2015). At the same time, while International Standards on Auditing (ISA) are applied in most jurisdictions (the USA being a notable exception), it cannot be assumed that the requirements of the ISAs will be consistent with country-specific assurance practice or regulation (ibid). Added to this is the challenge of co-ordinating the efforts of regulatory bodies which may be limited to specified jurisdictions and operate according to different legal frameworks (Malsch and Gendron, 2011).

Given the inherent limitations of external regulation, ensuring that auditors have sufficient guidance on how to conduct high quality engagements is essential. At the time of writing this book, the IAASB is working on an exposure draft of a revised quality control framework dealing with, *inter alia,* governance at the level of the audit firm, clarified responsibilities for engagement leaders, alternate models for ensuring quality control and application guidance for small and medium audit practices (IAASB, 2018). This is complemented by in-progress projects on how to improve engagement quality control reviews (ISQC 2) and strengthen quality management and control at the engagement level (revisions to ISA 220) (ibid). Work is also underway to provide more detailed guidance on the audit of estimates (ISA 540), testing balances and transactions in a group environment (ISA 600) and assessing the risk of misstatement at the overall and assertion-level (ISA 315). Table 1 provides a summary of recently completed projects.

Table 1: Summary of recently completed projects		
Project	**Year completed**	**Details**
Code of Professional Conduct	2018	The Code of Professional Conduct was updated by IESBA to align with updated guidance to professional accountants. It incorporated the NOCLAR provisions and created a conceptual framework which can be used to resolve ethical dilemmas (refer to Chapter 3).
ISA 810, ISA 800 and ISA 805	2016	Explains how enhancements to the standards dealing with the auditor's report on a client's financial statements (see below) are applied in the context of summarised financial statements (ISA 810) or to engagements where ISA 800 or ISA 805 are applicable.
Disclosures	2015	The changes clarify presentations and disclosures in financial statements from a core part of the financial statements and must be expressly considered during the audit process. Additional guidance focuses on: • The need for the auditor to understand the information system which supports or generates disclosures in a client's financial statements; • Assessing the risk of material misstatement in both qualitative and quantitative disclosures;

▶

Table 1: Summary of recently completed projects		
Project	**Year completed**	**Details**
		• Obtaining sufficient appropriate audit evidence for disclosures found in a set of financial statements; and • Evaluating the overall presentation of financial statements prepared according to a given financial reporting framework.
ISA 720	2014	Provides clarification on the auditor's responsibilities in connection with information accompanying a client's financial statements.
Reporting	2014	Arguably one of the most material changes to the ISA's, the project aims to provide additional information on the audit process and key findings. For example: • A discussion of key audit matters; • Reporting on the going concern status of the audit client; and • Disclosing the name of the partner/ engagement leader who is responsible for the audit. For details refer to Chapter 17.
ISA 315	2019	The IAASB revised ISA 315 to address a number of concerns expressed by practitioners and to modernise the standard, taking into account the advances in technology. The standard provides updated guidance related to the understanding of information technology and systems used by clients. In particular, guidance has been issued to allow for a more principle-based approach to identifying risks of material misstatement. Refer to Chapters 10 and 11.

2. Assurance on extended forms of corporate reporting

An area which is receiving increasing attention from regulators and standard-setters is the use of different types of assurance services for emerging forms of corporate reporting. How external assurance can be used to support integrated reporting is an example.

In most jurisdictions, integrated reporting is voluntary and mandatory assurance is limited to the financial statements which accompany or form part of an integrated report. Nevertheless, the International Integrated Reporting Council (IIRC, 2013) notes that:

'The reliability of information is affected by its balance and freedom from material error. Reliability (which is often referred to as faithful representation) is enhanced by mechanisms such as robust internal control and reporting systems, stakeholder engagement, **internal audit or similar functions**, and **independent, external assurance**' (p. 21, emphasis added).

Existing professional assurance standards are not always suited to testing the information found in integrated reports. Challenges being encountered when attempting to make parts of an integrated report the subject matter of an assurance engagement include:

- The IIRC's framework on integrated reporting is principles-based and there is no generally accepted standard for determining the format or content of an integrated report. This means that suitable criteria for expressing an opinion on an integrated report are not available.
- Not all companies have the resources or expertise to develop accounting systems and internal controls to support a formal integrated reporting process. As a result, auditors cannot test controls over and underlying data included in an integrated report in the same way as when auditing financial statements.
- Many of the test procedures used to gain sufficient appropriate audit evidence for a financial statement audit are difficult to apply to non-financial information or qualitative disclosures.
- Integrated reports should provide prospective information to stakeholders but it will not be possible for auditors to test and reach an objective conclusion on many forecasts, estimates or projections which may be included in an integrated report.
- The costs of assuring an integrated report may be prohibitively high.
- Audit firms have become specialists in financial reporting but may not have the necessary expertise and experience to assure an integrated report.
- The risk of legal liability may discourage assurance providers from expressing an opinion on an integrated report.

(Cohen and Simnett, 2015; Maroun and Atkins, 2015; Simnett and Huggins, 2015; Maroun, 2018a; Conradie et al., 2020)

In response to these challenges, the IIRC (2014a; 2014b; 2014c), IAASB (2015) and the academic community started to explore possible approaches for assuring integrated reports. Recommendations emerging from initial engagement with stakeholders and preliminary research findings include the following:

- Assurance providers need to participate proactively in the development of integrated reporting guidelines and be open to exploring creative approaches for providing some form of assurance over an integrated report.
- Companies need to explore how traditional external assurance services can be complemented by the work of internal auditors, monitoring by those charged with an entity's governance and testing performed by other experts to ensure the reliability of integrated reports.
- Standard-setters and practitioners should explore alternate assurance models. Possibilities include an approach to assurance which focuses on the systems underlying the integrated report or the methods followed to collect and analyse data included in an integrated report, rather than on the reliability of the disclosures themselves.
- Universities should examine their academic programmes to ensure that students are being trained to think broadly about how assurance functions and how best to test different types of information.

(Cohen and Simnett, 2015; IIRC, 2015; IOD, 2016; Farooq and De Villiers, 2018; Maroun, 2018b; Conradie et al., 2020)

Integrated reporting is still in a developmental stage but is showing signs of becoming an important method by which companies communicate with their stakeholders (De Villiers et al., 2014; Howitt, 2016). It represents an emerging area in corporate reporting which is likely to result in significant attention from standard-setters, regulators and academics in the future. The same may be true for sustainability reporting, as most of the world's largest companies are preparing some type of sustainability report (KPMG, 2017). Many of the challenges encountered when assuring an integrated report apply equally to sustainability reporting. Consequently, as sustainability and integrated reporting become more prominent, there will be a clear need for detailed guidance on how to assure this type of reporting (Farooq and De Villiers, 2017; 2018).

3. Changes in technology

The final driver of change to the assurance industry discussed in this book is the effect of emerging forms of technology. Companies are relying to an ever greater extent on automated systems for storing, managing and collecting data on different aspects of their business. The integration of these systems in almost every aspect of a business, coupled with the possible use of artificial intelligence, raises several questions for the future of the audit profession.

- Are current risk-based models which focus on audit risk at the financial statement and assertion level sufficient for a globalised and increasingly digital business environment? Alternate approaches to assessing and responding to audit risk which recognise that an organisation is only part of a broad network of firms and different stakeholders are already being explored and may be useful for dealing with the complexity of future business models (Peecher et al., 2007; Maroun, 2018b).

- Do auditing standards provide sufficient guidance on the use of computer-aided techniques to collect and analyse data? Many of the professional reporting and assurance standards were developed before the widespread use of complex information systems. Key principles may need to be expanded to explain how, for example, data analytics may be used to perform substantive or control tests. Similarly, how will technologies like quantum-computing, blockchains and artificial intelligence affect the planning and execution of an audit engagement? Following from this, the inherent limitations of the audit model may need to be revisited as the possibility of using embedded software to test all balances and transactions continuously becomes a reality (Kokina and Davenport, 2017; Chan and Vasarhelyi, 2018).

- How will stakeholders understand the role and function of the audit process? As new technology allows changes in the nature, timing and extent of the testing performed by auditors, will users expect the auditor to do more than just express an opinion on a client's financial statements?

- Related closely to the above, the focus of the assurance process may need to change. As the importance of complementing financial information with details on an organisation's social and environmental performance grows, stakeholders may expect auditors to go beyond providing a conclusion on the fair presentation of financial statements. This is especially true if advances in technology make it easier and more cost-efficient to collect and analyse different types of data on financial and non-financial metrics.

- Finally, how assurance is framed and studied by practitioners, students and academics will need to be reconsidered. Assurance is currently defined narrowly in terms of the extent to which a defined subject matter adheres to a set of objective criteria (IAASB, 2009). This may not hold in the future. As combined assurance becomes more prominent and technology allows expanded monitoring and accounting systems, exactly how information is 'assured' may need to be reconceptualised.

4. Areas for future research

Given the changing nature of financial statement audits and other types of assurance, there are significant opportunities for future research. These can be grouped broadly into studies on the functioning of existing forms of assurance and research, inspired by a normative agenda, which advances policy and practice recommendations.

For example, as more data become available on company performance, characteristics and the nature of assurance services, it becomes possible to re-examine already tested inter-connections between metrics such as auditor types, audit tenures and earnings quality, both over time and across jurisdictions. As explained by Hay (2015, p. 168):

'Replication of previous studies is not conducted frequently enough in auditing research. Replications and extensions of previous research studies should be conducted more often and should be accepted by journals. More repeated examinations of data through replications will allow more use of systematic reviews and meta-analyses and so lead to more robust conclusions.'

It is also important not to lose sight of the fact that assurance is wider than just the audit of financial statements. Much of the prior research has focused on the latter. More needs to be done to understand the drivers of other types of assurance – such as environmental, social and governance (ESG) assurance or performance audits – and how these are being executed in a practical context (Farooq and De Villiers, 2017; Maroun, 2018a). The process of examining assurance in innovative settings should be complemented by a concerted effort to explore how assurance practices can evolve; challenges which are expected and how current assurance models can be improved to meet the needs of a changing business environment. As is usually the case, a period of accelerated change can be difficult for standard setters and practitioners but it offers scholars opportunities to contribute significantly to policy development and the body of academic knowledge.

5. References

Bishop, C. C., Hermanson, D. R. & Houston, R. W. 2013. PCAOB Inspections of International Audit Firms: Initial Evidence. *International Journal of Auditing,* 17 (1), 1–18.

Carcello, J. V., Hollingsworth, C. & Mastrolia, S. A. 2011. The effect of PCAOB inspections on Big 4 audit quality. *Research in Accounting Regulation,* 23 (2), 85–96.

Chan, D. Y. & Vasarhelyi, M. A. 2018. Innovation and practice of continuous auditing. *Continuous Auditing: Theory and Application.* Emerald Publishing Limited.

Chandler, R., Edwards, R. & Anderson, M. 1993. Changing Perceptions of the Role of the Company Auditor, 1840–1940. *Accounting and Business Research,* 23 (92), 443–459.

Cohen, J. R. & Simnett, R. 2015. CSR and Assurance Services: A Research Agenda. *AUDITING: A Journal of Practice & Theory,* 34 (1)**,** 59–74.

Conradie, P., Christian, J., Simbarashe, N., Lange, Y. & Kadwa, O. 2020. The rationale purpose requirement impact on South Africa. Johannesburg: South African Institute of Chartered Accountants.

De Villiers, C., Rinaldi, L. & Unerman, J. 2014. Integrated Reporting: Insights, gaps and an agenda for future research. *Accounting, Auditing & Accountability Journal,* 27 (7)**,** 1042–1067.

Edwards, J. R. 2001. Accounting regulation and the professionalization process: A historical essay concerning the significance of P. H. Abbott. *Critical Perspectives on Accounting,* 12 (6)**,** 675–696.

Farooq, B. & De Villiers, C. 2018. Assurance of sustainability and integrated reports. *In:* DE VILLIERS, C. J. (ed.) *Sustainability Accounting and Integrated Reporting.* Oxfordshire, UK: Taylor & Francis.

Farooq, M. B. & De Villiers, C. 2017. The market for sustainability assurance services: A comprehensive literature review and future avenues for research. *Pacific Accounting Review,* 29 (1)**,** 79–106.

Francis, J. R. 2004. What do we know about audit quality? *The British Accounting Review,* 36 (4)**,** 345–368.

Hay, D. 2015. The frontiers of auditing research. *Meditari Accountancy Research,* 23 (2)**,** 158–174.

Howitt, R. 2016. IIRC Newsletter – Highlights from 2016. Available: https://us4.campaign-archive.com/?u=b36f6aeef75cea67e62812844&id=ce981ad463&e=ee7e66415f [Accessed 5 August 2018].

Humphrey, C., Kausar, A., Loft, A. & Woods, M. 2011. Regulating Audit beyond the Crisis: A Critical Discussion of the EU Green Paper. *European Accounting Review,* 20 (3), 431–457.

IAASB 2009. FRAME : International Framework for Assurance Engagements, 2009 Edition, Volume 2A. *SAICA Members' Handbook.* 2009 ed. Pietermaritzburg: LexisNexis.

IAASB. 2015. Exploring assurance on integrated reporting and other emerging developments in external reporting. Available: https://www.iaasb.org/system/files/publications/files/ IAASB-Integrated-Reporting-Working-Group-Publication_0.pdf.

IAASB. 2018. *Quality Control at Firm Level – ISQC 1* [Online]. Available: https://www.iaasb. org/projects/quality-control-firm-level-isqc-1 [Accessed 20 August 2018].

IIRC. 2013. The International Framework: Integrated Reporting. Available: http:// www.theiirc.org/wp-content/uploads/2013/12/13-12-08-THE-INTERNATIONAL-IR-FRAMEWORK-2-1.pdf [Accessed 1 October 2013].

IIRC. 2014a. Assurance on <IR>: an exploration of issues. IIRC assurance paper. Available: http://www.theiirc.org/wp-content/uploads/2014/07/Assurance-on-IR-an-exploration-of-issues.pdf [Accessed 15 August 2016].

IIRC. 2014b. Assurance on <IR>: an introduction to the discussion. IIRC assurance paper. Available: http://www.theiirc.org/wp-content/uploads/2014/07/Assurance-on-IR-an-introduction-to-the-discussion.pdf [Accessed 16 August 2016].

IIRC. 2014c. IIRC Stakeholder Feedback Survey. Available: http://integratedreporting.org/wp-content/uploads/2016/12/IIRC-Stakeholder-Survey-Report-Findings.pdf [Accessed 15 August 2016].

IIRC. 2015. Assurance on <IR> Overview of feedback and call to action. Available: http://integratedreporting.org/wp-content/uploads/2015/07/IIRC-Assurance-Overview-July-2015.pdf [Accessed 20 July].

IOD 2016. *King IV Report on Corporate Governance in South Africa*, Lexis Nexus South Africa, Johannesburg, South Africa.

Kokina, J. & Davenport, T. H. 2017. The emergence of artificial intelligence: How automation is changing auditing. *Journal of Emerging Technologies in Accounting,* 14 (1), 115–122.

KPMG. 2017. The road ahead. The KPMG Survey of Corporate Responsibility Reporting 2017. Available: https://assets.kpmg.com/content/dam/kpmg/xx/pdf/2017/10/kpmg-survey-of-corporate-responsibility-reporting-2017.pdf [Accessed 20 November 2017].

Löhlein, L. 2016. From peer review to PCAOB inspections: Regulating for audit quality in the US. *Journal of Accounting Literature,* 36, 28–47.

Malsch, B. & Gendron, Y. 2011. Reining in auditors: On the dynamics of power surrounding an "innovation" in the regulatory space. *Accounting, Organizations and Society,* 36 (7), 456–476.

Maroun, W. 2014. Reportable irregularities and audit quality: Insights from South Africa. *Accounting Forum,* 39 (1), 19–33.

Maroun, W. 2018a. A Conceptual Model for Understanding Corporate Social Responsibility Assurance Practice. *Journal of Business Ethics,* In press.

Maroun, W. 2018b. Modifying assurance practices to meet the needs of integrated reporting: The case for "interpretive assurance". *Accounting, Auditing & Accountability Journal,* 31 (2), 400–427.

Maroun, W. & Atkins, J. 2015. The Challenges of Assuring Integrated Reports: Views from the South African Auditing Community. London: The Association of Chartered Certified Accountants.

Maroun, W. & Gowar, C. 2013. South African Auditors Blowing the Whistle without Protection: A Challenge for Trust and Legitimacy. *International Journal of Auditing,* 17 (2), 177–189.

Myers, J. N., Myers, L. A. & Omer, T. C. 2003. Exploring the term of the auditor-client relationship and the quality of earnings: A case for mandatory auditor rotation? *The Accounting Review,* 78 (3), 779–799.

Peecher, M. E., Schwartz, R. & Solomon, I. 2007. It's all about audit quality: Perspectives on strategic-systems auditing. *Accounting, Organizations and Society,* 32 (4–5), 463–485.

Power, M. K. 1994. *The Audit Explosion,* London, Demos.

Simnett, R. & Huggins, A. L. 2015. Integrated reporting and assurance: where can research add value? *Sustainability Accounting, Management and Policy Journal,* 6 (1)**,** 29–53.

Vakkur, N. V., McAfee, R. P. & Kipperman, F. 2010. The unintended effects of the Sarbanes-Oxley Act of 2002. *Research in Accounting Regulation,* 22 (1)**,** 18–28.

Van Zijl, W. & Maroun, W. 2017. Discipline and punish: Exploring the application of IFRS 10 and IFRS 12. *Critical Perspectives on Accounting,* 44**,** 42–58.

Zeff, S. A. 2003. How the U.S. accounting profession got where it is today: Part I. *Accounting Horizons,* 17 (3)**,** 189–205.